D0853953

THE POLITICAL ECONOMY OF THE WELFARE STATE IN LATIN AMERICA

This book is one of the first attempts to analyze how developing countries through the early twenty-first century have established systems of social protection and how these systems have been affected by the recent processes of globalization and democratization. The book focuses on Latin America, a pioneer in welfare state development in the developing world, to identify factors associated with the evolution of welfare state policies during the preglobalization period prior to 1979 and studies how globalization and democratization in the last thirty years affected governments' fiscal commitment to social spending. In contrast with the Western European experience, more developed welfare systems evolved in countries relatively closed to international trade, while the recent process of globalization that has swept the region has put substantial downward pressure on social security expenditures. Health and education spending has been relatively protected from greater exposure to international markets and has actually increased substantially with the shift to democracy.

Alex Segura-Ubiergo is Resident Representative in Senegal and the Gambia for the International Monetary Fund (IMF), where he has served as an economist since 2001. Dr. Segura-Ubiergo is the recipient of the Mancur Olson Award for the best dissertation in political economy in 2001–2002. He holds degrees in economics and political science from the Autonomous University of Barcelona and a Ph.D. obtained with distinction from Columbia University, where he held a Fulbright Scholarship.

The Political Economy of the Welfare State in Latin America

Globalization, Democracy, and Development

ALEX SEGURA-UBIERGO

International Monetary Fund

CAMBRIDGE
UNIVERSITY PRESS

HN
110.5
.A8
S42
2007

CAMBRIDGE UNIVERSITY PRESS
Cambridge, New York, Melbourne, Madrid, Cape Town, Singapore, São Paulo

Cambridge University Press
32 Avenue of the Americas, New York, NY 10013-2473, USA

www.cambridge.org
Information on this title: www.cambridge.org/9780521871112

© Alex Segura-Ubiergo 2007

This publication is in copyright. Subject to statutory exception
and to the provisions of relevant collective licensing agreements,
no reproduction of any part may take place without
the written permission of Cambridge University Press.

First published 2007

Printed in the United States of America

A catalog record for this publication is available from the British Library.

Library of Congress Cataloging in Publication Data
Segura-Ubiergo, Alex.
The political economy of the welfare state in Latin America : globalization, democracy,
and development / Alex Segura-Ubiergo.
p.   cm.
Includes bibliographical references (p.) and index.
ISBN-13: 978-0-521-87111-2 (hardback)
ISBN-10: 0-521-87111-5 (hardback)
1. Welfare state – Latin America.   2. Welfare state – Latin America – Case studies.
3. Public welfare – Latin America.   4. Globalization – Economic aspects – Latin America.
5. Democratization – Latin America.   6. Latin America – Politics and government.   I. Title.
HN110.5.A8S42   2007
330.12′6 – dc22   2006037428

ISBN   978-0-521-87111-2 hardback

Cambridge University Press has no responsibility for
the persistence or accuracy of URLs for external or
third-party Internet Web sites referred to in this publication
and does not guarantee that any content on such
Web sites is, or will remain, accurate or appropriate.

Als meus pares, el meu avi, i a la Mariella

University Libraries
Carnegie Mellon University
Pittsburgh, PA 15213-3890

Contents

Tables and Figures

Tables

Figures

Acknowledgments

This is a book about economics and politics, two disciplines that have been strongly related since the time Adam Smith and David Ricardo referred to modern-day economics as political economy more than two hundred years ago. Over the years, I have accumulated debts with experts in both fields; they have taught me that economic analysis without a careful regard for political and institutional issues remains largely incomplete (and, I would add, uninteresting), while political analysis can also benefit in substance and rigor from the solid micro-foundations and the strong methodological traditions of economics.

While I cannot list all the people whose ideas have influenced my thinking over the years, I would like to single out some individuals who either provided direct comments to my manuscript or influenced my thinking in one way or another. This book is certainly a better one thanks to them. To be sure, all remaining faults and weaknesses are mine alone.

My first debt of gratitude is to Professor Carlos Mulas-Granados, admired colleague and best friend, who has shared my passion for economics and politics since we met at Columbia University almost ten years ago. He introduced me to some of the recent literature on the political economy of the welfare state, which he had become acquainted with thanks to seminars he had taken with Gøsta Esping-Andersen and Francis Castles – two giants of the study of the welfare state – at the Juan March Institute in Madrid. This book would not have been possible without him.

My second debt of gratitude is to Robert Kaufman, Alfred Stepan, Alfred Fishlow, and Robert Shapiro from Columbia University. Professor Kaufman was the first to introduce me to Latin American political economy. The idea for this book developed in a political economy seminar that he led at Columbia University. We coauthored an article in *World Politics* that became the foundation for some of the more detailed quantitative research that is presented in this book. I could not be more grateful for the advice and guidance, at all levels, that he has continually provided over the years, to the very last stages of this book. Alfred Stepan taught me most of what I know about political institutions, and convinced me (given my obsession for econometrics and quantitative methods) that analytical arguments should not hide behind seemingly sophisticated formulas. "If you cannot say it in simple words, it cannot be an important argument," he used to tell me. I hope that I have been able to follow his advice in this book. His infectious passion for interdisciplinary knowledge and his encyclopedic knowledge of political institutions around the world have always impressed me tremendously. Alfred Fishlow's scholarship on economic history has been another source of inspiration since I was a young student of economics in Spain and read with fascination his work on railroads and the American economy. It was a great honor to have him as a member of my dissertation committee at Columbia University. His work also had a great influence on this book, especially on Chapter 2. Robert Shapiro was the best professor of statistics and quantitative methods that I have ever had. He taught me that methods are nothing without good underlying theories and was always an example of dedication and commitment.

Third, I would like to thank three great economists I had the honor to work with during my first assignment at the International Monetary Fund: Marcelo Selowsky, Montek Ahluwalia, and David Goldsbrough. In different ways they all taught me something that has made this book better. Montek Ahluwalia, the first Director of the IMF's Independent Evaluation Office, is an intellectual giant with an elegance in presenting compelling arguments that is rarely seen. David Goldsbrough was widely seen as one of the best senior managers of the institution: he has an admirable combination of intelligence, modesty, and friendliness and a rare capacity to lead effective teams. However, my greatest debt is to Marcelo Selowsky, a distinguished economist from the University of Chicago and former World Bank chief economist for Latin America and later Eastern Europe and Central Asia. His intuitive approach to economics (yet based on strong analytical fundamentals), his imaginative thinking, and his capacity to grasp "the big picture" are unparalleled. If I have been able to use even a fragment of these skills, this book will be a success.

Other people that I would also like to thank for reasons that I cannot name individually include Francisco Rivera-Batiz, Jagdish Baghwati, Edmund Phelps, Xavier Sala-i-Martin, Helen Milner, Arturo Sotomayor, Alina Rocha Menocal, Emilio Pineda, and Marta Noguer from Columbia University; Pau Rabanal and Marc Siscart from New York University; Julio Cotler, Carolina

Trivelli, Martin Tanaka, Hildegarde Venero, and Johanna Yancari from the Institute of Peruvian Studies in Peru; and Eduardo Ley, Antonio Spilimbergo, Sanjeev Gupta, Gerd Schwartz, and Reza Vaez-Zadeh from the International Monetary Fund. Eduardo Ley and Antonio Spilimbergo do deserve a special mention for pushing me to continue working on the manuscript during the final stages of the review process, when working on a book combined with a full-time job became an almost impossible task. Eduardo convinced me to put aside my passion for the Spanish guitar to complete the book. Without him, perhaps my musicianship would now be better, but I would certainly have an unpublished manuscript in my hands.

Scott Parris, editor for economics and finance at Cambridge University Press, also deserves a special mention. Scott believed in my book manuscript from the start, and he always provided words of encouragement and praise that helped me through the different rounds of manuscript revisions. I will always be very grateful for that. I am also grateful to Katie Greczylo, who managed the editing process with incredible attention to detail, clarity, and consistency.

Finally, I would also like to gratefully acknowledge the generous support received from the Fulbright Commission in Spain, which made it possible for me to pursue my doctoral studies in the United States, where the initial ideas for this book first developed.

The analysis and opinions in this book are those of the author alone and do not necessarily reflect the views of the IMF.

This book is dedicated to my parents and grandfather, who always encouraged me to pursue my studies; and my wife, Mariella, who endured with patience and loving sympathy (in Barcelona, New York, Lima, Washington, and Dakar) all the time I spent away from her working on this book.

1

Introduction

The welfare state is the culmination of a centuries-old struggle for social protection and security in the industrialized countries. It may justly be regarded as one of their proudest achievements in the post-war period. It set a model and a standard for aspiration for the newly industrializing and transitional countries as also for the poorer countries.[1]

Let us narrowly define the welfare state as a repertoire of state-led policies aimed at securing a minimum of welfare to its citizens – that is, protecting them against the risks of unemployment, sickness, maternity, and old age – and providing an adequate accumulation of human capital through public investments in health and education. As such, the importance of the welfare state can hardly be overstated. Welfare states are a fundamental part of advanced modern capitalism in the West. They affect income inequality and poverty rates, they shape labor markets, they change public perceptions of how citizens perceive what the role of the state in the economy should be, and they influence the long-term prospects for economic growth through their investments in human capital and their legitimizing role for the political system.[2] It is therefore not surprising that in recent years there has been a proliferation of studies related to the origins, development, and crises of the welfare state.

Researchers have focused on the economic and demographic transformations related to the expansion of welfare effort[3]; on the effects of state

---

[1] See Ghai (1996).
[2] This discussion draws on Pierson (2000a), who provides a review of the literature on the main effects associated with welfare states. Pierson discusses mainly political effects. The economic effects of welfare states have been also extensively studied by, among others, Atkinson (1999), Barr (1992, 2004), Feldstein (2005), Sala-i-Martin (1999), and Mulligan and Sala-i-Martin (2003).
[3] See, for example, Boix (2001) and Pampel and Williamson (1989).

structure[4]; on the importance of policy legacies[5]; on how the distribution of power among political parties and interest associations generates different "types" of welfare states[6]; on the connection among economic openness, domestic vulnerability, and the establishment of social safety nets[7]; on the relationships among deindustrialization, technological change, and welfare state expansion[8]; and on the impact of aging on the sustainability of the welfare state.[9] Hence, it is not an exaggeration to claim that over the last three decades, the welfare state has been one of the most widely studied objects of inquiry in the political economy literature of advanced capitalist countries.[10]

Unfortunately, however, the welfare state has been one of the least studied topics in the political economy of the developing world.[11] Why, how, and with what consequences have some developing countries institutionalized much more extensive systems of social protection than others? Why do some countries at similar levels of economic development give much more fiscal priority to social security and human capital expenditures than others? How have the recent processes of economic globalization and democratic transition transformed the scope and role of the state for social insurance and human capital accumulation? These are important questions that have received little attention in the study of the political economy of third-world development.[12]

---

[4] The most notable examples are Huber, Ragin, and Stephens (1993); Pierson (1995); and Castles (1998).

[5] Heclo (1974), Skocpol (1986), Orloff (1993), and Pierson (1996).

[6] See Stephens (1979), Korpi (1983), Esping-Andersen (1991), and Hicks and Swank (1992).

[7] See, for example, Cameron (1978), Katzenstein (1985), Rodrik (1997), and Garrett (1998, 2000a, 2001).

[8] Iversen (2000) and Iversen and Cusack (2000).

[9] See, for example, Heller (2003), Diamond (2005), and Modigliani and Muralidhar (2005).

[10] In addition, the political economy literature comprises a number of related works that have influenced our understanding of political and institutional factors that affect economic policies, including welfare state development. These include, among others, Acemoglu (2003, 2005), Acemoglu and Robinson (2000, 2001, 2006), Acemoglu and Johnson (2005), and Aghion, Alesina, and Trevi (2004).

[11] This is somewhat understandable because social safety nets and systems of public investment in health and education are relatively weak in the developing world, especially in the poorest countries. However, even within the set of developing countries, there is significant variation in the scope and role of the state for social insurance. Further research on this topic is therefore needed to understand why some states in the developing world have more advanced systems of social protection than others, which is precisely one of the main objectives of this book.

[12] Most of the existing literature is somewhat descriptive or based on single case studies that make it difficult to establish causal patterns. The most widely cited source of social security analysis in Latin America is Mesa-Lago (1978, 1989, 2000). Although Mesa-Lago

In an attempt to advance our understanding of these questions, this book has three aims: first, to examine the different paths through which countries in the developing world – especially in Latin America[13] – have constructed (or failed to construct) their welfare systems; second, to analyze the effects of globalization and domestic politics on governments' fiscal commitment to social security, health, and education; and third, to offer a methodology that combines Qualitative Comparative Analysis (QCA), time-series cross-section (TSCS) data, and three in-depth case studies – Chile, Costa Rica, and Peru – to provide new insights into these questions and go beyond the limitations of previous approaches to the subject matter.

The focus on Latin American countries is appropriate for two reasons. First, because unlike in many other developing countries, some Latin American countries have long had welfare systems modeled along European lines, with benefit pension plans, health services, and family allowances. In Chile, Uruguay, and Argentina, for example, these programs began to evolve in the 1920s and even preceded the United States in health-maternity insurance, family allowances, and unemployment compensation.[14]

The second reason is the great process of economic and political change that has swept Latin America during the past three decades. The programs of economic reform and structural adjustment of the 1980s led to the

---

is a fundamental source of information on social security systems in Latin America, his analysis tends to be somewhat descriptive. The same occurs in other excellent single case studies that bring to the fore the importance of specific country-level factors but have more limited value to make broader generalizations, such as Malloy (1979), Raczynski (1994), and Filgueira (1995). Hence, in the context of the developing world, there is little quantitative and comparative research on the origins and development of income security programs and other policies usually associated with the welfare state. Also, unlike researchers who focus on OECD countries, students of developing countries have hardly made use of some of the most advanced statistical techniques (e.g., regression with panel data) or recent developments in the use of the comparative method (e.g., Boolean algebra), which are able to overcome the problem of "too many variables, too few cases." Some exceptions would be Huber (1996), who provides a qualitative comparative analysis of the origins and recent development of social policies in five major Latin American countries; and Brown and Hunter (1999), Kaufman and Segura-Ubiergo (2001), Huber et al. (2004), and Hunter and Brown (2005), who use quantitative methods.

[13] The reasons for choosing Latin America as the main regional focus of this study are provided herein.

[14] See Mesa-Lago (1989, xv). Also, if we focus on more recent data, in the 1990s, pension spending as a percentage of GDP reached 15 percent in Uruguay – a larger percentage than in every OECD country except Italy. Argentina, Brazil, Chile, Nicaragua, and Panama ranged from 4 to about 6 percent of GDP. These figures are similar to those of a number of OECD countries such as Australia (4.6), Canada (5.4), Iceland (5.7), Ireland (7.1), and New Zealand (6.2). For a comprehensive analysis of pension systems around the world, see Palacios and Pallares-Miralles (2000, 29–42).

abandonment of the previous model of development based on import sub-
stitution industrialization (ISI).[15] The ISI model, which had characterized
at least the largest Latin American economies since the 1930s and 1940s,
has given way to a new economic model based on a much closer integration
of Latin American societies into international trade and capital markets. At
the same time, Latin American countries were among the first to join the
so-called third wave of democratization.[16] Thus, the fact that these democratic transitions took place more or less concurrently with the process of
economic integration into trade and capital markets brings to the fore the
question of whether democracies can mitigate the potentially negative effects
of globalization on social spending. In short, the focus on Latin America
is appropriate because, as Mesa-Lago noted, it "has been a leader of social
security development in the Third World."[17]

The book is structured in three interrelated but substantively and meth-
odologically different parts. The first part, focusing on the preglobalization
period (i.e., 1920–1979), analyzes why some Latin American countries have
historically developed more comprehensive systems of social protection than
others. Using QCA,[18] two alternative paths to the welfare state in Latin
America are identified: with and without favorable economic conditions.
Favorable economic conditions include economic development and protection from international market competition. Under these circumstances,
only one political condition – democracy or left-labor power – was necessary
to develop a welfare state. Four of the five cases of relatively more developed
welfare systems followed this path: Argentina, which had a strong left-
labor movement but little history of continuous democracy; Brazil, which
had relatively weak Left parties and dependent labor unions, but remained

---

[15] ISI was an inward-looking model of economic development that rested on a mix of policies regarding tariffs, licenses, quotas, and exchange rates that shielded domestic producers
(especially in manufacturing) from international-market competition. For a comprehensive analysis of ISI policies within a cross-regional comparative framework, see Haggard
(1990).

[16] The original notion of the "third wave" of democratization comes from Huntington (1991).
Huntington is referring to the wave of democratization that started in Portugal in 1974,
swept Southern Europe and Latin America in the 1980s, and also transformed the political
systems of most Eastern European countries and some African countries in the 1990s.
For a review of the enormous literature on the third wave of democratization, see Geddes
(1999).

[17] Mesa-Lago (1989, xv).

[18] For a detailed analysis of the method of QCA, see Ragin (1987). For a comparison of
QCA versus other quantitative and qualitative methods of inquiry in comparative cross-
national research, see Janoski and Hicks (1994). For a more recent application of QCA to
the consolidation of welfare systems in advanced industrial countries, see Hicks (1999).

continuously democratic for eighteen years during the period under study; and Chile and Uruguay, which had both a long history of continuous democracy and a strong left-labor movement. However, in the absence of left-labor power, the "type" of welfare system that developed (as in Brazil) was more fragmented and regressive than when both political conditions where present (as in Chile and Uruguay). Alternatively, when economic conditions were unfavorable (i.e., low levels of economic development and high levels of trade openness), both political conditions – democracy and left-labor power – were necessary to develop a welfare state. This is the path followed by Costa Rica – the only country in Latin America that constructed a welfare state in the absence of a relatively high level of development.

The second part studies the relationship among globalization, domestic political institutions, and one of the most important aspects of the welfare state: social expenditures. The focus is on the 1973–2003 period – the longest period for which relatively reliable cross-national time-series of fiscal data are available for most Latin American countries.[19] The analysis uses a TSCS data set based on annual observations of public expenditures on health, education, and social security programs. The discussion revolves around a few fundamental economic and political hypotheses.

The economic hypotheses study the relationships among economic growth, the fiscal capacity of the state, and the growing integration into trade and capital markets on governments' fiscal commitment to social security and human capital expenditures. The political hypotheses analyze the effects of democracy and the balance of power between political parties and interest associations on the consolidation and development of different levels of welfare effort. The results show that growing levels of trade openness have been associated with significant reductions in social spending. However, this effect is not the same for all categories of social spending: the negative impact of trade openness operates entirely through its effect on social security expenditures, with no statistically significant impact on health and education. By contrast, the shift to democracy had either no impact or a negative impact on social security expenditures (which tend to be relatively regressive in the region) but was associated with an increase in

---

[19] As of mid-2005, the 1973–2003 period maximizes the number of annual observations that can be obtained from the IMF's *Government Finance Statistics* series. Most countries began to systematically report data on government expenditures to the IMF in 1972–1973. Data coverage after 2003 is not generally available for most countries. The study of this period is particularly important because it covers both the process of international-market integration (usually known as "globalization") and the "third wave" of democratic transitions that began in the mid-1970s.

health and education spending (which tends to reach a broader segment of the population). Openness to capital markets had a negative effect on social spending only when the fiscal deficit was relatively high, making it difficult to reduce it without cuts in social programs.

The third part of the book is based on three case studies of Chile, Costa Rica, and Peru. The rationale for the case studies and justification for the selection of them are also provided. The remainder of this chapter is organized in four sections. The first section is a brief review of the main theories of the welfare state; the second section explains how the idea of the welfare state can be applied to the developing world and situates the Latin American welfare states in comparative perspective with other regions; the third section describes the methodological approach followed in the book; and, finally, the last section summarizes each chapter.

1.1 The Welfare State: Review of Main Theories

In advanced industrial democracies, the welfare state can be seen as the culmination of a long process that began in the eighteenth century with the establishment of legal–civil rights, continued in the nineteenth century with the emergence of political rights, and culminated in the twentieth century with the consolidation of what Marshall called social citizenship.[20] However, the welfare state did not necessarily emerge gradually as the natural or automatic consequence of economic and political development. In fact, the origins of the modern welfare state in most countries can hardly be understood without taking into account the role of reformist political elites who either responded to the demands of an increasingly mobilized working class or acted preemptively to defuse labor agitation. The most notable example is Germany, where, in the 1880s, Chancellor Otto Von Bismarck – founder of the first modern welfare state – pursued a variety of political motives through state-sponsored social insurance.[21] According to Steinmetz, Bismarck had a combination of motives that included bypassing the Reichstag, splitting the liberals, and binding workers directly to the state.[22]

After World War II, the welfare state and its attendant income security programs became an intrinsic part of capitalism's postwar "Golden Age" – an era in which "prosperity, equality and full employment seemed in perfect

[20] See Marshall (1963).
[21] For an extensive review of the rise of social spending in the 1880–1930 period, see Lindert (1994). He argues against the conventional wisdom that the leader in welfare state development was not Germany but rather Denmark and Ireland (p. 15).
[22] For a detailed analysis of Bismarck's motives, see Beck (1995) and Steinmetz (1996).

harmony."[23] Some of the first conceptualizations of the "welfare state" are due to the English historian Asa Briggs.[24] According to Briggs, a state can only qualify as a "welfare state" if it undertakes three kinds of activity. First, it must provide individuals and families with the necessary income guarantees to escape poverty. Second, it must remove or significantly mitigate social risks associated with sickness, old age, and unemployment. And, third, it has to offer all citizens access to a certain range of social services.[25] As Castles points out, in contemporary welfare states, the first and second objectives have been accomplished through social security transfers, which provide assistance to the poor and income maintenance to those who fall under a wide variety of social risks. The third objective has been accomplished through high-quality public health and educational systems that have progressively been regarded as a social right of citizenship.[26] According to these criteria, the welfare state is a postwar creation.[27]

But, what factors account for the development of the welfare state? Scholars have generally identified four main theoretical perspectives. On the one hand, the "logic of industrialism" theory and economic-openness theory, which emphasize economic factors; on the other, the class analytical tradition and state-centric approaches, which emphasize political factors. First, theories that refer to the "logic of industrialism" emphasize how the welfare state emerges in the process of industrialization to respond to exogenous economic imperatives. Industrialization is associated with a deep transformation of socioeconomic structures and with transitions from agriculture to industrialism, from rural life to urban life, and from personal relations to abstract exchange relations.[28] This process involves dislocations in the family and work relations. As Pampel and Williamson noted, because many

---

[23] See Esping-Andersen (1991, 1).

[24] For a discussion of Briggs's contribution, see Castles (1998). This discussion draws on Castles's analysis.

[25] Another broadly used definition of the welfare state was provided by Wilensky, who argued that the essence of the welfare state is a series of "government-protected minimum standards of income, nutrition, health, housing and education, assured to every citizen as a political right, not charity" (1975, 6–7).

[26] Castles (1998, 146).

[27] These criteria need to be applied with care, however. A stringent application would lead to a small sample of welfare states even in advanced capitalist democracies. The criteria provide a general view to analyze the great deal of variations among countries at each level of development in the scope of their income-maintenance programs and social services. According to this view, the idea of the welfare state can be applied to any country. We need, then, to explore how and to what degree a given country satisfies these functions of income maintenance, protection against poverty, and social-service provision.

[28] Hicks (1999, 17).

vulnerable persons are unable to obtain traditional support from family members, the state expands to provide social welfare support.[29] A related argument is Wagner's well-known law of "increasing state activity."[30] According to this law, the size of the public sector grows with real per capita income as a response to the expanded administrative needs of an increasingly complex industrial society.[31] Furthermore, economic development fosters changes in the demographic structure of society that are important for the growth of the welfare state. Because of the loss of traditional family support, an increasing part of the social welfare effort of governments is directed to the aged in the form of pension transfers.[32] This is, first and foremost, a functionalist theory. The state expands because of exogenous technological and industrial pressures and responds (almost automatically) to the economic and demographic needs of the population. As such, this theory cannot specify the mechanisms that link industrial needs and the problems of the aged with welfare state expansion.

The second economic perspective (not necessarily in opposition to the first) emphasizes the relationship between economic openness and the welfare state. This perspective focuses on why and how social welfare expands to compensate the losers of international-market competition. Supported by a substantial body of empirical research on advanced industrial countries, the main argument is that globalization is associated with the expansion of the welfare state. The mechanism that connects globalization with the expansion of the welfare state can be summarized in three steps: first, growing exposure to international markets increases economic insecurity and inequality[33]; second, as a result, vulnerable economic actors – for example, those who have lost their jobs or work in industries that cannot face up to the challenges of international competition – will use political channels such as trade unions and political parties to press the governments for

---

[29] Pampel and Williamson (1989, 26).

[30] Wagner, A. 1883. *Finanzwissenschaft.* Translated and reprinted as "Three Extracts on Public Finance." In R. A. Musgrave and A. T. Peacock, eds., *Classics on the Theory of Public Finance.* London: Macmillan.

[31] For a more recent analysis of Wagner's Law and how economic development combined with other political factors is associated with an expansion of the public sector, see Boix (2001, 1–17).

[32] Wilensky (1975).

[33] According to the Hecksher-Ohlin-Samuelson factor-endowments model, expanding levels of trade will increase the demand for the relatively abundant factor of production and reduce the demand for the relatively scarce one. Because in developed countries skilled labor is the relatively abundant factor and unskilled labor the relatively scarce one, expanding trade, especially with developing countries, is likely to widen the wage differential between skilled and unskilled workers.

compensation; and, third, governments will respond to these pressures by expanding the welfare state to protect the domestic economy, control political unrest, and put into place programs designed to raise the skills of the labor force and make it more competitive in international markets. Until recently, this theory had been considered one of the most important determinants of welfare expansion in advanced industrial economies. However, recent work by Iversen and Cussack has cast some doubt on this hypothesis. These authors argue that most of the risks associated with modern industrial societies are the result of technologically induced structural transformations in national labor markets, such as increases in productivity, changes in consumption patterns, and saturated demand for products from the traditional sectors of the economy. According to these authors, it is these structural sources of risk that fuel demands for state compensation and risk sharing.[34]

The third and fourth theoretical perspectives highlight political factors. The "class analytical tradition" or "power-resource theory" focuses on how working-class actors, union organization, and worker representation by broadly socialist parties are the key determinants for development and expansion of the welfare state. In this perspective, what matters for welfare state development is working-class mobilization, combined with various political–institutional conditions.[35] This theory further assumes that the basic cleavage in society is between capitalists and the working class, and that it is reflected in political behavior: low-income people will vote for parties of the Left and high-income people will vote for parties of the Right.[36] The degree of working-class power and the size and centralization of labor unions determine whether left-oriented parties will be elected and will expand social welfare to favor the working class.[37] The core of this theory is best captured by Huber and Stephens, who argue that the struggle of the welfare state is a struggle over distribution. Hence, what is crucial is the organizational power of those standing to benefit from redistribution – that is, the working and middle classes.[38] An initial empirical problem with this theory, however, is that authors seem to disagree as to whether what matters

---

[34] Iversen and Cussack (2000, 303).

[35] Hicks (1999, 20).

[36] For the classical statement about the relationship among class identity, party systems, and voter alignments in a number of advanced industrial democracies, see Lipset and Rokkan (1967); for an analysis of class identity and the welfare state, see Korpi (1983).

[37] The main problem with this theory is that in most countries, the unionized constituency of leftist parties is too small to gain control of the government without strategic alliances with other groups. These alliances may compromise Social Democratic ideals associated with the welfare state. For a comprehensive analysis of this argument, see Przeworki (1985).

[38] Huber and Stephens (2001, 17).

is the percentage of Left votes, Left seats in parliament, or union organization. Some recent empirical analyses demonstrate, however, that the best predictor of welfare state generosity is the long-run partisan character of the government.[39]

Finally, the fourth theoretical approach to the origins and development of the welfare state focuses on the paternalistic actions of state autocrats and the policy-making capabilities and orientation of state institutions.[40] This perspective highlights two fundamental state characteristics associated in different ways with the welfare state. The first is *state centralization*, which makes it easier for state managers to develop and implement welfare policies. Some have argued, for example, that federalism – with its decentralization of finances and dispersion of authority – dampens the degree of expansion of the public economy,[41] or that competitive deregulation in a decentralized system could fuel a downward spiral in social provision, leading to "lowest common denominator" social policies.[42] According to this view, the concentration of decision making in the central government minimizes the veto power of subnational governments or the blocking potential of a fragmented opposition. Second, the welfare state may also expand as a function of the bureaucratic strength of administrative agencies. As Niskanen noted, government bureaucracies struggle to expand their budgets in order to be in a better position to reach their goals.[43] Hence, welfare state expansion will also be related to the power of welfare state agencies. Evidence from the American States and the industrialized democracies provides some empirical support to the idea that budget-maximizing state bureaucrats may act collectively to maximize public spending.[44]

1.2 The Welfare State: Latin America in Comparative Perspective

Whereas economists and political scientists are still debating the "origins," "worlds," "developments," and "consequences" of welfare state expansion, a growing number of studies from the Organization for Economic Cooperation and Development (OECD) have now changed their analytical focus to emphasize the "transitions," "contradictions," or "crises" of the welfare state.

---

[39] Huber, Ragin, and Stephens (1993) and Huber and Stephens (2001).
[40] See Hicks (1999) and Hicks and Swanke (1992).
[41] Cameron (1978, 1253).
[42] Pierson (1995, 452).
[43] Niskanen (1987).
[44] See Korpi (1989).

And, it has become increasingly fashionable to talk about the dilemmas, or even "trilemmas," facing the welfare state in an era of globalization.[45]

It is unfortunate, however, that despite the enormous amount of work on welfare states in advanced industrial democracies, research on the relationship between economic and political factors affecting different levels of welfare effort in the developing world is practically nonexistent. This is unfortunate if we take into account that some middle-income countries such as Argentina, Chile, and Uruguay had been pioneers in the early adoption of income security programs. For example, by 1920, all three countries had adopted at least one income security program (e.g., work accident, health, pension, or unemployment).[46] Thus, it may be true that talking about the "welfare state" outside the realm of advanced industrial countries requires some qualifications. And, it would likely be problematic to talk about the "welfare state" in very poor countries. There are a number of middle-income countries – many of which are found in Latin America – that preceded some of the OECD countries in terms of early establishment of income security programs.[47] It is therefore puzzling that researchers have almost completely excluded them from their analyses. We still know little about how these debates concerning the origin, development, and future of the welfare state in OECD countries apply to the middle-income countries of Eastern Europe, East Asia, and Latin America – the latter being a region of special interest because of its being the leader of social security development in the developing world.[48]

Two of the most important attempts to map the origins of the welfare state in Latin America are the works of Mesa-Lago and Huber.[49] However, to date, little work has been done to systematically test theories developed in the context of the advanced industrial countries of the OECD in other regional settings. Mesa-Lago provides some important clues, but his analysis is somewhat descriptive to establish clear causal patterns. On the other hand, Huber, who builds on Mesa-Lago's work, presents an analysis that provides

---

[45] The word *trilemma* was used for the first time by Iversen and Wren (1998).
[46] Mesa-Lago (1989, 3–8).
[47] For example, according to Mesa-Lago (1989, xv), Chile, Uruguay, Argentina, and Brazil "preceded the United States in health-maternity insurance, family allowances and unemployment compensation."
[48] Hence, the study of Latin America is particularly interesting because (1) it is probably the only developing region in which we can find at least some countries that have attempted to establish welfare systems similar to their European counterparts, and (2) it has experienced a recent process of democratization and globalization that allows us to explore the interaction between these two phenomena and welfare reform.
[49] See Mesa-Lago (1978, 1989) and Huber (1996).

some support for the "power-resource" theory. According to her, the development of social insurance in Latin America began virtually uniformly with the military, civil servants, and judiciary. Then, coverage extended to the best organized and strategically located sectors of the middle and working classes (e.g., journalists, bank workers, teachers, railroad and port workers, and the merchant marine) and only later for larger sectors of the working class in sectors such as mining, public services, and manufacturing.[50] This sequential extension of social benefits would reflect the organizational capacity and distribution of power within society. It does not seem coincidental, for example, that the military – which has always played a prominent role in Latin American politics – was the first social sector to receive protection.

Even less is known about East Asian welfare states. As Goodman and Peng observed, despite the burgeoning literature on East Asian countries, little is known to date about their social welfare systems. This fact probably reflects the idea that systematized social welfare has been a relatively new development among industrialized East Asian countries.[51] There is some notion that welfare policy has been dominated by economic rather social considerations and that ruling elites have only accepted the idea of social welfare when confronting a political crisis. Some analysts also refer to the influence of Confucian values and how the welfare role has been typically assumed by the family, the local communities, and the large corporations. But, little is known about what impeded the development of more comprehensive systems of social protection.

As Tables 1.1 and 1.2 illustrate, if we use social expenditures as a proxy for welfare state development (which, as acknowledged herein, has important limitations), East Asian countries are among the least developed welfare states in the developing world. The tables can also be used to further reinforce the intrinsic importance of choosing Latin America as the main regional focus for the study of the welfare state in the developing world.[52] An analysis of Eastern Europe based solely on social expenditures would demonstrate that all East European countries in the sample are highly developed

---

[50] Huber (1996, 147).

[51] Goodman and Peng (1996, 192).

[52] An important limitation of these tables is that they are based on central government budgeted expenditures. This can be an important problem to the extent that a significant share of social spending is executed by regional and local governments or by parapublic entities (e.g., public enterprises). However, the facts that the tables are based on averages over a period of about thirty years (in most cases, decentralization has increased significantly only in the last decade) and that social security expenditures continue to be highly centralized in most cases provide a reasonable degree of confidence that they offer an appropriate measure of relative rankings in social spending levels.

Table 1.1. *Average Social Expenditures as a Percentage of GDP around the World*[a]

Scale	OECD		Eastern Europe[b]		Latin America		East Asia	
30	Netherlands	31.7						
	Belgium	28.6						
	France	27.9						
			Poland	26.7				
25	Austria	25.5	Czech Republic	25.6				
	Sweden	23.6	Hungary	23.5				
	Italy	22.1						
20	Denmark	20.1						
	Germany	18.9						
	Finland	18.0						
	UK	17.3						
	Norway	16.8			Uruguay	16.9		
	Spain	16.0						
			Romania	15.0	Argentina	14.9		
15	Portugal	14.5	Bulgaria	14.7	Chile	14.6		
					Brazil	14.2		
	Switzerland	13.5			Costa Rica	13.4		
	Greece	13.5						
	Australia	11.5						
10	Canada	11.4						
	USA	10.2						
	Japan	10.0						
					Venezuela	7.6	Malaysia	7.8
					Mexico	6.4		
					Bolivia	6.2		
05							Singapore	5.7
					Ecuador	4.8		
					Peru	4.3	Korea	4.3
					Dominican Republic	4.2		
					El Salvador	4.2		
					Paraguay	4.0		
					Guatemala	3.0	Philippines	3.1
							Indonesia	2.9
00								
Average		18.9		20.3		8.7		4.7

[a] Average central government expenditures on social security programs, health, and education during the 1973–2000 period.
[b] Data for Eastern Europe are available for the 1990s only.
Source: Government Finance Statistics, IMF.

Table 1.2. *Average Social Expenditures as a Percentage of Government Spending around the World*[a]

Scale	OECD		Eastern Europe[b]		Latin America		East Asia	
70			Czech Republic	71.2				
	Germany	68.1	Poland	68.0				
	France	66.9						
	Switzerland	65.1						
					Uruguay	63.3		
60	Netherlands	60.8			Costa Rica	59.1		
	Sweden	58.4						
			Bulgaria	57.6				
	Spain	56.3						
	Finland	56.1						
	Italy	54.4			Chile	54.3		
	Denmark	53.3						
	Ireland	51.3						
50	Australia	47.0	Hungary	47.2	Argentina	47.8		
	Norway	46.1						
	Japan	45.2						
	USA	45.7						
	Canada	45.0						
	UK	44.7						
					Brazil	42.3		
	Portugal	41.3						
40					Bolivia	38.1		
					Paraguay	37.6		
					Mexico	36.9		
	Greece	35.9	Bulgaria	35.4				
					Ecuador	34.5		
					El Salvador	30.0	Singapore	29.7
30					Guatemala	29.7	Korea	29.5
					Dominican Republic	28.3		
							Philippines	27.5
					Peru	24.1		
							Thailand	21.2
20							Malaysia	20.4
							Indonesia	19.5
Average		52.6		55.8		37.6		24.6

[a] Average central government expenditures on social security programs, health, and education during the 1973–2000 period.
[b] Data for Eastern Europe are available for the 1990s only.
Source: Government Finance Statistics, IMF.

welfare states. In East Asia, all countries seem to have weak systems of social protection. By contrast, Latin American countries can be divided into two groups. The first group, including Argentina, Brazil, Chile, Uruguay, and Costa Rica, has relatively well-developed welfare states with social expenditures that range from 13.5 to 17 percent of gross domestic product (GDP) and from 42 to 63 percent of government expenditures, respectively. The second group of (less developed) welfare states includes Bolivia, Dominican Republic, El Salvador, Ecuador, Guatemala, Mexico, Paraguay, Peru, and Venezuela. In this group, social expenditures range between 3 and 7.6 percent of GDP and between 24 and 38 percent of government expenditures, respectively. Hence, Latin America seems to reproduce a wide variety of degrees of welfare state development. For example, at the high end of expenditures, Uruguay matches Norway and Costa Rica matches Switzerland in average social spending as a percentage of GDP (around 17 percent). At the low level, Latin American countries also reproduce the whole range of variation of East Asian countries: Venezuela's[53] social expenditures as a percentage of GDP are similar to those of Malaysia (7.5 to 8 percent), Peru matches Korea (4.3 percent), and Guatemala and the Philippines have historically spent practically the same, according to this criterion (3 percent).

Hence, the data suggest that in terms of social spending levels, Latin America could almost be considered a representative sample of the different degrees of welfare state development in the developing world. The most advanced welfare states in Latin America, such as Uruguay, spend as much as Norway and Spain and exceed substantially the levels of Japan and the United States – two of the richest OECD countries. However, the least developed welfare states in Latin America (e.g., Guatemala and Paraguay) are similar in terms of social spending levels to the Philippines or Indonesia – the two smallest welfare states in East Asia.

Finally, a note of caution should be introduced about the use of social expenditures to study welfare states. As Esping-Andersen pointed out, expenditures are epiphenomenal to the theoretical substance of the welfare state. By comparing welfare states based on their spending levels, we are assuming that all spending counts equally. Yet, some welfare states, like the Austrian one, for example, spend a large share on benefits for privileged civil servants.[54] This warning comes even more to the fore with the observation

---

[53] As noted, the analysis is based on historical averages of budgeted social expenditures. It does not include, for example, the recent expansion of social programs in Venezuela financed off-budget through the state oil company as a result of the current high oil prices.
[54] Esping-Andersen (1991, 19).

that social expenditures grew in Britain during the Thatcher period. This might be surprising considering that Thatcher's tenure is usually considered one of the major periods of welfare state retrenchment in Britain. The puzzle is, however, easily resolved if one takes into account that this increase in social expenditures was linked to the effect of automatic stabilizers, such as unemployment benefits, which usually come into action during periods of relatively lower economic activity.

There is, therefore, a limit to what we can learn by simply looking at expenditures. Expenditures do not tell us enough about the actual coverage, scope, and quality of delivery of social services. It is, therefore, important to move from the black box of expenditures to the content of welfare states, which includes questions such as the conditions of eligibility and the quality of benefits and services.[55] Social expenditures are a useful proxy for the resources that states are willing to devote to social protection; however, a focus on expenditures has to be complemented with a more qualitative type of analysis. The next section explains how this task can be accomplished through the cases studies.

1.3 Methodology

The book draws on three different albeit complementary methodologies: QCA, TSCS analysis, and in-depth case studies of three countries: Chile, Costa Rica, and Peru.

First, QCA is used to study the reasons why some Latin American countries have historically developed more extensive systems of social protection than others during the 1920–1973 period. QCA uses the Boolean approach. It analyzes matrices of binary 0–1 qualitative data describing the presence or absence of traits for a group of nations – in this case, the set of Latin American countries. This is a relatively new analytical technique used by scholars engaged in the qualitative study of macrosocial phenomena.[56] Its greatest advantage stems from its capacity to bridge the methodological gap that separates intensive, case-oriented research[57] and extensive, variable-oriented research, providing a middle road between generality and complexity.

---

[55] Esping-Andersen (1991, 20).

[56] For a comprehensive coverage of this methodology, see Ragin (1987). For an application of QCA to the study of pensions systems, see Ragin (1994, 320–345). For an application of Boolean algebra to the origins of the first income security programs, see Hicks (1999).

[57] Case-oriented research typically examines a limited number of cases exploring many causal and outcome conditions in different configurations. By contrast, variable-oriented research examines only a few variables across a large number of cases (Ragin, 1994).

This methodology is used to investigate the effects of economic development, trade openness, democracy, and left-labor power on the expansion and development of the welfare state in Latin America. In particular, which combinations of economic and political factors led to welfare state expansion in Latin America? Is economic development a *sine qua non* condition for the expansion of the welfare state in Latin America? What is the comparative role of democracy and left-labor power? Does trade exposure contribute to or hamper welfare state expansion? These are some of the questions that are considered.

Second, a TSCS data set that includes fourteen Latin American countries from 1973 to 2003 is used to explore the relationships among globalization, democracy, and the balance of partisan power on social expenditures. The main structural equation is given by the following:

$$\Delta Y_{i,t} = \alpha + \Delta X_{i,t-1}\beta_k + \phi(Y_{i,t-1} - X_{i,t-1}\Upsilon) + \varepsilon_{i,t},$$

where $Y_{i,t}$ is social expenditures in country i during year t, Δ is the first differences operator, X is a vector of independent variables, and $\varepsilon_{i,t}$ is a white-noise error term. This analysis is based on a pooled time-series research design in which annual time series from a cross-section of countries are stacked on top of one another and analyzed jointly within the same data set. This implies a combination of time-series (i.e., temporal observations on a unit of analysis) with cross-sections (i.e., observations on a unit of analysis at single time points). This statistical technique has a number of advantages. First, it produces a relatively large *n* (i.e., 14 countries by 30 years = 420 country-years) and can therefore simultaneously test for the effect of a large number of independent variables. This helps to overcome "degrees of freedom" problems, making possible analyses that would otherwise be problematical. Second, it combines attention to both longitudinal and cross-sectional variation and can therefore produce useful generalizations across both time and space.[58]

Finally, this book clearly recognizes that there are important limitations to what we can learn from large-n studies. Quantitative analysis forces the researcher to think in terms of variables and measurements whose validity and reliability are often open to question. For example, although social expenditures are a useful proxy for the resources that states are willing to devote to social protection, there is a limit to what we can learn by simply

---

[58] See Janoski and Hicks (1994, 18). In practice, however, TSCS data tend to have less explanatory power because researchers are forced, in most cases, to include country-specific fixed effects in their regressions to control for omitted variables. The inclusion of fixed effects is based on the "within" estimator, which virtually eliminates the capacity of making cross-sectional inferences.

looking at expenditures. As noted previously, expenditures do not tell us enough about the actual coverage, scope, and quality of delivery of social services. Similarly, measuring democracy on a numeric scale may mask important qualitative aspects of democratic institutions that have significant importance for welfare outcomes. It is not easy to compress a concept as complex as democracy into a simple numerical scale. Thus, the study of TSCS data is complemented with in-depth studies of three cases: Chile, Costa Rica, and Peru.

These countries have been chosen for three interrelated reasons. First, according to the World Bank, in the 1970s, Chile, Costa Rica, and Peru were at roughly the same level of development in terms of their GDP per capita[59] (Table 1.3). In the 1970s and 1980s, GDP per capita levels in these three countries were rather similar. However, both the degree of welfare effort (i.e., as measured by social expenditures) and social welfare outcomes (e.g., infant mortality and illiteracy) were much worse in Peru than in Chile or Costa Rica. No comparison among Latin American countries with similar GDP per capita levels produces such contrasting differences in terms of welfare state development and social welfare outcomes. If economic development is one of the most important factors in the expansion of the welfare state, why did Costa Rica and Chile develop a more comprehensive system of social protection than Peru?

Second, these countries were selected because they provide some of the best examples to understand the causal mechanisms underlying the relationships among globalization, democracy, and the welfare state. If we measure globalization simply in terms of a country's degree of trade openness, then Chile experienced the highest relative increase in its "degree of globalization" in Latin America, moving from an average ratio of imports plus exports to GDP of 30 percent in 1950–1979 to more than 55 percent in 1980–2000. Trade openness also increased sharply in Costa Rica, from an average of 58 percent of GDP in 1950–1979 to an average of 78 percent in 1980–2000. In contrast, Peru is the only country in Latin America in which the average level of trade openness actually declined substantially from 37 to

[59] In the *World Development Report* (2000), the average GDP per capita in 1995 U.S. dollars for the 1970s in these three countries were as follows: Peru ($2,785), Costa Rica ($2,338), and Chile ($2,146). It is important to note, however, that other sources give Chile a level of development about 30 percent higher than Peru or Costa Rica; see, for example, Thorp (1998, 353). Also, the focus herein is on a narrow definition of economic development that does not include social development. As Table 1.3 demonstrates, if we broaden our definition of development to include social outcomes such as infant mortality and illiteracy rates, Peru would score much lower on all these indicators than Chile or Costa Rica.

Table 1.3. *Comparative Economic and Social Indicators: Chile, Costa Rica, and Peru*

	1973–1981			1982–1989			1990–2000		
	Chile	Costa Rica	Peru	Chile	Costa Rica	Peru	Chile	Costa Rica	Peru
Fiscal Revenues (in % of GDP)	31.9	17.8	15.4	26.4	23.0	11.3	20.6	22.1	11.9
Social Spending (in % total expenditures)[a]	51.5	64.0	28.6	59.9	61.6	29.5	62.8	72.7	40.5
Social Spending (in % of GDP)	15.5	12.5	4.4	16.0	13.7	4.1	12.3	14.6	6.3
Per-capita GDP (in PPP-adjusted USD)	2,074	2,607	23.4	3,819	3,933	3,208	7,228	5,610	3,985
Per-capita GDP in USD	2,147	2,339	2,785	2,468	2,237	2,488	3,802	2,564	2,297
GDP Growth (in percent)	1.7	3.2	3.7	5.9	2.4	−1.2	7.7	3.7	4.6
% Population >65	5.5	3.5	3.6	5.9	3.9	3.8	6.5	4.5	4.2
Illiteracy Rates (in percent)	9.2	9.1	22.4	6.8	6.8	16.6	5.3	5.4	12.8
School Enrollment (in percent)	91.5	87.9	90.7	90.0	85.3	93.4	87.9	88.2	90.7
Immunization: Diphtheria (in percent)[b]	97.0	83.3	17.7	92.0	84.1	45.1	92.7	89.0	86.4
Immunization: Measles (in percent)[b]	91.6	66.7	24.3	93.4	79.9	43.0	91.6	90.2	79.7
Infant Mortality (per 1,000 live births)	45.0	27.9	88.0	18.0	13.3	68.0	10.4	14.2	40.0

[a] Includes social security, health, and education expenditures.
[b] Children younger than 12 months.
Sources: World Bank, *World Development Indicators* (various issues) and IMF, *Government Finance Statistics* (various issues).

30 percent, if we compare the 1950–1979 period with the 1980–2000 period. Hence, this choice of countries includes two cases in the sample in which trade openness increased the most and the only country in which it declined substantially.

Third, if our purpose is to document how political institutions may shape or hamper the expansion of social welfare, these three countries provide some of the most useful contrasts in Latin America as well. Costa Rica has

been continuously democratic since 1949: it has a strong two-party system, high levels of voter turnout, and a relatively high dispersion of power
between the Executive and other branches of government and autonomous
institutions (AIs). As Chapter 6 demonstrates, this particular configuration
of domestic political arrangements allowed the Costa Rican welfare state to
withstand the pressures of globalization and economic reform in a way that
neither Chile nor Peru managed to accomplish. On the other hand, Chile
had a strong tradition of continuous democracy until the early 1970s but
experienced a democratic breakdown in 1973 and was followed by one of the
most brutal and repressive dictatorships in Latin America. Unlike in Costa
Rica, the extreme concentration of power in the Executive allowed General
Pinochet to implement a fast and radical program of economic reform and
to roll back the size of the welfare state in a way that can hardly be imagined
in a democracy. Then, in 1990, Chile experienced a transition to democracy,
civil and political society reemerged relatively fast, and the new democratic
government moved quickly to expand the welfare state while preserving the
healthy macroeconomic environment inherited from the previous authoritarian regime. Finally, Peru had a weak history of democratic practices prior
to the transition to democracy in 1980, remained democratic for twelve
years, and then suffered another democratic breakdown in 1992. In sharp
contrast with Costa Rica (and Chile after 1990), the Peruvian party system lacked institutionalization, voter turnout was relatively low, and power
tended to be highly concentrated in the president. As a result, democracy
in Peru had a much weaker effect on social welfare than in Costa Rica and
Chile (after 1990).

These three case studies enhance substantially the analysis and contribute
to a better understanding of the mechanisms through which globalization
and economic reform put pressure on the welfare state, how these effects
are mediated by domestic political institutions such as regime type, and the
balance of partisan power among political parties and interest associations.
The case studies also provide an opportunity to take the analysis of the
welfare state beyond the black box of social expenditures and look into, for
example, changes in the organization and delivery of social services.

1.4 Chapter Outline

Chapter 2 uses QCA to study the reasons why some Latin American countries historically have developed more extensive systems of social protection
than others. It focuses on the origins of welfare systems in Latin America,
which in some countries date back to the 1920s and 1930s, and gives special

attention to their expansion and development from the 1940s to the 1970s. The chapter investigates, in particular, the effects of economic development, trade openness, left-labor power, and democracy on the development of the welfare state in Latin America.

Chapter 3 discusses the main economic and political hypotheses related to changes in social expenditures in Latin America during the 1973–2003 period. The chapter analyzes the effects of economic development, fiscal constraints, and globalization, on the one hand, and democracy and the partisan orientation of the Executive on the other. It presents the main hypotheses and introduces some simple correlations and charts to illustrate the initial tentative relationships among the main variables.

Chapter 4 uses pooled time-series analysis to systematically test the hypotheses presented in Chapter 3. The chapter shows that growing integration into trade markets has exerted a consistently negative pressure on social spending, with the effect being driven by declines in social security expenditures. It also finds that democracy and popularly based governments did not seem to have a statistically significant impact on aggregate social spending. However, once expenditures are disaggregated by program, popularly based governments had a positive impact on social security programs, which tend to be regressive, whereas democracies tended to protect human capital expenditures (which reach a wider segment of the population) more than their autocratic counterparts.

Chapter 5 analyzes the evolution of the Chilean welfare system under Pinochet's military regime (1973–1989), during the first democratic government of Patricio Alwyin (1990–1994), and the subsequent administration of President Frei (1995–2000). The chapter shows that until the military coup of 1973, Chile had developed one of the most comprehensive welfare systems in Latin America, covering a wide variety of social risks and consolidating a relatively developed and universalistic educational and health system. From 1980 to 1987, inspired by the philosophy of state retrenchment, social expenditures declined dramatically by almost 50 percent, but they increased again in 1988–1989 when Pinochet felt the electoral pressures of a plebiscite to decide whether he would continue in power. After the transition to democracy in 1990, the new government embarked on a strategy of "growth with equity" and substantially increased public expenditures on health and education.

Chapter 6 studies the evolution of the Costa Rican welfare system – one of the most advanced and comprehensive in the region – from the early 1970s to the late 1990s. What makes Costa Rica a particularly interesting case study is that, unlike most other countries in Latin America, in the 1980s and 1990s it experienced neither a process of democratization[60] nor a fast and radical program of trade liberalization and market-oriented reform. Costa Rica has been continuously democratic for more than fifty years, and economic reforms took place within a context of constant negotiation and broad participation by multiple interest groups, business associations, multilateral organizations, and foreign governments. Furthermore, the case of Costa Rica provides an opportunity to understand the conditions under which the strong relationship between trade openness and reductions in social expenditures (which emerges as a key empirical finding in Chapter 5 and also is corroborated by the case of Chile) does not necessarily hold.

Chapter 7 studies the evolution of the Peruvian welfare system from the mid-1970s to the late 1990s. First, the chapter shows that although a sound and balanced macroeconomic policy is not necessarily a good social policy in itself, a bad macroeconomic policy is always a bad social policy over the intermediate to long term. The inability of the democratic governments of the 1980s to reestablish the equilibrium in the most basic economic indicators ended in macroeconomic chaos, a radical erosion of fiscal revenues, and the inability of the state to provide even the most basic social services. Second, just like in Chile, the case of Peru shows that a process of fast and radical economic reform, facilitated by an extreme concentration of power in the Executive, can have a strong negative effect on employment-based social protection (i.e., social security programs). Finally, the Peruvian experience also shows that authoritarian leaders who subject themselves to the pressures of elections face similar or even greater incentives to increase social expenditures than their democratic counterparts.

Chapter 8, the concluding chapter, recapitulates some of the main findings, suggests a number of areas for future research, and points to two of the greatest challenges currently facing Latin American welfare systems. The first challenge is how to reconcile current levels of welfare effort, or even expand them, respecting basic macroeconomic (especially fiscal) constraints. As the cases of Chile under Allende (1970–1973) and Peru under García (1980–1985) demonstrated, to expand social welfare without paying attention to basic macroeconomic fundamentals has devastating consequences for the economy at large and the welfare state in particular. The second challenge is how to increase the effectiveness of Latin American welfare systems. Although looking at the effects of the welfare state as an independent variable is beyond the scope of this study, the concluding chapter briefly

---

[60] Costa Rica has been uninterruptedly democratic since 1949 to the present. This is the longest period of continuous political democracy of any country in Latin America.

compares the relationship between the welfare state and one of its most studied effects: income inequality. Both the long-term expansion/sustainability
of the welfare state and its effects on social welfare outcomes are important
areas that deserve future research. If the book cannot provide sufficiently
convincing answers to all these questions, it at least points to some useful
directions that are worth pursuing in future research endeavors.

2

The Historical Evolution of Welfare Systems
in Latin America

Qualitative Comparative Analysis

Why have some Latin American countries historically developed more
extensive welfare states[1] than others? What is the relative importance of
economic development, trade openness, democracy, and left-labor power
on the evolution of Latin America's public welfare systems? This chapter
asks which combinations of economic and political factors contributed to
the expansion of welfare systems in different groups of Latin American countries. For analytical purposes, it is useful to distinguish between the *origins*
and *consolidation* of the welfare state, on the one hand, and its *expansion* and
development, on the other. A study of the origins of the welfare state, both
in advanced capitalist democracies and in Latin America, would require a
careful analysis of the economic and political factors that led to the passage
of the first social security and welfare laws in the 1920s and 1930s (earlier for some countries). By contrast, an analysis of the development of the

---

[1] As noted in Chapter 1, the welfare state can be defined narrowly as a repertoire of state-led
public policies aimed at protecting citizens against the risks of modern capitalist life – for
example, unemployment, old age, sickness – and improving the accumulation of human
capital and the equalization of opportunities. The first objective is usually accomplished
through social security programs (e.g., pension transfers, unemployment benefits, family
allowances, food stamps), whereas the second objective depends on the public provision of
health and education services. States can be more or less successful in the pursuit of these
goals. In some countries, especially in Scandinavia, these objectives have been reached with
such success that they have progressively been regarded as a social right of citizenship. In
other countries, large segments of the population lack access to even the most basic social
programs. However, from the perspective we are taking herein, the idea of the welfare state
does not need to presuppose that the state is actually succeeding in maintaining the income
of their citizens, reducing poverty, ensuring equal access to health and education, limiting
dependence on the market, and so forth. It only presupposes that the state does indeed
have a more or less developed repertoire of policies aimed at reaching at least some of these
goals. The different degrees in which the state attempts to deal with these social risks are
precisely what we want to investigate.

welfare state would focus on the socioeconomic and political factors that transformed initial social legislation into increasingly greater welfare entitlements and public health and educational systems. The analysis in this chapter refers briefly to the origins of Latin American welfare systems in the 1920 and 1930s but focuses more extensively on their consolidation and expansion from the 1940s to the late 1970s – a historical period in which the largest Latin American economies were following ISI policies that kept them relatively closed to international markets.[2]

The chapter is organized in five sections. The first section briefly describes the emergence of Latin American welfare systems and provides an analytical framework to classify countries into welfare and non-welfare systems. It argues that welfare systems in the region developed in a fragmented manner. They were first established for groups that controlled significant proportions of public power or critical economic resources. Then they extended to the best organized and strategically located sectors of the working classes, leaving without coverage most of the self-employed, who typically belonged to the informal sector. In most cases, however, social-protection policies were not the passive result of group pressures. Rather, they were linked to issues of statecraft and social control as part of a general strategy to promote social peace and co-opt significant sectors of the working class that were becoming increasingly mobilized.

The second section introduces the main independent variables, discusses initial theoretical expectations, and describes the nature of the probabilistic relationships among economic development, trade openness, democracy, left-labor power, and the expansion of welfare systems in the region. The third section uses QCA to better specify how these different configurations of conditions allowed certain Latin American countries to develop more extensive welfare systems than others. Why did Argentina, Chile, Uruguay, Costa Rica, and – to a lesser extent – Brazil evolve into more developed systems of social protection than Mexico, Venezuela, Peru, Bolivia, Ecuador, Paraguay, Guatemala, El Salvador, and the Dominican Republic?[3]

The fourth section of the chapter illustrates with brief descriptions of each case some of the causal mechanisms underlying the complex configuration

---

[2] This period may therefore be called the "preglobalization period." Subsequent chapters deal with the post-1980 (globalization) period – when the fast growth of international flows of goods and capital linked Latin American societies more closely to international trade and capital markets.

[3] See Chapters 1 and 3 for the reasons why some Latin American countries had to be excluded from the analysis. In any event, the countries included account for more than 90 percent of the territory and population of Latin America.

of conditions that may have contributed to (or hampered) welfare state development in Latin America. It pays special attention to Chile, Uruguay, Costa Rica, Argentina, and Brazil (i.e., the five more developed welfare states). In the process, some of the main findings of the QCA are challenged. This concerns especially the role of democracy in Brazil. Finally, the last section takes stock of the main findings and extends the discussion to the rest of the Latin American countries, where the role of the state for social protection never developed to the same degree.

2.1 The Emergence of Welfare Systems in Latin America

Welfare systems in Latin America have evolved through an incremental process over a long historical period that dates back to colonial times. After independence from Spain and Portugal, most of the new republican governments retained the old socioeconomic status quo and inherited a number of social-protective institutions. One of the most important aspects that shaped the historical development of welfare systems in Latin America was the top-down, rigidly stratified structure of colonial society in the region. As Mesa-Lago[4] observed,

> Class divisions were closely connected to occupation and race. At the top of the hierarchy were royal functionaries, high military officers, church dignitaries, large landowners and mine operators. Next came other civil servants, military men, priests, and those in the liberal professions (lawyers, physicians, accountants) (. . .) [third was] the artisan group [which] expanded dramatically in the second half of the sixteenth century and throughout the seventeenth century (. . .) At the bottom of the scale were those working in the mines, agriculture, construction and domestic service. The bulk of this group was composed of Indians (particularly in Mesoamerica and the Andean region) and imported African slaves (in the Caribbean).[5]

The development of social insurance in Latin America reflected rather closely this constellation of forces. Coverage started with the military, civil servants, and judiciary. For example, pensions for military officers and high-level civil servants were typically established in the early independence period. They often reflected deliberate efforts to bolster the status and loyalty of state elites.[6] Next followed the liberal professions and workers in the best

---

[4] Mesa-Lago's work (1978, 1989, 2000) provides an impressive amount of data and carefully designed case studies, which are fundamental for the analyst doing comparative work in Latin America. The historical section of this chapter draws substantially on his work.

[5] Mesa-Lago (1978, 7).

[6] See Kaufman (2000). This work is the first attempt to apply QCA to the study of welfare systems outside the world of advanced Western capitalism.

organized and strategically located sectors of the middle and working classes (e.g., journalists, bank workers, teachers, and railroad and port workers). Then coverage extended to some sectors of the working class within the last category (i.e., mines, agriculture, and manufacturing). However, most of the self-employed and those working in the informal sector either remained formally excluded from the social-insurance system by lack of legal coverage or were excluded *de facto* by their lack of effective contributions to the social security system.[7]

Despite this general trend, there is great variation among Latin American countries with respect to the timing and subsequent expansion of their welfare systems. Mesa-Lago distinguishes three categories of countries depending on the timing of the introduction of systems of social protection. In the first group, he identifies five pioneer countries (i.e., Chile, Uruguay, Argentina, Brazil, and Cuba) where the foundations for the social security systems began to evolve in the 1920s. A second group of countries followed suit in the late 1930s and 1940s (i.e., Colombia, Costa Rica, Mexico, Paraguay, Peru, Venezuela, and Panama). Finally, a third group of countries with a much lower level of economic development lacked even rudimentary welfare systems until at least the 1950s and 1960s.[8]

Although pressures from powerful groups played an important role in the early establishment of welfare systems, and the timing and quality of social-insurance schemes tended to follow the underlying distribution of potential power, we cannot simply assume that social-protection policies were the passive governmental result of group pressures.[9] Rather than being the passive object of class pressures, many Latin American states initiated top-down social policies as a mechanism to control (by way of co-optation) increasingly mobilized labor movements and urban middle classes. Although in some countries (e.g., Chile, Uruguay, and Argentina), bottom-up pressures from a growing critical mass of workers in the industrial sector played a substantial role, the adoption of early schemes of social protection developed initially as an ad hoc response of paternalistic elites trying to defuse labor agitation. These elites often acted not in response to specific class demands but rather

---

[7] A good summary of these changes is Huber (1996).

[8] Mesa-Lago (1989, 40) notes the close relationship between the timing of the initiation of the first social security programs and the historical depth and scope of the welfare system that later developed. All the countries within the group of early reformers have developed fairly extensive systems of social protection – at least for developing-world standards. However, only one latecomer (i.e., Costa Rica) has evolved into a relatively advanced welfare state.

[9] See Malloy (1979). Also, for a discussion of the importance of diffusion in the establishment of social security systems throughout the world, see Collier and Messick (1975).

in a deliberate effort to co-opt, control, and hence demobilize key groups from civil society.[10] In those countries that established welfare systems later (i.e., during or after World War II), the preemptory role of administrative elites was even more pronounced. As Malloy noted, late adopters such as Mexico and Costa Rica found it relatively easy to impose social-protection programs more in line with what was then the latest in international (i.e., World War II) thinking regarding social insurance.[11]

The next sections focus not so much on the factors that led to the *emergence* of the first social security and welfare programs but rather on the influence of different causal factors in the *development* (or underdevelopment) of Latin American welfare systems.[12] The first step, however, is to devise certain criteria to classify Latin American welfare systems. As Table 2.1 suggests, Latin American countries can be logically divided into two distinct groups: a first group in which the scope and role of the state's responsibility for social insurance is relatively well developed and a second group in which it is not. Table 2.1 uses four measures of welfare state development to create an index of "welfare effort" that may be useful for this purpose. The four indicators used to create the index of welfare effort are as follows: (1) *social spending as a percentage of GDP*, which is a measure of the overall level of public resources each country is directing toward the social sector; (2) *social spending as a percentage of total public spending*, which is an indicator of the priority that public health, education, and social security programs have within the government budget; (3) *social spending per capita*, an indicator of the actual resources that citizens receive in transfers or payments from the state; and (4) *the percentage of the active population that is covered by some social security scheme* – a rough indicator of the scope of the welfare system. These four indicators were combined using principal-components factor analysis to create a *welfare effort index*. Because there is a high intercorrelation among these four measures of welfare effort,[13] the index can be considered a relatively good summary indicator[14] of different yet interrelated measures

---

[10] For an analysis of some of the strategies the state may use to co-opt key social groups, especially trade unions, see Stepan (1978). Stepan argues that government policy had a major impact on the character of the mobilization of interest groups. In the case of Mexico, for example, the strategy of co-optation radically reduced the number of worker strikes.

[11] Malloy (1979, 150).

[12] The case studies toward the end of the chapter provide a narrative that aims to capture both the emergence and development of welfare systems in different Latin American countries.

[13] Pearson's correlation coefficient among these four variables ranges between 0.70 and 0.85.

[14] Applying principal-components factor analysis to these four variables yields an eigenvalue of 3.54. The general rule of thumb of retaining only factors that have eigenvalues greater than 1 has been applied. Because the eigenvalue associated with the second factor is as low as 0.17, only one factor was retained. The new index of "welfare effort" explains around 91 percent

of welfare effort. Each measure of social welfare and the summary index of welfare effort obtained through factor analysis are provided in Table 2.1. The index has been standardized so that 100 represents the average degree of welfare effort for all countries in the sample.[15]

As Table 2.1 demonstrates, Latin American countries can be unequivocally divided into two groups depending on their "welfare effort" levels. The first group, which for convenience we may call *welfare states,*[16] includes Uruguay, Argentina, Chile, Costa Rica, and Brazil.[17] Within this group, average social

of the variation in the four component measures of welfare effort. Hence, the index can be considered a good summary indicator of the four subcomponents of welfare effort. This index is a useful mechanism to classify Latin American countries in terms of their welfare effort. Although three of the four components are based on social expenditures (and, therefore, critics might argue that it is better to analyze each component separately), each way of measuring social expenditures gives us a different dimension of welfare effort. Countries may rank high on one dimension and lower on the other. For example, Mexico has a lower level of social expenditures as a percentage of GDP than Bolivia but spends more per capita and a greater number of the total population is covered under the social security system. The index takes into account the notion that in trying to decide whether "welfare effort" is greater in Mexico or Bolivia, all these dimensions have to be considered at once.

[15] Thus, Uruguay, for example, with an index of 230 has a degree of welfare effort more than twice as large as the mean for the entire Latin American sample. This is consistent with the values of each component of the welfare index. In Uruguay, all measures of social expenditures are between two and three times greater than the Latin American average.

[16] Although the idea of the welfare state is best understood as a variable that is present to different degrees, rather than as a fixed property that is either present or absent, in this chapter we are particularly interested in explaining which historical factors led some countries to become "high welfare effort states" while others remained "low welfare effort states." Given that there are such large substantive differences between both groups of countries in terms of the role and scope of the state for social protection, a dichotomy (i.e., welfare versus non-welfare states) is a useful way of parsimoniously investigating why there are these historical differences between the two groups. The disadvantage is that a dichotomy cannot explain intragroup variation. Yet, to understand historical differences in degrees of welfare state development in Latin America, intragroup variation is much less important than intergroup differences.

[17] Some people may be puzzled by the decision to call Brazil a welfare state. As Lamounier (1999, 142) has argued, "no matter how one measures them, levels of income inequality and mass poverty in Brazil are among the worst in the world." However, the purpose of this chapter is not to understand why some states have been more successful and effective than others in reducing poverty, expanding health and education, and protecting citizens from the loss of income associated with sickness or old age. Rather, the objective is to discover why some states are trying to achieve these goals to a greater degree than others. In this regard, Brazil ranks high in terms of the resources the state has committed to the welfare system. Furthermore, the main determinants of Brazil's great economic inequality and low human development are rooted in its highly unequal patterns of land distribution (which dates back to its colonial past), high rates of population growth, and insufficient investment in *basic* welfare services. Thus, considering Brazil's level of welfare effort, and leaving aside the *type* of welfare system Brazil has constructed (i.e., one of limited efficiency and high regressivity when it comes to social security transfers), for the purposes of this chapter, Brazil can still be legitimately called a welfare state.

Table 2.1. *Relative Measures of Welfare Effort in Latin America, Averages 1973–2000*

Welfare Effort	Social Spending as a % of GDP[a]	Social Spending as a % of Public Spending[a]	Social Spending per Capita[a]	Coverage[b]	Welfare Index[c]
High Welfare Effort					
Uruguay	13.5	63–66	950	68.5	230.0
Argentina	14.7	48–53	836	78.9	181.2
Chile	13.8	54–57	581	67.3	163.8
Costa Rica	10.5	59–66	533	76.0	163.2
Brazil	12.5	42–65	459	48.0	138.9
Average	13.2	54–62	678	77.4	168.9
Low Welfare Effort					
Mexico	5.6	36–46	334	53.4	88.5
Venezuela	7.2	32–34	281	45.2	87.2
Bolivia	6.5	38–41	123	25.4	66.5
Ecuador	4.8	34–37	103	7.9	55.3
Paraguay	4.0	37–39	117	18.2	53.8
El Salvador	5.1	30–32	112	6.2	44.6
Peru	5.3	24–28	108	17.4	44.2
Dominican Republic	4.3	28–29	115	7.9	39.9
Guatemala	3.1	29–32	77	14.2	36.9
Average	4.9	32–36	149	21.7	56.6

[a] Social spending data are averages for the 1973–2000 period (data before the 1970s are not available), including public expenditures on health, educational, and social security programs (see Chapter 3 for a more comprehensive description). Social spending as a percentage of the budget includes two figures. The first figure is the gross level of social expenditures (which includes debt repayments), and the second one is the net level after deducting interest repayments on the debt. The average of the two figures was used in factor analysis.

[b] Refers to the percentage of the total population covered under the health program and the percentage of the economically active population covered by the pension program circa 1980. *Source:* Mesa-Lago (1989). For Brazil, data come from the Instituto Brasileiro de Geografía e Estatística, Anuario Estatístico do Brasil. Rio de Janeiro: IBGE.

[c] Factor analysis is a summary index of welfare effort, with 100 being the average for all countries. See explanation in the text for calculation procedures.

spending per capita in the 1973–2000[18] period was around \$532,[19] while as a percentage of GDP and as a share of the budget, social spending reached 51.6 and 12.6 percent, respectively. In addition, between approximately 50 and 75 percent of the population is covered by the public health and pension social security system. It is not surprising that the index of welfare effort

[18] Data refer to the 1973–2000 period.
[19] Measured in 1995 U.S. dollars.

within this group is well above the average, ranging from 138.9 (Brazil) to 230 (Uruguay).

In contrast, the second group of countries, which we call non-welfare states, has welfare-effort indices that range from 37 to 88. Within this second group, social spending per capita averaged $96.6, while social spending as a percentage of GDP and as a percentage of the budget averaged 5.2 and 34.7 percent, respectively. In terms of the percentage of the population actually covered by the social security system, only Mexico and Venezuela exceed Brazil – which has the lowest value within the group of welfare states. And, in some countries within the second group (e.g., El Salvador, Guatemala, the Dominican Republic), the percentage of the active population covered under some social security scheme does not even reach 10 percent. Our task in the following sections is to determine how different configurations of historical conditions within each subset of countries have contributed to the emergence of these differences in terms of overall levels of welfare effort.

2.2 Brief Review of Main Theoretical Perspectives: Defining the Independent Variables

Students of the political economy of advanced capitalism have long discussed the causes underlying the historical origins and development of the welfare state in advanced industrial countries. At least three sets of theories claim to explain the emergence and development of the welfare state in advanced industrial countries: (1) theories that emphasize the effects of economic development and industrialization; (2) theories that focus on the relationship between economic openness and welfare state expansion; and (3) theories that bring to the fore the importance of working-class actors, union organization, and workers' representation by broadly based Socialist parties.[20] Let us begin by briefly reviewing the main tenets of these theories and presenting the data that are used to assess their importance in the

---

[20] For a review of the importance of other (additional) theories, see Chapters 1 and 3. One important (additional) theoretical approach to the origins and development of the welfare state focuses on the paternalistic actions of state autocrats and the policy-making capabilities and orientation of state institutions. Although this is indeed an important part of the explanation of the emergence and expansion of the welfare state, it is difficult to operationalize these causal factors in a way that is amenable to cross-national comparative research. The importance of this approach is better captured by an in-depth historical knowledge of the cases. Therefore, this state-centered perspective is incorporated toward the end of the chapter, which provides a historical analysis of some of the most important cases.

specific context of Latin America during the preglobalization period (i.e., 1945–1979).[21]

Economic Development

Analysts of the welfare state have long studied the relationship between the process of economic development and the expansion of the welfare role of the state. Economic theories of the welfare state such as "the logic of industrialism" and "Wagner's Law" argue that the welfare state emerges in the process of industrialization, which generates deep transformations of socioeconomic structures that involve dislocations in the family and work relations. Because many vulnerable persons are no longer able to obtain traditional support from family members, the state expands to provide social welfare support and thus becomes a mechanism to meet the needs of the population. Wagner's well-known law of "increasing state activity" was one of the first analyses to pose this relationship.[22]

Table 2.2 presents data on GDP per capita by decade since the 1930s. The fourteen countries in the sample are divided into two groups depending on their relative level of economic development. The first group (high development) includes Venezuela, Uruguay, Argentina, Chile, and Mexico. Within this group, average GDP per capita[23] for the 1930–1999 period ranges between $695 and $1,017. Within the second group (low development), average GDP per capita for the period ranges between $286 and $551. To be sure, this distinction between high and low economic development is only valid to classify countries *within* Latin America. By developed-country standards (i.e., Western Europe, North America, and Australasia), even the income of the richest Latin American countries would be very low. For example, the average per capita income of the larger Latin American economies was 14 percent that of the United States in 1900 and 13 percent in the late 1990s.[24]

---

[21] For a more extensive and elaborate analysis of these theories and their relevance for Latin America, see Chapters 1 and 3.

[22] According to this law, the size of the public sector grows with real per capita income as a response to the expanded administrative needs of an increasingly complex industrial society. For a more recent and formal analysis of Wagner's Law, see Boix (2001, 1–17). However, there are other ways in which economic development may affect social welfare development. For example, Wilensky (1975) showed that sustained economic growth fosters changes in the demographic structure of society that are important for the expansion of the welfare state. Life expectancy increases and, because of the loss of traditional family support, an increasing part of the social welfare effort of governments is directed to the aged in the form of pension transfers.

[23] Measured in 1970 PPP values; Thorp (1998).

[24] Thorp (1998, 1).

Table 2.2. *GDP Per Capita in Fourteen Latin American Countries, 1930–1999*[a]

	GDP 1930s	GDP 1940s	GDP 1950s	GDP 1960s	GDP 1970s	GDP 1980s	GDP 1990s	Average
High Relative Development								
Venezuela	408	502	974	1,128	1,328	1,533	1,248	1,017
Uruguay		662	864	915	971	1,156	1,351	986
Argentina	559	645	773	852	1,191	1,377	1,402	971
Chile	502	482	576	679	851	959	1,392	777
Mexico	313	357	458	611	879	1,163	1,090	695
Low Relative Developement								
Costa Rica	278	325	371	469	655	884	880	551
Peru	270	309	370	485	613	702	562	419
Brazil	126	160	215	324	450	775	809	408
Paraguay		317	295	302	359	619	559	408
Dominican Republic			244	298	379	543	545	341
Guatemala	246	382	309	337	419	514	475	339
Ecuador	154	159	230	285	358	542	549	325
El Salvador	178	190	274	329	407	409	429	316
Bolivia			261	215	294	352	310	286

[a] GDP per capita in US$ at 1970 purchasing power parity (PPP) prices.
Source: Created with data from Rosemary Thorp (1998).

Although Latin American countries do not seem to have gained ground over the developed world during the course of the twentieth century, by the end of the century, income per capita in Latin America was five times higher than in 1900. In addition, the value added of the industrial sector (not shown in the table) grew from about 5 to 25 percent of GDP. One of our tasks in this chapter, therefore, is to analyze how this process of industrialization and economic growth has shaped welfare systems in Latin America.

One way of studying the relationship between economic development and welfare systems is to use the average GDP per capita figures for each country in Table 2.2 to generate a new table that classifies countries in terms of both their development and welfare effort. Table 2.3 suggests that there may be an important relationship between long-run economic development and the degree of welfare effort. Of fourteen cases, only four do not fall within the expected cell: Venezuela and Mexico, which combine high development with low welfare effort; and Brazil and Costa Rica, which combine low development with high welfare effort. All the other cases (71 percent of the sample) fall within the expected cell. In fact, some analysts would place Brazil within the high-development cell, which would elevate the predictive

Table 2.3. *Historical Relationship between Economic Development and Degree of Welfare Effort*[a]

	High Welfare Effort	Low Welfare Effort
Medium–High Development	Uruguay ($986)	Venezuela ($1,017)
	Argentina ($981)	Mexico ($695)
	Chile ($777)	
Low–Medium Development	Costa Rica ($551)	Peru ($ 419)
	Brazil ($408)	Paraguay ($408)
		Guatemala ($339)
		Dominican Republic ($341)
		Ecuador ($325)
		El Salvador ($316)
		Bolivia ($286)

[a] Figure in parentheses is average GDP per capita.
Source: Tables 2.1 and 2.2.

power of economic development to 78 percent. Despite the fact that average GDP per capita for the 1930–2000 period in Brazil was substantially lower than in the first group of countries, Brazil has historically enjoyed a degree of development of its industrial sector that would situate it much closer to the first group than the second. For example, in 1960, average value added of manufactured production as a percent of GDP in Brazil was around 26 percent, second only to Argentina (41 percent). The relatively lower figure of GDP per capita in Brazil is also a consequence of the huge demographic size of Brazil, with currently more than 180 million inhabitants, and the existence of some states (especially in the northeast) that are very poor.

Trade Openness

Latin America's share of world trade fell from 7 percent in 1900 to about 3 percent by the end of the twentieth century. Furthermore, in the late 1990s, more than half of the exports were still primary products. Table 2.4 presents average levels of trade openness by country and decade. Countries have been divided into two groups depending on the historical (i.e., 1950–1979) levels of openness of their economies. During the preglobalization period (before 1980), six Latin American countries (i.e., Argentina, Brazil, Mexico, Uruguay, Paraguay, and Chile) can be considered relatively closed to international trade. Within this group, export plus imports over GDP range between 14 and 30 percent. Within the second group of nine relatively

Table 2.4. *Trade Openness in Fourteen Latin American Countries, 1950–1999[a]*

Historical Openness	1950s	1960s	1970s	Average 50s–70s	1980s	1990s	Average 80s–90s	Absolute Change	Relative Change
High Openness									
Costa Rica	52.3	54.0	67.4	**57.9**	68.6	84.0	**77.4**	+19.5	+33.7%
El Salvador	45.5	51.5	66.2	**54.4**	47.2	53.5	**52.1**	−2.3	−4.3%
Bolivia	38.7	54.4	53.3	**48.8**	46.3	48.6	**48.1**	−0.7	−1.4%
Venezuela	49.2	43.8	46.9	**46.7**	43.2	54.4	**49.1**	+2.4	+5.1%
Dominican Republic	44.7	40.1	47.7	**44.2**	61.8	87.6	**70.1**	+25.9	+58.6%
Ecuador	33.9	34.1	49.1	**39.1**	50.8	56.7	**52.6**	+13.5	+34.5%
Peru	38.1	36.4	34.9	**36.4**	31.5	25.5	**29.9**	−6.5	−17.8%
Guatemala	27.7	32.7	44.0	**34.8**	32.5	43.0	**38.4**	+3.6	+10.3%
Low Openness									
Chile	25.6	28.5	37.9	**30.6**	55.8	59.5	**55.6**	+25.0	+81.7%
Paraguay	27.8	29.3	33.5	**30.2**	53.1	48.3	**48.3**	+18.1	+59.9%
Uruguay	27.5	28.1	33.2	**29.6**	45.7	43.3	**42.6**	+13.0	+3.4%
Mexico	26.1	17.7	16.6	**20.2**	31.6	45.4	**36.5**	+16.3	+80.7%
Brazil	13.6	12.7	16.6	**14.3**	17.4	17.5	**17.6**	+3.3	+23.0%
Argentina	13.6	14.5	13.7	**13.9**	15.8	16.1	**15.6**	+1.9	+13.7%

[a] Trade openness is the ratio of imports and exports to GDP.

Sources: Heston, Alan, and Robert Summers. *The Penn World Table (Mark 5): An Expanded Set of International Comparisons, 1950–1988, Quarterly Journal of Economics,* May 1991, 327–368. The actual data come from their Web site at http://pwt.econ.upenn.edu. Data for the 1990s come from the World Bank's *World Development Indicators,* various years.

more open countries, trade openness in the 1950–1979 period ranges from a low of 35 percent (Guatemala) to a high of 69 percent (Costa Rica). In the postglobalization period (after 1980), Chile, Paraguay, and Mexico joined the group of more open economies, while Peru with a relative decline of about 18 percentage points in trade openness became a more closed country.

Many influential analysts of advanced capitalist welfare states have argued that high levels of trade openness are historically associated with an expansion of social welfare.[25] In an influential article, Garrett[26] called this claim

---

[25] The literature on this topic is enormous. For the classical statements, see Cameron (1978) and Katzenstein (1985). For more recent debates with broader empirical samples and more sophisticated statistical techniques, see the work by Rodrik (1997, 1998) and Garrett (2000a, 2000b, 2001, 2004).

[26] Garrett (2000a).

the *compensation hypothesis.* According to this hypothesis, higher levels of
trade openness increase economic insecurity and inequality. As a result, vulnerable economic actors, such as workers who have lost their jobs because
of the pressures of international competition, are likely to use their political
resources (e.g., political parties and trade unions) to press governments for
compensation. Some important evidence from Western Europe shows that,
faced with heightened international competition, the role of government in
the economy has indeed expanded to protect those sectors of the economy
likely to suffer from the risks of exposure to international markets.

However, the historical relationship between trade openness and the welfare state in Latin America is very different from the one observed in
advanced capitalist economies. As Huber noted, welfare systems in Latin
America expanded the most in countries that followed ISI policies.[27] ISI was
an inward-looking model of economic development that rested on a mix of
policies regarding tariffs, licenses, quotas, and exchange rates that shielded
domestic producers (especially in manufacturing) from international-
market competition. On the one hand, ISI was associated with an increase
in the importance of the industrial sector in the economy, significantly
expanding the size of the working class, and – at least until the early 1970s –
producing high levels of economic growth.[28] On the other hand, ISI also
expanded the role of the state in the economy. It is hardly a coincidence
that with the exception of Costa Rica, all the countries in Latin America
with relatively well-developed welfare states had embraced ISI as their main
model of economic development after the Great Depression of the 1930s.[29]
As Huber noted, "ISI created urban constituencies for social insurance, that
is, employed middle and working classes with an interest in protection from
loss of earnings due to accidents, illness, and old age. Typically, these groups
were better organized than the self-employed, the unemployed, and the

---

[27] Huber (1996, 144).
[28] There are many analyses of the impact of ISI policies in Latin America. For a review
of the main issues involved in this model of development for Latin America, see Bulmer-
Thomas (1994). For cross-regional comparisons between Latin America and other regions,
especially East Asia, see Haggard (1990). See also Gereffy and Wyman (1990).
[29] In Costa Rica, ISI would also become important in the 1960s. By that time, however, the
basis of the welfare state had already been laid. We cannot, therefore, attribute a connection between ISI and welfare state development in this case. However, whereas it is true
that all the countries that can be considered welfare states embraced ISI as a post-1930s
model of development (with the noted exception of Costa Rica), the reverse is not true. For
example, Mexico also followed ISI policies to the same or higher degree than Argentina,
Brazil, Chile, and Uruguay and yet did not evolve into a welfare system of the same
scope.

Table 2.5. *Historical Relationship between Trade Openness and Welfare Effort in Latin America*[a]

	High Welfare Effort	Low Welfare Effort
Relatively Closed Economy	**Argentina (13.9)**	Mexico (17.7)
	Brazil (14.3)	Paraguay (30.2)
	Uruguay (29.6)	
	Chile (30.6)	
Relatively Open Economy	Costa Rica (57.9)	**El Salvador (54.4)**
		Bolivia (48.8)
		Venezuela (46.7)
		Dominican Republic (44.2)
		Ecuador (39.1)
		Peru (36.4)
		Guatemala (34.8)

[a] Figure in parentheses is the level of trade openness (ratio of imports plus exports to GDP).
Source: Tables 2.1 and 2.4.

workforce in the rural sector and thus had their needs met to a much larger extent."[30]

This point can be clearly observed in Table 2.5, which classifies countries in terms of both their levels of trade openness and welfare effort. The data show a fairly strong relationship between relatively low levels of trade openness and high levels of welfare effort. This is the exact opposite relationship of the one found by researchers of advanced industrial economies. With only one exception (i.e., Costa Rica), all countries that historically committed a high level of resources to social welfare were relatively closed to international markets from the 1940s to the 1970s.

Democracy

OECD[31] studies of the welfare state do not usually include democracy as an explanatory variable in the development of the welfare state. This

---

[30] Huber (1995, 144).
[31] The OECD groups thirty member countries sharing a commitment to democratic government and the market economy. In practice, OECD membership is typically restricted to countries with relatively high levels of economic development and political openness (i.e., democracy), such as members of the European Union (plus Norway, Switzerland, and Iceland), the United States, Canada, Australia, and New Zealand. In the mid-1990s, Mexico, South Korea, and some countries in Eastern Europe (i.e., Czech Republic, Hungary, Poland, and Slovak Republic) joined the OECD despite enjoying much lower levels of economic development and political openness than the other members. Most

is understandable because the great majority of OECD countries have remained democratic since (at least) the end of World War II. In Latin America, however, as well as in most of the developing world, the effect of democracy needs to be carefully incorporated into the analysis. Some countries, like Costa Rica, have remained continuously democratic since 1949; others, like Chile and Uruguay, had been continuously democratic for an even longer time, suffered democratic breakdowns in the early 1970s, and redemocratized in the 1980s. Yet, other countries, like Paraguay, El Salvador, Guatemala, and Bolivia, underwent transitions to democracy in the 1980s and 1990s without ever having been democratic before. Given the whole range of possible theoretical effects that we might expect from democracy,[32] regime type needs to be included as another independent variable that might affect the degree of welfare state development in Latin America.

We may expect democracy to be associated with an expansion of social welfare from both the demand and the supply side. From the demand side, democracy provides certain groups in civil society (e.g., trade unions, social movements, interest associations) with more extensive and open channels of participation. In a democracy, these groups can freely organize, mobilize, press, and demand different types of social benefits from the state. Their demands cannot be easily repressed or contained by force. On the supply side, democracy makes political leaders dependent on the popular vote. In so doing, it brings electoral pressures to the fore, making them a decisive mechanism of political choice. Assuming that political leaders are rational actors who want to gain or retain power, and to the extent that the poor constitute a relatively large proportion of the voting population in most developing countries, democratic political leaders are likely to be more sensitive to their demands concerning social needs and other tangible improvements in social welfare usually associated with the welfare state.

One way of appreciating the historical importance of democracy for welfare state development in Latin America is to divide those countries that had a relatively long history of democratic practices in the preglobalization period (1945–1979) from those that did not (Table 2.6). A country has been classified as having a relatively long democratic history if it remained continuously

---

studies of advanced capitalism are restricted to a set of about seventeen highly developed members of the OECD. This group does not include Turkey (which is a long-time member of the OECD but has a comparatively lower income level and a shorter history of continuous democracy), or Spain and Portugal, which became democratic in the mid-1970s.

[32] The discussion of the relationship between democracy and welfare state development is covered in detail in Chapter 3.

Table 2.6. *Democratic History of Fourteen Latin American Countries*

Country	Political Regime Type			Total Number of *Democratic* Years by Period	
	Democracy	Semidemocracy	Autocracy	Preglobalization (1945–1979)	Postglobalization (1980–1999)
Group I[a]					
Costa Rica	1949–1999			31/34	20/20
Chile	1945–1972		1973–1989	27/34	10/20
	1990–1999				
Uruguay	1945–1972		1973–1984	27/34	15/20
	1985–1999				
Venezuela	1947	1946	1945	23/34	20/20
	1958–1999		1948–1957		
Brazil	1946–1963		1964–1984	18/34	15/20
	1985–1999				
Group II[a]					
Ecuador	1948–1960	1961–1962	1945–1947	14/34	21/20
	1979–1999	1968–1969	1970–1978		
Peru	1963–1967	1945–1947	1948–1955	5/34	06/20
	1980–1982	1956–1961	1968–1979		
	1985–1987	1983–1984			
		1988–1991			
		1995–1999			
Argentina	1973–1974	1946–1950	1945	02/34	17/20
	1983–1999	1958–1961	1951–1957		
		1963–1965	1962		
		1975	1966–1972		
			1976–1982		
Dominican Republic	1978–1993	1966–1973	1945–1965	02/34	18/20
	1996–1999	1994–1995	1974–1977		
El Salvador	1992–1999	1984–1991	1945–1983	0/34	08/20
Bolivia	1982–1999	1956–1963	1945–1955	0/34	18/20
			1964–1981		
Guatemala		1945–1953	1954–1986	0/34	0/20
		1986–1999			
Paraguay		1989–1999	1945–1988	0/34	0/20
Mexico		1988–1999	1945–1987	0/34	0/20

[a] Group I includes countries with a moderate to strong history of continuous democracy in the preglobalization period. A country belongs to Group I if it has been continuously democratic for at least eighteen years in the 1945–1979 period. Group II includes countries with a weak to moderate history of continuous democracy (i.e., fewer than eighteen years of continuous democracy during the 1945–1979 period).

Source: Created with codings from Mainwaring, Brinks, and Pérez-Liñán (2001).

Table 2.7. *Relationship between Historical Experience with Political Democracy in the Preglobalization Period (1945–1979) and Degree of Welfare Effort*

	High Welfare Effort	Low Welfare Effort
Medium to Long Democratic History (≥ 18 years)	Costa Rica (31) Chile (27) Uruguay (27) Brazil (18)	Venezuela (23)
Short to Medium Democratic History (< 18 years)	Argentina (2)	Ecuador (14) Peru (5) Dominican Republic (2) El Salvador (0) Bolivia (0) Guatemala (0) Paraguay (0) Mexico (0)

Note: Parentheses indicate total number of democratic years during the preglobalization period (1945–1979).
Source: Tables 2.1 and 2.6.

democratic for at least eighteen years – that is, half the time during the pre-globalization period (1945–1979). Table 2.6 uses a new classification scheme of Latin American political regimes developed by Mainwaring, Brinks, and Pérez Liñán for this purpose.[33] The authors have classified Latin American political regimes using a trichotomy (i.e., democracy, semidemocracy, and autocracy). *Democracy* is defined as a regime "(1) that sponsors free and fair competitive elections for the legislature and executive; (2) that allows for inclusive adult citizenship; (3) that protects civil liberties and political rights; and (4) in which the elected governments really govern and the military is under civilian control."[34]

Again, a useful way of exploring the relationship between democracy and welfare state expansion is to classify countries in terms of both their democratic history in the preglobalization period (1945–1979) and their welfare effort levels. Table 2.7 shows that four of the five countries in the high

[33] Mainwaring, Brick, and Pérez-Liñán (2001, 37–65).
[34] See Mainwaring et al. (2001, 1). Semidemocracy is an intermediate category exhibited by a regime that has some of the components of democracy but lacks others or cases in which the principles are not respected to a sufficient degree. Examples could be (1) Argentina from 1955 to 1966, when certain electoral outcomes were ruled out a priori because the military proscribed the party that enjoyed the greatest amount of popular support, or (2) Guatemala in the 1980s and early 1990s, when civilian governments were under military "tutelage." See Mainwaring et al. (2001) for a more detailed account of these cases, as well as other examples.

welfare effort category remained continuously democratic for a relatively long period (i.e., at least eighteen continuous years) during the preglobalization period (1945–1979). The only exceptions are (1) Argentina, which was democratic only during a two-year period[35] but can be classified as a high welfare effort system; and (2) Venezuela, which remained continuously democratic for about twenty-three years in the period under study but did not become a high welfare effort system. Overall, using democratic history to predict welfare effort levels, we would correctly classify twelve of the fourteen cases (i.e., 86 percent).

Left-Labor Power

The importance of strong labor movements and Social Democratic parties for the development of the welfare state has long been recognized among students of advanced industrial economies. Many influential analysts of the welfare state have noted that Left parties with organic ties with labor unions are the main vehicles for the mobilization of the working class, which facilitates the establishment and subsequent development of the welfare state.[36] In one of the most recent and comprehensive studies of the welfare state to date, Huber and Stephens demonstrate that left-incumbency was the single most important factor for the expansion of the welfare state in Western Europe.[37] They show that working-class political power – typically measured in terms of labor unionization – and its mechanisms of political representation through Social Democratic parties became a crucial element of welfare state growth.

Assessing the importance of left-labor power for welfare state development in Latin America is more difficult for two reasons. First, there is no easy way of assessing labor strength. The most widely used indicator to measure

[35] As Table 2.6 shows, Argentina was semidemocratic for about thirteen years during the preglobalization period. Even if we counted these years as democratic, Argentina would still accumulate fewer than eighteen years of *continuous* democracy.

[36] See, for example, Castles (1985, 1998). The classic and one of the most influential statements in this respect is Esping-Andersen (1991). For a more recent analysis using QCA, see Hicks (1999). For sophisticated quantitative work using pooled time-series regression analysis, see, for example, Hicks and Swank (1992), Hicks and Misra (1993), and Huber and Stephens (2001). The latter work combines a large empirical sample with eight case studies to provide the most comprehensive examination of these issues to date.

[37] See Huber and Stephens (2001). The case of Australia vividly illustrates that a strong labor movement may not be enough for the growth of the welfare state. Unless the labor movement is linked to a political party (usually a Social Democratic one) that takes part in government by way of its electoral success, the welfare state may fail to develop. During 1950–1973, the Australian Labor Party (ALP) lost in every successive election by a small margin. It always achieved levels of electoral support close to 50 percent.

labor strength – labor unionization – is not readily available for the analyst interested in cross-national comparative analysis. Second, the lack of institutionalization[38] of Latin American political parties makes it more difficult to understand and track shifts in the partisan orientation of political parties over time.

To overcome this difficulty may be no easy task, but left-labor power is too important a variable to dismiss it because of data problems. Although quantitative data available to compare cases may have problems of validity and reliability, one can attempt to follow the leading study of labor movements in Latin America in trying to "establish a rough sense of orders of magnitude and an approximate ordering of the countries on the relevant variables."[39]

This chapter uses five interrelated variables to create two indices that assess the relative degree of power of the labor movements and the comparative importance of left-oriented parties in each country. First, four indicators that measure the likely relative size and organizational strength of the labor movement were used to create an index of "labor strength" that provides an approximate idea of the relative comparative power of labor unions in different Latin American countries during the preglobalization period (i.e., 1945–1979). Although these indicators can only be considered rough proxies, they are likely to capture at least some of the aspects that facilitate the emergence of stronger labor movements. The four indicators are (1) the size of the manufacturing sector (measured in terms of the value added to GDP ratio), (2) the per capita supply of electricity (per capita kilowatts/hour), (3) the percentage of the population living in urban areas, and (4) the size of the informal sector.[40]

The first and second indicators are proxies for the degree of labor-intensive industrialization the country has achieved. At a time (i.e., 1950s and 1960s) when the size of the service sector was still limited, higher degrees of industrialization were likely to be associated with a greater relative demand for

---

[38] One of the most comprehensive studies of Latin American party systems to date is Mainwaring and Scully (1995). In this work, the authors define the institutionalization of the party system according to a number of criteria such as the degree of electoral volatility, the difference in the percentage of the vote obtained in presidential and congressional elections, the relative attachment that citizens have with their parties, and the average age of the parties.

[39] See Collier and Collier (1992, 65).

[40] For a widely cited definition and analysis of the informal sector, see Portes, Castells, and Benton (1989, 12). The authors define the informal sector as "a process of income-generation characterized by one central feature: *it is unregulated by the institutions of society, in a legal and social environment in which similar activities are regulated*" (emphasis in the original).

workers. The growth of the manufacturing sector – which greatly expanded during the period of ISI after the 1930s – led to an increase in factory employment and a substantial expansion of the critical mass of workers.[41]

Similarly, the greater the size of the urban population, the greater the number of people who could be drawn into productive activities in the manufacturing sector. The growth of large cities and urban commerce contributed to the creation of the demographic base for labor movements in Latin America. It is not surprising that the earliest instances of worker organization and protest were typically found in large urban centers such as Rio de Janeiro, Buenos Aires, Santiago, Mexico City, Caracas, Montevideo, and Lima. Hence, we can have some confidence that higher degrees of industrialization and urbanization are likely to be associated with larger working classes. To be sure, these indicators do not tell us much about the capacity of organization of the working class, but they do suggest that unless the industrial sector (especially in manufacturing) was fairly developed, the size of the working class tended to be small. As a result, its power was likely to be relatively weak.[42] As an additional indicator that may help us measure the extent to which the labor movement will be better organized, a measure of the size of the informal sector has been added. The informal sector consists of production units that "typically operate at a low level of organization (. . .) Labour relations – when they exist – are based mostly on casual employment, kinship or personal and social relations rather than contractual arrangements with formal guarantees" (15th International Conference of Labour Statisticians). Following Roberts and Wibbels,[43] we can use a scale from 1 to 3 to determine the size of the informal sector (1 = small, 2 = medium, 3 = large). As noted previously, the assumption is that workers in the informal sector are notoriously difficult to organize; they have weak class identity and unstable political loyalties. A large informal sector, therefore,

---

[41] Collier and Collier (1992, 64) argue that the growth of manufacturing and factory employment created new contexts of work conducive to labor movements. In many countries, the manufacturing sector began to expand in the late nineteenth and early twentieth centuries. In 1925, for example, factory employment as a percentage of the economically active population was 8.3 percent in Argentina, 7 percent in Uruguay, and 6.1 percent in Chile. Brazil and Mexico followed suit at 3.7 and 3.2 percent, respectively. In other countries such as Colombia, Peru, and Venezuela, the percentage of workers in manufacturing did not exceed 1.5 percent (Collier and Collier, 1992, 67).

[42] The reverse is not necessarily true. The size of the working class may be large (because of a big industrial sector) but poorly organized. As we will see, however, evidence from the different Latin American countries suggests that industrialization and a larger working class correlated rather strongly with the degree of labor power.

[43] Roberts and Wibbels (1999).

can be expected to decrease the capacity for collective action of the labor movement.

The second dimension of "left-labor power" can be established by assessing the importance of center-left and Left parties. As noted previously, unlike in Western Europe where parties historically kept stronger links with civil society and more consistent ideological positions, to identify the partisan orientation of Latin American political parties can be a daunting task. Fortunately, in a recent study, Coppedge[44] attempted this task with reasonable success.[45]

Table 2.8 lists the four variables used to create the index of labor strength, the percentage of votes received by center-left and left-oriented parties, and an additive index of "left-labor power" that combines the index of "labor strength" and the percentage of votes for left-oriented parties.

Countries in Table 2.8 are ranked depending on the relative strength of their labor movement and the electoral success of center-left and left-oriented parties. The highest indices of left-labor power correspond to Argentina, Chile, and Uruguay. These countries enjoyed relatively high degrees of economic development, industrialization, and urbanization, which facilitated the emergence of a substantially large working class. They also had strong left-oriented parties that either were in government for significant periods or were a permanent influential force of the government opposition. Argentina, for example, had the best organized labor movement in Latin America. When the military allowed the Peronist party to freely participate in elections, it was generally capable of mobilizing the support of around 50 percent of the electorate. In Chile, the Left (i.e., Communists and Socialists) was comparatively strong and the labor movement active, relatively independent, and highly militant.[46] Uruguay, with the hegemony of the Colorado Party, in addition to a strong and independent union movement, also has among the highest levels of "left-labor" power.

The next case on the left-labor power scale is Venezuela. Although in numerical terms, Venezuela seems rather close to Argentina, Chile, and Uruguay, there are substantial differences between the former and the latter. First, in Venezuela, the industrial sector expanded slowly until the

---

[44] See Coppedge (1998).

[45] His work reports the percentage of the total valid vote won by various ideological blocs (i.e., left, center-left, center, center-right, or right) in twentieth-century Latin American lower chamber or constituent assembly elections. Apart from his own expertise as a leading expert in the study of Latin American party systems, Coppedge enlisted fifty-three country experts that provided him with useful information to improve the validity and reliability of the coding rules.

[46] See Roberts (1997).

Table 2.8. *Relative Strength of Labor Movement and Left-Oriented Parties in Latin America during the Preglobalization Period, 1945–1979[a]*

	Industrialization	Energy Supply	Urban Population	Informal	Labor Strength Index	Left-Vote	Left-Labor Power Index
Uruguay	22.6	284	80.1	1	82.0	46.5	128.5
Chile	23.0	493	67.8	1	90.9	36.9	127.8
Argentina[b]	41.1	272	73.6	1	100	26.2	126.2
Venezuela	15.5	155	61.2	1	50.6	69.6	120.2
Costa Rica	18.8	151	36.6	1	38.4	51.6	90.0
Bolivia	17.0	70	39.3	3	9.3	77.5	86.8
Peru	17.3	39	46.3	3	11.9	61.4	73.2
Mexico	18.6	166	50.8	2	37.5	26.4	63.9
Brazil	26.0	153	44.9	2	41.9	11.4	53.3
Ecuador	18.4	38	22.3	3	0.0	10.5	10.5
Dominican Republic	15.5	38	30.2	3	10.1	0	10.1
El Salvador	18.9	24	38.3	3	7.5	0	7.5
Guatemala	14.07	27	32.4	3	3.2	0	3.2
Paraguay	15.5	31	18.7	3	2.0	0	2.0

[a] The measurement of the variables is as follows: (1) *Industrialization:* size of the manufacturing sector (as measured by its value added) to GDP around 1960; *Source:* World Bank (2001). (2) *Energy Supply:* Per capita supply of electric energy (kilowatt hours per head); *Source:* Thorp (2000). (3) *Urban Population:* Percentage of urban population over the total population; *Source:* World Bank (2001). (4) *Informal:* Size of the informal sector (small =1, medium = 2, 3 = large); *Source:* Roberts and Wibbels (1999). (5) *Labor Strength Index:* Principal-components factor analysis index using the previous four variables. The first factor had an Eigenvalue of 3.27; the Eigenvalue associated to the second factor was 0.4 only. As a result, only one factor was retained. The factor, which I call "labor strength index," is a relatively good summary indicator of the four components because it accounts for about 80 percent in their joint variation. To facilitate interpretation, the index was standardized so that the maximum value (i.e., Argentina) equals 100 and the minimum value (i.e., Ecuador) equals 0. (6) *Left-vote:* Average percentage of votes received by the Center-Left and Left parties in all elections during the 1945–1979 period; *Source:* Coppedge (1997). (7) *Left-Labor Power Index:* Combined additive index of labor strength and percentage of votes received by left-oriented parties.

[b] In his classification of party systems, Coppedge (1997) does not classify the Peronist party as Left or Center-Left despite its long-term populistic relationship with the labor movement. The country experts that Coppedge consulted did not agree on how to classify this party. Thus, Coppedge placed the Peronist party in the "other" category. However, given the long-term association between the Peronist party and social welfare issues that started in 1943 when Perón was appointed Minister of Labor, I decided to classify the Peronist party as *Left.* Part of the problem with the classification of the Peronist party is that during the 1990s (under the presidency of Menem), the party leaned decisively to the Right and implemented a drastic neoliberal program of structural reform. During the period under study (1945–1979), the shift in the party's ideological position had not taken place yet. This is why I deem it appropriate to consider the Peronist party as Left for the purposes of this chapter.

mid-1950s. Second, Venezuela's degree of urbanization was much smaller than Argentina's, Chile's, or Uruguay's, and it only began to catch up in the 1960s (data presented in the table correspond to 1960). These conditions did not facilitate the emergence of a strong labor movement, which would explain why Venezuela's index of labor strength is half that of Argentina's. Venezuela's high score on the left-labor index is explained as a result of the tremendous electoral success of Acción Democrática, a Social Democratic party that received an average of 69 percent of the vote in all elections held between 1945 and 1979. In evaluating the Venezuelan case, however, we also need to consider that labor unions were not fully incorporated into the governing alliance until the 1960s and were in a subordinate position to a party that became increasingly conservative over time.[47] These are important differences that help us explain why Venezuela's welfare state was much less developed than Argentina's, Chile's, and Uruguay's.

The next country on the left-labor power scale is Costa Rica, which had a relatively small working class but a very strong Social Democratic party – the Partido Liberación Nacional (PLN) – which dominated Costa Rican politics after 1949. It held the majority in Congress from 1953 until 1978, as well as in most of the subsequent two decades.[48] Bolivia and Peru also score relatively high on the left-labor power index. Although the size of the labor movement was not too large and deeply affected by a large informal sector or urban workers, in Bolivia the Movimiento Nacional Revolucionario (MNR) and in Peru the Alianza Popular Revolucionaria Americana (APRA) were also influential forces of the Left during the period under study. The MNR was in power between 1952 and 1964 under Paz Estenssoro (1952–1956, 1960–1964) and Siles Suazo (1956–1960). By contrast, the APRA was never in power in Peru before the transition to democracy in 1980, but it was always an important force in the Peruvian political landscape.[49]

Most analysts would agree that in the rest of the countries, left-labor power has been historically weaker. In Mexico, the Left has been historically weak,

---

[47] See Kaufman (2000).
[48] Yashar (1997, 221).
[49] Kaufman (2000, 15) argues that, historically, "the APRA was the most important force on the left. It retained important pockets of strength in the coastal agroindustries, and exercised political influence for extended parts of the post-war period. From 1945–1948, it entered a power-sharing arrangement with Prado; then, after a period of repression, it was integrated into the governing coalition supporting Bustamonte from the late 1950s to the early 1960s. By the late 1960s, the APRA had moderated its demands for social reform considerably, and was one of the targets of the military regime that took power in 1968. But the military government attempted to mobilize a popular movement of its own, and by the mid-1970s, the unanticipated consequence was the formation of a very militant and independent movement of left parties and popular-sector organizations."

and labor unions, despite forming part of the governing coalition, were subordinated to the PRI – the hegemonic party that dominated Mexican politics from the 1930s to 2000. The orientation of the PRI itself is difficult to determine. Coppedge,[50] for example, classifies it as Center Right during the administration of López Mateos (1958–1964) and Díaz Ordaz (1964–1970), Center Left during the presidency of Luis Echeverría (1970–1976), and Center Right again thereafter. If we had to use the mean value of the left-labor scale to separate countries with a relatively strong labor movement from countries with a relatively weak one, Mexico would be divided right down the middle – thus illustrating the dilemma of whether to classify its left-labor movement as strong or weak. Indeed, the average value of the left-labor power variable for all countries in the sample is 64.9, virtually the same value obtained by Mexico (63.9). It is therefore necessary to consider different scenarios to assess whether classifying Mexico as "strong left" or "weak left" makes a difference in our general findings.

In all the other countries, with the exception of Brazil, the left-labor variable takes very low values. In Brazil, however, despite periods of labor militancy, the left-labor movement can safely be characterized as relatively "weak" during most of the postwar period.[51]

Table 2.9 shows that using the strength of the left-labor movement to predict welfare effort levels would place nine to ten countries within the expected cell, depending on whether we classify Mexico within the "weak" or "strong" left-labor power group. This means that, controlling for no other factors, using left-labor power to predict welfare state development would correctly predict 64 to 71 percent of the cases. This is a moderate degree of success

---

[50] See Coppedge (1997).

[51] Kaufman (2000, 13) also discusses in detail the Brazilian case. The other countries are much less economically developed, industrialized, and urbanized, and left-oriented parties were either nonexistent, electorally weak, or severely repressed. It is not surprising that they score very low on the left-labor power scale. In Ecuador, most of the preglobalization period (1945–1979) was dominated by Velasco Ibarra, a conservative who was president four times. In El Salvador, there was a persistence of military rule and the practical annihilation of the political Left since the 1930s. In Guatemala, despite the Left leanings of José Arévalo (1945–1951), who introduced a labor code and enacted a social security system that promised an expansion of benefits, subsequent military governments tremendously weakened and repressed Left forces. In the Dominican Republic, the left-labor movement was also unequivocally weak. The period under study was first dominated by the dictatorship of Rafael Trujillo (1930–1961), who governed the country as a sultan – that is, controlling the armed forces, government, the economy, and practically every element of Dominican society – and after 1963 by Joaquin Balaguer, a conservative who won the election after the United States invaded the island in 1966, fearing the revolutionary potential of the new Left. In Paraguay, under the dictatorship of General Stroessner (1954–1989), labor unions were strictly controlled and organized around only one government-recognized trade union – the Confederation of Paraguayan Workers (CPT).

Table 2.9. *Relationship between the Historical Strength of the Left-Labor Movement and Welfare Effort*

	High Welfare Effort	Low Welfare Effort
Medium to Strong Left-Labor Movement	**Argentina** **Chile** **Costa Rica** **Uruguay**	Peru Bolivia Venezuela Mexico (?)
Weak to Medium Left-Labor Movement	Brazil	**Mexico (?)** **Ecuador** **El Salvador** **Guatemala** **Dominican Republic** **Paraguay**

Source: Table 2.8.

when the sample is so small, but it does point to the potential importance of left-labor power for welfare state development. To fully understand, analyze, and evaluate the importance of this variable, however, requires that we assess its effects in conjunction with the effects of other variables – that is, economic development, trade openness, and democracy. This is precisely the purpose of the following sections.

2.3 Qualitative Comparative Analysis through the Boolean Methodology

The main problem with the analysis we have conducted so far is that the dependent variable is overdetermined. Each independent variable taken alone would have a high degree of success in predicting whether a country falls within one category or the other. As noted previously, development and left-labor power would correctly predict about 70 percent of the cases, trade openness would correctly predict 78 percent of the cases, and the correct predictions for democracy would reach 86 percent, an even higher degree of success. But, how can we know that it was democracy and not economic development or a strong left-labor movement rather than lack of economic openness that led to the gradual emergence of a high welfare effort system?

One way is to use regression analysis; indeed, this is the methodology that is used in the following chapters. Regression analysis allows researchers to measure the effect of a given independent variable controlling for the influence of all other independent variables. However, fourteen cases are too few to obtain robust results using regression analysis. One useful alternative is to use QCA, which uses matrix algebra to specify alternative paths along which a given outcome can be reached. QCA, which is based on Boolean algebra, is a useful tool to discover the relative importance of these variables and theories and to help us understand the unequal degree of historical development of the welfare state in Latin America. This methodology allows researchers to overcome the problem of "too many variables, too few cases." One of the pioneers in its development was Ragin,[52] who was the first to use the Boolean procedure in comparative analysis to specify causal relations between a set of hypothesized causes (i.e., independent variables) and an outcome (i.e., dependent variable). Ragin proposed to use a series of matrices of binary (0–1) qualitative data that describe the presence or absence of traits, for example, in a group of nations such as our set of Latin American countries. The first step in QCA is to create a "truth table" (Table 2.10), which is a widely used technique in Boolean analysis that provides a visual representation of the different combinations of causal conditions and the value of the outcome variable for the cases conforming to each combination. The truth table can be summarized using the following four structural equations[53]:

$$(1) \quad EtdL = WS$$
$$(2) \quad EtDl = WS$$
$$(3) \quad EtDL = WS$$
$$(4) \quad eTDL = WS$$

where "WS" stands for welfare state, "E" for economic development, "T" for trade openness, "D" for democracy, and "L" for left-labor power. Uppercase letters indicate that the condition is present, lowercase that it is not. In other words, uppercase corresponds to the "ones" in the truth table and lowercase letters represent the "zeros."[54]

Each equation illustrates one of the four ways in which a welfare state in Latin America emerged: (1) with economic development and left-labor power in the absence of democracy and economic openness (Argentina); (2) with economic development and democracy in the absence of left-labor power and economic openness (Brazil); (3) with economic development, democracy, and left-labor power in the absence of economic openness

---

[52] See, in particular, Ragin (1987, 1994).

[53] Researchers sometimes use just one equation to represent the alternative paths to a certain outcome. For example, we could have simplified these expressions by writing (1) EtdL + EtDl + EtDL + eTDL = WS, where each component describes one path and the "+" sign indicates "or."

[54] For a more extensive description of how the Boolean approach works, see Appendix 2.1.

Table 2.10. *Economic and Political Determinants of Welfare State Development in Latin America*

Conditions				Outcome	
Economic Development (E)	Trade (T)	Democracy (D)	Strong Left/Labor (L)	Welfare State	Countries
					WELFARE STATES
1	0	0	1	1	Argentina
1	0	1	0	1	Brazil
1	0	1	1	1	Chile
					Uruguay
0	1	1	1	1	Costa Rica
					NON-WELFARE STATES
1	1	1	1	0	Venezuela
0	1	0	1	0	Peru
					Bolivia
1	0	0	0	0	Mexico[a]
0	1	0	0	0	Dominican Republic
					El Salvador
					Ecuador
					Guatemala
0	0	0	0	0	Paraguay
1	1	1	1	?	
1	1	0	1	?	
1	1	0	0	?	
0	1	1	0	?	
0	0	1	1	?	
0	0	1	0	?	

[a] Mexico was initially classified as "weak left-labor power." However, the text also discusses different scenarios in which Mexico could also be classified as "strong left-labor power."

Notes: A "1" indicates that the condition or outcome is present; a "0" indicates that it is not. The last six rows describe theoretically possible but empirically empty combinations.

(Chile and Uruguay); and (4) with left-labor power, democracy, and economic openness in the absence of development (Costa Rica).

After the set of causal conditions has been identified and the cases have been represented in a truth table, the next step is to logically minimize the truth table to evaluate whether certain conditions are redundant and, hence, the number of paths can be reduced. This would be the case, for example, if two countries shared the same outcome and had three of four conditions in common. Variation in the fourth condition could then be considered unimportant for reaching this specific outcome, and the two cases (i.e., countries) could be said to share the same path. The first step in the minimization process, therefore, is to simplify rows that differ on only one causal condition and yet produce the same outcome. In our case, there are two sets of rows that can be combined. First, Row 1 and Row 3 can be combined. Both rows share in common economic development (E), lack of trade openness (t), and a relatively strong left-labor movement (L). The only difference is that Argentina, which represents the first row, does not have a relatively long history of democracy, whereas Chile and Uruguay, which represent the third row, do. But, if the same outcome was reached with the same combination of preconditions except democracy, we may conclude that *democracy is not a necessary precondition to develop a welfare state*. The combination of Rows 1 and 3 leads to the following reduced equation: $Et\_L = WS$. This equation indicates that one possible path to the welfare state (WS) in Latin America would be achieved through a combination of economic development (E), a relatively closed economy to international markets (t), and a strong left-labor movement (L). The dash in the third term of the reduced equation indicates that a long history of democracy could be present (Chile and Uruguay) or not (Argentina).

In the second place, Rows 2 and 3 can also be combined. According to the previous truth table, the only difference between Row 2 and Row 3 is that countries in Row 3 (i.e., Chile and Uruguay) had a relatively strong left-labor movement, whereas Brazil (the only country in Row 2) did not. Therefore, we can write a second reduced equation as follows: $EtD\_ = WS$. This equation suggests that the welfare state in Latin America could also develop with economic development (E), lack of trade openness (t), and a long history of democracy (D), irrespective of whether there was a strong left-labor movement. Finally, Row 4 cannot be combined with any other rows to yield a reduced expression because it differs in more than one condition with any other row. Hence, the third path to the welfare state, exemplified by Costa Rica, combines a long history of democracy and a strong left-labor movement with trade openness and absence of economic development.

As a result after this Boolean exercise, we can distinguish two paths toward the welfare state in Latin America – one with favorable and another with unfavorable economic conditions. The first path – with favorable economic conditions – combines economic development and a protected economy from international markets (no trade openness) with *either* democracy

(Brazil) *or* left-labor power (Argentina), or both (Chile and Uruguay). The second path combines democracy *and* left-labor power with trade openness *and* absence of development (Costa Rica).

The main implication of this analysis is that in countries that had relatively favorable economic conditions (i.e., a comparatively high level of development and a protected economy from international competition), only one of the two political conditions (i.e., democracy and left-labor power) was necessary to develop a welfare state. This is the case of Brazil, where development and a relatively closed economy that embraced ISI were combined with democracy to produce a welfare state.[55] The absence of left-labor power in Brazil did not hinder the development of the Brazilian welfare state. However, as discussed herein, it did affect the type of welfare state that was created – one of the most regressive in the region. By contrast, Chile and Uruguay combined the same economic conditions as Brazil (i.e., development and relatively closed economies) with both democracy and left-labor power. Despite the fact that Boolean analysis indicates that left-labor power may not have been a necessary condition for the development of the welfare state in these two countries, the presence of a much stronger left in Chile and Uruguay is useful to explain the differences in the character (i.e., less regressive than in Brazil) of the welfare state in these two countries. On the other hand, in the absence of development and with an open economy (theoretically unfavorable preconditions), both democracy and left-labor power were necessary to create a welfare state (as the case of Costa Rica illustrates). Figure 2.1 graphically represents these alternative paths. Then, the next section uses brief descriptions of some cases to gain a better understanding of these alternative paths to the welfare state in Latin America. This offers a more nuanced view of how the effects of the different

---

[55] Some critics may find the democratic classification of Brazil during the 1946–1963 period as problematic because the military exerted a considerable degree of influence about who was and was not acceptable as president. The manuscript follows Mainwaring et al. (2001), who classify this period as democratic. This is also consistent with Przeworski et al. (2000) and Marshall et al. (2005). However, it could be argued that the influence of the military on Brazil's democratic regime during this period prevented the type of bottom-up pressures for welfare state expansion that were observed in other countries, like Costa Rica. In fact, the chapter finds that democracy in the case of Brazil did not play a key role for the development of the welfare state. As a result, because little explanatory power can be attached to democracy in the case of Brazil, there is some doubt about whether the path exemplified by Brazil (i.e., economic development combined with a closed economy and democracy) would have any clear empirical referent. The answer to this question would require an analysis of countries in other regions.

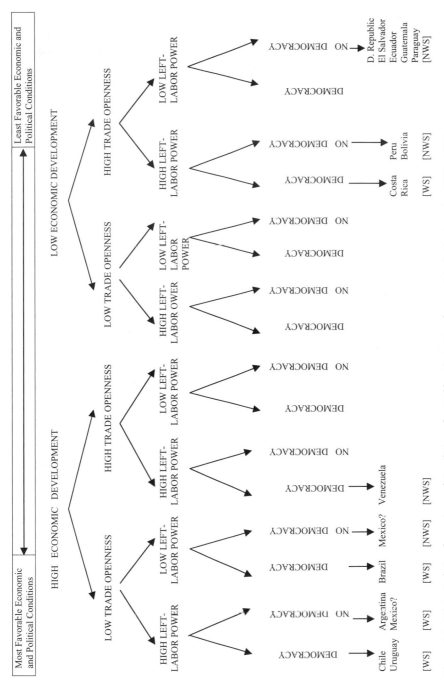

Figure 2.1. Historical Configurations of Conditions for Welfare State Development in Latin America, 1945–1979.
Note: WS = welfare state; NWS = non-welfare state.

independent variables operated. In some cases – most notably, the role of democracy in Brazil – they serve to explore the limits and even dispute some of the findings of the Boolean analysis just discussed. The chapter concludes with an analysis of the countries that did not evolve into welfare states, giving special attention to the perhaps more difficult cases of Mexico and Venezuela.[56]

2.4 Specifying the Alternative Paths to the Welfare State in Latin America

Path 1: With Favorable Economic Conditions

Chile

The first path to the welfare state in Latin America combined economic development and a relatively closed economy with *either* democracy (Brazil) *or* left-labor power (Argentina) or both (Chile and Uruguay). We begin with the cases of Chile and Uruguay, which present the most favorable configuration of conditions to develop a welfare state and were, until the 1970s, the two most universalistic and redistributive welfare states in the region.

By some measures, the beginnings of the Chilean welfare state date back to the mid- to late nineteenth century. In 1855, Manuel Montt, the first civilian president (1851–1861), faced army revolts coupled with a severe economic crisis. As a reward to the military, which had helped him settle the revolt, Montt established a system of public pensions for military officers.[57] But, Montt was a conservative who adapted the Napoleonic Civil Code, with its laissez-faire individualistic ideology, to Chile. As a result, the Code did not regulate labor conditions, and employees in practically all economic sectors received no protection against any risks (e.g., old age or sickness). It would therefore be premature to date the origins of the Chilean

[56] The cases of Mexico and Venezuela are especially important and warrant further study. Venezuela combined practically the same preconditions as Chile and Uruguay (i.e., democracy, left-labor power, and development) but, unlike the former, did not develop a strong welfare state. Mexico is also a particularly important case. If we classify its left-labor movement as strong, Mexico would have exactly the same preconditions as Argentina (at least if measured as a dichotomy, as required by Boolean analysis), yet Argentina evolved into a welfare state and Mexico did not. These differences are discussed in the last section of this chapter.

[57] The first pensions for the military were set up in the 1810s during the presidency of O'Higgins, but they were only for military veterans (Mesa-Lago, 1978, 22).

welfare state with Manuel Montt. However, during the last quarter of the nineteenth century, Chile's socioeconomic structure experienced profound changes. Workers began to organize and gradually changed from mutual-aid societies of workers in one trade to more militant and aggressive organizations of much broader scope. By the turn of the century, strikes had become a relatively common mechanism for workers' organizations to complain about poor labor conditions, job safety, and lack of labor regulations. The first strikes, led by skilled and semiskilled workers (e.g., dock, railroad, and construction), began in the larger cities (e.g., Santiago and Valparaiso) and then extended to other areas. The government had to use the army to repress the labor movement, which had become increasingly better organized and started to develop strong links with political parties.

In 1883, a powerful organization of industrialists, the Sociedad de Fomento Fabril (SOSOFA), came into existence. It quickly forged an alliance with other business groups to demand tariff increases and maintain the exchange rate despite the existence of substantial domestic inflation. During the same period, government expenditures rose and the education system was greatly expanded. At the start of the Balmaceda government in 1886, there were about 79,000 primary and secondary students in the country; at the end of his administration, the number had more than doubled.[58] As a result of these policies, there was continued industrial expansion. By 1914–1916, Chile's level of industrialization was 1.7 times the level predicted by its population and per capita income levels.[59]

Higher levels of industrialization quickly expanded the size of the working class, which led to growing labor tension and more worker demands. But, not all worker demands were equally powerful. Workers in strategic sectors of the economy had more bargaining power. This is why railroad workers,[60] who controlled the most important part of the transportation system, obtained old-age pensions in 1911, earlier than any other group and second only to the military. This increasing mobilization quickly put issues of social protection on the political agenda, and they became an important part of the presidential campaign of Arturo Alessandri in 1919. After winning the election, Alessandri greatly expanded the scope of the welfare state; however, he could not do it immediately. Facing opposition in the senate, he was

---

[58] Thorp (1998, 70).
[59] Muñoz (1968, 71).
[60] The railroad system was fundamental to transporting copper and nitrates (i.e, Chile's two main sources of economic wealth) from the mines to the cities and then exported abroad.

unable to pass his social-reform program for more than four years. In 1924, however, white-collar workers received protection against occupational diseases, and old-age pensions were also set up for civil servants, journalists, and the merchant marine. Unions were recognized and a Ministry of Labor, Hygiene, Assistance, and Social Welfare was created. Passing social legislation, however, was not easy for Alessandri, who faced strong opposition in the senate. Social legislation was finally approved after Alessandri appointed a general as head of his cabinet, following a tumultuous period of popular discontent and military conspiracies.

The new social legislation of the 1920s was not fully implemented until 1927–1931, when Colonel Carlos Ibáñez enforced the new legislation, which had been opposed by both business groups and the extreme left. Ibáñez was a welfare innovator because he compiled all the existing labor legislation into the first labor code in Latin America. The code, however, did not treat white- and blue-collar workers equally and, therefore, was conducive to a highly stratified system that reproduced social inequality.[61]

The expansion of the Chilean welfare state took place in the 1932–1973 period, an interval of about forty years of relative closure to international markets, continuous political democracy, and a strong left-labor movement. The Great Depression of the 1930s provoked a drastic change in the Chilean strategy of economic development. Before the Great Depression, the economic development strategy was characterized by dependence on external demand, especially of mining products. By contrast, after the 1930s, the state promoted a new strategy of development based on ISI, which included a combination of policies to protect national industry (e.g., import tariffs, subsidies, tax incentives), programs of investment in infrastructure, and the administration of public firms.[62] ISI encouraged the expansion of the state in the economy, providing the public sector with many additional functions and instruments.[63] At the same time, the welfare system expanded by

[61] Mesa-Lago (1978, 23–26).
[62] For a detailed analysis of the emergence and consolidation of social policies in Chile, see Raczynski (1994).
[63] As Thorp argued, "the core of protection was the combination of high tariffs on final goods, exemption from tariffs for many capital goods and intermediate products, and an overvalued exchange rate, which meant that products not subject to tariffs were extremely cheap" (1998, 137). In the case of Chile, state involvement in the economy became particularly important in the processing of natural resources. In 1939, the Corporación de Fomento a la Producción (CORFO) was established. CORFO was regarded as a technically strong, highly professional state organization responsible for formulating a national production plan. In 1958, it was reformed to give more emphasis to its role as provider of credit.

both covering increasing segments of the population and broadening benefits. This strategy received the support of the industrial bourgeoisie and urban workers and was concurrent with the rise to power of the Radical Party. Although its main basis of support was the white-collar urban middle classes, the Radical Party's predominance in the 1932–1952 period was not based on its electoral strength per se but rather on its capacity to forge alliances, especially with the Socialists.[64] The Radicals worked to fill important holes in the welfare system and to extend coverage to special subgroups. This is why they enjoyed, at least in part, the support of the Confederation of Workers of Chile (CTCH) and the Communists.[65] As Castiglioni noted, during this period, "expansion of coverage did not come due to governmental initiative but to social pressure, and reflected, especially, the victories of unionized workers."[66]

The next two phases of expansion of the Chilean welfare system comprise two periods. The first period (1953–1964) was preceded by the election of General Ibáñez in 1952. The role of labor was again very important. Fearing that Ibáñez might become a dictator again, a number of labor unions united to form the Central Única de Trabajadores de Chile (CUTCh), which integrated Communists, Socialists, and Radicals. As a result, Ibáñez responded with a strong welfare-reform agenda. Among other actions, he reorganized the white-collar health insurance (i.e., Servicio Médico Nacional de Empleados) and granted a minimum wage to blue-collar workers. The final phase of expansion (1964–1973) of the Chilean welfare system before the breakdown of democracy in 1973 was characterized by the implementation of an agrarian reform, which expanded the degree of social insurance available to agricultural workers. President Frei (1964–1970) reorganized the social security system for the military and made several attempts to unify and reduce the inequalities prevailing in the social security system. However, political opposition made reform impossible. Finally, President Allende (1970–1973) was able to maintain the support of the strong labor movement by increasing minimum pensions and refusing to reform the social security system.

Uruguay
The origins and development of the welfare state in Uruguay are similar to those of Chile, but there are also important differences. Both countries

---

[64] See Scully (1995, 113).
[65] Mesa-Lago (1978, 26).
[66] Castiglioni (2000, 3).

have been among the most economically developed in Latin America; both followed ISI policies after the 1930s, which promoted industrialization and protected domestic producers from international competition; and both had strong left-oriented parties, a well-organized and highly militant labor movement, and a relatively long history of continuous democracy until the early 1970s. The most important difference between the two cases is captured best by Castiglioni's analysis. She argues that "while in Chile the creation of the welfare state constituted a response to increasing pressure of certain organized social groups, most notably labor, in Uruguay the Colorado Party, which launched the first sets of social policies, sought to anticipate social pressures and to secure the electoral support of urban sectors by the development of the welfare state."[67]

Indeed, in Chile, like in many Western European countries, the welfare state emerged as a response to the bottom-up pressures exerted from increasingly better organized and powerful groups of civil society – especially the labor movement. In Uruguay, the welfare state emerged as part of a broader "nation-building" strategy. As Filgueira noted, in Uruguay,

rather than reacting to demands for social justice, the state attempted to mold the groups that could formulate such demands. Herein lies a trait peculiar to the Batllista state's social program. Its desire for social progress, influenced by democratic radicalism and a dose of social doctrine, was structured by a political logic that sought to craft a modern urban and industrial society by empowering and expanding the emerging middle classes and the small urban proletariat (. . .) [and hence] create consciousness and resolution in the subordinated sectors within a republican and democratic framework.[68]

The origins of the Uruguayan welfare state date back to the beginning of the twentieth century – especially during the 1904–1916 period. In 1904, the Colorado Party – which represented the urban, liberal, secular sectors – had just defeated the Blanco Party – which represented the rural, conservative sectors. The Colorado Party gained power on a platform that heavily emphasized social welfare, and social legislation was especially introduced during the presidencies of José Batlle (1903–1907 and 1911–1915). Batlle imported social welfare arrangements from Europe and initiated welfare reform before the beneficiaries of social legislation had become well organized and powerful. However, by the beginning of Batlle's second administration, only the military, civil servants, public-school teachers, and administrative personnel were protected by pension plans. As Perelli observed, Batlle aimed

---

[67]   Castiglioni (2000, 1).
[68]   Filgueira (1995, 9).

at constructing a model country based on a state dominated by urban middle classes but sensitive to the demands of the poor. After Batlle, through a combination of charismatic leaders, the strategic use of public expenditures to gain popular votes, and arrangements with the Blancos to share political power, the Colorado Party would manage to remain uninterruptedly in power until 1958.

As noted previously, the emergence of the welfare state in Uruguay was more the result of a progressive elite that acted preemptively, before the labor movement had become too vocal. At the same time, it is not possible to understand the expansion of the welfare state in Uruguay after the 1920s without considering the tremendous pressure and influence exercised by an increasingly well-organized and mobilized labor movement, which became especially powerful in the mid-1930s and 1940s. During this period, the government started to pursue a more aggressive industrialization program based on protectionist measures that included high import duties and import-licensing control. This resulted in a strong demand for labor. Employment in manufacturing increased by 70 percent in 1936–1948 and by 45 percent in 1948–1955 and coincided with a great rise in labor unionization. As Porzecanski pointed out, "the small, narrow, but numerous, trade unions of the 1910s and 1920s gave way to the broad-based, large-scale labor organizations of the 1940s."[69] As a result of a more militant and better organized labor force, the 1940s and 1950s saw a great expansion of pensions, the introduction of family allowances, the establishment of the first unemployment-compensation programs, and mandatory compensation in case of occupational accidents. In the 1960s, the conservative Blanco Party came to power. By that time, however, labor unions were already large and well organized, and even pensioners had been unionized in order to protect and expand their benefits. Blanco Party administrations could not roll back the welfare state if they wanted to maintain political stability. By the 1960s, the only major hole in the Uruguayan welfare system was the lack of health insurance.

Argentina

At the turn of the twentieth century, Argentina was not only the richest country in Latin America but also one of the richest countries in the world. By 1913, the industrial sector, led by the meat-packing and grain-product sectors, was already 17 percent of GDP.[70] As a result of fast and relatively early

---

[69] Porzecanski (1978, 76).
[70] Thorp (1998, 64).

industrialization, during the 1905–1916 period union activism increased dramatically. In 1921, President Yrigoyen passed social security legislation that benefited white-collar employees and other middle-class sectors from which he received political support. During the 1930s, the military government that had overthrown Yrigoyen passed a series of social security laws that provided a maternity fund for female employees on maternity leave (1934); a pension fund for journalists (1939); and old age, disability, and survivor's pensions for merchant marine and civil airline employees (1939). This coincided with a general change in the model of economic development. As in other countries in the region, Argentina – which had been a relatively open economy to international markets until the 1930s – embraced ISI. The immediate effects of this change are staggering. In 1928, the ratio of imports plus exports to GDP was around 60 percent. By the end of the 1930s, however, it had dropped to 35 percent, and it would continue to drop during the next decades so that by the mid-1950s, trade openness was less than 15 percent of GDP.[71] ISI fostered the expansion of import-competing sectors, reduced dependence from the external sector, and helped Argentina recover from the worldwide economic crisis that followed the Great Depression. As in other countries, it also expanded the size of the urban working class, which gradually increased its demands for improvements in working conditions and new social welfare benefits.

However, it was not until the 1940s that the Argentinean welfare state became consolidated and began to expand substantially. It did so under President Juan Perón (1946–1955), a charismatic army colonel who had been Minister of Labor in 1943 and became president in 1946 in one of Argentina's cleanest elections. As Minister of Labor, Perón had worked for new social and labor legislation, as well as the improvement and enforcement of the existing social welfare laws. He rose to power in 1946 courting the support of a strong labor movement, which had not developed strong organic ties with any political parties. Recognizing the importance of labor, Perón designed "justicialismo" as a strategy to keep his regime in power (1946–1955). Justicialismo, the main declared goal of which was social justice, consisted of an allegedly optimal blend of the best elements of capitalism with the best elements of communism. The relationship between Perón and the labor movement was based on a two-pronged strategy. On the one hand, Perón encouraged workers' organizations, sponsored the unionization of most of the labor force, and initiated social programs in their favor.

---

[71] Bulmer-Thomas (1994, 195).

On the other hand, however, Perón used a top-down corporatist strategy of control of civil society groups. He made sure that the demands of the labor movement could only be channeled through the state apparatus, which he controlled. For example, as McGuire pointed out, "Perón used the political branch [of the Peronist party], whose handpicked leaders were heavily dependent on his personal backing, as a counterweight to the union branch, whose leaders often had organizational, financial, and prestige resources of their own."[72]

One of Perón's most important actions in his efforts to develop a comprehensive welfare system for Argentina was to include social security in the justicialist constitution as one of the "Ten Rights of the Workers."[73] This was an attempt to universalize the coverage of the social security system, which had previously protected only a few privileged sectors (e.g., civil servants, the military, and some powerful white-collar groups). However, despite the fact that the system created by Perón had wide coverage for pensions and health care, it still showed great heterogeneity and inequality.[74]

Until the return of democracy in 1983, the military took direct or indirect control of the Argentine political system since Perón fall in 1955. The major labor union (i.e., CGT) split, with some factions remaining loyal to Peronism and others occasionally cooperating with the subsequent military regimes. Although the labor movement was severely weakened during military rule, it still remained one of the major political forces in Argentina, and the policy of using social policies to co-opt and control the labor movement and other pressure groups continued. For example, it was during the bureaucratic–authoritarian government of Onganía (1966–1970) that the welfare system received some degree of unification. In 1973, in the midst of a severe economic crisis, Perón returned to the presidency and launched a strong program of welfare reform that included the universalization of coverage to all the population, the expansion of benefits to cover all social risks, and the unification and standardization of the welfare system. But Perón's program was never fully implemented. As Mesa-Lago pointed out, "the change from an autocratic to a relatively democratic political system and the problems that Perón faced in maintaining a balance of power (in which labor played a crucial role) prevented the implementation of such a program."[75] After Perón's death in 1974 and the brief stay in power of his

---

[72] McGuire (1995, 210).
[73] Mesa-Lago (1978, 165).
[74] Huber (1995, 151).
[75] Mesa-Lago (1978, 168).

wife and former vice president, Maria Estela Martínez de Perón, the fragmentation of Argentine society intensified, which impeded the unification of the welfare system that Perón had envisaged and ultimately led to a new military intervention in 1976.

Brazil

Brazil's level of economic development at the time of the emergence of the first social legislation in the 1920s and 1930s was four to five times lower than that of Argentina, Uruguay, and Chile. In fact, using GDP per capita figures alone, Brazil would have to be classified, at least during the first half of the twentieth century, within the group of less developed Latin American countries.[76] Brazil is, however, by far the most populous country in Latin America, and per capita GDP figures may be misleading if used as the only indicator of economic development. Strong industrial growth in the 1900–1930 period led to a fivefold increase in industrial output. During the 1945–1972 period, typically considered the period of consolidation and expansion of welfare systems in the region, the value added of manufacturing in Brazil grew at an annual average rate of 8.4 percent of GDP – the fourth highest among a group of nineteen Latin American countries. Similarly, average GDP growth during the same period was 6.9 percent, the highest in the region.

The first social welfare laws, with some modest pension benefits, date back to 1923 (i.e., railroad workers), but it was only in the 1930s that the system began to expand to include other groups, such as public-utility workers (1931) and workers in commerce, banks, the merchant marine, industry, and transportation (1932–1937). Although the country's industrial development in the first two decades of the twentieth century had created some initial conditions for the adoption of social insurance, the origins of the Brazilian welfare system are not to be found, however, in a response to the demands of a highly mobilized and well-organized labor movement that pressed the government for social benefits (like in Chile and Argentina). Rather, it was associated with the expansion of the administrative capacity of the state and the concurrent objective of regulating social conflict and maintaining the stability of the political system. Governmental elites attempted to control the process of mobilization of increasingly key sectors of civil society such as organized labor. Granting social-insurance benefits

---

[76] In fact, among a group of sixteen Latin American countries, Brazil's income per capita in the 1920s and 1930s was the lowest. By the mid-1990s, however, Brazil's per capita GDP was the seventh highest (after Argentina, Uruguay, Venezuela, Mexico, Panama, and Costa Rica). See Thorp (2000, 353).

was one of the main tools in a strategy of co-optation of these groups into the officially sanctioned and controlled structures of the state.[77] Hence, the emergence and expansion of the Brazilian welfare system can be clearly distinguished from the Western European and Chilean models of welfare state formation in which the progressive incorporation of an increasingly better organized labor force led to a series of social policies that responded to demands for more equality and protection from the risks of modern capitalist life. In particular, the formation and expansion of Brazil's welfare system is strongly associated with the authoritarian period of Getlio Vargas (1930–1945).

In their study of the Brazilian welfare system, Draibe, Castro, and Azeredo captured well the essence of this strategy:

the organization of the social security system in the 1930s was a crucial component of the Vargas dictatorship, operating as a decisive source of power in the formation of his political regime. Conceived as a system that divided the working classes into specific sectors (. . .), which were organized in corporatist structures controlled by the central government, it simultaneously created barriers to entering the political arena – incorporating only those professional, unionized categories recognized by the state – and defined those who could make legitimate demands on social policies such as education, public health and housing.[78]

As in Chile, Uruguay, and Argentina, the expansion of the Brazilian welfare system from the 1930s to the 1970s coincided with a period of limited exposure to international markets. The ratio of imports plus exports to GDP, which was around 39 percent in 1928, declined to 33 percent in 1938, and by the 1950s and 1960s had dropped dramatically to less than 15 percent. The welfare system that Vargas created remained practically intact until the 1960s. During the democratic period (1945–1964), the labor movement became more dependent on the system of privileges administered by the state. Unions began to intensify their pressure to expand social benefits. Furthermore, different labor categories defended the privileges inherited from the previous authoritarian period and opposed attempts at unification discussed in congress. The corporatist strategy of labor co-optation that had developed during the presidencies of Getulio Vargas fostered a tradition of direct, unmediated, clientelistic ties between the state and groups in civil society, which hindered the institutionalization of the party system.

Hence, both a relative degree of economic development (and/or indus-trialization) and lack of openness to international markets facilitated the

---

[77] Malloy (1979, 155).
[78] Draibe, Guimaraes de Castro, and Azeredo (1995, 12).

expansion of the welfare system. However, unlike Chile and Uruguay, Brazil did not have a well-institutionalized left-oriented political party that could act as a constant supporter of a welfare-reform agenda. In addition, its labor movement was less well organized and powerful than in Argentina. According to our initial Boolean results, however, Brazil enjoyed a longer history of continuous democracy than Argentina. It is therefore necessary to analyze whether democracy played a fundamental role in the expansion of the Brazilian welfare system; the historical evidence suggests that it did not.

The Brazilian experience with democracy extended from 1955, after the death of President Vargas in 1954, to 1964, when President Goulart was overthrown by the military. However, the social security system implanted by Vargas remained largely unchanged during this period. Two fundamental characteristics of social policy during the democratic period need to be emphasized.[79] First, the main issues in the welfare-reform agenda were monopolized by an administrative elite of state bureaucrats. Second, the distribution of social benefits followed rather closely electoral cycles and the occupation of strategic posts in the state bureaucracy by social security institutions. Significant changes took place only after the breakdown of democracy in 1964. The new authoritarian regime undertook a process of welfare reform aimed at weakening organized labor. Labor representation in the social security system was abolished and the six major social security systems were merged into one.[80]

Path 2: With Unfavorable Economic Conditions

Costa Rica

Costa Rica's economy – traditionally based on the export of bananas and coffee – has enjoyed much lower historical levels of industrialization than Argentina, Brazil, Chile, and Uruguay – the other major welfare systems in the region. During the first forty years of the twentieth century, Costa Rica was characterized by political conservatism, lack of industrialization, limited political participation, and – with the exception of workers in the banana plantations – weak unions.[81] It is therefore not surprising that the first social welfare legislation for workers in Costa Rica arrived fifteen to twenty years later than in the other welfare systems in the region.

---

[79] See Draibe, Guimaraes de Castro, and Azeredo (1995, 13) for a more detailed description.
[80] Huber (1995, 150).
[81] Mesa-Lago (1989, 45).

During the Great Depression of the 1930s, world prices of coffee and bananas dropped dramatically. Costa Rica's dependence on these two agricultural exports intensified the magnitude of the recession and led to a dramatic reduction of fiscal revenues, which were heavily dependent on import and export taxes. Unlike Argentina and Brazil – which had large domestic markets – or Chile and Uruguay – which were more developed – Costa Rica was a small country, with relatively low levels of development and industrialization. Hence, an inward-looking strategy of ISI that would significantly reduce Costa Rica's trade openness was not an option. The deterioration of socioeconomic conditions during the 1930s led to labor unrest and fostered the growth of the Communist Party, which had been founded in 1931. Because of Costa Rica's lower level of industrialization, the urban working class was small and poorly organized, except in the banana-growing rural areas where unions were particularly strong.

In 1940, Rafael Calderón Guardia was elected candidate of the National Republican Party (NRP). The NRP was a conservative party that represented the ideological tradition of nineteenth-century liberalism associated with the ideas of a free market system, universal suffrage, freedom of expression, and separation of church and state.[82] Calderón was elected president in 1940. He was a physician who had traveled and studied extensively in Europe. It was there that he developed a strong Christian Democratic orientation and became familiar with the state-sponsored social policies that were already in place in some European countries. After being elected, one of Calderón's first moves was to separate himself from the more conservative sectors of the NRP and allied with the Communist Party, which was influential with the powerful unions of banana workers. One of his responses to the economic crisis was to initiate a reform process that would lay down the foundations for the Costa Rican welfare system. For example, in 1941, he created the Caja Costarricense de la Seguridad Social (Costa Rican Social Security Fund), which provided the first relatively comprehensive pension programs, as well as sickness and maternity health insurance. Also, in 1943, a Labor Code that protected workers from arbitrary lay-offs was enacted.

However, although the origins of the Costa Rican welfare state are associated with Calderón Guardia, its tremendous expansion from the 1950s to the 1970s cannot be understood without referring to José Figueres and the party he founded: the Partido Social Demócrata (Social Democratic Party, or PSD), which later became the Partido de Liberacion Nacional (National Liberation Party, or PLN). José Figueres was a wealthy landowner and vocal

---

[82] Mesa-Lago (2000, 399).

critic of Calderón. He opposed communism but favored social policies to improve the living conditions of the poor, which, he believed, provided fertile ground for the growth of communism. After a civil war in 1948, he headed an eighteen-month interim government that passed the 1949 Constitution. In 1953, he became the presidential candidate of the PLN party. After winning the election by a landslide, President Figueres raised taxes to finance state-supported social programs and took an ambitious series of measures that would turn Costa Rica into one of the most advanced welfare states in the region. First, in 1955, he established the Ministry of Labor and Social Security, which would offer services for unemployment and family allowances. Second, he expanded public expenditures on education, in line with the PLN's belief that education was the cornerstone of upward social mobility and democracy. Finally, he raised the minimum wage and created new jobs through the expansion of the public sector.

During the 1958–1970 period, the welfare state experienced tremendous growth. The PLN controlled the presidency during one term only (Orlich, 1962–1965), but it always was the dominant party in the Legislative Assembly, often enjoying an absolute majority. The anti-PLN coalition that governed during 1958–1961 and 1966–1970 expressed a combination of different ideological tendencies, from hardline economic liberalism to Christian Democratic ideas about public responsibility in the alleviation of poverty. As Clark argued, "opposition governments have usually featured the promise of reducing state intervention in the economy, combined with a commitment to welfare programs. But surprisingly, conservative governments made almost no progress in shrinking the size and scope of the state until the PLN did so itself in the 1980s."[83]

2.5 The Trajectories of the Group of Low Welfare Effort Countries (Non-Welfare States)

So far, we have explored which configuration of economic and political factors has been historically associated with the establishment and development of the welfare state in Latin America. However, without a closer examination of the cases that did not become welfare states, the analysis would be incomplete. What can we say about those countries whose level of historical welfare effort was much lower? The data presented in this chapter show that the group of non-welfare states can be further divided into two subgroups for analytical purposes. The first subgroup would include the

[83] Clark (2001, 27).

Dominican Republic, El Salvador, Ecuador, Guatemala, and Paraguay. These are countries at a comparatively lower level of economic development and industrialization, relatively more open to international markets (with the possible exception of Paraguay), with little or no experience with democracy, and weak left-labor movements. Hence, it is hardly surprising that these countries did not develop a welfare state. Practically all the conditions for the emergence of a welfare state were absent.

Then, there is a second subgroup of non-welfare states in which some of the conditions for the development of a welfare state were present. This subgroup would include Peru, Bolivia, Mexico, and Venezuela. In Peru and Bolivia, the Left was significantly stronger and more influential than in the other subgroup of countries (i.e., Dominican Republic, El Salvador, Ecuador, Guatemala, and Paraguay), but their low levels of development and absence of democratic history were quite similar. We may therefore conclude safely that the strength of the Left in Peru and Bolivia was insufficient to contribute to the development of a welfare state. There are at least two reasons why this can be reasonably considered the case. First, the level of industrialization in these two countries was relatively low and the size of the informal sector was large. Both factors combined to limit the development of better organized labor unions that could effectively press the state for social benefits, and it also limited the continuous supply of a strong basis of electoral support for these Left parties. In addition, the absence of continuous democracy during most of the period either impeded the access to power of the main party of the Left (i.e., APRA in Peru) or, once in power, forced it to adopt a development strategy that would leave little room for a redistributive agenda (i.e., MNR in Bolivia).[84]

Mexico and Venezuela are perhaps more difficult cases to explain. Let us begin with Mexico. If Mexico is coded as "strong" on the left-labor variable, then we run into a technical contradiction in the Boolean analysis performed previously. The problem in such a case is that Mexico and Argentina would have the exact same codings in all four independent variables used in the truth table. Yet, Argentina developed a welfare state whereas Mexico did not. This technical problem is easily resolved, however, if we relax the Boolean requirement of measuring variables using a dichotomy. On the one hand, it is true that in terms of economic development, trade openness, and left-labor

---

[84] As Gamarra and Malloy (1995, 405) stated, "The MNR's state capitalist model at first responded to popular demands but later because of the need to accumulate capital for investment, the party redirected the costs of development, placing the major burden on the working class represented by the COB." See Gamarra and Malloy (1995).

power, Mexico is much closer to Argentina than to Guatemala, Ecuador, Paraguay, El Salvador, and the Dominican Republic. On the other hand, however, if we go back to the original values of the each variable, the differences between Argentina and Mexico are sufficiently large to understand why the former became a more developed welfare state than the latter. The main difference between the two cases is that Argentina enjoyed higher degrees of economic development and industrialization, as well as a considerably smaller informal sector than Mexico. It is not surprising that Argentina's score on the "labor strength" index developed previously is more than twice as large as that of Mexico's. No area expert would question that the strength of the labor movement in Argentina was greater than in Mexico, as were its autonomy and independence from the state.

Despite the strong links between the Argentine labor movement and the Peronist party, the degree to which the PRI built a capacity to influence strike behavior, restrain wage demands, and mobilize the support of the system finds no parallel in Argentina. As Levy and Bruhn argued, the Mexican labor movement (especially the CTM) was characterized by leaders with absolute and seemingly perpetual dominance, corruption, and personalism, and a tendency to "sacrifice the interests of union members at the president's behest."[85]

In principle, the Mexican Revolution had created the conditions for a broad-based commitment to social development, but social policy soon became an instrument to support other national goals, such as economic growth, rather than a goal in itself that had to be sustained over time. In addition, the Mexican political system has been historically characterized by a low level of political mobilization and limited "pluralism," where the contest for power was restricted to supporters of the regime. The PRI was able to retain control by ensuring the support of the grassroots movements and by rigging the ballot box. This limited the need to expand the welfare state to "purchase" social control. When it was established in 1929, the PRI (then called PRM) drew heavily on the revolutionary discourse of social justice and borrowed from the Left the language of class conflict. But, the party's "catch-all" nature later developed a multiclass appeal capable of embracing vastly disparate social groups, from the poorest peasants and urban workers to the wealthiest entrepreneurs.[86]

Finally, the case of Venezuela is perhaps the most difficult one in light of the values of this country in almost all independent variables. First, Venezuela

[85] Levy and Bruhn (1995, 178).
[86] Craig and Cornelius (1995, 253).

had the highest average income per capita in Latin America during the twentieth century. Also, despite the recent political turmoil, it had been continuously democratic since 1959 (i.e., it ranks fourth after Costa Rica, Chile, and Uruguay in terms of continuous democratic history in the pre-globalization period). And, it scored high on the left-labor power scale, just after Chile, Uruguay, and Argentina. The key to understanding the Venezuelan case lies in its particular type of oil-dependent economic development. The great circulation of oil rents in the economy generated an extraordinary acceleration of the process of urbanization, which led to the expansion of the middle class. However, the industrial working class remained relatively small even for developing-country standards. The flow of oil revenue eliminated the need to generate a coherent industrialization-based economic development strategy.[87] This limited the size and power of the working class during the critical years of potential welfare state expansion. Although Acción Democrática (AD), a self-declared Social Democratic party, was in power for a significant period, reliance on oil led to a rent-seeking system with little incentive to build the extractive apparatus that domestic taxation requires.[88] When oil booms ended, the state was unable to raise taxes, regulate the economy effectively, and continue financing its spending programs. Venezuela's reliance on oil led to weak, corrupt, and inefficient state structures unable to develop the functions necessary for successful state development. Although it is true that after becoming democratic, a greater proportion of state spending was redirected toward social programs that benefited the middle and working classes, even during the years of economic boom, Venezuela never established a complete and consistent social safety net available to most citizens.[89]

2.6 Summary and Conclusion

This chapter studied why some Latin American countries developed more extensive systems of social protection (i.e., welfare states) than others from the 1930s to the 1970s. It focused on a period that preceded the current

---

[87] The small size of the industrial sector is surprising for a country that had the highest average GDP per capita in Latin America until about 1983. Comparative figures of the development of the manufacturing sector, for example, are striking. In the late 1960s, the value added of manufacturing to GDP ratio in Venezuela was only 15.5 percent – one of the lowest in the set of fourteen Latin American countries under study in this book.

[88] For an extensive analysis of these issues, see Karl (1997).

[89] For a more detailed analysis of why Venezuela failed to develop a more extensive system of social protection, see Hellinger and Melcher (1998).

process of increasing integration into trade and capital markets (globalization) and democratization that has been sweeping Latin America since the early 1980s. The latter is precisely the task of the following chapters.

The analysis began in the 1930s (somewhat earlier for some countries) – a period characterized by a great shift toward an inward-looking model of development (i.e., ISI) for the largest Latin American economies. And, it ended in the late 1970s, just before most Latin American countries started to join the so-called third wave of democratization and initiated processes of structural reform that would link them more closely to international trade and capital markets.

Our first task was to create an index of welfare effort, which was a helpful mechanism to identify those Latin American countries whose welfare system enjoyed a relatively higher level of development. This group, which was called for convenience "welfare states," included Argentina, Brazil, Chile, Costa Rica, and Uruguay. Among this group of countries, both the fiscal and macroeconomic priority of social spending, as well as the percentage of the active population covered by the social security system, were between two to four times greater than in other Latin American countries. The main research question was then to explain why the scope and role of the state for social insurance had developed much further in these countries than in the rest of Latin America. To this end, the chapter analyzed and critically evaluated the role of four independent variables: economic development, trade openness, democracy, and left-labor power. The chapter demonstrated that, with few exceptions, the economic and political environment within the group of welfare states was very different from the rest of Latin America.

First, the group of welfare states had a higher level of industrialization and income per capita, which increased the fiscal capacity of the state and its ability to support state-sponsored social programs. Second, the welfare state in these countries developed in the context of ISI, which relied on a set of protective measures (e.g., tariffs and import quotas, overvalued exchange rate, tax breaks for domestic industries) that shielded the domestic economy from international competition and fostered the expansion of the domestic industrial sector. This facilitated the emergence of a critical mass of workers that, depending on other labor market and political conditions, gained the capacity to act collectively in the pursuit of state-sponsored social programs. Hence, the relationship between trade openness and the development of the welfare state in Latin America was the opposite of the one found in advanced capitalist countries.

As demonstrated by many studies, the welfare state in countries such as Denmark, Austria, Belgium, and Sweden expanded in the post–World War II period as a compensation mechanism that protected those economic sectors that were increasingly exposed to the risks and volatility of international markets. By contrast, in Argentina, Brazil, Chile, Uruguay, and – to a lesser extent – Costa Rica, the development of the welfare state was inextricably linked to limited trade openness and the growth of the industrial sector associated with ISI.

Third, the group of Latin American welfare states had a longer history of continuous democracy and stronger left-labor movements than the group of non-welfare states. On the one hand, democracy opened new channels of participation for different groups in civil society that could organize and press the state for social benefits; provided a structure of incentives for politicians that could use social spending to increase their popularity and thus enhance their chances for (re)election; and generated a certain inertia of gradual social change whereby even conservative governments could not roll back social benefits easily. On the other hand, these countries also enjoyed stronger left-oriented political parties and/or relatively better organized and powerful labor unions than the group of non-welfare states.[90] Despite the fact that the strength of the Left and union movements among these countries would still be fairly small and limited if compared with their Western European counterparts, unions and/or left-oriented parties in Argentina, Chile, Costa Rica, Uruguay, and – to a lesser extent – Brazil were far more powerful and influential than in the rest of Latin America.

However, this chapter has shown that one cannot really understand the differential degree of welfare state development in Latin America by focusing on these independent variables individually. Taken alone, each variable would correctly predict whether a given country became a welfare state with 70 to 85 percent accuracy. This makes it impossible to determine whether it was economic development, lack of trade openness, continuous history of democracy, or a strong left-labor movement that drove the expansion of the welfare system. To overcome this difficulty, QCA was used to specify two alternative paths to the welfare state in Latin America – one with favorable economic conditions and another with unfavorable ones. With favorable economic conditions (i.e., economic development and protection from international market competition), only one political

---

[90] Among the group of welfare states, the case of Brazil is particularly difficult. On the one hand, the country remained formally democratic during a significant period but, as noted previously, the military exerted a considerable amount of influence, and democracy did not seem to have much explanatory power in the development of the Brazilian welfare system. On the other hand, Brazil's "left-power" can be considered weak if compared to Argentina, for example. Yet, in some of Brazil's urban centers, which heavily shaped political dynamics, the strength of labor power was considerably higher. This is why the strictly dichotomous codings used in Boolean algebra are particularly difficult to apply to the Brazilian case.

condition – democracy or left-labor power – was necessary to develop a welfare state. Four of the five cases followed this path: Argentina, which had a strong left-labor movement but little history of continuous democracy; Brazil, which had a relatively weak and dependent labor union but remained continuously democratic for eighteen years during the period under study; and Chile and Uruguay, which had both a long history of continuous democracy and a strong left-labor movement. Alternatively, when economic conditions were unfavorable (i.e., low levels of economic development and high levels of trade openness), both political conditions – democracy and left-labor power – were necessary to develop a welfare state. This was illustrated by the case of Costa Rica.

Some brief case studies of each of the five welfare states were also conducted, which were useful to put into context the general findings of QCA. In general, the case studies provided useful examples of how the different configurations of causal effects operated. One of the cases, however, casts serious doubt about the effects of democracy in the absence of left-labor power. In particular, the welfare state in Brazil emerged and developed during two authoritarian periods. It first emerged under Vargas's (civilian) authoritarian regime (1930–1945); it moderately expanded in a fragmented and selective manner during the democratic interlude (1945–1964); and it consolidated and expanded massively in the 1964–1977 period, again under an authoritarian regime. Finally, the chapter explored some of the reasons why the other set of Latin American countries did not develop a welfare state, giving special attention to the cases of Mexico and Venezuela.

APPENDIX 2.1: BASIC FEATURES OF QCA

The Boolean procedure of QCA uses dichotomous data on a series of independent variables or hypothesized preconditions (C) and one dependent variable or specified outcome (O). The data are arranged in a table (i.e., truth table), in which the first row lists all the conditions (i.e., independent variables) plus the specified outcome or dependent variable. An additional column on the right is reserved to list all the cases that will be used in the analysis (shown herein). An example may be useful to briefly illustrate how the procedure works.

Suppose we have a model with three dichotomous (i.e., nominal) independent variables and one dichotomous outcome or dependent variable.[91]

---

[91] The variables do not need to be initially dichotomous, but they have to be amenable to dichotomous treatment by the researcher.

Table 2.11. *Observable Combinations of
Preconditions and Outcomes in a Set of Eight Cases*

Cases	Independent Variables/Conditions			Dependent Variable/Outcome
	X_1	X_2	X_3	Y
N_1, N_8	1	1	1	1
N_2	0	0	0	0
N_3	1	1	0	1
N_4	1	0	1	1
N_5	1	0	0	0
N_6	0	1	0	0
N_7	0	0	1	0

Let X_1, X_2, and X_3 denote the set of independent variables or preconditions, and let Y denote the dependent variable or specified outcome of interest. Our purpose is to determine which precondition alone or in combination with others may lead to the specified outcome of interest (i.e., Y = 1).[92] By definition, each variable can take only two values: 1 if the property or condition of interest is present and 0 if it is not. As with the use of dummy variables in regression analysis, the numbers (0, 1) do not have any quantitative meaning. They are only useful as a coding device that helps the researcher identify cases in terms of whether a given property is present.[93] Suppose that we have eight cases, N_1 through N_8 (N = 8), and the outcome of interest is present in four and absent in the other four. Then, the truth table (Table 2.11) tells us that:

1. When all three preconditions are present, the outcome is also present. In other words, if $X_1 = 1$ and $X_2 = 1$ and $X_3 = 1$, then Y = 1. In the previous example, two cases (N_1 and N_8) have all the preconditions plus the outcome. If there were any cases in which the three preconditions were present and the outcome was not, then the truth table would become inconsistent.

[92] This amounts to observing the dependent variable taking a value of 1 – that is, having the property of interest we are investigating.
[93] An important issue in QCA is how to dichotomize variables that are not strictly dichotomous. The process of dichotomization often involves subjective decisions insofar as the researcher has to (1) decide whether the conditions or outcome is present based on a limited amount of conflicting information, and/or (2) transform quantitative variables into dichotomous ones selecting a (more or less) arbitrary cutting point.

2. When *either* $[X_1$ and $X_2]$ *or* $[X_1$ and $X_3]$ are present, the outcome is also present. In other words, $Y = 1$ if (a) $X_1 = 1$ and $X_2 = 1$ *or* (b) $X_1 = 1$ and $X_3 = 1$. We find one case in the first configuration (N_3) and one case in the second (N_4).
3. None of the other combinations lead to the outcome of interest in the dependent variable. This implies that $Y = 0$ (outcome is not present) when (a) none of the conditions are present ($X_1 = 0$, $X_2 = 0$, and $X_3 = 0$) as illustrated by N_2 and when only one of the conditions is present (as in N_5, N_6, and N_7).

Ideally, all possible combinations of preconditions or independent variables have to be included in the truth table. This requirement prevents the logical structure of our theory from being limited by a restricted range of observed cases. As Hicks noted, "incomplete coverage of all possible combinations of conditions might yield a Boolean expression (of outcomes in terms of conditions) that is inaccurate or unnecessarily complicated (or both) relative to the expression from the full table."[94] In our particular example, this means that we need to consider *one* additional combination of conditions that has no observable empirical referent. The second truth table (Table 2.12) adds this additional combination to the previous truth table.

The additional row illustrates a theoretically possible (albeit empirically inexistent) combination of independent variables. It suggests that a combination of X_2 and X_3 is not sufficient to observe Y. In this particular example, we only needed to add one extra combination of independent variables, but in other practical situations, many more may be required.[95]

Once the full truth table has been constructed, the next step is to reduce it by means of the elimination of all redundant primitive terms. This step, which helps us identify the conditions that are necessary and/or sufficient, can be accomplished through a series of paired comparisons. For example, for positive outcomes on the dependent variable, we find the following sequence of ones and zeros: 111, 110, 101. We may reduce these three equations into two reduced ones: 11-, 1-1 (where "-" means any value). In other words, to observe a positive outcome on the dependent variable, not all three preconditions are necessary. X_1 combined with X_2 *or*

---

[94] Hicks (1999, 70).
[95] For example, in his analysis of episodes of welfare state consolidation in advanced industrial democracies, Hicks (1999) adds four empirically unobservable but theoretically possible combinations of independent variables.

Table 2.12. *All Observable and Theoretically Possible Combinations of Preconditions and Outcomes in a Set of Eight Cases*

Cases	Independent Variables/Conditions			Dependent Variable/Outcome
	X_1	X_2	X_3	Y
N_1, N_8	1	1	1	1
N_2	0	0	0	0
N_3	1	1	0	1
N_4	1	0	1	1
N_5	1	0	0	0
N_6	0	1	0	0
N_7	0	0	1	0
	0	1	1	0

X_3 suffices to produce Y, irrespective of the value of the other precondition. A table of so-called prime implicants for both positive and negative outcomes can be constructed to help us in the task of generating the reduced equations.

Prime Implicated Variables and Reduced Equations

	Prime Implicated Variables	Reduced Equations
For Positive Outcomes	1 1 -	$X_1 X_2 = Y$
(Y = 1)	1 - 1	$X_1 X_3 = Y$
For Negative Outcomes	0 0 -	$x_1 x_2 = y$
(Y = 0)	0 - 0	$x_1 x_3 = y$
	- 0 0	$x_2 x_3 = y$

In this table, "1" indicates that the condition is present, "0" that the condition is absent, and "-" that the condition can be either present or absent without affecting the result. On the reduced equations, uppercase letters denote that the condition/outcome is present; lowercase letters indicate that it is not. When a variable does not appear in the equation, it follows that it plays no role. We are particularly interested in the row of results associated with a positive outcome on the dependent variable, which summarizes our main finding: that a positive outcome on the dependent variables is associated with the presence of X_1 in combination with X_2 or X_3.

The use of this Boolean procedure to conduct QCA has a number of advantages. First, it provides both inductive and deductive help in the specification of the multiple combinations of causal elements that generate a given outcome (e.g., in the following application, the emergence of the "welfare state" in Latin America). In so doing, it implements a "successive approximation of a set of 'leading' hypotheses to a body of data by means of a process of theoretically informed hypothesis formulation, testing, and revision, reminiscent (despite an advance in technical sophistication) of what Rueschemeyer et al. (1992) (. . .) have termed *analytical induction.*"[96] Second, as noted previously, it is appropriate to analyze a limited number of cases in which statistical techniques would be affected by problems of "degrees of freedom." Finally, the method helps to systematize comparisons of nations and bring into sharper focus historical and institutional differences that affect a given outcome. In short, QCA is a method of systematic comparisons that permits an "attractive fusion of quantitative-formal and qualitative, comparative, and case study approaches."[97] However, this method may be insufficiently deterministic and/or too prone to model under specification and development of spurious relationships. Hence, the usefulness of the method is greatly enhanced if, as I have tried to do in this chapter, the findings that emerge from Boolean analysis are also supported by some specific knowledge of the cases.

[96] Hicks (1999, 49).
[97] Hicks (1999, 50).

3

Theoretical Framework and Main Hypotheses

This chapter presents an analysis of the economic and political factors that are hypothesized to have affected the evolution of social spending in Latin America over the last three decades. The chapter draws on the welfare state literature to identify the correlates of social spending and adapts them to the reality of the developing world and to the middle-income countries of Latin America in particular. To this end, possible causal factors are divided into two sets of economic and political hypotheses. The purpose of the chapter is to lay down the theoretical foundations for the empirical analysis presented in Chapter 4. The chapter is organized in two parts. The first part discusses the hypothesized effects of three fundamental groups of economic factors on the fiscal and macroeconomic priority of social spending[1] in Latin America[2]: (1) economic development, (2) fiscal constraints, and (3) trade

---

[1] The fiscal priority of social spending is measured by the ratio of social spending to public spending; the macroeconomic priority is determined by the ratio of social spending to GDP.

[2] One of the most important economic variables in any OECD study of the welfare state is unemployment. As Huber and Stephens (2001, 6) noted, the crisis of the welfare state in many countries in recent years has followed increases in unemployment: "higher levels of unemployment meant that more people were drawing on welfare state benefits and fewer people were paying contributions, which cause severe fiscal stress." Unfortunately, however, unemployment data in Latin America are not generally available to be used in TSCS analysis. Hence, this variable has not been included in the analysis of Latin American welfare states. However, it is worth noting that the main problem in Latin American labor markets is not unemployment but rather inadequate employment or subemployment. In addition, unlike in the OECD, unemployment schemes in many Latin American countries are either nonexistent or poorly developed. As a result, unemployment expenditures are not in Latin America a fundamental component of social spending. For an analysis of unemployment insurance systems in Latin America in comparative perspective, see Cortázar (2001).

openness and capital mobility. The second part discusses two sets of political factors: (1) regime type (democracy/nondemocracy) and (2) the partisan orientation of the Executive Branch.

In the discussion of different hypotheses, the chapter develops two theoretical ideas that are key to understanding why welfare state development in Latin America has been affected by radically different dynamics from those that most researchers attributed to Western European countries, where most of the study of the welfare state has so far focused. First, the chapter explores why in Latin America the relationship between globalization and welfare state development is likely to have been affected by diametrically different forces from those observed in Western European cases. This is important because Latin American countries have been pioneers in the development of social-protection structures in the developing world, and this finding could, therefore, have implications for the study of welfare state development in other parts of the world. In particular, whereas the welfare state developed in advanced European democracies as a mechanism for offsetting the social costs of international integration, in Latin America, welfare structures first developed in a context of limited trade exposure (under the ISI model of development). They were then likely to have contracted rather than expanded with increasing integration to international trade – a dynamic that is exactly the opposite of that long observed by researchers of OECD countries. This chapter develops two mechanisms behind this relationship: one that operates through the value attached to macroeconomic stability by economic agents, and especially by producers of tradable goods, and a second one that operates through the changes that trade liberalization introduces on labor markets and the relative importance of different economic sectors in the economy.

The second theoretical contribution of the chapter is to unravel the complex relationship between democracy and welfare state development in an effort to understand the expected effect of democracy on social spending in Latin America. The point of departure is the well-established expectation from the median voter theorem that democratization shifts the position of the median voter to the left, increasing the distance between median and mean income. Most studies focused on OECD countries have interpreted this to mean that democracy will increase voters' preferences in favor of higher social spending. This assumes, however, that social spending is an instrument to redistribute income. If this is not the case, as it tends to occur in Latin America where social security programs have often been found to be regressive, a positive relationship between democracy and social spending can no longer be expected.

3.1 Economic Determinants of Welfare State Development

Economic Development and the Welfare State

There are two widely cited perspectives that describe the relationship between economic development and the size of the public sector.[3] The first is known as Wagner's Law, the second as Baumol's Cost Disease. It is now common for most empirical students of the welfare state to cite at least one of these perspectives and then introduce some measure of economic development (typically GDP per capita) as a "control" in their quantitative studies. Unfortunately, however, researchers hardly specify the mechanisms that connect economic development and the size of the public sector. Although "economic development" is a variable that appears in a wide variety of research situations in the social sciences, its effect on the size of the public sector is far from obvious. This subsection briefly reviews Wagner's Law and Baumol's Cost Disease and provides some descriptive evidence about the relationship between economic development and the size of the welfare state in Latin America.

Wagner's Law

According to Wagner's Law,[4] the public sector expands as a result of the process of economic development. Because social spending accounts for between one and two thirds of public expenditures, we should observe an expansion of social expenditures with economic development as well. Wagner's Law posits that there are three ways through which economic development can lead to an expansion of the public sector. First, industrialization leads to an expansion of public activity over private activity because in an increasingly complex society, the need for expenditures on regulatory activities grows. Second, the demand for collective or quasicollective goods – in particular, education and culture – is income elastic; that is, its demand increases as income grows. As a consequence, the state has to increase its supply of these goods, which would otherwise be undersupplied by the market. Finally, because of the existence of economies of scale in certain economic activities, economic-growth concerns push the state to take over the operation and management of natural monopolies.[5]

---

[3] Although they refer to the public sector in general (and not to public social programs in particular), it has become commonplace to refer to them in the analysis of the relationship between economic development and welfare state expansion.

[4] For Wagner's original article, see Wagner (1883).

[5] For a good empirical analysis especially designed to test Wagner's Law with a broad cross-national sample, see Ram (1987).

Boix[6] takes Wagner's Law one step further. He shows with a formal model and a wide cross-national sample of countries that at low levels of development, the public sector remains marginal in the economy. In premodern societies, for example, peasant families own small plots of land and are affected by similar risks. Communal arrangements to share risks and the support of the family and church tend to be the most important mechanisms of social security. Hence, at low levels of economic development, the family and community-based risk-sharing mechanisms substitute for the state.

However, the process of economic modernization leads to an expansion of manufacturing and service-oriented jobs that transforms the traditional economic structure. This change has two effects. On the one hand, it shifts the distribution of economic risks, concentrating them in specific segments of the population – for example, unemployment and work-related accidents among industrial workers. On the other hand, economic prosperity improves the material conditions and general economic well-being of the population, which leads to longer life expectancy. In addition, as the demographic structure of society changes and the percentage of old people grows, pressures for intergenerational transfers in the form of pensions and health-care programs are intensified.[7]

Baumol's Cost Disease

Baumol provided the second theoretical perspective that connects economic development and the size of the public sector.[8] According to Baumol, real wages in the private and public sectors grow at roughly the same speed. However, because the public sector is labor-intensive and mainly service-oriented, productivity grows at a lower speed than in the private sector. Hence, the relative size of the government in the economy grows. As Snower argued, "the output of many welfare state services is simply the unmediated labor input: doctors cannot significantly reduce the time spent with each patient without reducing the level of care; nor can teachers raise class size without reducing the quality of education."[9] Thus, given that (1) the productivity of these social services will tend to rise more slowly than productivity in other sectors of the economy, and (2) average wages in the welfare sector are not likely to fall below the average wage level, the cost of the welfare state will rise relative to average costs in other economic sectors. And, the economy will need to allocate an increasingly greater share of GDP to welfare state services.

---

[6] See Boix (2001).
[7] Boix (2001, 4–5).
[8] Baumol (1967).
[9] Snower (1996).

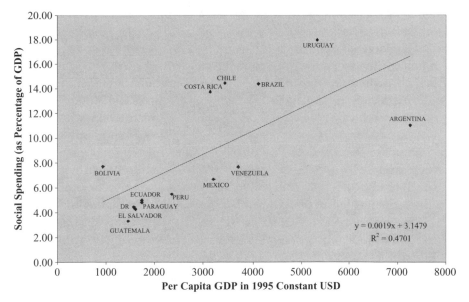

Figure 3.1. Economic Development and Social Spending as a Percentage of GDP, Average 1973–2003.

Although some recent research by Holsey and Bordering[10] seemed to confirm Baumol's finding, Boix has demonstrated that this mechanism is not automatic: higher productivity levels in non-welfare services may also expand the tax base to finance the state, which would prevent the public sector from automatically taking a bigger share of the economy.

Figures 3.1 and 3.2 provide some initial evidence of the relationship between economic development and the size of the welfare state in Latin America, as measured by social spending levels.[11] The two figures suggest a positive relationship between per capita GDP and welfare effort because higher levels of economic development are associated with significantly higher levels of social spending.

However, there is a lot of variation in the sample. For example, Costa Rica and Chile, with a similar level of development as Mexico (about USD $3,500 per capita), have levels of social spending that are almost twice as large as those of Mexico. A similar observation can be made if we turn to

[10] Holsey and Bordering (1997).
[11] This evidence is presented for descriptive purposes only to justify, along with the theoretical discussion that accompanies it, the hypotheses that are being presented. It is not intended to make causal statements given that the sample is small and that no other controls are being introduced. The proper testing of this relationship is carried out in Chapter 4 in the context of multivariate regression analysis.

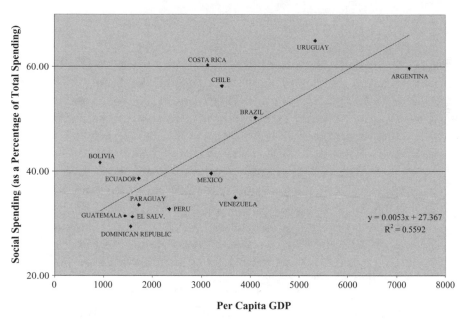

Figure 3.2. Economic Development and Social Spending as a Percentage of Total Public Spending, Average 1973–2003.

social spending as a percentage of government spending, which provides a measure of the budget priority of social programs. As Figure 3.2 illustrates, the relationship continues to be positive, with richer countries giving social spending a greater priority in the composition of the budget.

Two conclusions can be drawn from Figure 3.2. First, although there seems to be a positive relationship between economic development and the budget priority of social spending, countries at a similar level of development can give a different priority to social spending in the composition of the government budget. The cases of Peru and Costa Rica provide a particularly interesting contrast of how countries that have a relatively similar level of development can differ in their commitment to social spending. If we take the average values of per capita GDP in purchasing power parities (PPPs) for the 1973–2003 period, Costa Rica is about $1,000 richer than Peru. In 1973, however, per capita GDP was similar in both countries ($1,949 in Costa Rica and $1,817 in Peru), yet Costa Rica devoted 58.7 percent of the budget to social spending, whereas Peru devoted only about 30 percent. In other words, despite having roughly the same level of development, the priority of social spending in the composition of the budget was twice as large in Costa Rica. This suggests, as the following chapters demonstrate, that there is a need to explore what other economic and political differences lead countries at a relatively similar level of development to give more priority to social spending than others.

One limitation of the preceding analysis is that it does not tell us what the actual mechanism is that connects economic development and the size of the welfare state. If our purpose is to know whether the relationship is caused by Wagner's Law or Baumol's Cost Disease, then data on the differential productivity rates of the private and public sectors in Latin America would be needed. These data are not, unfortunately, available to undertake such exercise. Despite this limitation, we can conclude from the previous analysis that limited economic development is likely to constrain the expansion of social spending. Richer countries, to be sure, will have more resources to protect their citizens through more generous social programs. However, at any given level of development, there is ample margin for the state to provide more or less social protection. This is especially true if we take the priority of social spending in the public budget as our measure of welfare effort. The stark contrast between Costa Rica and Peru in the early 1970s provides a clear indication that this is the case.[12] The preceding discussion leads to our first hypothesis, which can be formulated simply in the following way:

[H1]: Higher levels of per capita GDP are likely to have been associated with higher levels of social spending. Everything else being equal, average welfare effort in Latin America increased faster in countries where per capita GDP rose more during the sample period.

The Role of Budget Constraints: Revenue Effort and Fiscal Deficits

As noted previously, the share of social spending in a country's budget can vary substantially from one country to the next. However, once the percentage of the budget to be allocated to social spending has been set, welfare effort can only increase with increases in public spending. And, over the long term, increases in public spending can only be financed with increases in the extractive capacity of the state.[13] Short-term deviations are

---

[12] See Chapter 6 for a detailed analysis of Costa Rica and Chapter 7 for a study of the Peruvian case. These two chapters analyze which other economic and political factors allowed Costa Rica to develop and maintain a more extensive system of social protection than Peru.

[13] Countries can also finance expenditures through grants, but given Latin America's level of development, grants constitute a less important way of financing expenditures than in other regions, like Africa.

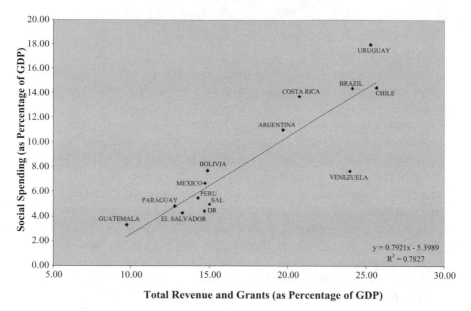

Figure 3.3. Revenue Effort and Social Spending Levels in Latin America, Average 1973–2003.

possible if countries finance higher public expenditures via fiscal deficits, but as public debt begins to accumulate and other macroeconomic imbalances emerge (e.g., inflation, large current account deficits), this ceases to be a possibility. In fact, one of the main reasons behind the first-generation structural adjustment programs in Latin America was precisely the existence of persistently large fiscal deficits during most of the 1970s and 1980s.[14]

Figure 3.3 shows the relationship between revenue effort and social spending as a percent of GDP in Latin America, using averages for the entire

---

[14] This occurred because budget deficits were typically financed through seigniorage (i.e., printing money), which is clearly inflationary. There are, however, other ways of financing fiscal deficits (e.g., through domestic or foreign borrowing) that are not necessarily inflationary. The relationship between the public deficit and the different ways of financing can be summarized as follows: [Public deficit financing = Money financing + Domestic debt financing + External debt financing]. Each form of financing leads to serious macroeconomic imbalances if used excessively. As noted, financing deficits through the printing of money leads to inflation; excessive domestic borrowing leads to higher interest rates, a credit squeeze, and the crowding out of private investment. Finally, external borrowing may lead to a current account deficit and an appreciation of the real exchange rate. If foreign reserves are low, it may end up in a balance-of-payment crisis; if debt is too high, it may provoke an external debt crisis. For a review of the previous equation with a comprehensive analysis between fiscal deficits and macroeconomic performance, see Easterly and Schmidt-Hebbel (1993).

Table 3.1. *Regional Averages of Central Government Revenues and Social Spending as a Percentage of GDP in Four Different Regions, Average 1970–2000*[a]

	Tax Revenues (in Percent of GDP)	Social Spending (in Percent of GDP)
Eastern Europe	35.7	20.4
OECD	32.5	18.9
Latin America	17.2	8.0
East Asia	20.4	4.7

[a] Ideally, it would be better to use data on the "consolidated general government," which includes the central and any subcentral (i.e., state and municipal) levels of government. Unfortunately, however, reliable cross-national data across regions beyond the central level of government are not available for a substantial number of countries. This may be an important problem in federal countries and also in unitary countries with a long tradition of strong municipal government (e.g., Scandinavia). Fortunately, however, systems of taxation are usually more centralized than systems of public expenditures. Hence, the figures presented here are still a relatively good measure of regional differences in the capacity of the state to collect taxes. The three largest states in Latin America (i.e., Mexico, Brazil, and Argentina) are federal, but until the late 1980s (later in the case of Mexico), subnational governments collected a small amount of public revenues. Other federal states in the OECD such as Belgium and Austria are also very centralized in terms of tax revenue, although the degree of decentralization is greater in Canada and the United States. Tax-revenue collection is also highly centralized in East Asia.

Sources: Created with data from *Government Finance Statistics*, various issues.

sample period (1973–2003). The results need to be interpreted with care because they are based on a small sample and no other controls have been introduced. The graph shows a strong relationship, with a tentative regression line explaining about 80 percent of the long-term variation in social spending in the sample.[15] Countries that have deviated from the average predicted line tend to fall into two possible categories: (1) those with large taxable natural resources (e.g., Venezuela with large oil-related revenues), or (2) those with a high fiscal priority for social spending, usually associated with a long welfare state tradition (e.g., Costa Rica and Uruguay).

When compared to other regions, the weakness of Latin American governments to collect taxes is notorious. Table 3.1 provides comparative evidence of average tax collection and social spending as a percentage of GDP in four different regions during the 1973–2000 period. The amount of total revenues (in terms of GDP) collected by Latin American countries is, on average,

---

[15] This regression is presented only for illustration purposes. With only fourteen observations and the inclusion of no other controls, these are simply tentative relationships that are tested more in-depth in the next chapter.

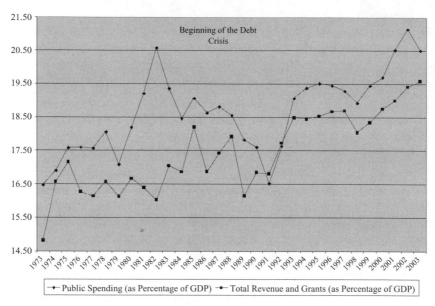

Figure 3.4. Trends in Revenue and Expenditures in Latin America, 1973–2003.

about half the amount of their OECD and Eastern European counterparts and 3 percentage points lower than in East Asia. Table 3.1 also shows a strong link between the resources that states can commit to social programs and their revenue effort. A notable exception is East Asia, where the revenue-to-GDP ratio is about 3 percentage points higher than in Latin America, and yet social spending is about 3 percentage points lower. This has to do with the historically low level of development of East Asian welfare states, where other family- and private-sector–based forms of social protection are prevalent. However, the relationship holds strongly across the other regions (i.e., Latin America, OECD, and Eastern Europe) and within regions themselves.

Although the analysis of averages over long periods is necessary to identify long-term trends, it is also useful to study short-term fluctuations in revenues and expenditures. The short-term changes in revenue and expenditures determine the behavior of fiscal deficits, which can temporarily loosen the link between the extractive capacity of the state and expenditure levels. As Figure 3.4 illustrates, average fiscal deficits (i.e., the gap between the revenue and expenditure lines) were rather large between the late 1970s and most of the 1980s, but they narrowed significantly during the 1990s. Hence, the relationship between welfare effort and revenue collection was stronger in the 1990s, a decade when hard budget constraints became more widespread.

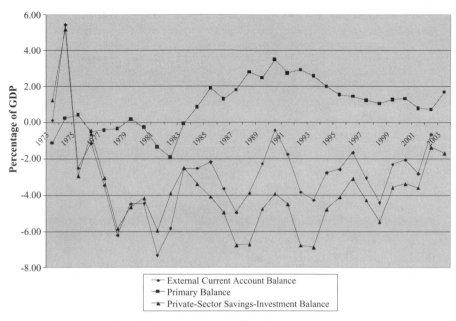

Figure 3.5. External Current Account, Fiscal, and Private-Sector Balances in Latin America, 1973–2004.

The process of fiscal adjustment that began in 1982 was in large part driven by the need to support an external current account adjustment. Countries that had received large capital inflows during the 1970s saw sudden reversals in capital flows after the Mexican default in 1982, which marked the start of the debt crisis. Deprived of capital to finance their current account deficits, Latin American countries had to reduce their fiscal deficits. Some countries resisted and did not reduce their fiscal deficits in response to the reduction of external capital flows. However, these countries resorted to domestic (i.e., monetary) financing of the fiscal deficit and ended up with serious episodes of hyperinflation. The relationship between the adjustment in the external current account and in the improvement in the government's fiscal position is illustrated in Figure 3.5. The primary fiscal balance (which excludes interest payments) reached equilibrium in 1983 (one year after the start of the debt crisis) and registered substantial surpluses for the rest of the decade and until the mid-1990s. After 1995, it began to decline but has always remained positive.

By contrast, the private-sector savings-investment balance continued to deteriorate shortly after the start of the debt crisis in 1983 until the late 1980s, suggesting that private spending (consumption and investment) continued

Table 3.2. *Sources of Tax and Nontax Revenue in the OECD and Latin America*[a]

	1970–1990		1990–1994	
	OECD	Latin America	OECD	Latin America
Total Revenue (%)	100	100	100	100
Income Tax	36.9	21.7	35.0	20.4
Social Security Taxes	31.5	21.6	32.2	23.5
Indirect Taxes	20.4	29.3	20.4	26.3
Trade Taxes	1.4	8.8	1.0	5.2
Nontax Revenue	7.8	17.1	8.1	15.9

[a] (1) Income taxes include personal income taxes, corporate income taxes, and corporate profit taxes, including taxes on corporate capital gains; (2) social security taxes include payroll taxes and selective employment taxes directly linked to the social security system; (3) indirect taxes include sales taxes (i.e., value added tax) and excise taxes (i.e., taxes on specific products and services such as tobacco, alcohol, electricity, gas, and energy); (4) trade taxes include import and export duties (i.e., taxes on imports and exports) and other taxes on international trade and transactions; and (5) nontax revenues include net profits from public enterprises, interest, dividends, fines and private contributions, donations, or gifts to the government (excluding grants from abroad). For a detailed analysis of different sources of revenue, see IMF, 1986, *A Manual on Government Finance Statistics*; Washington, DC: IMF. A new version of the manual was published in 2001, but this classification remains largely valid.
Sources: Created with data from Gavin et al. (1996, 5). Each figure represents the percentage of total government revenue that is collected through each source.

to increase at a relatively strong pace despite the economic crisis. This trend, however, was reversed after 1988.

The analysis of the evolution of tax revenues presented in Figure 3.4 is also useful in one additional sense. Trends in fiscal revenues in Latin America show a significant degree of volatility and are much more sensitive to fluctuations in the business cycle than in advanced industrial countries. This is the case because governments in Latin American countries rely more on indirect taxes, international trade taxes, and nontax revenues than their OECD counterparts. As Gavin, Hausman, Perotti, and Talvi demonstrated, the higher the proportion of nondirect taxes on total tax receipts, the greater the sensitivity of public revenues to fluctuations in the business cycle.[16] As Table 3.2 demonstrates, the share of income taxes in total revenue is significantly lower in Latin America than in the OECD, and the pattern has not changed substantially in recent years. Conversely, indirect tax revenues are much higher in Latin American countries than in their OECD counterparts.

[16] Gavin et al. (1996).

For example, during the 1970–1990 period, the share of indirect taxes in total revenue was almost 10 percentage points greater in Latin America than in the OECD. Similarly, Latin American countries relied more on nontax revenues and trade taxes. As noted, although income taxes are also sensitive to fluctuations in the business cycle, their degree of sensitivity tends to be significantly smaller than other types of taxes.

To the extent that social expenditures depend on the extractive capacity of the state, the greater volatility of public revenues in Latin America is likely to have resulted in significantly procyclical patterns of spending. In other words, when the economy was doing well, revenue collection was buoyant and the government had a greater capacity to finance social programs. Yet, in times of economic recession, the structure of taxation in Latin America is likely to have led to a more significant depression of tax revenues and, hence, a lower capacity to finance public expenditures than would have been observed in OECD countries. This leads us to our second economic hypothesis:

[H2]: Social spending will vary positively with the ratio of taxes to GDP and negatively with fiscal adjustment. The higher the amount of revenues collected, the greater the capacity of the state to devote resources to social programs. Conversely, improvements in the fiscal balance (i.e., smaller fiscal deficits or higher surpluses) will be associated with lower social spending levels.

Globalization: The Critical Importance of Trade Openness and Capital Mobility

In the last three decades, world trade has grown much faster than world output, and cross-border flows of capital have grown even more rapidly.[17] This process, which is often referred to as *globalization*,[18] is affecting the autonomy and capacity of states to pursue independent monetary and fiscal policies. There are three broad implications of these trends. First, in a context of high capital mobility, policymakers cannot preserve monetary policy autonomy and fixed exchange rates at the same time. Second, economies are more sensitive to external shocks, as the Asian financial crisis clearly showed in 1997–1998. Finally, there is some evidence that internationalization has

---

[17] A good source to study these changes from an international political economy perspective is Keohane and Milner (1996).

[18] There are many definitions of globalization. For our purposes, following Garrett (1998, 2001, 2004), *globalization* is simply defined as the process of international integration of markets of goods, services, and capital.

decreased state intervention in the economy and pressed governments in developing countries to cut budget deficits.[19] Within this context, this subsection presents the main hypotheses that describe the relationship between globalization and social spending in Latin America. The point of departure is a theoretical discussion of the main arguments that relate globalization to the welfare state.

Trade Openness and the Welfare State: How Does Trade Integration Affect Welfare Effort?

The relationship between trade integration and the welfare state has a relatively long history in the economics and political science literatures. Although the link has been questioned recently,[20] it remains one of the most widely cited explanations for the development of the welfare state, at least in the literature of OECD countries. If one focuses on advanced industrial economies, for which data on both public expenditures and trade integration are available since the early 1960s, the growth of government expenditures as a percentage of GDP and the rising levels of trade have followed remarkably similar paths, at least until the mid-1990s. This is the period on which most researchers studying OECD countries have focused. However, the trends were reversed after 1994, with trade openness and the size of government moving in different directions (Figure 3.6).

In Latin America, a radically different dynamic seems to be at work, as shown in Figure 3.7. With few exceptions, increases in trade openness and the size of government tend to move in opposite directions. The trends can be divided into three phases: (1) in the first phase (1973–1981), public spending increases and trade openness decreases steadily; (2) in the second phase (1982–1991), trade openness increases and public spending decreases steadily; and (3) in the third phase (1992–2003), both trade openness and public spending trend upward, but even in this case, annual changes tend to move in opposite directions in a majority (i.e., 60 percent) of the cases.[21]

For the group of OECD countries (Figure 3.6), the average level of trade integration increased from about 60 percent of GDP in the 1970s to 70 percent by the mid-1990s and 90 percent of GDP by 2003 – over the entire

---

[19] Garrett (1995, 682).

[20] Iversen and Cusack (2000) argued that it was not globalization but rather technological change and deindustrialization that led to the expansion of the welfare state.

[21] Although both variables trend upward during this phase, they only move in the same direction between 1992 and 1995 and 2000 and 2002.

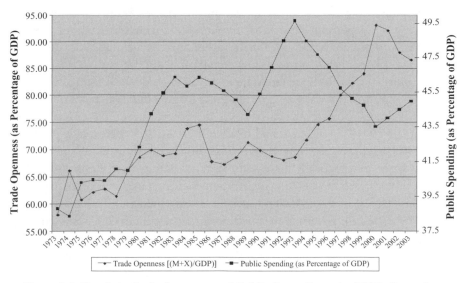

Figure 3.6. Trends in Trade Openness and Public Expenditures in OECD Countries, 1973–2003.

period, this represents an absolute growth of 30 percentage points and a relative growth of about 50 percent. Similarly, total government spending went up from about 39 percent of GDP in 1973 to 50 percent by the mid-1990s and then declined to 45 percent of GDP by 2003 – an absolute increase

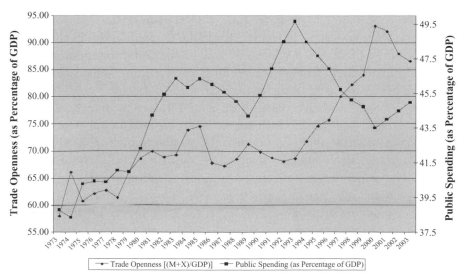

Figure 3.7. Trends in Trade Openness and Public Expenditures in Latin America, 1973–2003.

over the entire period of 6 percentage points (which results in a relative increase of 15 percent). The most remarkable characteristic about these trends is not their upward movement; rather, it is the fact that, at least until the mid-1990s, they seem to follow remarkably similar paths, consistent with most studies of the welfare state in advanced industrial countries.

In Latin America, trade integration grew from about 39 percent of GDP from its lowest point in the early 1980s to 55 percent of GDP (its highest point) by 2003 – an absolute and relative increase of 16 percentage points and 40 percent, respectively. By contrast, however, government spending levels have not practically increased over the same period. From its 1982 peak of 20.5 percent of GDP, government spending declined dramatically during the rest of the 1980s and, despite steady increases during most of the 1990s, by 2003 government spending (at 21 percent of GDP) had barely surpassed the levels of two decades before. Also, in contrast with the OECD cases, the most important characteristic of these trends in Latin America is the fact that they seem to move in opposite directions during most of the time intervals. Hence, we need to ask about the mechanisms underlying these different trend patterns. In short, why should the public sector expand as the level of trade integration rises in the OECD and remain unaffected or contract in Latin America? To answer this question, it is useful to draw on a distinction made by Garrett between a *compensation hypothesis* and an *efficiency hypothesis.*[22]

The compensation hypothesis focuses on the role of the welfare state as a mechanism for offsetting the social costs of international integration and for contributing to the development of "human capital." In addition to the evidence presented in Figure 3.6, in OECD countries this hypothesis is supported by studies that show a strong empirical association among economic openness, large public sectors, and generous welfare systems. Katzenstein,[23] for example, argued that it is no coincidence that small, highly open economies such as Sweden, Austria, and the Netherlands have large public sectors. Governments in these countries have used the public sector to protect those sectors of the economy likely to suffer from the risks of exposure to international markets. Katzenstein shows how the share of social security expenditures in national income was identical in both the small European and the large industrial states (i.e., about 13 percent of GDP). By the beginning of the 1970s, however, the large industrial states were spending only 14.3 percent of GDP in social security programs, while the

---

[22] Garrett (2001).
[23] Katzenstein (1985, 55).

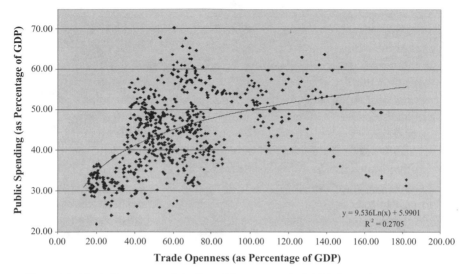

Figure 3.8. Trade Openness and the Size of Government in OECD Countries, 1973–2003.

small open economies had increased spending levels to about 20.3 percent of GDP.[24]

Combining both cross-section and time-series data, Figure 3.8 shows a rather strong positive relationship between trade integration and the size of the welfare state in the OECD. A logarithmic curve explains about 30 percent of the variance in the level of social spending, a rather significant effect for a single variable.[25] In line with many previous studies, this suggests that in OECD countries, there clearly is a strong and positive relationship between trade openness and the size of the welfare state as measured by public spending levels.[26] The evidence for the Latin American sample (Figure 3.9) is radically different. The simple bivariate scatter plot shows

[24] Similar arguments are made by Cameron (1978) and Garrett and Mitchell (2001), among others.

[25] Although this graph only shows a bivariate relationship, a partial-regression scatterplot that looks at the effect of trade controlling for GDP per capita and other demographic and economic factors yields similar results. Because the results do not seem to change much after introducing other control variables, the bivariate scatterplot, which is easier to interpret, has been retained. Partial regression scatterplots are based on the errors of a multivariate regression equation and the scales on the X and Y axes are distorted. The partial regression scatterplot applied to the Latin American sample yields a more negative and statistically significant slope than the one presented in the bivariate scatterplot.

[26] Cameron (1978), Katzenstein (1985), and Rodrik (1998) use public expenditures rather than social expenditures as a proxy for welfare state development. However, if we are interested in the welfare role of the state, social spending seems a more appropriate measure.

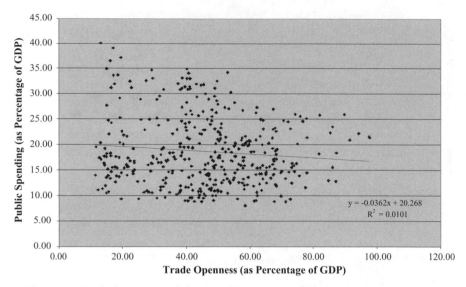

Figure 3.9. Trade Openness and the Size of Government in Latin America, 1973–2003. *Sources:* Created with data from the IMF's *Government Finance Statistics* and *World Economic Outlook.*

no evidence of a positive relationship between trade openness and social spending. In fact, the relationship tends to be negative, even if weakly so. A partial regression scatter plot (not shown) turns the relationship strongly negative, suggesting that some other mechanism different from the compensation hypothesis may be at work. This leads us to the introduction of an alternative theoretical perspective known as the efficiency hypothesis. This hypothesis presents a completely different picture of the relationship between trade openness and the welfare state. It operates through two possible mechanisms concerning the impact of trade liberalization: (1) on the value attached to macroeconomic stability by economic agents, and especially by producers of tradeable goods; and (2) on labor markets and the relative importance of different economic sectors in the economy.

Trade Liberalization and Macroeconomic Stability. Trade liberalization increases the social cost of macroeconomic instability. In more open economies, business groups exposed to international competition are more likely to press the government to reduce fiscal deficits, without which competitiveness in international markets could be seriously eroded. In particular, looser fiscal deficits increase aggregate demand and, depending on how they are financed, they can crowd out private investment, undermine price stability, create an unsustainable external current account position, and/or generate strong debt sustainability concerns. Under flexible exchange rates, fiscal deficits may lead to an appreciation of the currency, which makes it more difficult for export-oriented firms to remain competitive in international markets. Under fixed exchange rates (and high capital mobility), they usually lead to a deterioration in the external current account balance, a contraction in the money supply,[27] and an increase in interest rates. This has two effects: first, it raises the borrowing costs for the private sector and consequently reduces private investment; and second, it leads to a gradual loss of the central bank's net foreign assets, which undermines the credibility of the exchange rate peg and may lead to speculative attacks against the currency, ultimately generating a currency crisis. As a result, there is a general deterioration of the business environment.

Furthermore, whenever fiscal adjustment is needed, business groups will prefer expenditure cuts and resist increases in tax rates (including payroll taxes and social security contributions that are generally used to directly finance certain social spending programs) because these affect negatively their production costs and consequently erode their competitiveness. Given the strong opposition to tax increases, the composition of the needed fiscal adjustment is likely to rely on expenditure cuts, including social spending, that account for between 40 and 70 percent of total public spending.

Changes in Labor Markets and the Structure of the Economy. Trade liberalization changes the structure and incentives of previously dominant companies in import-competing sectors (characteristic of the ISI model described in Chapter 2) and increases the relative importance of new companies in export-oriented sectors. The ISI model relied on an expansion of internal markets with rising real wages as part of the strategy. Under this model, companies in import-competing sectors did not have good incentives to be cost-efficient because they were shielded from international competition by a system of tariffs and import quotas. The expected effect of the elimination of this system of protection depends on a variety of factors, including the structure of the market and the broader institutional framework. However, economic theory provides a rather straightforward answer: the removal of import protection will put pressure on firms to reduce costs. Successful firms may achieve this through investment in new technology, which produces a downward shift in the supply curve. This allows them to offer the

---

[27] Unless the central bank sterilizes this effect through an open-market operation.

same quantity of goods for a lower price. Conversely, firms that are not able to reduce costs in line with the new long-term lower market prices will be forced to exit the industry. The magnitude of these effects is likely to depend on the initial levels of inefficiency, which will be lower in cases where there was a significant amount of domestic competition.[28]

This simple framework is useful to understand the Latin American experience. There is some evidence that productivity in the tradeable sector increased in a number of countries.[29] This suggests that surviving firms in import-competing sectors have been forced to be more competitive. However, higher productivity was not the result of new investment, taking advantage of easier access to higher quality imported intermediate and capital goods. Rather, the evidence suggests that this higher productivity reflected significant reductions in real wages and in employment in the manufacturing sector. In particular, while the value added of the manufacturing sector increased by close to 4 percent per year during most of the 1990s, manufacturing employment decreased by about 1 percent per year. This decline was in fact much higher (i.e., 2 to 3 percent per year) in some subsectors such as transportation equipment and textiles.[30] Real wages in the manufacturing sector also declined, whereas the gap between skilled and unskilled workers widened.[31]

The reduction of manufacturing employment was associated with an increase in the size of the service sector, as well as a significant expansion of the informal sector in many countries.[32] According to one recent study, most of the employment growth was in the informal sector. This means that large shares of the Latin American labor force now operate outside of minimum standards of protection.[33] Workers in the informal sector are outside the protection of the legal system, usually have no social benefits, may be subject to hazardous working conditions, and have no rights of union organization.

---

[28] In practice, as Paus et al. (2003, 3) argue, the effect of trade liberalization on the behavior of individual firms may depend on many other factors that are difficult to anticipate. For example, exit barriers may slow the long-term adjustment process; firms in import-competing sectors may decrease rather than increase investment because competition reduces their market size and thus the payoff to lowering the marginal cost.

[29] See Paus et al. (2003).

[30] Stallings and Peres (2000, 167).

[31] These developments seem to contradict the theory of comparative advantage. The reasons behind this development are beyond the scope of this book. For an interesting explanation of this phenomenon, see Inter-American Development Bank (2004).

[32] See Heckman and Pages (2004).

[33] Buvinic, Mazza, and Deutsch (2004, 186).

The reduction in employment levels in manufacturing[34] was facilitated in some countries by the introduction of greater labor-market flexibility. This increased flexibility may have helped to support an expansion of the workforce, but it also contributed to greater instability and lack of social benefits.[35] Hence, as employment in the manufacturing sector declined and the informal sector expanded, the level of social protection in the new jobs went down. As Heckman and Pages suggested, the new openness to international trade increased the demand for labor flexibility. Without significant labor-market reforms, it was argued that Latin American economies would not be able to compete internationally.[36] This was the main motivation behind the reforms that introduced temporary contracts (in some cases, without full social benefits) in Argentina, Colombia, Ecuador, Nicaragua, and Peru. As the case study of Peru will show, the number of workers hired under these contracts increased enormously. The change of philosophy was so radical that the 1993 Constitution even replaced the right of workers to a permanent job with the right of firms to dismiss workers.[37]

At the same time, there is evidence that all these changes in the structure of production (i.e., declining employment in manufacturing, expansion of the informal sector) and labor markets (i.e., higher flexibility and a greater percentage of contracts with lower social benefits) have weakened trade unions in Latin America. Affiliation rates have declined in all countries in the region, with particularly large declines in Mexico, Argentina, Venezuela, Costa Rica, and Uruguay.[38] This has occurred from an already weak position. Union density in Latin America (14.7 percent) is less than half the level

---

[34] Note that the point about reductions in employment concerns only the manufacturing sector. No causal link is being established between trade liberalization and lower overall employment. In fact, overall unemployment levels in the region increased during the 1990s, but this was mostly the result of an increase in labor-force participation (especially women).

[35] Buvinic et al. (2004, 183).

[36] Heckman and Pages (2004, 8).

[37] However, the effect of labor reform on the reduction of workers' social benefits should not be exaggerated. In many countries, labor reform has been an area of relatively slower progress than other structural reforms (Heckman and Pages, 2004). By the mid-1990s, although reform programs had affected almost every sector, labor markets in some sectors of economic activity continued to be highly regulated. For example, many Latin American countries continued to rely on labor legislation that favored lifelong employment protection, especially for civil servants in the public sector (Edwards and Cox, 1997, 1). Conversely, there is evidence that in the face of labor-market rigidities that made it difficult for employers in some countries to reduce work benefits, employers shifted most of the cost of providing protection to the workers. In this regard, Heckman and Pages note that employees currently bear between 50 and 90 percent of nonwage-related labor costs.

[38] Heckman and Pages (2005, 11).

of industrial countries (36.6 percent). In addition, the scope and level of centralization is much lower. Collective bargaining enjoys a high degree of centralization only in Argentina and Brazil. Also, unions in Latin America have a more reduced level of autonomy from the state (e.g., the state intervenes in union registration and accreditation as well as in the process of collective bargaining). For example, in Mexico, collective bargaining takes place at the firm level, but a high level of centralization is achieved through the penetration of the dominant political parties (for many years, the PRI) into the union through a strong corporatist structure. In addition to the weakness of labor unions, the low institutionalization of the party system in many countries implies that the traditional OECD-type of "organic" links between unions and left-oriented parties is relatively weak. As a result, the capacity of Latin American unions to effectively articulate demands for compensation against these structural changes in the economy and labor markets is much lower than in advanced industrial democracies. Furthermore, the fact that only a limited percentage of the working-age population is unionized implies that the actual incentive for political leaders to respond to demands for compensation is also more limited.

As a result of the trends analyzed herein, the percentage of workers covered by the social security system declined substantially in many Latin American countries. For example, the percentage of salaried workers with social benefits declined from 34.5 to 17.4 in Bolivia, from 49.8 to 43.2 percent in Mexico, from 37 to 31 percent in Peru, from 33.6 to 18.5 percent in Nicaragua, and from 70.6 to 66.3 in Costa Rica.[39] To the extent that declines in social benefits can be linked to reductions in social spending, these trends provide another mechanism to understanding why social security expenditures (which are usually funded through payroll taxes and only cover workers in the formal sector of the economy) may also have declined as a result of trade liberalization.

However, it is important to introduce three caveats to this analysis. First, the trends described in manufacturing employment and labor markets concern mostly the 1980s and 1990s, while the relationship between trade openness and social spending (mostly social security spending) remains strong throughout the entire period, covering also the 1970s. Hence, the evidence can only explain one part of the period under study. Second, separating in practice the effect of trade liberalization on the structure of employment in the economy is difficult. In particular, although the expansion

---

[39] Cox and Edwards (2002). The only countries where there is some evidence that this percentage increased slightly are Brazil and Colombia.

of the informal sector may be linked to the decline in employment in the manufacturing sector (associated in part with trade liberalization), the informal sector may also have increased because of other factors such as the economic crisis, changes in the political environment, and changes in the quality of regulatory and law-enforcement institutions. Unfortunately, data on employment in manufacturing and the size of the informal sector have problems of coverage, validity, and reliability, which makes it impossible to test this mechanism in a more formal way using econometric techniques (e.g., a two-stage estimation procedure or interaction effects). The importance of this explanation, however, becomes clear during the discussion of the case studies, especially the cases of Chile and Peru. Finally, the link between the social benefits enjoyed by workers and social spending levels may not always be a direct and automatic one. This is most clearly illustrated by public expenditures on pensions. For example, whereas the percentage of workers enjoying pension rights as a characteristic of their labor contract may decline (e.g., if a higher percentage of workers belongs to the informal sector), it is also possible that governments decide to increase payroll taxes and social security contributions of the workers who remain in the formal economy in order to be able to pay for the entitlements of the workers who are retiring. In fact, there is some evidence that social security contributions increased in a number of countries to face actuarial imbalances and/or transitional costs in their pension systems.[40]

The empirical validity of the compensation and efficiency hypotheses in the Latin American context is tested in Chapter 4 using data from the IMF's *Government Finance Statistics*. Unlike Cameron or Rodrik,[41] the analysis is based on social expenditures rather than total government expenditures. If our purpose is to study welfare effort, social expenditures seem a more appropriate indicator than general public spending. Public expenditures include, for example, defense spending and debt repayments – programs that can hardly be considered "social." Rodrik justifies this choice because of the lack of data on social expenditures for an important cross-section of countries. However, focusing on the middle-income countries of Latin America, it is possible to compile data on social expenditures for the 1973–2003 period.

---

[40] Hence, this means that in a less than fully funded pension system, it is theoretically possible to envisage a situation in which a lower percentage of the labor force enjoys social benefits and yet social expenditures are increasing as more people reach retirement age. The empirical evidence suggests, however, that this possibility is unlikely. For example, the econometric model used in Chapter 4 shows that the variable that measures the percentage of people older than age sixty-five is not statistically significant in most cases.

[41] See Cameron (1978) and Rodrik (1998).

[H3]: Higher trade openness is not likely to have encouraged increases in social spending in Latin America. Although the growing integration into international markets of goods and services may have been a significant factor in the expansion of the welfare state in OECD countries, in Latin America, efficiency concerns are likely to have been more important than demands for compensation.

In addition to this general hypothesis that reflects the previous theoretical discussion and preliminary empirical analysis, trade openness can have other related effects that are presented in two additional sets of subhypotheses.

[H3a]: The negative effect of trade openness is likely to affect social security expenditures but not necessarily health and education expenditures.

Most social security expenditures are financed through payroll taxes that have a direct impact on the cost of labor. Therefore, one might expect business groups to press especially hard for holding them down. By contrast, health and education expenditures generally have a smaller direct impact on labor costs and can, in fact, be viewed as investment in human capital that may raise the skills of the workforce and enhance the competitive position of the firms. Even more important, most social security expenditures go to pension benefits, which are typically the most regressive component of social spending. Although the social security category includes antipoverty programs and targeted assistance to the poor, pension payments themselves flow mainly to the middle class and to workers in the formal sector of the economy, whereas the costs of financing large pension-fund deficits are socialized through general taxation or inflation. Thus, with the possible exception of a few comprehensive pension systems such as those in Uruguay and Costa Rica, cutbacks in the pension component of social security spending may be less likely to generate widespread popular protest than has been the case in many European countries.

[H3b]: The negative effect of trade on social spending in Latin America is likely to have been greater in the group of more developed welfare states.

As Chapter 2 illustrated, the development of the welfare state in Latin America was closely associated with the model of economic development known as ISI, which was an inward-looking model of economic development that rested on a mix of policies regarding tariffs, licenses, quotas, and exchange rates that shielded domestic producers (especially in manufacturing) from international market competition. Despite the fact that the model has been criticized on many counts, ISI managed to increase the importance of the industrial sector in the economy, significantly expanding the size of the working class, and, at least until the early 1970s, producing high levels of economic growth.[42] ISI also expanded the role of the state in the economy, and it is hardly a coincidence that with the exception of Costa Rica, all the countries in Latin America with relatively well-developed welfare states had embraced ISI as their main model of economic development for significant periods – especially after World War II. However, as Bulmer-Thomas noted,[43] the fact that the manufacturing sector was shielded from international competition led to higher costs and inefficiencies. Hence, trade liberalization in countries such as Argentina, Brazil, Chile, and Uruguay, which had relied heavily on inward-looking ISI economic strategies, is likely to have had the greatest constraining effect on social spending. This is likely to be the case because the need to reduce labor costs (as analyzed in the previous subsection) in this group of countries is greater than in countries that had received less protection from international-market competition.

Capital Mobility

As Rodrik has argued,[44] the point that government policies lose effectiveness in highly open economies should not be controversial. There are many reasons behind this argument. First, after the seminal works by Mundell and Fleming, it is a well-established fact in international economics that under full capital mobility and fixed exchange rates, governments cannot pursue an independent monetary policy – that is, the money supply and interest rate are endogenous and need to be adjusted mechanically to maintain the exchange rate peg. Under flexible exchange rates, monetary policy can be relatively independent but fiscal policy loses its effectiveness.[45] Second, with no

---

[42] For a study of how ISI led to high levels of economic development during the 1950s and 1960s in Latin America (especially in Brazil and Mexico), see Gereffy and Wyman (1990).

[43] Bulmer-Thomas (1994).

[44] Rodrik (1998).

[45] This can be demonstrated easily with the standard IS-LM-BP model of any basic macroeconomics text. A fiscal stimulus leads to an expansion of aggregate demand, an initial increase in income (i.e., the IS curve would shift to the right), an increase in the demand for money, and consequently (with other policies unchanged) an increase in interest rates. The increase in interest rates attracts higher capital inflows and is associated with an appreciation of the currency. The appreciation of the currency would then lead to lower exports and a shift of the IS curve back to its original position.

restrictions to capital mobility, governments are constrained in raising taxes on footloose factors. For example, a domestic tax on capital would be entirely shifted to immobile factors of production. The possibility for investors to move their holdings from one country to another affects their capacity to punish or reward governments for their policies. With limited capital mobility, investors do not have a credible threat of exit. Faced with deteriorating economic conditions, they can stop additional investments but they cannot move their assets to alternative investment markets. By contrast, in an environment of high capital mobility and high asset liquidity, investors can credibly threaten to liquidate their assets and move them elsewhere if they are not satisfied with government policies. The possibility of financial flows, therefore, changes the nature of the relationship between financial markets and governments.[46] Hence, in the presence of higher capital mobility, we can expect sharper responses to government policy outcomes.[47] Mosley summarizes this logic well in her recent book on global capital and domestic policies:

> Governments must sell their policies not only to domestic voters, but also to international investors. Because investors can respond swiftly and severely to actual or expected policy outcomes, governments must consider financial market participants' preferences when selecting policies. Investors' credible threat of exit (...) greatly increases their voice.[48]

However, whereas the impact of higher capital mobility on the effectiveness of monetary and fiscal policies is well known, it is less clear why international investors should care about more specific economic policies, such as the level and composition of public spending. To pursue this question, it is useful to distinguish in principle between debt and equity instruments as a source of international capital flows. On the one hand, large-portfolio asset managers who invest mostly in government debt are likely to have a relatively narrow focus emphasizing mostly the tradeoff between the interest rate premium and the risk of debt default. The main focus for this type of investors is likely to be debt-sustainability considerations and the behavior of the main macroeconomic aggregates that affect debt dynamics (i.e., GDP growth, primary fiscal deficit, inflation, domestic interest rates, and the exchange rates). By contrast, equity-based capital flows stem from international investors who seek to take ownership of certain domestic economic assets, either by buying shares from an existing firm or by investing in the

---

[46] See Andrews (1994).
[47] Mosley (2000, 742).
[48] Mosley (2003, 9).

establishment of a new company.[49] In this case, investors may be more likely to look at a broader set of economic and institutional factors. This could include tax policies (e.g., corportate income-tax rates, tax exemptions) and expenditure policies (e.g., social security expenditures financed through payroll contributions, availability of subsidies, publicly financed training programs, and health services). In practice, recent research by the World Bank has shown that the single most important indicator to attract foreign investment is the quality of institutions that protect property rights and ensure the enforceability of contracts.[50]

The theoretical relationship between capital mobility and general public spending or social spending, therefore, is not straightforward. Different types of capital flows may focus on different issues, with only equity-based capital flows likely to go beyond general macroeconomic indicators. Furthermore, even in this case, as noted previously, investors are more likely to focus on the general business climate (e.g., macroeconomic stability, tax policies, and quality of institutions) rather than specific expenditure policies.

It is not surprising that the empirical evidence on the effect of capital mobility on public spending so far has been mixed. Rodrik found that higher capital mobility is associated with lower government spending.[51] In contrast, Quinn showed that increases in his financial liberalization index were associated with higher levels of government spending.[52] Garrett reported a negative albeit statistically insignificant relationship between capital mobility and government spending in a large cross-national sample covering the 1985–1995 period.[53] Swank, focusing on advanced industrial economies, showed that there is no evidence that rises in international capital mobility are systematically associated with retrenchments in social welfare provision.[54]

The fact that increases in capital mobility have not had a clear-cut effect on social spending in the literature to date should not be too surprising given the distinct preferences of different types of investors and the potentially different effects on different spending categories. It seems clear, therefore, that the relationship between capital mobility and social spending cannot be studied by focusing only on its direct effects. The work of Mosley suggests

---

[49] In the first case, capital flows would be considered portfolio investment or foreign direct investment (FDI), depending on the size of the operation. The second case is a typical example of FDI.

[50] World Bank (2004).

[51] Roderick (1998).

[52] Quinn (1997).

[53] Garrett (2001).

[54] Swank (2002, 86).

that, given their general interest and the cost of obtaining information, investors are, in general, likely to exert a strong influence but only on a limited range of economic indicators.[55] Similarly, I hypothesize that when the budget deficit is small and debt sustainability is not a big concern, investors are not likely to focus on a government's particular expenditure policies. After all, if the government's medium-term solvency position is not at risk, why should investors who purchase public debt (and, hence, help finance higher expenditure levels than would otherwise be possible) be concerned about how much the government spends on particular programs?[56]

As recent research has shown, investment flows to developing countries depend critically on the quality of institutions that define the legal framework and business environment (e.g., a well-defined legal framework, respect for property rights and the enforceability of contracts, good governance), as well as the stability of the macroeconomic environment (World Bank, 2004). But, international financial markets have a narrow focus and do not usually get into the details of government policies if they are satisfied with the main economic aggregates.[57] This is hardly surprising because gathering information is costly, and only those indicators that may affect the rate of return to investment, which includes a probabilistic estimate of the risk of default, are likely to play a prominent role. However, when fiscal deficits are high and debt sustainability becomes a concern, investors who provide external financing for the public deficit are more likely to focus on particular expenditure policies. This is likely to be the case because in such circumstances, investors look for signs of a sustainable fiscal adjustment, which usually requires structural reforms, often including permanent changes in social policies and welfare entitlements. Without these reforms, the government's commitment to fiscal discipline is less credible (because fiscal consolidation may simply be a one-off temporary adjustment that is quickly reversed), and external financing to sustain existing spending levels is likely to decline. This discussion leads us to the next hypothesis:

[H4]: The effect of capital mobility on social spending is likely to be contingent on the medium-term sustainability of current fiscal policies. In particular, capital mobility is likely to exert a negative pressure on social spending only to the extent that fiscal deficits are relatively high; and hence, debt sustainability becomes a key concern for investors.

---

[55] Mosley (2003).

[56] This argument is also valid for investors who purchase equity instruments. If the deficit is high and debt sustainability becomes an issue, they will become concerned about macroeconomic stability above all other considerations.

[57] See Mosley (2003).

3.2 Political Determinants of Welfare State Development in Latin America: Democracy and Popularly Based Governments

This section examines the political determinants of social spending in Latin America. It presents a theory that relates *political* variables to the welfare state and introduces two additional hypotheses that are tested in the following chapter using TSCS regression analysis. The first subsection discusses the definition and measurement of democracy; the second subsection analyzes the possible theoretical relationship between democracy and social expenditures; the third subsection explores the relationship between the partisan basis of electoral support of the Executive and social spending[58]; and the fourth subsection discusses other important institutional factors that may affect social spending but cannot be included in the quantitative analysis of Chapter 4 because of lack of data or other methodological problems. Although their importance cannot be ignored, their effect will be best captured through the qualitative analysis and more detailed case studies of Chapters 5 through 7.

The Relationship between Democracy and the Welfare State

The Role of Democracy in the Previous Welfare State Literature
Quantitative studies of the political economy of the welfare state in advanced capitalist countries do not usually include democracy as an important explanatory factor in the development of the welfare state. This is understandable because most of these countries – usually long-standing members of the OECD – have remained continuously democratic since at least the end of World War II. In Latin America, as well as in most of the developing world, however, differences in democratic and economic contexts offer the opportunity to test the influence of additional variables and evaluate new sets of hypotheses. The case of democracy is particularly interesting because Latin American countries were among the first to join the so-called third wave of democratization.[59]

If we turn to the available empirical evidence focusing on Latin America, earlier quantitative cross-national analyses seemed to lend support to the argument that democracies are associated with higher levels of social spending than autocracies. Ames, for example, found that electoral competition

---

[58] As explained later in this chapter, because of problems of data validity and reliability as well as a number of statistical estimation problems, other potentially important political variables such as state centralization, unitary versus federal constitutional structures, electoral laws, or voter turnout cannot be included in the analysis.

[59] Huntington (1991).

associated with democracy tends to increase social spending.[60] Unfortunately, he concluded, middle-class constituencies seem to get more of this spending than the poor themselves.

In a study of regime type, regime age, and public policy outcomes in twenty Latin American countries, Sloan and Tedin concluded that democracies performed better than autocracies on a range of health and educational indicators. Then they emphasized the role of democracy in opening up new arenas of representation and bringing about policy changes that may potentially improve the welfare of the population.[61] However, as Moon pointed out, democratic processes do not always bring about an orientation favorable to the interests of the poor. Political resources of groups "vary so dramatically that even 'one man, one vote' procedures fail to equalize them."[62]

Other studies do not look at the direct effect of democracy on social spending but rather at how democracy interacts with other variables to raise the levels of social spending. Within the Latin American context, some of the most important work on the relationship between social spending and democracy are the studies by Avelino, Brown, and Hunter. In a first paper[63] using a panel of seventeen Latin American countries, they argued that the study of the possible effects of democracy on social spending is particularly relevant at a time when many researchers were abandoning the simple distinction between authoritarianism and democracy. They then showed how democratic and authoritarian regimes react in a different way when faced with the same economic constraints: at low levels of per capita income and negative rates of economic growth, authoritarian governments usually cut down social spending at a much faster rate than democracies. Similarly, when general economic conditions improve, nondemocratic regimes also increase spending at a higher rate. In a more recent paper,[64] Avelino, Brown, and Hunter show again that democracy has a positive and statistically significant effect on social spending in virtually all their model specifications.

Hence, all these studies provide some empirical evidence in favor of a positive link between democracy and social spending. However, other studies by Kaufman and Segura-Ubiergo and Huber, Mustillo, and Stephens found no statistically significant effect of democracy on *aggregate* social spending.[65]

---

[60] Ames (1987).

[61] In the case of Sloan and Tedin (1987), the results on social spending are important, but the authors focus more on the relationship between regime type and economic growth (concluding that growth is greatest under bureaucratic authoritarian regimes than in democracies, but democracies grow more than military dictatorships).

[62] Moon (1991, 135).

[63] Brown and Hunter (1999).

[64] Avelino, Brown, and Hunter (2005).

[65] See Kaufman and Segura-Ubiergo (2001) and Huber, Mustillo, and Stephens (2004).

The empirical evidence about the effect of democracy on social spending is, therefore, somewhat mixed.

Theoretical Perspectives on the Link between Democracy and Social Spending

To develop a set of theoretically grounded and empirically testable hypotheses about the relationship between regime type (i.e., democracy/nondemocracy) and social spending, this chapter follows a modified version of the standard median voter models[66] generalized by De Mesquita et al.[67] The following discussion seeks to capture in a simple framework the relationship between regime type and social spending, taking into account three key factors: (1) the structural changes introduced in the Latin American political environment by the general shift to democracy during the period, (2) the fact that political preferences toward social spending may differ depending on the type of social program (e.g., social security versus health and education), and (3) the high degree of inequality characteristic in the region.

The point of departure is Meltzer and Richards' seminal insight that the size of government depends critically on the relation of mean income to the income of the decisive voter. The argument is a straightforward one: political competition takes the level of social spending toward the ideal point of the median income voter. According to this perspective, "any voting rule that concentrates votes below the mean provides an incentive for redistribution and, thus, leads to an increase in the size of government."[68] This theory makes two key predictions. First, a change in the economic environment that causes the income distribution to grow more unequal increases political support for redistributive policies. This implies that citizens favor redistributive policies to a greater degree as the need for them expands.

Second, democratization is associated with an extension of the franchise that leads to a broader inclusion of voters below mean income. In the case of Western European countries during the second wave of democratization in the nineteenth and twentieth centuries, the spread of the franchise implied that wealth and income requirements were reduced or eliminated. This increased the number of voters with relatively lower income, increased the distance between mean and median income, and shifted the position of the median voter decisively to the left. It is within this context that Meltzer and Richards note that social security systems grew in most countries after the

---

[66] Downs (1957), Romer (1975), Roberts (1977), and Meltzer and Richards (1981), more recently extended by Moene and Wallerstein (2001).

[67] De Mesquita et al. (2003).

[68] Meltzer and Richards (1981, 916).

franchise was extended. In other words, democracy annulled the traditional correlation between the right to vote and socioeconomic class, whereas the distribution of economic assets remained markedly unequal and highly correlated with socioeconomic class.[69]

Despite its general appeal for its elegance and simplicity, Meltzer and Richards' hypothesis only holds if it can be demonstrated that social spending systems redistribute wealth from higher to lower income groups – that is, in the direction of the median voter. However, whether this is the case actually depends on the specific type of social program. In fact, as Moene and Wallerstein[70] argued, support for some kinds of welfare spending may increase as inequality rises while support for other kinds is lower when inequality is higher. Everything depends, therefore, on how much the median voter gains from welfare expenditures. If median income decreases but the median voters perceive that social spending does not benefit them sufficiently (in terms of the cost borne in the form of higher taxes), then support for social spending will decline. This would clearly be the case, for example, if some social programs were actually regressive. Although this possibility may seem difficult to conceive in advanced OECD countries, it actually reflects the situation of social security systems in many countries in Latin America. This distinction is crucial to understand the effect of democracy on social spending or rather on different types of social spending components (e.g., social security, health, and education).

What then is the expected effect of democracy on social spending in Latin America? According to the previous discussion, to answer this question we need two types of information. First, we need to know the extent to which democratization has shifted the position of the median voter in Latin American countries. This depends on the initial distribution of income and the level of political participation (one key indicator being voter turnout) in each country. The level of inequality reflects deep-seated structural characteristics of the economy that change slowly. What continues to be striking in the case of Latin American countries is the persistently high levels of inequality that range from about 0.44 (Peru) to 0.6 (Brazil) – and the inequality has not shown a generalized improvement in the region in the last decades. In particular, trends in income inequality in Latin America have varied significantly from country to country over the last two decades. In a sample of the nine largest Latin American economies, Morley[71] finds that the gini index of income inequality improved in four countries, deteriorated in

---

[69] See Korpi and Palme (2003, 427).
[70] Moene and Wallerstein (2001).
[71] Morley (2001).

three countries, and remained relatively constant in two countries. These high levels of inequality suggest that in Latin America, democratization would increase the distance between the median voter and mean income more than in other more equal regions that also underwent a recent process of democratization (e.g., Southern Europe and Eastern Europe) and hence create greater pressures for redistribution.

The second type of information necessary to understanding the effect of democratization on social spending has to do with the nature of social programs themselves. This is critical to understand the preferences of the median voter. Given structural rigidities in expenditure policies, the nature and scope of social programs reflect prior commitments and structural rigidities that cannot usually be changed quickly. Hence, if certain social programs are perceived as regressive by the median voter, political support for them will decline.

Within this context, the first effect of democratization is to expand the size of the "selectorate" – that is, "the set of people whose endowments include the qualities or characteristics institutionally required to choose the government's leadership and necessary for gaining access to private benefits doled out by the government's leadership."[72] In Latin America, democratization implied that the selectorate expanded from a restricted alliance of business and military groups, best described by O'Donnell's notion of the *bureaucratic–authoritarian state*, to a much broader segment of the population. In other words, the wave of political democratization that, beginning in the mid-1970s, transformed one regime after another in Latin America extended the selectorate from a restricted elite of privileged military and business groups to the entire (adult) population. However, although the theoretical selectorate may have become the entire adult population, the "effective" selectorate depends on the level of voter turnout. If citizens have the right to vote but do not exercise it, they cannot be considered members of the effective selectorate. Figure 3.10 shows the evolution of the average level of voter turnout as a percentage of the total voting-age population in Latin American parliamentary and presidential elections. It is not surprising that, given the wave of democratization that started in the mid-1970s, average voter turnout has increased from below 40 to around 65 percent of the voting-age population. This suggests that the selectorate in the region has indeed substantially expanded.

The first effect of a regime shift toward democracy is therefore clear: it expands the size of the selectorate. The median voter theorem predicts that

---

[72] De Mesquita et al. (2003, 42).

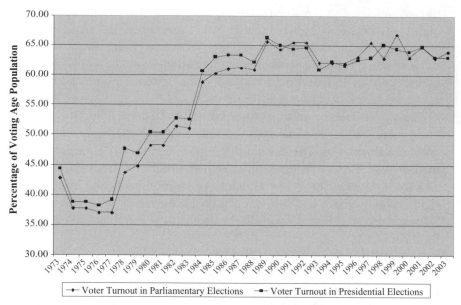

Figure 3.10. Average Voter Turnout in Latin America, 1973–2003.
Note: As a general rule, voter turnout is zero in years when the regime is not democratic because regular elections are usually not held in nondemocratic regimes. The exceptions are Brazil (up to 1985), Mexico (up to 1999), and Peru (between 1992 and 2000). In these cases, elections were held even if the regime cannot be considered democratic for other reasons. The graph also assumes that in years between two elections, voter turnout remains constant at the level of the last election. This convention is necessary to compute the sample average given that electoral cycles differ across countries. *Sources:* Institute for Democracy and Electoral Assistance and author's calculation.

this expansion of the selectorate will shift the position of the median voter to the left in favor of higher social spending, as long as the median voter stands to benefit from these programs. By bringing electoral pressures to the fore, making them a decisive mechanism of political choice, democracy introduces electoral accountability. In a democracy, the voters with median income are therefore decisive and, hence, democratic governments are likely to respond to their preferences. At the same time, it is also critical to recognize that this effect may also take place (at least in part) when an authoritarian regime holds regular elections (i.e., Brazil 1964–1984, Mexico until 1999, and Peru between 1993–2000) or makes its continuity directly or indirectly contingent on the outcome of a popular vote such as a constitutional referendum (Chile in 1988). Although some of these elections are not sufficiently free and fair, and the country may fall short of other necessary characteristics to qualify as a democracy, the fact that an election is held also expands the size of the selectorate. As the case studies of Chile and Peru demonstrate, this leads to a significant change in the incentives of the autocratic leader who will try to use social spending to influence the outcome of the election.

There is, however, another critical effect of democracy that does not depend directly on electoral processes. The median voter theorem, which focuses on micro-behavior at the individual level at the time of electoral contests, does not take explicitly into account other collective-action processes that democracy is also likely to bring about. In particular, democratization opens up new channels of participation for groups in civil society such as trade unions, social movements, and interest associations that can freely organize and articulate their preferences to the state, including a demand for social spending in a variety of ways. Broad-based mobilization allows those who stand to benefit from social programs to take advantage of a richer repertoire of political participation choices. This can take a variety of forms beyond the act of voting itself (e.g., community activity, lobbying, strikes).

To be sure, this does not necessarily mean that these groups will automatically seize this opportunity, but at least democracy provides an opportunity that was not previously available. Ultimately, for this influence to be effective, individual interests need relatively autonomous mechanisms of interest aggregation such as political parties, trade unions, and pressure groups, which may lack sufficient institutional strength to be effective instruments in many developing countries. In addition, we should not take the interests of the poor for granted. An additional complication is that sometimes the greatest problem in low-income democracies is not the lack of organizations that represent the interest of the poor but rather the fragmentation and lack of collective identity of the poor themselves, which leaves them without interests to be represented.[73]

Also, as previously noted, the median voter argument hinges critically on the nature (i.e., progressivity/regressivity) of social programs. Research by the Economic Commission for Latin America and the Caribbean (ECLAC) has shown that social security expenditures in Latin America are markedly regressive. The bulk of social security expenditures are pension transfers that flow disproportionately to the middle and upper classes. A significant portion of the lower-middle and lower classes does not have employment in the formal sector of the economy. Therefore, they do not contribute to the social security systems through payroll taxes and are not entitled to pension transfers. Although they may receive some noncontributory transfers through pro-poor funds and programs such as FONCODES in Peru, Progresa/ Oportunidades in Mexico, and Bolsa Escola in Brazil, these programs still

---

[73] The author thanks Julio Cotler, a leading Peruvian sociologist, for suggesting this point.

constitute a small part of the total social security expenditures. Even in Argentina, for example, a country with one of the highest relative levels of social spending in the region, assistance programs to the poor are only about 4.2 percent of total social expenditures.[74] Targeted poverty relief remains, therefore, minuscule when compared to other areas of social spending.

This suggests that democracy would be associated with a reduction of support for social security expenditures (which benefit a small percentage of the population) and increase support for health and education expenditures (which reach a larger segment). Social safety nets and transfer programs that would benefit the relatively lower-income median voter still constitute a small component of social spending in most Latin American countries. As Lloyd-Sherlock noted, "Latin American social security programs typically only protect a minority of their populations and largely exclude the poorest and neediest sectors: rural and informal sector workers, part-time workers and the unemployed."[75]

In contrast, our theoretical framework predicts that democracy is likely to be associated with increases in public health and education expenditures. Research by the ECLAC, among others, has shown that public health and education are the most progressive categories of social expenditures. The first most progressive type of expenditure is primary education, followed by health and nutrition expenditures and provision of basic social services. Secondary education is also quite progressive, reaching levels of progressivity similar to those of health and nutrition expenditures. Within the group of "human capital expenditures" (i.e., health and education), the only type of expenditure that is markedly regressive is tertiary/college-level education.[76] Hence, given the greater progressivity of health and education expenditures, we might expect the median voter to prefer increases in this type of expenditure.

The preceding discussion leads to the formulation of the following hypothesis concerning the expected effect of democracy on social spending:

[H5]: The effect of democracy on aggregate social spending is ambiguous given that radically different dynamics are likely to affect different categories of social spending. Democracy is likely to be negatively associated with social security expenditures (which tend to be regressive and benefit a limited segment of the population) and positively associated with increases in health

---

[74] Lloyd-Sherlock (2000).
[75] Lloyd-Sherlock (2000, 110).
[76] Economic and Social Commission on Latin America and the Caribbean (2001, Chapter IV).

and educational expenditures (which tend to reach a broader proportion of citizens).

This hypothesis, therefore, tries to take seriously Esping-Andersen's observation that "the existence of a social program and the amount of money spent on it may be less important than what it does."[77]

The Measurement of Democracy

In the definition of *democracy*, there are a number of issues. The first issue concerns the scope of the concept. This book follows the work of Mainwaring, Brinks, and Pérez Liñán,[78] who recently presented the most comprehensive classification of Latin American political regimes since 1945. Democracy, according to these authors, is a regime "(1) that sponsors free and fair competitive elections for the legislature and executive; (2) that allows for inclusive adult citizenship; (3) that protects civil liberties and political rights; and (4) in which the elected governments really govern and the military is under civilian control." This procedural definition leaves outside the semantic field of democracy a number of *normatively desirable* political and economic outcomes. This is appropriate because if we include too many desirable aspects of economic and political life in the definition of democracy (e.g., accountability, equality, participation, dignity, rationality), the set of true democracies might be small, if not an empty one.[79] As Przeworski et al. argued, it is better to define democracy in a relatively narrow way and then examine empirically its relationship with social expenditures or other economic outcomes, such as equality, economic growth, and so forth.[80] To do otherwise invites circular reasoning.

[77] Esping-Andersen (1990, 2).
[78] Mainwaring, Brick, and Pérez-Liñán (2001).
[79] See Alvarez et al. (1996).
[80] However, procedural definitions of democracy are not without problems. First and foremost, procedural definitions of democracy find it harder to justify what it is about democracy that makes it a preferable form of governing a society. In other words, as a mechanism to select and check political leaders and guarantee a minimum body of civil rights, democracy is useful in protecting society against tyranny. But, it is far less appealing than a normative idea of democracy that envisions a community of equal citizens whose political arrangement promises economic efficiency, political equality, and human development. However, it should also be noted that the consensus about the institutional ingredients that a procedural definition should include is limited because different scholars are often eager to present their own recipe. This can be observed, for example, in the definitions proposed by some of the most important democratic theorists of the procedural school (e.g., Schumpeter [1950], Dahl [1971], Linz [1975], Przeworski [1991], and Linz and Stepan [1996]). As a result, seemingly small or inconsequential differences may have important effects when applied to the empirical task of classifying countries as democratic or autocratic. In any event, however, it is remarkable that there is a high correlation between the different data sets that have taken on the task of classifying political regimes

The second issue concerns measurement. Should scholars engaged in quantitative comparative research treat the distinction between democracy and nondemocracy as a dichotomy or in terms of gradations?[81] Some authors believe that democracy should be treated as a continuous property. Bollen and Jackman, for example, argued that democracy is a property that regimes can display in different degrees. According to these authors, treating democracy as dichotomous increases measurement error.[82] This argument would probably be consistent with Dahl's view of democracy as "an underlying, hypothetical continuum that extends from the greatest to the least opportunity for oppositions."[83] In contrast, Sartori argued that conceptualization precedes measurement. In his view, it is not possible to know how democratic a country is if we cannot establish whether the core property (i.e., democracy) is present in the first place.[84] This view is also shared by Przeworski et al., who argue that any regime in which the main executive and legislative offices are not filled through contested elections should not be considered democratic *to any degree*.[85] Responding to Bollen and Jackman's question about measurement error, Przeworski et al. argued that a graded scale will lead to smaller measurement error when the distribution of cases is unimodal and approximately symmetric. However, if the distribution of cases follows a U-curve, as they suggest tends to be the case, a dichotomy is best at minimizing measurement error.

Dahl's view that a dichotomous approach may "impose upon the moral and empirical complexities of the world a false Manichean orderliness" is rather powerful.[86] However, Sartori's point that conceptualization precedes measurement is even more convincing. We first need to decide whether a country is democratic before asking how democratic it is. Gradations of democracy may be useful but only after a country has been classified as democratic according to some criterion. At a minimum, democracy requires free and fair elections as well as the protection of basic civil rights and

---

such as Mainwaring et al., Polity IV, Freedom House, Przeworski et al., and Bollen and Jackman. Most quantitative cross-national studies that have used democracy as a variable report similar results irrespective of the source used to classify political regimes. This is not surprising if we consider that the correlation among these alternative sources is close to 0.90.

[81] For a critical review of this issue, see Adcock and Collier (1999). The discussion draws on their analysis.

[82] Bollen and Jackman (1989).

[83] Dahl (1971, 231).

[84] Sartori (1984).

[85] Przeworski et al. (2000).

[86] Dahl (1989, 316).

liberties. Although different countries may achieve these goals to different degrees, there is a threshold below which a country cannot be considered democratic *to any degree*. In addition, given the tremendous processes of political change associated with the third wave of democratization, if our purpose is to decide whether democracy "makes a difference," a dichotomous treatment is more useful to assess the real differences between the newly established democracies and the authoritarian regimes they replaced. A dichotomy allows researchers to investigate whether democracies or autocracies are more prone to go to war, generate higher levels of economic growth, or promote the expansion of the welfare state, in a way that a continuous treatment does not.

However, despite the author's inclination to use a dichotomous measure of democracy, the existence of different theoretical positions suggests that in the empirical evaluation of the effects of democracy, continuous measurements should also be considered in alternative estimations to evaluate whether the main empirical findings are sensitive to the way in which democracy is measured.

Parties, Unions, and Popularly Based Governments

Most OECD studies highlight the importance of left-oriented parties and strong labor unions for the development of the welfare state. As Esping-Andersen noted, the history of political-class coalitions is the most decisive cause of welfare state variations.[87] Left parties with organic ties to labor unions are the main vehicles for the mobilization of the working class and the establishment of the welfare state.[88] From this perspective, "working-class mobilization, combined with various political–institutional conditions, was a pervasive source of early welfare state formation."[89] Working-class political power and its mechanisms of political representation through Social Democratic parties became a crucial element of welfare state growth. As Shalev noted, the welfare state is a class issue, with the working class being its principal defender.[90]

This theory assumes that there is a fundamental social cleavage between capital and the working class. This cleavage is reflected in political behavior, with high-income classes voting for parties of the Right and low-income

---

[87] Esping-Andersen (1991, 1).
[88] See, for example, Stephens (1979) and Castles (1985, 1998).
[89] Hicks (1999, 19).
[90] Cited in Pampel and Williamson (1989, 34).

classes voting for parties of the Left.[91] The theory further assumes that when Social Democratic parties that represent the working class are in government, social welfare spending, which theoretically provides more benefits for low-income classes, will be higher. As Castles noted, when the government is dominated by Rightist parties that do not represent the working class, social spending tends to be much lower.[92] According to him, the degree of unity of conservative parties is even more important than the actual power of the Left. In any event, a well-organized capitalist class, depending on its degree of political organization, will resist social reform.[93] In general, the power-resource theory fits advanced industrial democracies quite well. Empirical studies show that the percentage of cabinet seats held by left-oriented parties is a statistically significant predictor of higher levels of social spending.[94] It is no coincidence, for example, that among advanced industrial democracies, Sweden, Austria, and Norway have combined high levels of social security expenditures with the highest rates of labor unionization and the most stable leftist control of government.[95]

Without a sufficient level of economic development, however, the size of the industrial working class remains relatively modest. If economic underdevelopment is also accompanied by the absence of political democracy

---

[91] This theory has received many different names in the literature: "power resources theory," "working class strength theory," "social democracy theory," or "class analytical theory." All these labels, however, refer to the importance of strong, encompassing, highly centralized labor unions and their connections with social democratic parties for the expansion of the welfare state.

[92] Castles (1982).

[93] We should be careful, however, in assuming that the capitalist class will systematically oppose the expansion of the welfare state. Social spending includes categories such as education or health care that may improve the skills of the labor force and, hence, make it more competitive. The opposition of employers to the welfare state usually depends on how social spending is financed. If social security programs are financed through payroll taxes and employers have to bear the brunt of these costs, they are likely to oppose high social spending. But, there is no a priori reason to assume that employers will oppose high social spending that may improve the skills of the labor force if they are not directly responsible for the financing of these programs. And, they may even agree to contribute to the financing of these programs if they raise the levels of human capital of their labor force and, hence, their productivity. However, in practice, countries with high social spending levels tend to impose high and progressive tax rates on personal income. This is the reason why high-income classes, to which employers usually belong, generally oppose high social spending levels. For a study of the conditions that generate different attitudes among employers toward the welfare state, see Swank and Martin (2001).

[94] See, for example, Hicks and Swank (1992) and Huber and Stephens (2001).

[95] At the same time, however, Huber and Stephens (2001) argue that Christian Democratic incumbency is also associated with high levels of social expenditures. This is why in terms of expenditures, Italy, Germany, and Austria also rank very high.

(as it is often the case), the existing working class is either too small to yield any political power or has no access to open channels of political representation, making it difficult for them to gain or exert significant political power for welfare reform.

In principle, some elements of the "power resource" theory might also be useful to explain the timing and subsequent expansion of welfare systems in Latin America. However, welfare systems throughout the region reflect the historical weakness of these forces relative to their European counterparts.[96] A highly mobilized labor movement was a key ingredient in the expansion of the welfare state in advanced industrial democracies. In Latin America, by contrast, by the time their welfare systems were established, no country had reached 20 percent of the labor force in unions or a left parliamentary vote of at least 20 percent – the criteria established by Hicks[97] to distinguish strong labor movements in advanced industrial democracies.[98] In addition, as Malloy noted, "labor (...) was never really capable of defining the central issues of the 'social question' or of directly participating in fashioning structural or programmatic solutions to the problem."[99]

Conversely, unlike in Europe, the Latin American Left has been historically weak, and whenever it was "too strong," as in Chile in the early 1970s, military coups returned it to its "natural state of weakness." Furthermore, if we turn our attention to the last three decades – that is, the period for which systematic information on social spending is available – we need to take into account an important fundamental difference between Latin America and Europe: the lack of institutionalization of party systems.[100]

Although in Latin America, party systems differ considerably from country to country, "in most Latin American countries parties have long been

---

[96] Kaufman (2000, 1).

[97] Hicks (1999).

[98] Kaufman (2000, 5).

[99] Cited in Kaufman (2000, 6).

[100] For the analysis of the institutionalization of the party system in the developing world, I follow the seminal studies of Mainwaring and Scully (1995) and Mainwaring (1999). More institutionalized party systems are characterized by the following attributes. First, they are more stable; hence, patterns of party competition manifest regularity and relative predictability. Second, they have stronger roots in society. This is important because it allows parties to structure political preferences over time; furthermore, parties tend to be more consistent in their ideological positions, and there is a certain regularity in how people vote. Third, in more institutionalized party systems, the major political actors accord legitimacy to parties. As a consequence, the elites and the citizenry believe in parties as fundamental, desirable, and necessary institutions of democracy. Finally, when parties are institutionalized, they are usually not subordinated to the interests of a few ambitious leaders; in other words, they show autonomy vis-à-vis the individuals who created them.

118 *Theoretical Framework and Main Hypotheses*

characterized by vague programs, extensive reliance on patronage, unreliable electoral bases, and unstable political organizations."[101] This situation was aggravated in the 1980s when in addition to the effects of the economic crisis, Latin American political parties were also affected by at least three additional phenomena. First, there was the crisis of the traditional Left that accelerated after the collapse of the Soviet Union. In all cases but one, the South American Left abandoned its commitment to revolutionary ideals and embraced the tenets of liberal democracy. Second, there was a trend toward anti-statist, free-market neoliberalism, which challenged the previous state-driven ISI model. Neoliberal policies were pursued by the military regimes in Argentina (1976–1983), Uruguay (1973–1984), and Chile (1973–1990). Despite the failures in Argentina and Uruguay, the Chilean success (especially after 1985) was used as an example of the positive effects of reducing "excessive" statist intervention. Leaders from Mexico, Venezuela, Argentina, Bolivia, Peru, and elsewhere looked at the Chilean case and studied the success of the export-oriented model of the East Asian newly industrializing countries (NICs). These tendencies provoked in some countries a split in the traditional parties of the Right. It separated the traditional Right, which had an important stake in the old ISI model and still believed in a strong role for the state and the new liberal Right, with its strong commitment to the market and the principles of neoclassical economics.[102]

Given this situation of crises and weak institutionalization of party systems, how can we test for the influence of the "power-resource" or "social democratic" model in the context of Latin America? Unfortunately, lack of institutionalization of party systems and insufficient data, as well as problems of validity and reliability, make it difficult to classify governments as "left" or "right," as it is typically done in OECD studies.[103] In addition, cross-national differences of labor strength within the region are extremely difficult to measure systematically. Not only are data on labor unionization scarce but also, as noted previously, Latin American unions are generally weak and belong to the formal sector, which in most countries leaves out between one and two thirds of the workforce. A recent study by Rudra

---

[101] Kaufman (1997, 14).

[102] This section draws on Mainwaring and Scully (1995).

[103] An interesting attempt in this respect is the work of Coppedge (1998), who has systematically classified votes for the major parties in each national election for a sample of ten Latin American countries as Right, Center, or Left. His classification is, however, difficult to use for the researcher doing comparative work. First, because unlike what would happen with the European cases, his codings are open to question by Latin American specialists. Second, he only has data for ten countries, which would lead to the exclusion from the analysis of about one third of the cases.

attempts to circumvent this measurement problem by focusing on variations in labor-market conditions as a proxy for the bargaining power of organized labor. In a global sample of least developed countries (LDCs), she finds that social security spending varies positively with the ratio of skilled to unskilled labor and negatively with the pool of "surplus" labor.[104] Conversely, we still lack more direct and reliable indicators of organizational strength (e.g., membership and cohesion) that characterize studies of the OECD.

This book, drawing on previous research by Kaufman and Segura-Ubiergo,[105] focuses on the political orientation and constituent base of the parties supporting incumbent presidents. As the following discussion shows, social security transfers advocated by "popularly based" parties in Latin America may sometimes benefit their labor constituencies but have a negative impact on the incomes of rural and informal-sector workers. Even when the transfers pursued by such parties do not reach the very poor, however, we can hypothesize that social security spending is more likely to be sustained under presidents who have been elected with their support. Table 3.3 describes the codings used for popularly based presidents.

Presidents have been coded as popularly based if they come from parties with close historical links with labor unions (e.g., the Peronists in Argentina or Acción Democrática in Venezuela) and/or if their parties have long-standing programmatic orientations toward "the popular sector" (e.g., the MNR in Bolivia and the PLN in Costa Rica).

The coding does not take into account whether individual presidents themselves were conservative or left-leaning in their own social-policy preferences. It may well be the case that some popularly based presidents such as Carlos Menem in Argentina did in fact lean decisively to the right. The question is instead whether their policy behavior is constrained by their constituent base or partisan supporters; this is an issue that should be resolved empirically rather than by definition. Again, this approach parallels a question typically asked about OECD countries: namely, whether "left" parties behave differently from conservative ones once they arrive in government. A number of autocratic regimes have also been coded as popularly based, according to the way specialists have characterized their principal support coalitions or their strategies for building political support. One example is the military regime that took power in Peru in 1968; a second is the dominant-party regime in Mexico. Although we may have more

---

[104] Rudra (2002).
[105] Kaufman and Segura-Ubiergo (2001).

Table 3.3. *Codings for Popularly Based Presidents, 1973–2003*

Country	Presidents	Period
Argentina[a]	Isabel M. de Perón (Peronist party)	1974–1975
	Carlos S. Menem (Peronist party)	1990–1999
	Eduardo Duhalde	2002–2003
Bolivia	Hernán Siles Suazo (MNR)	1983–1984
	Víctor Paz Estensoro (MNR)	1985–1989
	Jaime Paz Zamora (MIR)	1990–1993
	Gonzalo Sánchez de Lozada (MNR)	1994–1997
	Gonzalo Sánchez de Lozada (MNR)	2003
Brazil	Luis Ignacio "Lula" Da Silva (Worker's Party)	2003
Chile	Salvador Allende (Socialist Party of Chile)	1973
	Patricio Alwyn(Eduardo Frei (Concertación)	1990–2000
	Ricardo Lagos (Concertación)	2001–2003
Costa Rica	José Figueres (PLN)	1973
	Daniel Oduber (PLN)	1974–1977
	Luis Alberto Monge (PLN)	1982–1985
	Óscar Arias (PLN)	1986–1989
	José María Figueres (PLN)	1994–1997
Dominican Republic	Antonio Guzmán Fernández (PRD)	1979–1982
	Salvador Jorge Blanco (PRD)	1983–1986
	Peña Gómez (PRD)	1997
	Leonel Fernández Reyna (PRD)	2001–2003
Mexico	Luís Echeverría (PRI)	1973–1976
	José López Portillo (PRI)	1977–1982
	Miguel de la Madrid (PRI)	1983–1988
	Carlos Salinas (PRI)	1989–1994
	Ernesto Zedillo (PRI)	1995–2000
Ecuador	Guillermo Rodriguez Lara (*)	1973–1976
	Poveda/Duran/Franco (*)	1976–1979
	Rodrigo Borja (Democratic Left)	1989–1992
	Lucio Gutiérrez (Patriotic Society Party)	2003
Peru	Velasco Alvarado (*)	1973–1975
	Alan García (APRA)	1985–1990
Uruguay	Julio María Sanguinetti	1995–2000
	Jorge Luís Batlle	2001–2003
Venezuela	Carlos Andres Pérez (AD)	1974–1978
	Jaime Lusinchi (AD)	1984–1988
	Carlos Andrés Pérez (AD)	1989–1992
	Hugo Chavez	1999–2003

(*) Popularly based military president or junta. During years in which there is a change of president, the old year is coded under the new president if he/she takes office before June 30 and under the old president otherwise.

[a] Juan Perón took office in October 1973. The previous president from the Peronist party, Hector Cámpora, had been sworn in in May and resigned in July. Thus, he was not in power long enough to introduce any significant policy changes. The year 1973 has therefore been coded as "not popular." Isabel Perón became president in July 1974, replacing her husband Juan Perón who had just died. She was deposed by military coup in March 1976. Only 1974 and 1975 have therefore been coded as "popular."

Sources: Kaufman and Segura-Ubiergo (2001) and author's codings based on discussions with Robert Kaufman.

confidence in the validity of this coding in democratic regimes, it is of interest to see whether "popular bases" determine behavior independently of regime type. This analysis laid out the ground for the second main political hypothesis:

[**H6**]: Everything else being equal, popularly based presidents are likely to increase social security spending, which directly benefits their constituency in the more unionized formal sector of the economy, and reduce or leave unchanged health and education spending, which reaches a more general and diffuse segment of the population. This might be either the result of an attempt to maintain their "popular" bases of support or their long-term programmatic commitment to social issues such as poverty reduction.[106] Furthermore, the increase in social spending associated with popularly based presidents is likely to be greatest in the case of social spending as a percentage of public spending, which is the specification of social spending more amenable to quick change/manipulation.

Relevant Political Factors Excluded from
the Quantitative Empirical Analysis

A number of quantitative studies of the welfare state in advanced industrial democracies have analyzed the effects of some additional political factors such as voter turnout and constitutional structures. This section briefly discusses why these factors, although theoretically important, have not been the object of hypotheses to be tested through the quantitative analysis of the next chapter. This does not mean that their importance has been ignored. However, because of data or methodological problems, they could not be included in the empirical analysis and their importance is incorporated in the qualitative discussion of the case studies in Chapters 5 through 7.

Voter Turnout

The importance of voter turnout in models of the median voter was discussed previously. Some scholars have even downplayed the effects of partisanship factors and stressed the greater importance of voter turnout for welfare expansion.[107] The argument is that political parties in highly competitive electoral systems tend to make pro-welfare appeals such as promises of "income security." According to Hicks and Swank, who summarize the

---

[106] Poverty-reducing expenditures are part of the social security spending category although, as discussed previously, they are usually a relatively small component.

[107] See, for example, Pampel and Williamson (1989).

main arguments related to this position, "increases in voter turnout pressure governmental incumbents to spend more on welfare because rises in turnout reflect the entry into politics of new, lower-status voters."[108] This argument is similar to a position advanced by V. O. Key, who had argued that what prevented the emergence of programs for the poor in the United States' southern states was one-party politics, which hampered the development of institutionalized mechanisms for the expression of lower-bracket viewpoints.[109] Hence, higher levels of voter turnout are likely to be associated with a broader representation of interests in the political system and a greater capacity for popular voice to influence policy development.[110]

However, studies that include voter turnout as an independent variable do not usually include democracy. Indeed, one of the reasons to include voter turnout as an explanatory variable in OECD studies is the fact that most countries have remained continuously democratic for most if not all the period under study. Hence, in studies of advanced industrial countries, democracy is not a variable but a constant. In the case of the developing world, it is difficult to separate the effect of voter turnout from that of democracy. Some countries, such as Brazil (1964–1985) and Peru (1992–2000), held elections at regular intervals. However, these elections were insufficiently competitive or fair to allow us to classify the country as democratic.[111] Yet, most authoritarian countries in Latin America eliminated electoral competition and did not hold general elections at regular intervals. This means that there is a high correlation between democracy and voter turnout, leading to serious problems of multicollinearity.[112]

---

[108] Hicks and Swank (1992, 660).

[109] Key (1949, 308).

[110] Castles (1998).

[111] Furthermore, even if the elections had been free, fair, and competitive, this would not be a sufficient condition to call the regime democratic. Free and fair elections are a necessary but not a sufficient condition for democracy. For a discussion of the fallacy of "electoralism" (i.e., to define democracy only in terms of elections), see Linz and Stepan (1996, 4).

[112] The correlation coefficient between democracy and voter turnout for the entire TSCS data set is 0.60 (averaging over cross-sectional and inter-temporal variation). However, when we include fixed effects (as the next chapter argues we need to do), all cross-sectional differences will be captured by the fixed effects; hence, the only effects that will remain are "within-country" effects. In this case, the correlation between democracy and voter turnout for many countries exceeds 0.80. This high correlation level would lead to a serious problem of multicollinearity if both democracy and voter turnout were used in the same regression equation. Although multicollinearity is not a sufficient reason to drop a variable when it theoretically belongs in the model in the first place, I believe that in the context of the third wave of democratization, deciding whether democracies protect social spending more than autocracies must take precedence. Once this question has been addressed, we can ask whether different types of democracies (or autocracies) are more likely to keep higher

In addition, there are not only statistical but also substantive reasons not to include voter turnout as an explanatory factor. First, in some countries, voting is compulsory; hence, higher levels of voter turnout might not reflect higher levels of mobilization per se but rather a simple attempt on the part of citizens to avoid having to pay fines. Second, in an attempt to prevent possible conflicts and increase the degree of social cohesion, governments may decide to increase social spending levels not when participation is high (which might reflect a high degree of satisfaction with the system) but rather when it is actually low. Hence, it might be argued that democratic governments in Colombia and Guatemala, where voter turnout rarely exceeds 35 to 45 percent, might have a greater incentive to increase social spending levels than governments in Uruguay and Costa Rica, where voter turnout typically exceeds 80 to 85 percent of the voting-age population. Finally, if social spending might be used to attract to the ballot box groups of voters that would otherwise not vote, higher levels of political participation might reflect the fact that social spending had been high rather than the other way around. In other words, there might be an important problem of endogeneity between social spending and voter turnout. All these substantive and methodological reasons prevent the inclusion of voter turnout in the multivariate analysis of social spending presented in the next chapter.

Constitutional Structures

A number of studies of social spending focused on constitutional impediments to welfare state development such as federalism, electoral laws, and the widespread use of referenda. For example, in his widely cited study of the relationship between an open economy and public spending, Cameron noted in passing that federalism "dampens the degree of expansion of the public economy."[113] Castles and McKinlay showed that federal institutions led to lower levels of welfare spending and that the effect of this variable was even greater than that of left incumbency.[114] In a similar vein, Pierson argued that federal institutions prevent the formation of class alliances that are necessary for welfare expansion or reform.[115] Similarly, in her study of health policies, Immergut noted how the spending initiatives of

---

levels of social spending than others. But, this will best be assessed through qualitative analysis. It is no coincidence that despite having rather similar levels of development, Costa Rica has much higher levels of social expenditures than Peru and that voter turnout in Costa Rica is more than 20 percentage points greater than in Peru.

[113] Cameron (1978, 1253).
[114] Castles and McKinlay (1979, 169–186).
[115] Pierson (1995, 453–454).

Swiss governments may be challenged by citizen plebiscites, thus potentially allowing a relatively small group of citizens to block policies.[116]

However, the most important study of the relationship between constitutional structures and social spending is probably that by Huber and Stephens.[117] The authors construct an index of institutional *veto points* depending on (1) the existence and strength of federal institutions; (2) whether there is a presidential form of government; (3) the strength of the upper house, if there is one; and (4) the existence of provisions for referenda. They show how this index of "constitutional structure" has a strong negative effect on social spending.[118]

Thus, there are good reasons to believe that certain constitutionally embedded political structures have an important constraining effect on welfare state development. In practice, there are both substantive and statistical reasons to exclude these variables from the *quantitative* analysis of social spending in Latin America.[119] Let us take for example the case of federalism. The three largest countries in Latin America (i.e., Brazil, Mexico, and Argentina) are formally federal. However, if we accept Stepan's definition of federalism, as I do herein, a country cannot really be considered fully federal unless it is also democratic. Federalism requires a constitutionally embedded division of power and responsibilities between the center and the subunits. This means that within its domain of authority, the subunit has the ultimate power to decide. Yet, in a nondemocratic state, we can have no guarantee that the center is going to respect the exercise of authority of the subunits. Although the subunit may be endowed with certain initial powers, the center usually has overwhelming control of state institutions so that the subunit (1) is penetrated by the center in a way that greatly reduces its autonomy, and/or (2) can always lose its power by decree, co-optation, or force if the center so decides. As Stepan has demonstrated, in a nondemocratic state, federalism does not structure politics in the same way as in a democratic state. Only a system that is a democracy "can build the relatively autonomous constitutional, legislative, and judicial systems to meet the (. . .) requirements for a federation."[120] This means that in Latin America, we cannot easily separate the effect of federalism and that of democracy.

---

[116] Immergut (1992).

[117] Huber and Stephens (2001).

[118] In their pooled time-series analysis, the standardized regression coefficient associated with this variable is the highest of their entire set of regressors.

[119] It is important to reiterate that the importance of these variables is pursued in the qualitative case studies that follow Chapter 4.

[120] Stepan (2001, 318–319).

The largest countries in Latin America – Brazil, Mexico, and Argentina – are usually considered federal, yet we can only refer to them as truly federal after they became democratic. Hence, Brazil and Argentina cannot be considered federal until the mid-1980s and Mexico cannot be considered federal until the late 1990s.

However, there are also statistical reasons that prevent the inclusion of these institutional variables. Constitutional structures tend to remain fixed for long periods. This is a problem if our statistical techniques call for the introduction of fixed effects. As the next chapter demonstrates, the inclusion of fixed effects removes the effect of all time-invariant parameters, making it impossible to assess their effect in regression analysis. If the need to avoid omitted variable biases makes the inclusion of fixed effects necessary, as the next chapter shows, then this variable cannot be included in the analysis. This does not mean that constitutional structures are not important. Rather, the implication is that their influence needs to be assessed by other means, such as qualitative case studies. In particular, the case study of Costa Rica is particularly useful in analyzing the influence of this variable.

3.3 Conclusion

This chapter presented a theoretical discussion and some initial hypotheses to assess the importance of a number of economic and political variables on the size and evolution of social spending in Latin America. First, it hypothesized that economic development is likely to impose relatively strong constraints on the ability of the state to finance social programs. Yet, at any given level of development, there is significant room for the state to give more or less priority to social programs. Second, it showed that there is likely to be a strong positive relationship between the extractive capacity of the state to mobilize revenues and social spending and a negative association between fiscal adjustment (often necessary to ensure debt sustainability, bring inflation under control, or sustain an external current account adjustment) and social spending. In this regard, the close correlation between the ability of the state to raise revenues through an adequate system of taxation and the aggregate level of social spending was noted. A comparison with other regions showed that Latin America's fiscal capacity is still far behind, even when compared with East Asian countries, which devote fewer resources to social spending.

The chapter also showed that whereas trade integration may have been an important factor in the expansion of the welfare state in the OECD countries, the logic of compensation is less likely to apply in Latin America.

Growing integration into international markets has not, it seems, led to an expansion of the welfare role of the state (in fact, it has reduced it, as the following chapters demonstrate). Moreover, the hypothesized negative effect of trade integration on social spending is likely to have been greater in countries that had followed an ISI development strategy for a relatively long time. Regarding the political hypotheses, this chapter discussed how democracy can best be defined and operationalized and what its effect on social spending might be. On the one hand, democracy expands the size of the selectorate and brings electoral pressures to the fore. This shifts the position of the median voter decisively to the left. On the other hand, the preferences of the median voter for social spending cannot be taken for granted. The (relatively poor) median voter in Latin American countries is not likely to favor social security expenditures, which tend to be regressive. By contrast, support for health and education, which reaches a much broader segment of the population, is likely to increase with democratization.

Finally, the chapter discussed the importance of studying the partisan orientation of the chief executive. In particular, social spending may be higher, it was hypothesized, when the president belongs to a popularly based party that either has close historical links with labor unions or long-standing programmatic orientations toward the popular sector. In the end, whether democracies and popularly based governments commit more resources to public social spending is something that will have to be determined empirically, which is precisely the purpose of the next chapter.

4

Determinants of Social Spending
in Latin America

A Time-Series Cross-Section Analysis, 1973–2003

This chapter uses time-series cross-section[1] data to analyze the economic and political determinants of social spending in Latin America over the last three decades (1973–2003). The chapter is divided into four sections. The first section describes data sources and research design; the second section defines the dependent and independent variables; the third section is a general discussion of pooled time-series techniques[2] and presents the econometric model; and the fourth section discusses the main results of the empirical analysis using, first, aggregate social spending as the dependent variable, and then disaggregating the results into social security and human capital expenditures (health and education). The chapter also includes two appendices. Appendix 4.1 is a summary of the main variables and data sources; Appendix 4.2 describes the *Error Correction Model* (ECM) – the statistical model used in the regression analysis of this chapter.

---

[1] TSCS data refer to observations on a number of cross-sections (e.g., countries) over a certain period. In the particular case of this chapter, we analyze annual observations of data on fourteen Latin American countries during a period of about thirty years (1973–2003). Part of the chapter is devoted to a full description of the data-collection process and a detailed analysis of the range of statistical techniques that can be used with this type of data.

[2] In pooled time-series research designs, annual time-series from a cross-section of countries are stacked on top of one another and analyzed jointly within the same data set. This implies a combination of time-series (i.e., temporal observations on a unit of analysis) with cross-sections (i.e., observations on a unit of analysis at single time points). The unit of analysis is, therefore, an intersection of time and space, which is usually called a "country-year."

This chapter draws in part on previous research with Robert R. Kaufman. See, in particular, Kaufman and Segura-Ubiergo (2001).

4.1 Data Sources, Research Design, and Model Specification

The analysis is based on a data set including fourteen Latin American countries during the 1973–2003 period. The full data matrix, therefore, comprises 14 countries × 31 years (hence, the maximum number of observations is 434). The use of lagged variables and some missing data actually led to the analysis of panels of different sizes. This depended on the country and year coverage of the relevant variables. However, gaps were generally small (i.e., never exceeding two to three years) and almost always at the beginning or the end of the series – thus, limiting possible negative effects on the dynamic modeling of the time-series.[3]

The sample-selection criterion was a simple one: all Latin American countries that have reported sufficiently disaggregated data on public expenditures to the IMF for a minimum of twenty years during the 1973–2003 period[4] were included. According to this criterion, the following countries were selected: Argentina, Bolivia, Brazil, Chile, Costa Rica, Dominican Republic, El Salvador, Mexico, Uruguay, Ecuador, Guatemala, Paraguay, Peru, and Venezuela.[5] Lack of sufficient data prevented the inclusion of one major South American country (i.e., Colombia) and several countries in Central America and the Caribbean (i.e., Cuba, Haiti, Honduras, Nicaragua, and Panama). Despite this limitation in terms of scope, the sample still represents 85 to 90 percent of the GDP, population, and territory of Latin America. The greatest strength of the sample is the length of its temporal dimension. The analysis presented in this book is based on the longest time-series of data on social expenditures available to date in Latin America.[6]

---

[3] The only two countries in which the gap was initially larger were Peru and Venezuela, where IMF data were not available for most of the 1990s. In these cases, the trends for the 1990s were constructed using data from the United Nations ECLAC. This is a reasonable procedure given that for the years in which both the IMF and the ECLAC data series were available, the correlation exceeded 0.85. The author thanks David Brown for help in obtaining the ECLAC data.

[4] The IMF began publishing its annual series, *Government Finance Statistics* (GFS), in the early 1970s. The GFS is one of the most comprehensive sources of data on public finances available to researchers doing comparative work on public-sector economics. As of mid-2005, the most recent year of data coverage for most countries was 2003.

[5] The series for Colombia contained many gaps at the central government level, despite sometimes surprisingly detailed information at the subnational level. In addition, Panama and Nicaragua had to be excluded from the final panel because data on some of the key independent variables were not available.

[6] Another comprehensive source of social spending data in Latin America is the United Nations ECLAC. At the time of this writing, ECLAC had a database of social expenditures that covered seventeen Latin American countries during a period of about twenty years (1980–1999). This database has been used in a number of studies, including Brown and Hunter (1999), Avelino (2000), and Avelino, Brown, and Hunter (2005). The main

There are, however, limitations to the validity and reliability of the data that need to be acknowledged from the start. Some countries in the sample have relatively weak statistical agencies and, hence, the quality of the data is likely to be lower than in their OECD counterparts. In addition, during times of macroeconomic instability, it may be particularly difficult to ensure the consistency and integrity of the data series.[7] Fortunately, the IMF makes a systematic effort to regularly update and correct its data series. Although this is, to be sure, no guarantee of integrity, it provides a reasonable degree of confidence that the social spending data used in the analysis do indeed reflect general budget priorities set within the Latin American public sectors.[8] Another advantage of using GFS data is that the IMF uses the same classification scheme across countries, which ensures a certain degree of cross-country comparability. The GFS does not provide specific information on social spending, but it disaggregates public-spending data by function of government. Social spending can then be simply defined as public expenditures on education, health care, and social security.[9]

To construct the series of information on social spending, three budget components were selected: (1) Social Security and Welfare Affairs and

limitation with the use of the ECLAC series of social spending is that it begins in 1980; hence, it does not permit empirical research on the determinants of social spending to have a preglobalization benchmark. It was precisely in the 1980s when trade and capital mobility started to rise dramatically in Latin America. Furthermore, from a statistical point of view, the temporal dimension of the ECLAC data series may be too short to appropriately model time dynamics. This is the typical small-n/large-n problem. The larger the number of cases, the better our ability to test for the effect of an increasingly greater number of substantively important independent variables and the better our ability to obtain consistent parameter estimates. As Greene (2000) and Beck (2000) pointed out, many of the good properties of time-series estimators are in T (number of years), not in N (number of countries). This is why a relatively small T is a potentially important problem.

[7] This is especially true when countries undergo extreme episodes of hyperinflation (e.g., Peru, Argentina, and Brazil in the late 1980s) and the value of the currency (and often its name) keeps changing rapidly.

[8] An important related issue that escapes the control of any data-collecting organization arises when countries cheat or misreport information. Although this is a potentially serious problem, IMF data are less affected because the IMF intervenes in the aggregation of different expenditure categories according to well-defined categories of spending. For a review of the procedures and a systematic analysis of the categorization of revenue and expenditures, see IMF, *Manual on Government Financial Statistics* (1986), and the new *Manual on Government Financial Statistics* (2001). The analysis is based on the 1986 Manual (rather than the more recent 2001 one) because the entire data series (with the exception of 2003) was collected following the guidelines of the 1986 Manual.

[9] Some studies include housing expenditures as part of social spending. These expenditures, however, are small (i.e., typically less than 5 percent of social spending). Given their limited size, a decision was made to exclude them in the calculation of social spending because data coverage was much less extensive.

Services,[10] (2) Health Affairs and Services,[11] and (3) Education Affairs and Services.[12] The sum of these three categories formed the raw aggregate measure of social spending.[13]

Once the data set on social expenditures had been created,[14] an ECM was used to test the economic and political determinants of social spending in Latin America, as described by the hypotheses presented in Chapter 3. In the ECM, every independent variable is included in both "levels" and "first differences."[15] Then, the model is simply estimated through Ordinary Least

[10] Social security includes transfer payments, including payments in kind to compensate for reduction or loss of income or inadequate earning capacity; sickness, maternity, or temporary disablement benefits; old age, disability, or survivor's pensions; pro-poor programs; unemployment compensation benefits; family and child allowances; and welfare services for children, old persons, and the handicapped.

[11] Includes hospital affairs and services (i.e., general and specialized hospital and services, medical and maternity center services, nursing and convalescent home services, clinics, and paramedical practitioners) and public health affairs and services (e.g., the administration, management, operation, and support of disease-detection services such as laboratories and population-control services).

[12] Includes pre-primary, primary, secondary, and tertiary educational affairs. Expenditures related to the administration, management, inspection, and operation of pre-primary, primary, secondary (i.e., high school level), and tertiary (i.e., university level) educational affairs.

[13] The other categories of spending were *general public services* (executive and legislative organs, financial and fiscal affairs, foreign economic aid); *defense affairs and services* (military and civil defense administration and research); *housing and community amenity affairs and services* (housing and community development, water supply affairs and services, sanitary affairs including pollution abatement and control, and street lighting); *fuel and energy affairs and services* (expenditures related to fuel, electricity, and other affairs and services); *agriculture, forestry, fishing, and hunting affairs and services; mining and mineral resource affairs and services; transportation and communication* (road, water, railway, and air transport affairs and services); and *other economic affairs and services* (hotels and restaurants, tourism, general economic and labor affairs).

[14] The different measures of social spending were constructed as follows. First, from the GFS of the IMF, raw data series on expenditures on health care, education, and social security in local currency units were obtained. These three categories were added together and divided (1) by the overall public expenditures of the consolidated central government to obtain the share of social spending in the public budget (i.e., variable WELFPUB), and (2) by figures for the GDP in local currency units (obtained from the International Financial Statistics) to obtain social spending as a percentage of GDP (i.e., WELFGDP). Finally, for each year, WELFGDP (i.e., welfare spending as a percentage of GDP) was multiplied by GDP per capita in constant 1995 U.S. dollars (obtained from the World Bank's *World Development Indicators*) to obtain social spending per capita.

[15] A "level" variable is measured in absolute values, whereas a variable measured in "first differences" provides the value of the changes in the value of a level variable from one year to the next. In other words, if the variable of interest is, for example, GDP per capita, in "levels," the variable would simply give us for every year the level of GDP per capita; in first differences, the variable would measure increases and decreases in GDP per capita from year T to year T + 1.

Squares (OLS). Appendix 4.2 provides a detailed description of this model. The main advantage of the ECM specification is that it allows researchers to capture both long-term relationships (through the level variables) and short-term effects (through the first-difference variables). Another advantage of ECMs is that they tend to be more robust than other models to the possible existence of unit roots in the data. Hence, they are less likely to be affected by spurious relationships generated by trending variables.[16]

Panel data are affected by two other potentially serious estimation problems – namely, *panel heteroskedasticity* and *spatial correlation.*[17] Compared to alternative estimation methods such as Generalized Least Squares (GLS) and Maximum Likelihood (ML), the proposed methodological procedure (i.e., ECM with panel-corrected standard errors) tends to establish a higher threshold of conventional statistical significance.[18]

Finally, the chapter takes seriously the issue of parameter heterogeneity.[19] This is a fundamental issue in the use of pooled time-series techniques that is, unfortunately, insufficiently taken into account in most studies using panel data. Because its importance is often not well understood, this issue is discussed with some detail herein.

Dealing with Heterogeneity in Causal Processes

Panel data[20] combine the possibility of studying inter-individual differences (i.e., cross-sectional analysis) with intra-individual dynamics (i.e., time-series analysis). It can therefore produce useful generalizations across

---

[16] For a detailed analysis of ECMs, see Banerjee et al. (1993). A technical summary of the main issues is also provided by Greene (2000). For a comprehensive survey of applications to political-economy analysis, see Freeman (1992). For a more recent defense of ECMs and why they should be used more often in pooled time-series research designs, see Beck (2000).

[17] Panel heteroskedasticity refers to the unequal variance of the error process in different countries. Spatial correlation refers to the correlation of the errors between different units (countries) at the same point in time. Both are problems that violate the classical Gauss-Markov assumptions of linear regression models. The presence of panel heteroskedasticity and/or spatial correlation does not bias the regression coefficients but leads to an inefficient (and inconsistent) estimate of the error variance-covariance matrix. This means that the standard errors associated with each regression coefficient will not be correct. Hence, we cannot properly test for the effect of our vector of independent variables.

[18] For a detailed description of how panel-corrected errors are estimated and why they are necessary, see Beck and Katz (1995).

[19] Pooled time-series analysis assumes that the effect of each independent variable is the same in every country at every point in time.

[20] Panel data or pooled time-series analysis is being used interchangeably.

both time and space.[21] However, as Hsiao and Sun pointed out, the ability to exploit the information contained in panel data depends critically on the plausibility of pooling: "if individual observations are more appropriately viewed as generated from heterogeneous populations, there is no justification to pool the data, hence [we] cannot explore the many advantages associated with the use of panel data."[22]

Heterogeneity in the dependent variable per se is not an impediment to pooling as long as this heterogeneity is captured by our set of regressors or independent variables. The problem arises when the heterogeneity among cross-sectional units over time is not completely captured by the explanatory variables. In such a case, as Hsiao pointed out, "it makes no sense to pool the data."[23]

This suggests that the issue of "poolability" should be seriously discussed in every article using TSCS data.[24] The advantages of pooling cannot

---

[21] In practice, however, many models require the use of fixed effects to control for country-specific factors that can be correlated with the regressors, thereby biasing the results. Once fixed effects are included in the regression, the estimates are simply capturing the temporal dimension and no causal inferences can be made about purely cross-sectional differences.

[22] Hsiao and Sun (2000, 181) argue that the decision to pool or not to pool the data depends on whether y_{it}, the ith individual observation of the dependent variable at time t, conditional on x, the independent variable(s) of interest, can be viewed as a random draw from a common population. This is the so-called exchangeability criterion. It implies that the individual and time subscript, $_{it}$, is simply a labeling device. Observations on the dependent variable should be exchangeable so that a priori $E(y_{it}|x) = E(y_{js}|x)$. In other words, the expected probability of observing y_{it} or y_{js}, conditional on x, the independent variable(s) of interest, should be the same. If this condition is satisfied, by pooling the data, we can obtain more robust and precise parameter estimates. However, if individual outcomes are more appropriately viewed as stemming from a heterogeneous population, then the subscript $_{it}$ contains important information that can be used to determine the specific heterogeneous population from which the particular observation is generated.

[23] Hsiao and Sun (2000, 182).

[24] In the simple linear regression framework, we can write a generic pooled time-series equation as follows:

$$y_{it} = x_{it}\beta + \varepsilon_{it} \qquad \text{(Equation 1)}$$

where $_{it}$ is a subscript denoting unit i observed at time t, y is the dependent variable, x is a vector of independent variables, β is a vector of regression coefficients, and ε is the residual, representing the effect of all excluded variables. One of the standard Gauss-Markov assumptions to ensure that OLS is Best Linear Unbiased Estimator (BLUE) is that ε is a random variable, independent of or uncorrelated with x. This assumption is violated if the heterogeneity among cross-sectional units over time is not captured by x. A possible test to determine this is the F-test, which compares the following two generic models:

$$Ho : y_{it} = x_{it}\beta + \varepsilon_{it} \qquad \text{(Equation 2)}$$

$$H_1 : y_{it} = x_{it}\beta_i + \varepsilon_{it} \qquad \text{(Equation 3)}$$

and tests the null hypothesis that $\beta_i = \beta$.

be exploited if cross-sections that are fundamentally not comparable are aggregated and jointly analyzed within the same data set. This point is well captured by Ward's warning that:

> Comparing China or Taiwan, for example, in the same regression analysis may well have the same effect on your regression coefficients as weighting your analysis by including three Indias, two Benins, and half a dozen Japans. Regression coefficients (...) are only meaningful if the data base contains observations on comparable units.[25]

Some solutions, such as comparing the results of individual country regressions with the coefficients of the pooled model, were not possible because of problems of limited degrees of freedom in some of the individual time-series.[26] Following Hsiao and Sun's recommendation,[27] a more direct approach to deal with parameter heterogeneity has been taken, by trying to limit it a priori, on theoretical grounds. In particular, the sample has been divided into two groups of countries on an a priori theoretical judgment. The first group, which is referred to as "welfare states," includes Argentina, Brazil, Chile, Costa Rica, and Uruguay. These countries were early welfare state developers and, as noted in Chapter 2, have historically committed significant resources to social spending. They also tend to be richer, have less exposure to international trade, and have had on average a longer history of continued democratic institutions. The quality and coverage of the available data, especially on the dependent variable, tend to be higher as well. By contrast, the other countries (with the exception of Mexico and Venezuela) are significantly poorer, more open to international trade, historically less democratic, and have slightly less reliable/complete statistical information. There are, therefore, theoretical reasons to expect causal effects to be different in these two subsets of countries. As a result, dividing the sample on theoretical grounds may be a useful way of dealing with the problem of parameter heterogeneity. Hence, each regression table is presented with a column for the general results of the completely pooled model and two additional columns, one for the first group of countries (i.e., welfare states) and another for the second group (i.e., non-welfare states). These methodological steps should make us reasonably confident that the problem of parameter heterogeneity has been appropriately limited.

---

[25] Quoted in Sayrs (1989, 15).

[26] However, the main findings were consistent with individual-country regressions when the most relevant variables were used.

[27] See Hsiao and Sun (2000).

4.2 Description of the Variables

The Dependent Variable

The dependent variable is social spending as a percentage of GDP and as a percentage of government expenditures. The findings are presented for both specifications of the dependent variable because each captures somewhat different kinds of welfare effort. Whereas the fiscal share of social expenditures (WELFPUB) reflects priorities set within the public sector, social spending as a percentage of GDP (WELFGDP) indicates allocative priorities within the national economy as a whole.[28] A third possible measure of welfare effort is social spending per capita (WELFCAP), which measures the actual amount of resources that citizens receive in transfers from the state and/or direct or indirect benefits from public investments in health and education. Although some descriptive statistics are presented for this variable, the main regression focus is on the previous two specifications. This is appropriate given that social spending per capita and as a percentage of GDP are highly correlated (Table 4.1), and the latter is the most widely used measure of welfare effort.

---

[28] One important shortcoming of the data set is the fact that it only captures expenditures executed by the central level of government. This should not be a problem for social security expenditures, which tend to be highly centralized. But, it may be a problem for the measurement of health and education expenditures in countries that have experienced an important degree of fiscal decentralization. The only country that has detailed data on social spending at the subnational level throughout the period of study is Argentina. In this case, subnational governments' social spending amounted to about 35 percent of all social spending in the 1970s and about 37 percent in the 1990s. In all the other cases, there is only data on total spending of subnational governments (with no details on disaggregated spending patterns, at least until the late 1990s). Note that the possible bias in the measurement is not a function of the level of decentralization across cases but rather depends on (1) whether decentralization has increased over time, and (2) a significant share of this decentralization has affected health and education expenditures. It would not matter, for example, if health and education expenditures are highly decentralized but the degree of decentralization has not changed over time. This would be the case of Argentina, for example. Because the results did not change using one measurement or the other, central government has been used for the case of Argentina as well to ensure consistency with the other cases. Qualitative evidence suggests that this bias may be important in the cases of Bolivia, Peru, and Mexico. However, it is likely to affect only the last few years of the sample (i.e., from the mid-1990s onward), as this is the period when decentralization accelerated. The conceptual implications are discussed later in the text. In practice, the overall results do not seem to have been substantially affected by this. Running different regressions that excluded countries where decentralization was higher did not yield significantly different results. But, as discussed in the concluding chapter, the relationship between decentralization and social spending remains largely unexplored and this is, therefore, an area where further research is clearly needed.

Table 4.1. *Pearson's Correlation Coefficient among Three Different Specifications of Social Spending in Latin America*

	WELFCAP	WELFPUB	WELFGDP
WELFCAP	1.0000		
WELFPUB	0.7704	1.0000	1.0000
WELFGDP	0.8651	0.8259	1.0000

Note: WELFCAP = social expenditures per capita; WELFPUB = social expenditures as percentage of public expenditures; and WELFGDP = social expenditures as a percentage of GDP.

Sources: IMF's *Government Finance Statistics* and author's calculations.

Figures 4.1 and 4.2 are graphs of the evolution of social spending (as a percentage of the budget and as a percentage of GDP) in Latin America in the 1973–2003 period. After declining during the economic crises of the 1980s, social spending within Latin America as a whole rose substantially during the 1990s, a period in which the region also became increasingly integrated into the world economy. On the surface, the concurrence of spending

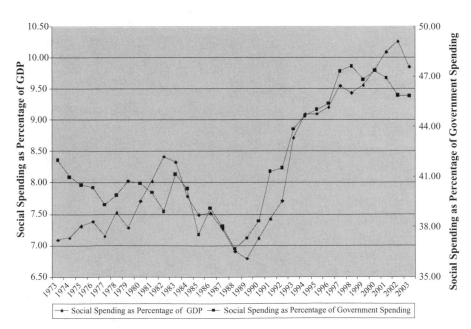

Figure 4.1. Evolution of Social Spending in Latin America, 1973–2003.
Notes: The left scale indicates the average level of social spending as a percentage of GDP. The right scale measures the average level of social spending as a percentage of government spending. *Sources: Government Finance Statistics* and author's calculations.

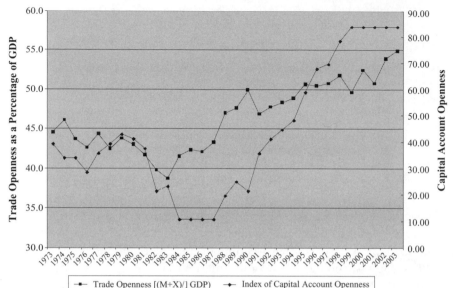

Figure 4.2. Trade Integration and Capital Account Openness in Latin America, 1973–2003.
Sources: Government Finance Statistics and author's calculations.

increases and economic opening would appear to support the compensation hypothesis. It is impossible to assess the causal connection between the two trends, however, without also taking into account the effect of other factors that can also influence social spending, which is what this chapter seeks to accomplish.

It is important to emphasize, moreover, that the rate of change varied considerably from one country to the next. During the thirty-year period covered by our model, the average annual change in spending per capita was $5.87, whereas the standard deviation was $51.57. The changes as a percentage of the budget and of GDP averaged 0.10 and 0.08 percent, respectively, while the standard deviations were 4.45 and 1.08. During the upward trend of the 1990s, annual rates of change of social spending as a percentage of GDP varied from a low of 0.005 percent in El Salvador to a high of 0.7 percent in Bolivia and Uruguay, and even by the end of the decade, spending in El Salvador, Guatemala, and Venezuela remained below pre-1980 highs. This shows that there is enormous variation in the dependent variable.

Globalization

Exposure to international markets is measured in two ways. Following conventional practices in most of the literature on globalization, trade integration is calculated as [imports + exports]/GDP.[29] This measure is affected by the size of the economy and by changes in the exchange rate, but the inclusion of country dummies and exchange-rate variables as regressors correct for these effects.[30]

For openness to international capital markets, an index of capital account liberalization has been created using data from the IMF's Exchange Arrangements and Exchange Restrictions Yearbooks.[31] The index captures four types of restrictions that reflect the extent of sectoral control on foreign investment, limits on profit and interest repatriation, and controls on external credits by national borrowers and capital outflows. The use of this policy index, instead of a more direct measure of capital flows, is due to the fact that flows often indicate macroeconomic volatility rather than openness, especially in an extraordinarily unstable region like Latin America. As with the use of trade ratios, this choice follows a practice common in the literature on globalization.[32] As Figure 4.2 vividly illustrates, both levels of trade

[29] Including Cameron (1978), Hicks and Swank (1992), Rodrik (1998), Garrett (2000a, 2000b), Huber and Stephens (2001), and Boix (2003).

[30] Avelino, Brown, and Hunter (2005) measure trade openness using PPP exchange rates to compute GDP figures (the denominator in the trade-openness indicator). This is, however, an unconventional and problematic measure of trade openness for five reasons. First, all the studies of the welfare state available to date have measured trade openness as imports plus exports over GDP (not PPP-based GDP). Hence, their measure does no allow comparability of results with previous research (including in the context of OECD countries). Second, there is a broad consensus in the economic literature that PPP does not hold in the short term (e.g., Froot and Rogoff, 1996; and Taylor and Taylor, 2004). Only with the use of long data sets (i.e., 60 to 700 years) have economists been able to show some support for long-term PPP. There is, therefore, no evidence that PPP holds in the relatively short period of this sample (1973–2003), and this is even more questionable in their even shorter sample (1980–1999). Third, the PPP theory states that prices of traded goods will equalize *if and only if* there is an absence of tariffs and other barriers to trade. During most of the 1970s and 1980s, barriers to trade in most Latin American countries remained relatively large, even if the process of globalization that we describe in this book began to eliminate them gradually. Even by the early 1990s, in many countries the average tariff rate was 35 to 40 percent. Fourth, according to the Balassa-Samuelson critique, any events that shift relative prices of traded and nontraded goods pose problems for PPP. This may include devaluations, asymmetric changes in production technology, and changes in expenditure patterns – events that have been common during the period under study in Latin America. Finally, PPP may be useful for analyzing differences in cross-national standards of living, but they are not useful to analyze the real economic effects of changes in economic policies within the same economy. This is particularly important with the inclusion of fixed-effects, which only captures "within-country" changes over time.

[31] The author thanks Harald Jens Anderson from the Monetary and Financial Systems Department and Misa Takebe of the IMF's Independent Evaluation Office for advice on indices of capital account openness. Initial research had used an index by Morley, Machado, and Pettinato (1999), but this index has not been updated since 1995.

[32] See Garrett's discussion of these issues (2000a). For similar arguments applied to the OECD, see the seminal work of Quinn (1997).

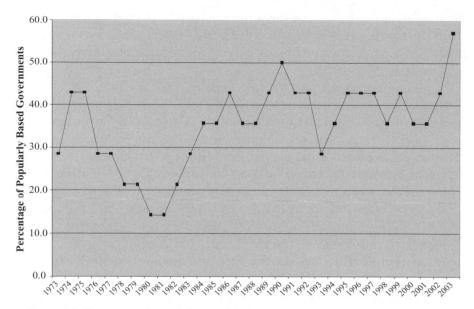

Figure 4.3. Percentage of Popularly Based Governments in Latin America, 1973–2003. *Source:* Codings from Chapter 3.

integration and capital mobility start growing dramatically in the 1980s, especially after 1982 – the year when the debt crisis began after Mexico's default. After 1982, country after country started programs of structural adjustment that included as part of the reform "package" trade and capital-market liberalization.

Popularly Based Presidents

To gauge the relative balance of partisan power, all democratic heads of state have been coded taking into account the political orientation of their party base. As discussed in the previous chapter, presidents are coded as popularly based if they come from parties with close historical links with labor unions (e.g., the Peronists in Argentina or Acción Democrática in Venezuela) and/or if their parties have long-standing programmatic orientations toward "the popular sector" (e.g., the MNR in Bolivia and the PLN in Costa Rica). Figure 4.3 shows the percentage of popularly based governments in Latin America.

As shown in the graph, the percentage of popularly based governments declined in the 1970s from a high of 40 percent to a low of 10 to15 percent in 1980. However, the percentage increased sharply during the 1980s to a high of 50 percent in 1990.

Democracy

As noted in Chapter 3 and Appendix 4.1, the analysis relies on a dichotomous measure of democracy. Yet, the sensitivity of the results to the measurement of democracy is also checked using continuous measurements from the Polity IV data sets.[33] Countries have been coded as democratic or nondemocratic following the classification proposed by Mainwaring et al. described in Chapter 3, which can be considered the most reliable and comprehensive classification of political regimes for Latin America.[34] As Figure 4.4 illustrates, the percentage of democratic countries in Latin America has experienced a phenomenal increase. Whereas about only 20 percent of countries were democratic in the early 1970s, by the mid-1990s, the percentage of democratic countries in the region had risen to about 90 percent; by 2001, the entire sample was democratic. This is also consistent with the 2001 statement of the Organization of American States, which declared that with the exception of Cuba, the whole region was largely democratic.

Other Relevant Economic and Control Variables

In the course of this research, the impact of a large number of economic and control variables[35] was examined, including population size, urbanization, percentage of the population over sixty-five, dependents (i.e., population younger than age fourteen and older than sixty-five over the total population), public debt, interest repayments, economic shocks (i.e., inflation, exchange rate, GDP shocks, and terms of trade), logged GDP, GDP growth, and output gaps. The decision on which controls to include in the final model was based on the strength of the initial theoretical expectations, the completeness of data coverage, and Chow and Aiken information tests to determine the contribution of the controls to the total variance explained

---

[33] See Keith Jaggers and Ted Robert Gurr, "Regime Type and Political Authority, 1800–2003," at http://www.cidcm.umd.edu/inscr/polity/, consulted May 2005. For a detailed description of this variable and the codings, see Chapter 3.

[34] Mainwaring, Brick, and Pérez-Liñán (2001). Updated to 2003 in Mainwaring and Pérez-Liñán (2005). What is distinctive about this classification is that unlike most others, it has been specifically created for Latin America by Latin American experts. Hence, the validity and reliability of the codings is much greater than in other data sets of broader scope but created by researchers with less specific knowledge about the cases. Mainwaring et al. use a trichotomy: democracy, semidemocracy, and autocracy. Countries classified under the "democracy" heading were considered democratic, countries under the "autocratic" label were coded as nondemocratic. As noted in Appendix 4.1, for cases coded "semidemocratic" following previous research by Kaufman and Segura-Ubiergo (2001), a particular country-year has been coded as democratic if DEMOC-AUTOC $\geq$ 6 in the Polity IV database.

[35] For a more detailed description of these variables as well as data sources, see Appendix 4.1.

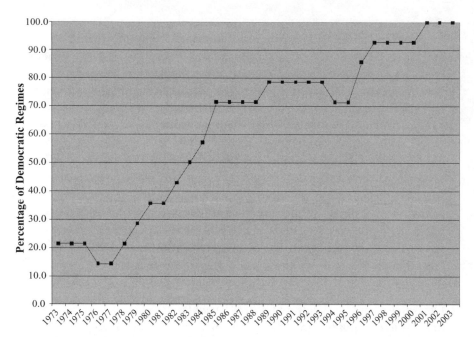

Figure 4.4. Percentage of Democratic Regimes in Fourteen Latin American Countries, 1973–2003.
Sources: Mainwaring et al. (2001, 2005) and Polity IV database.

in the model. It should be emphasized, however, that none of the controls excluded from this model altered the basic substantive findings.

The final specification of the model incorporates the effects of demographic composition by including controls for the age of the population or, where relevant, the percentage of both child and elderly dependents. GDP per capita controls for Wagner's Law, which holds that the size of government increases with the wealth of the economy. A measure of the "output gap," usually used to compute the deviation between observed and underlying trend growth, is also included. It is derived by comparing the actual value of GDP in a given year with the value predicted by the underlying growth trend and can be used to assess the effects of the business cycle on social spending. A positive sign would indicate that these effects are pro-cyclical, while a negative relation would show a counter-cyclical pattern. As a control, the output-gap measure helps to limit the possibility that the effects of other variables are actually caused by these cyclical relationships.

As noted in Chapter 3, changes in social spending are severely constrained by the capacity of the state to collect taxes; tax revenues as a percentage of GDP have therefore been included in the model as a fiscal constraint variable.

Another fiscal constraint variable is the share of interest payments in GDP, which reduces the available resources for primary expenditures (of which social spending is a subcomponent). Finally, terms of trade and exchange-rate fluctuations are also included. A deterioration in the terms of trade has an unequivocal negative impact on economic activity and is therefore included as a variable that controls for "external shocks." On the other hand, a measure of the real exchange rate [estimated by multiplying the nominal rate in each country by the ratio of local consumer price inflation to the U.S. Consumer Price Index (CPI)] has also been added to the model. The theoretical effect of this variable is, however, indeterminate. On the one hand, a depreciation/devaluation can be associated with higher exports and a stimulation of economic activity. This can in turn improve tax collection and lead to higher social spending. On the other hand, however, a depreciation of the currency can also have a contractionary effect if countries are highly indebted in foreign currency. In this case, there would be a "balance sheet effect," whereby the book value of external debt for the government and the private sector would increase dramatically. As a result, their ability to deal with the higher value of the debt (in domestic currency) can lead to a severe economic crisis where social spending would decline.

The model also takes into account the effects of time and country-specific fixed effects. Decade dummies are used to account for the important differences in regional and international conditions over the course of our period. The first covers the years prior to the debt crisis, from 1973 to 1981. This was a decade in which the majority of Latin American states were authoritarian, economic growth tended to be positive, flows of capital into Latin America were at their highest, and no major programs of economic reform (with the exception of Chile) had been initiated. The second decade dummy extends from 1982 to 1990, years that were generally marked by economic recession, painful structural adjustments, and transitions to democracy in most countries in the region. The last decade dummy, which was used as the "base" category, covers the period of economic recovery that took place during the first half of the 1990s.[36] The decision to use these three decade dummies has

---

[36] As previously noted, the decade dummy for the 1990s is the base category and, therefore, has been excluded from the regression analysis. The interpretation of the other decade dummies is based on a comparison with the 1990s. If, for example, the coefficient for the decade dummies in the 1980s is negative and statistically significant, this means that, controlling for everything else in the model, there are specific factors that make social spending in the 1980s lower than in the 1990s. Although we have not been able to include these factors in the analysis (otherwise, we would have included them in the regression as independent variables), we are at least controlling for them with the dummies.

therefore been made on theoretical grounds, given that different dynamics seem to have been at work during these three decades. To the extent that these differences are captured by the other independent variables, the decade dummies should not be statistically significant, but they are included to control any remaining decade-specific factors that are not included in the model and could also affect social spending (e.g., the 1990s was the decade where the so-called Washington Consensus structural reforms reached its zenith; it was also the decade where fiscal decentralization and the emphasis on health and education by international development partners became stronger). Finally, country dummies are included in all specifications of the model. These control for time-invariant country-specific factors that might impact a country's economic openness and/or welfare spending over the long term – for example, the size of the population and territory, wealth, or long-term political history – and which may not have been included in the regression model.

4.3 The Model

The proposed ECM takes into account the important distinction between analysis of cross-national differences and the analysis of changes within individual countries over time.[37] Cross-national differences in the size of the welfare state, Garrett argues, are likely to be invariant over time because they are influenced by historical factors at work over long periods or by structural conditions that change only slowly. The causes of such differences are best assessed statistically through analyses in which the key explanatory variables (e.g., openness, Left strength) are expressed as long-term properties of the system. In this chapter, however, the analysis is based on *changes* in social spending, which are presumably influenced more directly by dynamic processes of globalization and by contemporaneous political pressures. The use of an ECM is well suited for just such a purpose.

Particular care has been taken to deal with the most common problems that affect TSCS models. Thus, this study follows the methodology suggested by Beck and Katz[38] whereby the use of OLM[39] with panel-corrected

---

[37] See Huber, Ragin, and Stephens (1993) and Garrett (2001) for a discussion of these issues.
[38] Beck and Katz (1995, 1996).
[39] It can be argued that using OLS in a dynamic model with fixed effects does not provide in theory the most consistent and efficient estimates. In a classic paper, Nickell (1981) demonstrated that this introduces a bias that is a function of (1) the amount of serial correlation in the model, and (2) the number of time periods. This can be a particularly important problem in the typical panel data set with a large-N/small-T structure. A

standard errors deals with the problem of panel heteroskedasticity and spatial correlation. In addition, as noted previously, the use of an ECM deals with problems of serial correlation and unit roots.[40] Finally, country and time dummies are included to control for omitted variables (i.e., country-specific and time-specific fixed effects). Results from the F-test indicate that the fixed effects belong in the model. Unfortunately, however, the inclusion of dummy variables tends to deflate the statistical significance of the other regressors. This method, therefore, carries some risk that causal hypotheses will be rejected prematurely.[41] Conversely, it also increases our confidence that results that do emerge as significant are not the consequence of unsound statistical assumptions or inappropriate econometric methods.[42]

The generic version of the model can be specified as follows[43]:

$$\Delta Y_{i,t} = D\alpha + Y_{i,t-1} \cdot \phi + \Delta X_{i,t-1} \cdot \beta_k + X_{i,t-1} \cdot \beta_j + T\lambda + \varepsilon_{i,t} \quad (4.1)$$

where $Y_{i,t}$ measures social expenditures in country i during year t, X is a vector of independent variables, D is a vector of country dummy variables or fixed effects, and T is a vector of time effects. Specifications of the dependent variable are measured as first differences, and the independent variables include the lagged level of social expenditures, the lagged level of each independent variable, and the yearly changes (Δ) in the independent variables. Note that this model with the dependent variable in first differences would

generalized method of moment estimator (GMM) such as the one proposed by Arellano and Bond (1991) tends to be the solution. However, this is less of a problem when there is no residual serial correlation (as demonstrated, e.g., with a Lagrange multiplier test) and T is relatively large. In our sample, the bias is estimated to be less than 3 percent. As a result, OLS still seems a more preferable alternative given that GMM is more difficult to interpret in an ECM framework, and some properties of the GMM estimator combined with other model corrections (e.g., panel-corrected standard errors) are unknown.

[40] See the following section for an explanation of why this model with first differences on the left-hand side and a lagged dependent variable in levels is equivalent to a more conventional model with both the dependent variable and the lagged dependent variables measured in levels. The only advantage of the former is that it produces a meaningful R-squared that is not driven by the lagged dependent variable.

[41] Sayrs (1989).

[42] The failure to address these technical problems has called into question the findings of a number of earlier studies. For example, in a replication of Hicks and Swank's (1992, 25) influential study of OECD spending, only four of thirteen political and institutional variables reach conventional levels of significance when panel-corrected standard errors are used (Beck and Katz, 1995).

[43] This model is equivalent to the one described by Beck and Katz (1996), in which the authors analyze the importance of separating short-term from long-term effects in dynamic political economy models (see Appendix 4.2).

be exactly the same as a model with levels on the left-hand side to which researchers are perhaps more familiarized. Adding Y_{t-1} on both sides of the equal sign in equation (4.1) leads to:

$$Y_{i,t} = D\alpha + Y_{i,t-1} \cdot (1 + \phi) + \Delta X_{i,t-1}\beta k + X_{i,t-1} \cdot \beta_j + T\lambda + \varepsilon_{i,t} \quad (4.2)$$

Equations (4.1) and (4.2) are equivalent. The regression coefficients of all exogenous variables remain the same, with the only difference being in the coefficient of the lagged dependent variable (see Appendix 4.2 for a more detailed explanation). Equation (4.1), however, has the advantage of yielding an R-square that is substantively meaningful as an indicator of the total amount of variance in the dependent variable explained by the model. By contrast, in Equation (4.2), the R-square coefficient is substantively meaningless because it is almost completely driven by the lagged dependent variable.

The fundamental aspect of this type of model is that it is based on the idea that the dependent and independent variables are in a long-term equilibrium relationship but that there are also important short-term or temporary effects.[44] As noted previously, the "Δ variables" on the right-hand side of the equation measure first-difference changes that are used to estimate annual changes in the dependent variable. Their overall impact on spending depends on the magnitude of the regression coefficient (β_k) associated with the first-difference variable and the extent to which the change persists over time, which in turn depends on the coefficient of the lagged dependent variable (ϕ). In other words, if a 10 percent change in Δ trade is sustained in subsequent years, it will have a larger effect than if the change is subsequently reversed.

The coefficients (β_j) of the *levels* variables ($X_{i,t-1}$) measure long-term effects on the dependent variable. They allow us to assess whether trends in independent variables are causally related to long-term trends in the dependent variable. When the regression coefficient (β_j) is statistically significant, it indicates that there is a long-term causal relationship between these trends. The strength of that relationship is estimated by dividing the regression coefficient (β_j) by ($-\phi$), the yearly rate at which the unpredicted annual changes in the Y variable return to the trend line (see Appendix 4.2).

The inclusion of both first-difference and "levels" variables is a statistical requirement of the ECM. The interpretation of their causal role, however, requires theoretical and conceptual judgments. The demographic measures

---

[44] See Greene (2000, 733–755) for a theoretical discussion. Recent applications of this model include Huber (1998) and Iversen and Cusack (2000).

used as control variables, for example, change slowly from year to year, and their effects are most likely to work through the levels variables. In other cases, both first-difference changes and long-term trends may have substantive meaning. For example, the first-difference variables for democracy or popularly based governments can be presumed to measure the effects of a regime transition or change of government in a given year, while the levels variables measures the longer term effect of these changes within a given country. To the extent that the effects of trade on spending work through the lobbying efforts of business groups exposed to international competition, they are most likely to be felt over the long term. However, as we suggest in the following discussion, governments that link structural reforms to spending reductions may also produce important short-term effects captured by first-difference variables.

4.4 Analysis of the Results

Aggregate Social Spending

Table 4.2 presents the results of a first set of regressions that look into the determinants of aggregate social spending in Latin America. Two measures of welfare effort are analyzed: namely, social spending as a percentage of public spending (WELFPUB) and social spending as a percentage of GDP (WELFGDP). For each measure of the dependent variable, results are presented in terms of a general pooled time-series regression that includes all Latin American countries for which data were available (GENERAL), one set of results comprising the sample of relatively more developed welfare states (WELFARE), and another regression with the less developed welfare states (NONWELFARE). To enhance the clarity of the presentation, the control variables and country dummies are not displayed.

Overall, the models explain between 37 and 56 percent of the variance in social spending – a reasonably good fit for a model that uses first differences as the dependent variable. A model using only *level* variables typically leads to much higher R^2. But this is only because, as noted previously, the lagged dependent variable artificially inflates the total amount of variance explained.

The results presented in Table 4.2 suggest three broad sets of conclusions concerning (1) the impact of globalization (trade and capital openness variables), (2) the relative importance of fiscal constraint variables (revenue effort, primary deficits, and interest payments), and (3) the effects of political–institutional variables (i.e., democracy and popularly based governments).

Table 4.2. *Determinants of Social Spending in Latin America, 1973–2003*

	WELFGDP			WELPUB		
	General	Welfare	Non-Welfare	General	Welfare	Non-Welfare
L.OUTPUTGAP	0.0064	0.0060	-0.01480	0.0287	0.0208	-0.1289
	[0.0196]	[0.0344]	[0.0181]	[0.0847]	[0.1210]	[0.1255]
L.GDPCAP	0.0001	0.0002	0.0001	0.0005	0.0005	0.0029
	[0.0001]	[0.0002]	[0.0002]	[0.0005]	[0.0007]	[0.0016]
L.AGE65	0.0690	0.3663	-0.1456	-0.8074	1.3632	-1.9061
	[0.1526]	[0.4293]	[0.1508]	[0.6755]	[1.5282]	[1.0075]
L.TT	-0.0034*	-0.0001	-0.0017	-0.0189***	-0.0209	-0.0125
	[0.0018]	[0.0047]	[0.0015]	[0.0085]	[0.0194]	[0.0095]
D.TT	-0.0027	-0.0011	-0.0024	-0.0231***	-0.015	-0.0261**
	[0.0022]	[0.0056]	[0.0021]	[0.0113]	[0.0231]	[0.0134]
L.REX_RATE	-0.0001	0.0010**	-0.0002***	-0.0014***	0.0005	-0.0018
	[0.0001]	[0.0005]	[0.0001]	[0.0006]	[0.0020]	[0.0007]
D.REX_RATE	-0.0001	0.0019***	-0.0003***	-0.0018***	0.0050*	-0.0028
	[0.0001]	[0.0007]	[0.0001]	[0.0008]	[0.0027]	[0.0008]
L.TRADE_Y	-0.0129**	-0.0596***	-0.0038	-0.0487***	-0.1598***	-0.0522*
	[0.0058]	[0.0178]	[0.0049]	[0.0272]	[0.0646]	[0.0326]
D.TRADE_Y	-0.0167**	-0.0748***	0.0049	-0.0402	-0.1978***	0.0383
	[0.0072]	[0.0172]	[0.0061]	[0.0336]	[0.0667]	[0.0394]
L.KCTOT	0.0035**	0.0052	0.0025*	0.0253***	0.0213	0.0227***
	[0.0018]	[0.0054]	[0.0015]	[0.0091]	[0.4875]	[0.0112]
D.KCTOT	0.0030	0.0052	0.0067***	0.0227***	-0.0036	0.0381***
	[0.0024]	[0.0048]	[0.0023]	[0.0114]	[0.0181]	[0.0162]
L.REVEN_Y	0.1604***	0.2139***	0.1194***	-0.0500	-0.1600*	0.0466
	[0.0302]	[0.0447]	[0.0289]	[0.0651]	[0.0923]	[0.1064]
D.REVEN_Y	0.3012***	0.3399***	0.2306***	-0.5496***	-0.4652	-0.6107***
	[0.0294]	[0.0388]	[0.0291]	[0.1180]	[0.1414]	[0.1775]

146

	(1)	(2)	(3)	(4)	(5)	(6)
L.PRBAL	−0.1193***	−0.1526***	−0.1056***	0.1966***	0.2832***	0.0191
	[0.0315]	[0.0401]	[0.0306]	[0.0807]	[0.1103]	[0.1504]
D.PRBAL	−0.2670***	−0.2898***	−0.2405***	0.5922***	0.5050***	0.5021***
	[0.0260]	[0.0345]	[0.0261]	[0.0807]	[0.1373]	[0.1711]
L.INTPAY_Y				−0.5581***	−0.6067***	−0.6870***
				[0.1247]	[0.1688]	[0.1946]
D.INTPAY_Y				−1.1629***	−0.9473***	−1.5503***
				[0.1255]	[0.1559]	[0.1981]
L.DEMOCRACY	0.0405	−0.4031	0.1411	0.5091	−1.2102	0.7627
	[0.1287]	[0.3403]	[0.1139]	[0.6341]	[1.2527]	[0.7671]
D.DEMOCRACY	0.1520	0.1559	0.1786	1.1455	0.8092	1.1963
	[0.1841]	[0.4803]	[0.1487]	[0.8962]	[1.8122]	[0.9640]
L.POPULAR	0.0678	−0.1498	0.0866	0.4713	−0.1109	0.7872
	[0.1213]	[0.2433]	[0.1183]	[0.5776]	[0.9472]	[0.7021]
D.POPULAR	−0.0755	−0.1764	0.1174	0.2564	0.1711	0.8697
	[0.1515]	[0.2384]	[0.1623]	[0.7102]	[0.9889]	[1.0061]
LaggedDV	−0.3579***	−0.4802***	−0.2634***	−0.3571***	−0.5513***	−0.3469***
	[0.0640]	[0.0813]	[0.0577]	[0.0503]	[0.0807]	[0.0597]
Observations	402	174	228	402	174	228
R-Squared	0.4542	0.5601	0.4557	0.3680	0.4816	0.4066
WaldChi2	293.65	218.96	181.94	248.58	162.69	164.84
Prob>Chi2	0.0000	0.0000	0.0000	0.0000	0.0000	0.0000

Notes: Panel-corrected z-statistics in parentheses. * Significant at 10%; ** significant at 5%; *** significant at 1%. In all tables, variables preceded by "L" are measured in levels; variables preceded by "D" are measured in first differences (the first differences of the first three control variables were, in most cases, not significant and are therefore not shown). Estimation with an ECM that is robust to unit roots (see Appendix 4.2). Lagrange multiplier test indicates that model is not affected by serial correlation. Model was estimated with fixed effects (i.e., Least Squares Dummy Variables model). Country dummies are not shown to save space. The country dummy for Argentina was omitted to avoid perfect collinearity. An F-test for the significance of the fixed effects indicated that at a 5 percent (or better) level of significance, the fixed effects belong in the model. The correlation between the fixed effects and the regressors is about 0.8. Hence, the model cannot be estimated with random effects. The "xtpcse" command in STATA 8.0 was used. Alternative estimation techniques such as "rreg" (robust regression), Maximum Likelihood (ML), Generalized Method of Moments (Arellano-Bond estimator), and Generalized Least Squares (Prais-Winsten correction for serial correlation, common rho) did not produce major substantive changes in the reported results.

The Impact of Globalization

The results provide strong evidence that growing trade integration has had a consistently negative effect on social spending, in both the short and long terms. Everything else being equal, a 10-percentage-point increase in exports plus imports over GDP was associated with a long-term reduction of 0.35 and 1.5 percent of social spending as a percentage of GDP[45] and as a percentage of public spending, respectively. This effect is rather large if we consider that a 10-percentage-point increase in trade openness during the period under study is a relatively small one.[46]

Consistent with our theoretical expectations, the impact of trade integration is much larger in the group of so-called welfare states (WELFARE). Indeed, for this group of countries, the same 10-percentage-point increase in trade integration would be associated with a reduction of social spending of about 1.25 and 3.50 as a percentage of GDP and as a percentage of public spending, respectively. Hence, the effect is between two and three times larger than the average for the entire sample. As noted in previous chapters, welfare states in Latin America developed in the context of ISI – a model of development that rested on a mix of policies regarding tariffs, licenses, quotas, and exchange rates that shielded domestic producers (especially in manufacturing) from international-market competition. All the countries within the *welfare state* group embraced ISI for significant periods. Although ISI led to a significant degree of industrial development, the distortions and inefficiencies associated with this model of development seem to have put stronger downward pressure on social expenditures than in the group of non-welfare states, which were, on average, more exposed to international-market competition.

On the other hand, the results suggest a positive relationship between higher levels of capital account openness and social spending, even if the results tend to be less robust than with the trade variables. The magnitude of the effect is, however, very small to allow us to draw any strong conclusions. Indeed, a 10-percentage-point increase in the index of capital account openness[47] would be associated with an increase in social spending of less than 0.1 percent of GDP and 1 percent of total spending. Despite the fact that

---

[45]   The result is obtained by dividing the regression coefficient by the lagged dependent variable, as explained in Appendix 4.2.

[46]   The average increase in trade openness from the lowest point in the sample (corresponding with the start of the debt crisis in 1982) and the highest point in the late 1990s is about 40 percentage points of GDP.

[47]   The range of the index is 0–100, which is rather similar to the range of the trade-openness variable (10 to 95 percent of GDP). Hence, it is reasonable to compare the effect of both variables with the same simulation of a 10-point increase in the independent variable.

the magnitude of the effect is small, the results are not intuitively obvious. We return to the analysis of this variable in the next section once its impact is decomposed into its direct and indirect effects using interaction terms in the regression.

Fiscal-Constraint Variables

The three "fiscal-constraint" variables – revenue effort, primary balance, and interest payments – have a strong and almost always statistically significant effect. First, higher revenue collection is strongly associated with higher social spending as a percentage of GDP. This is not surprising given that the extractive capacity of the state determines to a large extent the degree to which governments can finance public expenditures over the long term, including social spending, in a sustainable noninflationary manner. Overall, for each permanent increase of 1 percentage point of GDP in tax revenue, social spending increases, on average, by about 0.5 percent of GDP[48] – the effect being similar in all groups of countries.[49] As expected, by contrast, the degree of revenue effort seems to have no impact on the fiscal priority of social spending, with only one of the regression coefficients being (barely) statistically significant.

Second, fiscal adjustment, as measured by *levels* and *changes* in the primary fiscal balance, has a different effect depending on the measure of welfare effort under study. On the one hand, a reduction in the primary deficit has a consistently negative effect on social spending as a percentage of GDP. For example, a reduction of 1 percentage point of GDP in the primary deficit would be associated with a contemporaneous (i.e., short-term) reduction of social spending of 0.27 percent of GDP. If this reduction were to be permanent (i.e., long-term effect captured by the level variable), the long-term reduction of social spending would increase to about 0.33 percent of GDP. There is, therefore, no doubt that during times of budgetary restraint, social spending is negatively affected in absolute terms. However, as indicated by the second set of regressions (WELFPUB), it seems that the magnitude and pace of the decline of social spending would be slightly less pronounced than for other categories of spending. Indeed, a fiscal adjustment of 1 percent of GDP would be associated with an increase in the fiscal priority of social spending in total spending of about 0.5 percentage point. Although this

---

[48] This results from dividing the parameter estimate for the *level* revenue variable (0.1604) by the lagged dependent variable in absolute value (0.3579).

[49] Although the short-term effect is larger in the group of welfare states, the speed of adjustment to long-term equilibrium is also faster within this group. Hence, once each "level" coefficient has been divided by the lagged dependent variable, the effects are similar in both groups.

effect is relatively small, it suggests that governments facing strong pressures to cut overall spending have tried to protect social spending more than other categories of spending. The reasons behind this relationship become apparent once the analysis of social spending is disaggregated into social security and human capital expenditures in the next sections.

Finally, not surprisingly, the results suggest that the higher the share of interest payments in total spending, the lower the share of social spending in the overall budget. In other words, countries that face higher interest payments have less room to accommodate social spending in their expenditure envelopes. This difference can be illustrated with an example. In Brazil, average interest payments over the period were about 7 percent of GDP, compared with only 1 percent of GDP in Chile. Everything else being equal, if Brazil had been able to reduce interest payments to the level of Chile, social spending as a percentage of total public spending would have been 3 percentage points higher.

Political Variables

Neither democracy nor the partisan orientation of the president was statistically significant in any of the model specifications with aggregate social spending. This might be an indication that there is significant heterogeneity in the sample (hence, the large standard errors in the coefficients) or simply that our hypothesized causal relationships have not been confirmed by the data. Fortunately, however, as it becomes apparent in the next sections, the explanation lies in the radically different effects that the set of independent variables had on the different types of social spending (i.e., social security versus health and education).

Control Variables

As expected, a permanent deterioration in the terms of trade (as captured by the *levels variable*) had a negative and statistically significant effect on social spending in virtually all model specifications. Movements in the exchange rate had different effects depending on the group of countries. A depreciation had a positive effect on social spending in the group of welfare states but a negative one on the group of non-welfare states. Without further empirical evidence, it is not possible to establish the reasons behind these different effects. As discussed in the previous sections, a depreciation has an indeterminate effect on growth (and, hence, on social spending), depending on the balance between growth-enhancing increases in competitiveness (via higher exports) and growth-reducing balance-sheet effects (via increases in the amount of foreign-exchange denominated public debt).

The percentage of citizens older than sixty-five was not statistically significant in most model specifications. This suggests that contrary to OECD countries, pension entitlements in Latin America (given the low coverage of social security systems) accrue to a limited percentage of the active population. Reaching retirement age is, therefore, no guarantee of receiving a substantial pension for most Latin American citizens. Finally, no particularly pattern of cyclicality of social spending was found in years where actual GDP growth deviated from its trend. However, two caveats need to be introduced about this finding. First, part of the cyclicality of expenditures is already captured by the "revenue effort" variable (because in years where actual growth is below trend growth, revenue collection also tends to be lower). Second, the lack of significance of this variable could simply signal substantial heterogeneity across countries or time periods.

Disaggregated Results of Social Security and Health and Education

Public expenditures on social security, health, and education have typically been combined in analytical overviews of social spending in Latin America. There are, however, reasons to believe that they might be influenced by different political logics. Hence, this section disaggregates social spending into component categories to reexamine the effects of the globalization and political variables on social security transfers and on human capital expenditures on health and education. There are several reasons why social security expenditures might be most susceptible to the "efficiency" pressures of trade integration and perhaps less likely to be defended by democratic regimes. First, most of the spending in this category goes to pension payments. These are financed in part through payroll taxes that have a direct and transparent impact on the cost of labor; consequently, we might expect business groups to press especially hard to hold them down. Even more important, pension benefits are typically the most regressive component of social spending.[50] The social security category does includes antipoverty programs and targeted assistance to the poor; however, pension payments themselves flow mainly to the middle-class and formal-sector workers, while the costs of financing large pension-fund deficits are socialized through general taxation or inflation.[51] Thus, with the possible exception of a few comprehensive pension systems such as those in Uruguay and Costa Rica, cutbacks in the

[50] See Economic and Social Commission on Latin America and the Caribbean (1999) and Stallings and Peres (2000, 142–149).
[51] Mesa-Lago (1989, 15–18).

Table 4.3. *Determinants of Social Security Expenditures in Latin America, 1973–2003*

	SSEXP_Y			SSEXP_E		
	General	Welfare	Non-Welfare	General	Welfare	Non-Welfare
L.OUTPUTGAP	0.0101	0.0100	0.0066	0.0435	0.0665	0.0329
	[0.0185]	[0.0340]	[0.0545]	[0.0705]	[0.1255]	[0.0669]
L.GDPCAP	0.0001	0.0001	−0.0001	0.0001	−0.0002	−0.0003
	[0.0001]	[0.0001]	[0.0001]	[0.0004]	[0.0006]	[0.0008]
L.AGE65	0.1482	0.1029	−0.1037	−0.4421	1.2158	−1.3980**
	[0.1659]	[0.4227]	[0.0811]	[0.6434]	[1.5931]	[0.5794]
L.TT	−0.0045***	−0.0042	−0.0014**	−0.0282***	−0.0366**	−0.0122***
	[0.0014]	[0.0048]	[0.0007]	[0.00629]	[0.0188]	[0.0052]
D.TT	−0.0003	0.0050	−0.0020*	−0.0115	0.0126	−0.0167**
	[0.0019]	[0.0059]	[0.0011]	[0.0086]	[0.0236]	[0.0074]
L.REX_RATE	−0.0001	0.0012**	−0.0002***	−0.0016***	0.0012	−0.0020***
	[−0.0001]	[0.0005]	[0.0001]	[0.0004]	[0.0021]	[0.0005]
D.REX_RATE	−0.0001	0.0016**	−0.0002***	−0.0016***	0.0034	−0.0024***
	[0.0001]	[0.0007]	[−0.0002]	[0.0006]	[0.0027]	[0.0006]
L.TRADE_Y	−0.0178***	−0.0545***	−0.0043*	−0.0802***	−0.1602***	−0.0493***
	[0.0055]	[0.0195]	[0.0024]	[0.0237]	[0.0736]	[0.0185]
D.TRADE_Y	−0.0201***	−0.0684***	−0.0001	−0.0769***	−0.2183***	0.0089
	[0.0074]	[0.0201]	[0.0031]	[0.0308]	[0.0772]	[0.0221]
L.KCTOT	0.0037**	0.0089	0.0020***	0.0264***	0.0356*	0.0152***
	[0.0017]	[0.0055]	[0.0008]	[0.0072]	[0.0197]	[0.0057]
D.KCTOT	−0.0001	−0.0041	0.0027**	0.0074	−0.0057	0.0138*
	[0.0024]	[0.0052]	[0.0012]	[0.0098]	[0.0196]	[0.0081]

	(1)	(2)	(3)	(4)	(5)	(6)
L.REVEN_Y	0.1151***	0.1736***	0.0560***	0.0795	0.0769	0.1355
	[0.0209]	[0.0331]	[0.0141]	[0.0566]	[0.0821]	[0.0758]
D.REVEN_Y	0.1784***	0.2468***	0.0631***	-0.0989	-0.0314	-0.2310**
	[0.0263]	[0.0369]	[0.0173]	[0.1027]	[0.1402]	[0.1063]
L.PRBAL	-0.0908***	-0.1331***	-0.0477***	-0.0476	-0.0103	-0.0790
	[0.0206]	[0.0295]	[0.0133]	[0.0663]	[0.0977]	[0.0879]
D.PRBAL	-0.1581***	-0.2149***	-0.0644***	0.1138	0.0473	0.1883*
	[0.0220]	[0.0317]	[0.0138]	[0.0903]	[0.1322]	[0.0950]
L.INTPAY_Y				-0.1970***	-0.2512**	-0.1886*
				[0.0865]	[0.1280]	[0.1026]
D.INTPAY_Y				-0.5376***	-0.5725***	-0.4512***
				[0.0888]	[0.1233]	[0.1270]
L.DEMOCRACY	-0.1387	-0.5032	-0.0060	-0.6301	-2.6886**	-0.0377
	[0.1226]	[0.3589]	[0.0545]	[0.5023]	[1.3496]	[0.3906]
D.DEMOCRACY	-0.0093	0.1333	0.0735	0.4346	0.4593	0.5304
	[0.1685]	[0.4761]	[0.0804]	[0.6880]	[1.7806]	[0.5320]
L.POPULAR	0.1983	0.0885	0.1717**	1.2376**	1.4331	0.8713**
	[0.1333]	[0.2845]	[0.0738]	[0.5537]	[1.1144]	[0.4275]
D.POPULAR	0.2093	0.3155	0.1120	1.2763**	1.9773*	0.3586
	[0.1732]	[0.2890]	[0.0804]	[0.6188]	[1.1450]	[0.5181]
Lagged DV	-0.3693***	-0.4497***	-0.2328***	-0.3826***	-0.5132***	-0.2872***
	[0.0640]	[0.0700]	[0.0540]	[0.0511]	[0.0714]	[0.0493]
Observations	402	174	228	402	174	228
R-Squared	0.3523	0.4816	0.3200	0.3404	0.4431	0.3840
Wald Chi2	159.23	154.00	88.90	201.16	150.98	115.26
Prob>Chi2	0.0000	0.0000	0.0000	0.0000	0.0000	0.0000

Notes: Panel–corrected z–statistics in parentheses. * Significant at 10%; ** significant at 5%; *** significant at 1%.

Table 4.4. *Determinants of Human Capital Expenditures in Latin America, 1973–2003*

	HUMANCAP_Y			HUMANCAP_E		
	General	Welfare	Non–Welfare	General	Welfare	Non–Welfare
L.OUTPUTGAP	−0.0044	−0.0047	−0.0237*	−0.0211	−0.0422	−0.1469
	[0.0120]	[0.0230]	[0.0148]	[0.0647]	[0.1002]	[0.0995]
L.GDPCAP	0.0001	0.0001	0.0004**	0.0005	0.0009***	0.0033***
	[0.0001]	[0.0001]	[0.0002]	[0.0003]	[0.0004]	[0.0013]
L.AGE65	−0.0858	0.1780	−0.0831	−0.3506	−0.3038	−0.4957
	[0.1118]	[0.2243]	[0.1120]	[0.5443]	[0.9556]	[0.7602]
L.TT	0.0010	0.0046	−0.0004	0.0083	0.0193	0.0008
	[0.0011]	[0.0028]	[0.0012]	[0.0067]	[0.0131]	[0.0077]
D.TT	−0.0023	−0.0064	−0.0003	−0.0116	−0.0263	−0.0094
	[0.0017]	[0.0043]	[0.0017]	[0.0096]	[0.0198]	[−0.0094]
L.REX_RATE	−0.0001	−0.0002	−0.0001	0.0001	−0.0006	0.0004
	[0.0001]	[0.0003]	[0.0001]	[0.0004]	[0.0018]	[0.0005]
D.REX_RATE	−0.0001	0.0002	−0.0001	−0.0001	0.0017	−0.0004
	[0.0010]	[0.0004]	[0.0001]	[0.0006]	[0.0022]	[0.0006]
L.TRADE_Y	0.0048	−0.0053	0.0015	0.0317	−0.0034	0.0010
	[0.0043]	[0.0158]	[0.0039]	[0.0231]	[0.0689]	[0.0257]
D_TRADE_Y	0.0036	−0.0082	0.0058	0.0387	0.0051	0.0278
	[0.0066]	[0.0159]	[0.0050]	[0.0325]	[0.0692]	[0.0322]
L.KCTOT	−0.0001	−0.0036	0.0005	0.0001	−0.0150	0.0052
	[0.0010]	[0.0031]	[0.0011]	[0.0063]	[0.0132]	[0.0088]
D.KCTOT	0.0031	0.0028	0.0041**	0.0156	0.0033	0.0229
	[0.0020]	[0.0037]	[0.0019]	[0.0106]	[0.0164]	[0.0139]

L.REVEN_Y	0.0538***	0.0326**	0.0778***	-0.1304***	-0.2471***	-0.1193
	[0.0131]	[0.0168]	[0.1685]	[0.0501]	[0.0728]	[0.0987]
D.REVEN_Y	0.1239***	0.0897***	0.1685*	-0.4462***	-0.4344***	-0.3995***
	[0.0209]	[0.0259]	[0.0240]	[0.1007]	[0.1153]	[0.1438]
L.PRBAL	-0.0359***	-0.0116	-0.0782***	0.2474***	0.3050***	0.0930
	[0.0145]	[0.0149]	[0.0228]	[0.0607]	[0.0813]	[0.1186]
D.PRBAL	-0.1103***	-0.0707***	-0.1824***	0.4713***	0.4642***	0.3192***
	[0.0180]	[0.0220]	[0.0203]	[0.0923]	[0.1080]	[0.1326]
L.INTPAY_Y				-0.3936***	-0.3496***	-0.4227***
				[0.0850]	[0.1113]	[0.1213]
D.INTPAY_Y				-0.6335***	-0.3675***	-1.0707***
				[0.1020]	[0.1105]	[0.1638]
L.DEMOCRACY	0.1831*	0.1006	0.1780***	1.1666**	1.5354*	0.7139
	[0.0992]	[0.2103]	[0.0922]	[0.5459]	[0.8988]	[0.5834]
D.DEMOCRACY	0.1605	-0.0003	0.1237	0.7275	0.2392	0.5641
	[0.1146]	[-0.2553]	[0.1193]	[0.7275]	[1.1074]	[0.7499]
L.POPULAR	-0.1349	-0.2629	-0.1208	-0.7032	-1.7312**	-0.2554
	[0.1110]	[0.2010]	[0.0999]	[0.5591]	[0.8863]	[0.6038]
D.POPULAR	-0.2773**	-0.4867**	0.0093	-0.9825	-1.6969*	0.4941
	[0.1449]	[0.2184]	[0.1339]	[0.6936]	[0.9750]	[0.8175]
Lagged DV	-0.3919***	-0.5152***	-0.3652***	-0.3774***	-0.5999***	-0.3364***
	[0.0764]	[0.1035]	[0.0658]	[0.0591]	[0.0613]	[0.0491]
Observations	402	174	228	402	174	228
R-Squared	0.3486	0.4132	0.4379	0.3164	0.4455	0.3484
Wald Chi2	132.42	79.43	180.86	145.56	98.69	114.87
Prob>Chi2	0.0000	0.0000	0.0000	0.0000	0.0000	0.0000

Notes: Panel-corrected z-statistics in parentheses. * Significant at 10%; ** significant at 5%; *** significant at 1%. See Table 4.2.

pension component of social security spending may be less likely to generate wide popular protest than has been the case in many European countries.

Conceivably, the political constraints and opportunities are different in the case of human capital expenditures on health and education. Although health insurance is also sometimes a component of the wage bill, these expenditures generally have a smaller direct impact on labor costs. From the point of view of employers, they may have more substantial payoffs as human capital investments.

There is also a greater likelihood of strong political opposition to cutbacks in these areas. Despite inequities and the severe inadequacy of social-service delivery systems, human capital expenditures do appear to reach a larger segment of the population than pensions. In-depth country studies of Argentina, Brazil, Chile, and Colombia, for example, show that spending on health and education constitutes about 75 percent of the total social expenditures received by families in the lowest income quintile and has a positive impact on the overall distribution of income.[52] In short, as Latin American economies become more integrated into global markets, incumbent governments may face stronger political incentives to protect health and education expenditures than those for social security. In fact, the simple correlation (i.e., Pearson's r = −0.55) between these measures as a percentage of the budget does imply a rather sharp tradeoff. Particularly in an era of "hard budget constraints," governments appear to be under considerable pressure to establish priorities.

Tables 4.3 and 4.4 show how expenditures on social security and expenditures on health and education are affected by the variables used in the general model. As for the general model, we can quickly come to appreciate the importance of dividing the sample into welfare states and non-welfare states countries. Again, the main difference between these two sets of countries is not in the direction of the relationships (which is generally consistent with general initial theoretical expectations) but rather in the magnitude of the effects.

The results are generally (although not always) consistent with our initial theoretical expectations.

Globalization

Trade openness has a strong and consistently negative effect on social security expenditures and a positive (although not statistically significant effect) on health and education spending.

---

[52] See Mostajo (2000).

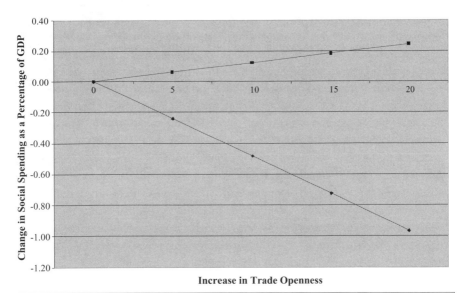

Increase in Trade Openness

--◆-- Social Security Expenditures (as Percentage of GDP)   --■-- Health and Education Expenditures (as Percentage of GDP)

Figure 4.5. Effect of Trade Openness on Social Security and Human Capital Spending as a Percentage of GDP.
Note: Increase in trade openness measures the increase in the ratio of imports and exports to GDP.

Figures 4.5 and 4.6 simulate the long-term effect of higher trade openness on social security and human capital expenditures, as a percentage of GDP and as a percentage of total spending, respectively. The figures illustrate the strong negative effect exerted by higher trade openness on social security expenditures both as a percentage of GDP and as a percentage of total spending. For example, a 20-percentage-point increase in trade openness (which was experienced by a number of countries in the sample) would be associated with a reduction of social security spending of about 1 percent of GDP and 4 percentage points of public spending, respectively.

By contrast, the effect of trade openness on health and education spending would seem to be positive. This effect does not, however, reach conventional levels of statistical significance. Consistent with our theoretical expectations, the effect of higher trade openness on the group of welfare states is much larger than in the group of non-welfare states. This is illustrated by Figures 4.6 and 4.7. For example, in the group of welfare states, a 20-point increase in trade openness is associated with a reduction of social security spending of 2.5 percent of GDP and 6 percentage points of public spending, respectively. By contrast, in the group of non-welfare states, the same increase in

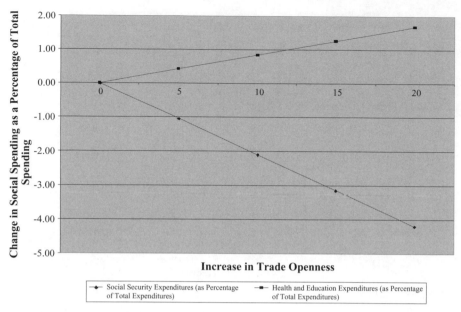

Figure 4.6. Effect of Trade Openness on Social Spending as a Percentage of Public Spending.

trade reduces social security spending by a smaller 0.4 percent of GDP and 3.5 percentage points of public spending.

Higher levels of capital account openness had no effect on health and education expenditures and a positive (and somewhat counterintuitive) effect on social security spending. However, the magnitude of the effect is relatively small. In particular, a similar simulation exercise as with the trade variable (i.e., a 20-point increase in the capital-openness index) would be associated with an increase in social spending of about only 0.15 percent of GDP and of less than 1 percent of public spending. One possible explanation is that higher capital mobility (if accompanied by higher capital inflows) could help finance a higher level of expenditures (including social spending). However, this is also likely to depend on the level of the fiscal deficit. When deficits are small, capital inflows may help finance the fiscal deficit, but when deficits are large (and, hence, debt sustainability becomes an issue), capital mobility could have a negative effect on expenditure levels as investors become increasingly concerned and are no longer willing to finance the fiscal deficit. As a result, the impact of capital openness on expenditure levels is likely to be contingent on the level of the fiscal deficit. The empirical validity of this claim becomes apparent in the following section, which discusses interaction effects.

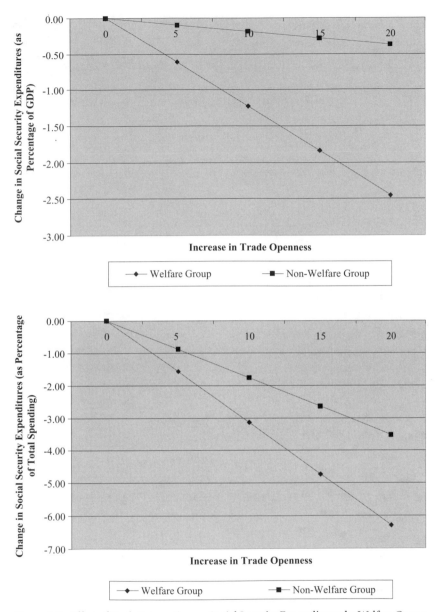

Figure 4.7. Effect of Trade Integration on Social Security Expenditures by Welfare Group.

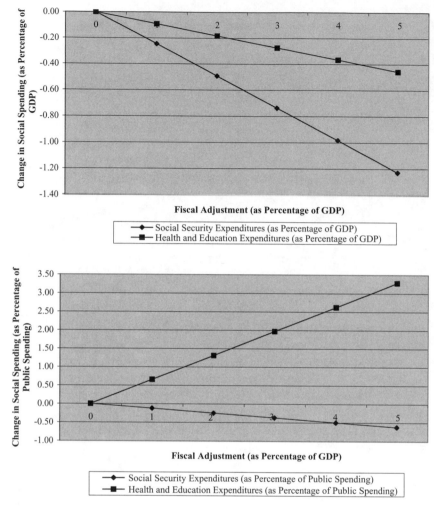

Figure 4.8. Effect of Fiscal Adjustment on Social Security and Human Capital Spending.

Fiscal Constraints

Although there do not seem to be important differences regarding the effects of revenue effort and interest payments on different categories of social spending, the effect of fiscal adjustment is markedly different depending on the measure of welfare effort. Fiscal adjustment has a negative effect on both social security and human capital expenditures as a percentage of GDP. The effect on social security expenditures is, however, up to four times larger (see Figure 4.8). For example, whereas a fiscal adjustment of 1 percent of GDP is associated with a reduction of social security expenditures of 0.25 percent of GDP, the same fiscal adjustment is associated with a reduction of human capital expenditures of only 0.07 percent of GDP. In addition, whereas fiscal adjustment has a negative (although statistically insignificant) effect on social security expenditures as a percentage of total public spending, its effect on the fiscal priority of health and education spending is markedly positive. In the short term, a fiscal adjustment of 1 percent of GDP increases the share of health and education in total spending by almost 0.5 percentage points. If the same increase is permanent, the long-term effect would be an increase in the fiscal priority of human capital spending of about 0.7 percentage points. Although this is a relatively small effect, it does suggest that, everything else being equal, Latin American governments facing fiscal pressures for adjustment have protected health and education spending more than other types of spending.

Political Variables
The effects of both democracy and popularly based presidents tend to be stronger when welfare effort is measured as a share of public spending than when it is measured in terms of GDP. Because the former is the variable that measures budget priorities, we should therefore expect political pressures to have a more direct effect on social spending with this measure of welfare effort. Whereas permanent increases in social spending as a percentage of GDP may require long-term changes in the structure of the economy – usually accompanied by expansions in the size of the public sector – that are often difficult to carry out in the short term, the fiscal priority of social spending can change much faster. For example, without significant changes in tax-revenue collection, governments can still shift priorities from defense to social services.

Democracy tends to have a negative effect on social security expenditures and a positive effect on human capital spending (Figure 4.9). But, there are differences across groups of countries. The effect of democracy is particularly important in the group of welfare states, where the long-term impact of a permanent shift to democracy is a reduction of the share of social security expenditures in total spending of more than 5 percentage points. The effect of democracy operates over the long term. In other words, a transition to democracy has no immediate contemporaneous effect (as shown by the lack of significance of the first-difference variable), but the negative effect on social security expenditures over the long term if democracy is sustained is rather important. By contrast, democracy is associated with an increase in the share of human capital spending in total spending of about 2.5 percentage points. And although democracy has no statistically significant effect on

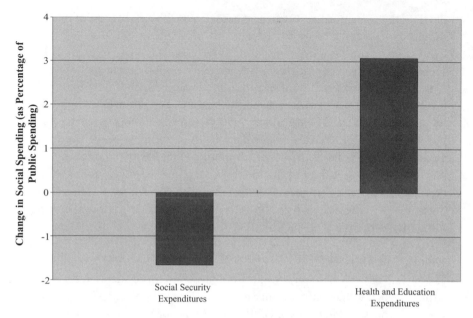

Figure 4.9. Effect of Democracy on the Fiscal Priority of Social Spending.
Note: The fiscal priority of social spending is the share of social spending in total government spending.

social security expenditures as a percentage of GDP, it has a positive and significant effect on human capital expenditures as a percentage of GDP. Over the long term, the shift to democracy increases the share of human capital spending in GDP by about 0.5 percentage points.

The effect of popularly based presidents is radically different from the effect of democracy. On average, popularly based presidents are associated with an increase of 3.2 percentage points in the fiscal priority of social security expenditures. They also tend to be associated with a decrease in the fiscal priority of human capital expenditures, but the results are less consistently robust and are only statistically significant in the group of welfare states. Within the latter, popularly based presidents are associated with a reduction of about 3 percentage points in the share of health and education spending in total public spending.

Extension: Interaction Effects

In addition to the direct effects analyzed previously, a model with interaction terms was used to test whether there were important indirect effects among the groups of variables. The results presented in Table 4.5 are useful to answer the following three types of questions:

1. First, is the negative effect of trade openness on social security expenditures stronger when the fiscal deficit is also higher? If so, this would provide further evidence in favor of the efficiency hypothesis.
2. Second, is the impact of capital mobility also contingent on the level of the fiscal deficit? As discussed previously, with small fiscal deficits and debt sustainability not being a serious concern, there would be little reason to expect an impact of capital mobility in one direction or another. However, as fiscal deficits become larger, international investors would be less willing to provide deficit financing, which would be conducive to cuts in social expenditures.
3. Finally, is the impact of fiscal adjustment or that of the globalization variables contingent on some of the political variables (e.g., regime type and the partisan orientation of the president)?

Table 4.5 summarizes the effect of all the indirect effects that have been studied. The model is based on exactly the same specification as in the previous baseline models. For ease of presentation, however, only the interaction terms of interest necessary to assess the indirect effects are presented. The table provides strong evidence in favor of our initial theoretical expectations.[53]

First, the effect of fiscal adjustment on social spending (social security expenditures, in particular) does depend to an important degree on the level of trade openness. Figure 4.10 represents this effect: a fiscal adjustment

[53] Note that the indirect effect cannot be captured by looking at the coefficient associated with the interacted term only. For example, to compute the effect of fiscal adjustment on social security spending (denoted as $\partial Y / \partial$ PRBAL) contingent on the level of the fiscal deficit, two steps are necessary. First, the following formula needs to be used: $\partial Y / \partial$ PRBAL $= \beta_1 + \beta_2$ TRADE, where Y is social security spending, PRBAL is the primary balance, and TRADE is the ratio of imports and exports to GDP. Applying the formula to Table 4.5, we obtain $\Delta Y = 0.4477 - 0.0069^*$TRADE. Second, given the dynamic nature of the model, each coefficient needs to be divided by the lagged dependent variable (see Appendix 4.2). This yields the following adjusted formula: $\Delta Y = 1.1 - 0.2^*$TRADE. The results can be now plotted in Figure 4.10. For example, when TRADE = 0, a reduction of the fiscal deficit of 1 percentage point of GDP is associated with a reduction of -1.1 percentage points in the share of social security expenditures in total spending. By contrast, when TRADE = 100, the same fiscal adjustment has an impact three times as large (i.e., reduction of 3 percentage points in social security expenditures as a share of total spending). For a recent overview of how to interpret interaction effects in regression analysis, see Kam and Franzese (2005) and Brambor, Clark, and Golder (2006).

Table 4.5. *Indirect Effect of Globalization, Fiscal Constraints, and Political Variables on Social Security and Human Capital Expenditures*

	SSEXP_E			HUMCAP_E		
	General	Welfare	Non-Welfare	General	Welfare	Non-Welfare
KCTOT	0.0467***	0.0500	0.0489***	−0.0125	−0.0165	−0.0356
PRBAL	0.4477*	1.0235***	0.2291	−0.2166	−0.3996	0.1337
TRADE	−0.1230***	−0.1312	−0.1221***	0.0798***	−0.0816	0.0796
PRBAL_TRADE	−0.0069**	−0.0176***	−0.0035	−0.0007	0.0090**	−0.0084
PRBAL_KCTOT	−0.0802*	−0.1736***	0.0470	0.1390***	0.1084***	0.1193
PRBAL_DEM	−0.0911	0.0357	−0.2677***	0.1164	0.0771	0.1760
PRBAL_POP	0.0806	−0.0145	−0.1735	0.0042	−0.0178	0.3085
TRADE_DEM	0.0228	−0.0583	0.0342	0.0067	0.1844***	0.0116
TRADE_POP	0.0398	0.1075	0.0231	−0.0722***	−0.1610***	−0.0992
TRADE_KCTOT	0.0115	0.0073	0.0162**	−0.0079	−0.0025	−0.0228
Lagged DV	−0.3998***	−0.5715***	−0.3300***	−0.4159***	−0.6898***	−0.3696
Observations	402	174	228	402	174	228
R-squared	0.3628	0.4974	0.4222	0.3558	0.5320	0.3906
Wald Chi2	225.28	187.14	136.07	167.55	129.88	140.43
Prob>Chi2	0.0000	0.0000	0.0000	0.0000	0.0000	0.0000

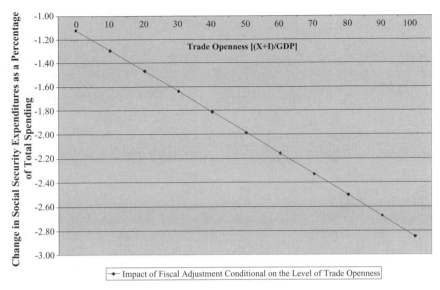

Figure 4.10. Impact of a 1 Percent of GDP Fiscal Adjustment on Social Security Expenditures, Conditional on the Level of Trade Openness.

of 1 percent of GDP would be associated with a reduction of social security expenditures (as a percentage of total spending) of slightly more than 1 percent if trade openness is relatively low (say, around 10 percent of GDP). However, the impact becomes increasingly larger at higher levels of trade openness, reaching about 3 percentage points of total spending when trade openness approaches 100 percent of GDP. By contrast, the effect on health and education expenditures would tend to be positive, but it is statistically significant in only one of the specifications (and not so in the more robust general model). These results are consistent with the efficiency hypothesis and suggest that to the extent that social security expenditures affect labor costs, globalization has been increasing the pressure to reduce the share of this type of expenditure in total spending when fiscal deficits are high.

Second, the results confirm that the effect of capital mobility is contingent on the level of the fiscal deficit. As Figure 4.11 illustrates, when the budget is in balance, capital mobility has a positive impact on social security expenditures. However, the effect becomes gradually more negative as the fiscal deficit deteriorates. This effect does not apply to health and education expenditures, as shown by the positive interaction coefficient (PRBAL_KCTOT) in Table 4.5. This suggests that at higher levels of capital mobility, the quality of fiscal adjustment becomes an important issue, with more open countries

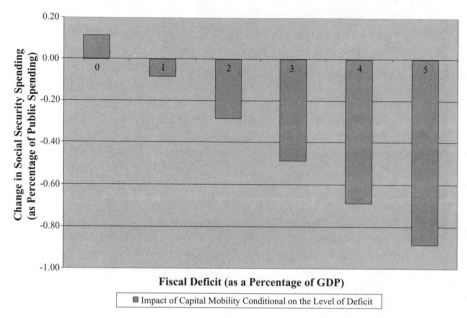

Figure 4.11. Impact of Capital Mobility on Social Spending, Conditional on the Size of the (Primary) Fiscal Deficit.

being more inclined to protect health and education expenditures. Finally, the indirect effects of the political variables also go in the expected direction, but the results are not as robust and statistically significant as with the previous interaction terms. On the other hand, higher levels of trade seem to have a more positive effect on the fiscal priority of health and education expenditures in democracies than in nondemocracies. This effect is, however, only significant for the groups of welfare states. By contrast, under popularly based presidents, higher levels of trade tend to have a positive effect on the fiscal priority of social security and a negative effect on the fiscal priority of health and education spending. However, the effect on social security expenditures does not reach conventional levels of statistical significance. Overall, these results indicate that the effect of fiscal adjustment on social security expenditures is contingent on the degree of trade openness. At higher levels of trade openness, fiscal adjustment has a larger (i.e., negative) effect on social security expenditures. This suggests that with higher trade integration, efficiency concerns lead to a preoccupation for the sustainability of the fiscal adjustment, which requires structural reforms (including welfare reform) to make the adjustment sustainable. Second, the effect of capital mobility on social security spending is contingent on the degree of fiscal discipline. When the budget is in equilibrium or the deficit is small, capital mobility has a slightly positive or slightly negative effect, but the impact is, in any event, moderate and does not reach conventional levels of statistical significance. This suggests that investors do not worry too much about the composition of expenditures in situations of reasonable fiscal discipline. However, when the fiscal deficit becomes larger, capital mobility exerts a strong downward pressure on social security expenditures, suggesting that investors worry about the sustainability of the adjustment, which may require welfare reform. Third, fiscal adjustment under a democracy reduces the fiscal priority of social security expenditures.

4.5 Conclusion

This chapter used TSCS data to test the main economic and political hypotheses presented in the previous chapter. First, it has shown that integration into international markets of goods and services exerted a consistently negative pressure on social spending. The effect of higher trade openness, however, was not the same for all categories of spending. In particular, the negative effect of trade seemed to operate through its impact on social security programs. Because social security benefits depend on formal employment, and they are usually financed through payroll taxes that have a direct impact on labor costs, it is precisely with this type of expenditure where we might have expected domestic producers subjected to increasing international competition to press governments especially hard to reduce them. Without further qualitative analysis, the chapter cannot yet establish what the precise causal mechanism has been. This is the object of the case studies in the chapters that follow. For example, governments may also have decided to cut down this type of expenditure in anticipation of the expected future pressures from business groups worried about the competitiveness of their export sectors (or their domestic production networks subject to import competition). However, trade had no effect on human capital expenditures. In all groups of countries and model specifications, the null hypothesis of no effect of the trade variable on health and education expenditures could not be rejected.

Second, the effect of trade openness was contingent on the degree of historical development of the welfare state. For both theoretical and empirical reasons, the chapter divided the sample of Latin American countries into two groups: a group of so-called welfare states and a group of non-welfare states. The former included Argentina, Brazil, Chile, Costa Rica, and Uruguay – five countries in which the fiscal and macroeconomic priority of social spending was relatively high for Latin American standards. These countries were at higher levels of economic development, had a stronger history of continuous democratic institutions prior to 1973, and experienced lower historical levels of exposure to international markets – which was closely associated with their ISI model of development. ISI was, as it was shown, an inward-looking model of development that sought to promote industrialization by shielding domestic producers from international competition through a series of import quotas, tariffs, and overvalued exchange rates. It was in the context of ISI that the five Latin American welfare states developed. Hence, it is not surprising that the growing integration of trade and capital markets (i.e., globalization) in the late 1970s and 1980s had a greater negative effect on the group of Latin American welfare states than on the other group of countries (i.e., Bolivia, Dominican Republic, Ecuador, El Salvador, Guatemala, Mexico, Paraguay, Peru, and Venezuela) in which, with the exception of Mexico and post-1968 Peru, ISI policies did not figure prominently as a major model of industrialization and economic development. This confirms our initial hypothesis that the weight of efficiency pressures would be greater in ISI countries because of their higher levels of previous market distortion and economic inefficiency.

Third, fiscal-constraint variables were key explanatory factors for understanding the evolution of social spending. Higher revenues were strongly correlated with higher social spending; fiscal adjustment tended to reduce total social spending as a percentage of GDP (while increasing the fiscal priority of health and education expenditures); and higher interest payments (the consequence of many years of fiscal profligacy and high public-debt levels) naturally reduced budgetary resources available for social spending. In addition, the effect of fiscal adjustment on social spending was greater at higher levels of trade openness.

Fourth, no strong evidence was found about the effect of the progressive elimination of governmental restrictions to the free flow of capital, in line with many previous studies that documented ambiguous results for this variable. However, this chapter showed that part of the puzzle about the effects of this variable may have to do with the fact that it operates in an indirect manner. The results suggest that when fiscal discipline is maintained (and, hence, debt sustainability is not an issue), investors do not seem to have a strong view about public-expenditure composition. However, when fiscal deficits are higher, cuts in social expenditures are viewed as necessary to make the fiscal adjustment credible and sustainable.

Fifth, in line with our initial theoretical expectations, this chapter showed that there is not a direct and straightforward relationship between democracy and social spending. In fact, the findings of this chapter point unequivocally against a simplistic understanding of the relationship between regime type and social spending. In other words, arguments about the effect of democracy can no longer be restricted to pointing out that democratic incumbents are likely to face greater electoral pressures than their autocratic counterparts and that these pressures, in turn, will result in higher levels of social spending across the board. Any argument about the relationship between democracy and social spending requires at least two qualifications. First, democracy does not affect all types of social spending equally. In line with the theory presented in the previous chapter, the results presented in this chapter suggest that low-income groups are likely to press governments for higher levels of social spending only to the extent that these expenditures reach and benefit them directly. This is why the effect of democracy tended to be negative vis-à-vis social security expenditures (which, in Latin America, are regressive) and turned positive with respect to health and education expenditures (which tend to be more progressive). This corroborates the findings from a number of studies that have documented that social security spending in Latin America is based on legal employment in the formal sector, which makes most of the lower classes ineligible for these types of transfers (mainly pensions). It is, therefore, not surprising that low-income groups that presumably gain political power with democracy do not press governments to increase social security programs that will not benefit them directly. In contrast, the effect of democracy changes dramatically once we move from social security to health and education expenditures, which are generally progressive and reach a much larger segment of the population. Finally, as in most statistical studies, this chapter cannot clearly point out to the causal stories and mechanisms underlying the reported statistical associations. The findings presented herein leave open a variety of questions, many of which can only be answered by more qualitative research methods. In the first section and at various points throughout the chapter, a number of explanations for the relationships found among globalization, political pressures, and social expenditures were discussed. Do cutbacks in aggregate social spending and in social security transfers reflect producer pressures, the initiatives of government decision makers, or the indifference or even opposition of sectors that are excluded from benefits? Or, what is the exact mechanism through which democracy and popularly based governments affect different types of expenditures? These types of questions can only be resolved through careful qualitative analysis, which is precisely the purpose of the following chapters.

APPENDIX 4.1: DESCRIPTION OF VARIABLES

NAME	DESCRIPTION, MEASUREMENT, AND SOURCE
WELFPUB	Social expenditures as a percentage of central government spending. *Source:* Created with data from the *Government Finance Statistics* (IMF), various issues.
WELFGDP	Social expenditures as a percentage of GDP. *Source:* Created with data from the *Government Finance Statistics* (IMF), various issues.
SSEXP_E	Social security expenditures as a percentage of central government spending. *Source:* Created with data from the *Government Finance Statistics* (IMF), various issues.
SSEXP_Y	Social security expenditures as a percentage of GDP. *Source:* Created with data from the *Government Finance Statistics* (IMF), various issues.
HUMCAP_E	Health and education expenditures as a percentage of government spending. *Source:* Created with data from the *Government Finance Statistics* (IMF), various issues.
HUMCAP_Y	Health and education expenditures as a percentage of GDP. *Source:* Created with data from the *Government Finance Statistics* (IMF), various issues.
PRBAL_Y	Primary balance as a percentage of GDP (i.e., overall fiscal balance plus interest payments as a percentage of GDP). *Government Finance Statistics* (IMF).
INTPAY_Y	Interest payments as a percentage of GDP. *Government Finance Statistics* (IMF).
REVEN_Y	Tax and nontax revenues as a percentage of GDP. *Source:* Created with data from the *Government Finance Statistics* (IMF), various issues.
REX_RATE	Real exchange rate. Nominal exchange × (US CPI index/National CPI index). *Source:* For the nominal exchange rate, WDI. Formula for the real exchange rate comes from Krugman (2001). Increases in the index indicate a currency depreciation (in real terms) vis-à-vis the U.S. dollar.
GDPCAP	GDP per capita in 1995 constant U.S. dollars. *Source: World Development Indicators 2004* (WDI2004), World Bank.
OUTPUT GAP	Difference between real GDP in local currency units at constant prices and the underlying growth trend, as a percentage of the trend.

NAME	DESCRIPTION, MEASUREMENT AND SOURCE
	A Hodrick-Prescott filter (H-P) is used to estimate the underlying growth trend. The H-P filter uses long-run moving averages to de-trend the output series. The method is used frequently by financial and policy institutions such as the IMF and the OECD. It minimizes the sum squared of deviations of actual output around its trend, subject to a constraint on the variation of the growth rate of trend output. It calculates the trend as the solution to the following minimization problem:

$$\underset{\{y_t^T\}}{\text{Min}} \sum_{t=1}^{T} \left[\left(y_t - y_t^T\right)^2 + \lambda \left[\left(y_{t+1}^T - y_t^T\right) - \left(y_t^T - y_{t-1}^T\right)\right]^2 \right]$$

	where, for each period, the trend values y_t^T minimize this equation for a given value of the smoothing parameter λ.
AGE65	Percentage of the population over 65. *Source:* WDI.
TRADE	Imports plus exports as a percentage of GDP. *Source:* WDI.
TTRADE	Terms of trade. Base year 2000 = 100. *Source:* WDI.
KCTOT	Measures the degree of freedom from government restrictions on capital mobility. It is based on the extent to which there are (1) multiple exchange rate practices, (2) current account restrictions, (3) capital account restrictions, and (4) surrender requirements on exports proceeds. For every country-year, the index can take discreet values from 0 (least restrictive) to 4 (most restrictive). *Source:* IMF.
DEMOCRACY	Dummy variable with a value of 1 in democratic years and 0 in nondemocratic years. Countries have been coded as democratic using the Mainwaring and Perez-Liñán classification (2005) completed, as explained herein, by the 10-point democracy (DEMOC) and autocracy (AUTOC) scales in the Polity IV database. All countries that were coded as democratic in the Mainwaring and Perez-Liñán classification received a 1. In addition, these authors include a category called "semidemocracy." In these cases, following previous research by Kaufman and Segura-Ubiergo (2001), a particular country-year has been coded democratic if DEMOC-AUTOC ≥ 6 in the Polity IV database.
POPULAR	Dummy variable coded 1 for years in which a popularly oriented president was in office and 0 otherwise. *Source:* Chapter 3.

APPENDIX 4.2: THE ERROR CORRECTION MODEL[53]

The ECM is given by the following equation:

$$\Delta Y_{i,t} = \alpha + \Delta X_{i,t-1}\beta_k + \phi(Y_{i,t-1} - X_{i,t-1}\Upsilon) + \varepsilon_{i,t} \qquad (A2.1)$$

where, in this case, $Y_{i,t}$ is social expenditures in country i during year t, Δ is the first-differences operator, X is a vector of independent variables, and $\varepsilon_{i,t}$ is a white-noise error term. The model describes a short-term equilibrium relationship given by $\Delta Y_{i,t} = \alpha + \Delta X_{i,t-1}\beta_k + \varepsilon_{i,t}$ and a term ϕ ($Y_{i,t-1} - X_{i,t-1}\Upsilon$), which measures the deviation from this short-term equilibrium relationship. Equation (A2.1) shows that, first, a change in $X_{i,t-1}$ produces a contemporary change in $Y_{i,t}$. This short-term effect is determined by the k-dimensional vector of regressor β_k. Furthermore, when the impact of $X_{i,t-1}$ on $Y_{i,t}$ throws the model off its long-term equilibrium (given by the cointegrating vector $Y^*_{i,t-1} = X^*_{i,t-1}\Upsilon$, where the "*" indicates equilibrium), the discrepancy or "error" ($Y_{i,t-1} - X_{i,t-1}\Upsilon$) is corrected at a yearly rate of ϕ.

One way to show more intuitively how to interpret the different short- and long-term coefficients is to transform Equation (A2.1) through a simple mathematical operation. Let β_j be defined as $- (\phi\Upsilon)$, where both parameters ϕ and Υ come from Equation (A2.1); then it follows that $\Upsilon = \beta_j /- \phi$. Equation (A2.1) can therefore be rewritten as follows:

$$\Delta Y_{i,t} = \alpha + Y_{i,t-1}\phi + \Delta X_{i,t-1}\beta_k + X_{i,t-1} \cdot \beta_j + \varepsilon_{i,t} \qquad (A2.2)$$

Equation (A2.2) is then estimated through OLS. The interpretation of the coefficients is then as follows: the regression coefficient for an independent *level* variable is a measure of the long-term equilibrium relationship between a vector of cointegrated independent variables (i.e., sharing the same long-term trend) and the dependent variable. As noted previously, the long-term equilibrium relationship is given by $Y^*_{i,t-1} = X^*_{i,t-1}\Upsilon$. The parameter Υ (which measures this long-term equilibrium relationship) is not directly observable from Equation (A2.2) but can be found by dividing β_j by $-\phi$ (see previous discussion).

On the other hand, the importance of the short-term effects $\Delta X_{i,t-1}$ depends on the size of β_k and on how long the effects of changes in $X_{i,t-1}$ persist through time. A change in $X_{i,t-1}$ produces an immediate (contemporary) change in $Y_{i,t}$ that is measured by β_k. If at time t there is a change in

---

[53] This appendix draws on Kaufman and Segura-Ubiergo (2001).

$X_{i,t}$ in the opposite direction to the change in $X_{i,t-1}$, then there are no more effects. But, if the change in $X_{i,t-1}$ is sustained, then the impact will continue in subsequent periods and can be measured by $\Delta X_{i,t-1} \cdot (1+\phi)^t$, where t is the number of periods after the initial change. Thus, for example, three years after the initial change $\Delta X_{i,t-1}$, the effect will be $\Delta X_{i,t-1} (1+\phi)^3$. Because $0 < \phi < -1$, the smaller the value of ϕ, the longer the sustained changes in X will persist through time.

5

Chile

A Classic Latin American Welfare State under
Authoritarian Stress (1973–1989) and Democratic
Reinvention (1990–2000)

This is the first of three chapters that expand the quantitative findings of
Chapters 3 and 4 through a more detailed comparative analysis of three
cases – Chile, Costa Rica, and Peru. The purpose of these case studies is
twofold: first, to better specify some of the causal mechanisms underlying the main statistical relationships among globalization, domestic political institutions, and social spending; and second, to take the analysis of
Latin American welfare systems beyond the black box of social expenditures, thereby linking, for example, social spending patterns with changes
in the organization and delivery of social services.

The Chilean case provides specific evidence for two of the most important
findings obtained in Chapter 4 through multivariate regression analysis. The
first was the strong relationship between increasing levels of trade openness
and significant reductions in social expenditures, especially social security
expenditures. Chapter 4 concluded that in the debate between the efficiency
and the compensation hypotheses, in Latin America, the weight of evidence
favored the efficiency hypotheses. However, without further specific information from the cases in the sample, the causal mechanism behind this
association could not be established in depth. Did social spending decline as
a result of increasing pressures from business groups concerned about competitiveness in international markets? And/or did government officials make
decisions in anticipation of such pressures? How were decisions made within
the government? Were there distinctions being made between social security expenditures vis-à-vis health and education? The Chilean case points
to specific mechanisms regarding the effect of trade liberalization on the
structure of the economy and the functioning of labor markets that will
be useful to gain a better understanding of these questions. Some of these
mechanisms, as we will see, also apply to other cases; others are more specific
to the Chilean case.

The second main finding that emerged from Chapter 4 concerned the relationship between democracy and human capital expenditures (i.e., health and education). The quantitative evidence suggested that we cannot assume that democracy will be associated with higher social expenditures in the aggregate. However, public expenditures on health and education do tend to go up after democratization. Again, the causal mechanism underlying this relationship could not be clearly established. Democratic governments might, for example, have been more responsive to pressures from health workers and teachers unions, which tend to be among the strongest components of organized labor. Or, they may have used this type of expenditure (which reaches a relatively large segment of the population) to bolster their chances of electoral success. The Chilean case provides specific evidence to illustrate one particular aspect of democracy that has a strong effect on human capital expenditures: *electoral competition*. This is part of the explanation of why public expenditures on health and education increased steadily after the transition to democracy in 1990.

However, the case of Chile also provides crucial evidence to better understand the relationship between regime type and social welfare. Authoritarian leaders who subject themselves to electoral competition may also face substantial pressures to increase social expenditures. As demonstrated herein, the fiscal priority of social expenditures increased quickly in Chile during 1988–1989. It is no coincidence that, after more than sixteen years without elections in which Pinochet cut down social spending substantially, this increase in social expenditures in 1988–1989 coincided with a plebiscite in late 1988 (i.e., to decide whether Pinochet would continue as president for another period of eight years) and a presidential election in 1989 (in which Pinochet did not directly participate but provided strong support for the candidate of the Right). Hence, the Chilean case is useful not only to point out specific aspects of democracy that relate to social expenditures (especially human capital expenditures) but also the conditions under which authoritarian governments also face similar pressures to expand social welfare. This insight can also be appreciated in other cases, most notably in Peru – which is the subject of Chapter 7.

The remainder of this chapter is organized in four sections. The first section summarizes the historical antecedents of the Chilean welfare system. The second section analyzes patterns of social spending under Pinochet's military regime (1973–1989). The third section links the evolution of social expenditures under Pinochet to the reorganization of social services and its relationship with trade liberalization and economic reforms, especially during the 1980s. Finally, the fourth section analyzes the changes in the

Chilean welfare system associated with the transition to democracy in 1989–1990 and the establishment of a new democratic system that ended more than sixteen years of military rule.

5.1 Historical Antecedents of the System (1920–1973)

From the 1920s to the 1970s, Chile developed a welfare system[1] that offered wide coverage for most social risks. As discussed in Chapter 2, Chile had all the positive conditions associated with the development of a welfare state: a relatively high level of economic development and industrialization (at least for Latin American standards); a model of economic development based on ISI, which shielded domestic producers from international competition and fostered the expansion of the urban working class; a long history of uninterrupted political democracy until 1973; a well-institutionalized party system dominated by left-oriented and Christian Democratic parties concerned with social issues; and a relatively mobilized and well-organized labor movement. With the possible exception of Uruguay, no other Latin American country enjoyed such a favorable combination of conditions for the establishment and development of a welfare state.

Welfare state expansion from 1925 to 1973 was largely the consequence of pressures from organized sectors of civil society – for example, middle classes, urban workers, and miners – who became increasingly better organized and successfully pressed the state for improvements in their salaries, working conditions, pensions, education, health care, and housing. Political parties also played a prominent role. They tried to build loyal constituencies that would bring their leaders to power and promised social and economic benefits in return.[2] This combination of factors led Chile to develop one of the most comprehensive systems of social protection in Latin America. As Mesa-Lago demonstrated with a wide variety of indicators, at the beginning of the 1970s, "the Chilean system occupied one of the top positions in Latin America. It covered all social risks plus more than 70 percent of the population (it was practically universal when health care and welfare pensions were taken into account), it provided one of the most generous benefit packages as well as the most liberal entitlement conditions, and it stood out in terms of health levels and services."[3] The underlying philosophy of the

---

[1] For a more extensive analysis of the historical evolution of the Chilean welfare system, see Chapter 2.
[2] Raczynski (2000, 120).
[3] Mesa-Lago (1989, 105).

system was that the whole population should have access to free or highly subsidized services in health and education and a high degree of protection from market-generated social risks.

To be sure, such a high degree of welfare state development was costly. In the early 1970s, during the Socialist government of Salvador Allende, average public social spending represented about 20 percent of GDP. This was a high figure even if we compare it with the wealthier economies of Western Europe.[4] By Western European standards, however, the Chilean welfare system was excessively fragmented. At the beginning of the 1970s, the system had 150 different social security programs governed by more than two thousand legal texts![5] This was a consequence of the form in which the system had evolved: through a series of state concessions to pressure groups that had been flourishing during the long period of continuous political democracy that preceded the 1973 military coup. It is not surprising that the level of state benefits was higher for those groups – for example, the military, police, senior civil servants, and miners – that controlled key political and economic resources, and much lower for the rest – blue-collar workers, agricultural workers from rural areas, and the self-employed.[6] Thus, despite the (unsuccessful) efforts of the Socialist government of Salvador Allende (1970–1973) to universalize and standardize benefits, by the time the military junta headed by General Pinochet assumed power, the system still had significant inequalities in the distribution of welfare entitlements among different social groups.

5.2 A Welfare System under Stress: Comparative Patterns of Social Spending under Authoritarianism (1973–1989)

When the military junta – headed by General Pinochet[7] – took power in October 1973, it immediately launched an almost revolutionary crusade

---

[4] At around 20 percent of GDP, the level of social spending in Chile during the first three years of the Allende government (1970–1972) was similar to the level of Denmark and considerably higher than in Norway (16.8), the United Kingdom (17.3), Finland (18.0), and Germany (18.9). An economic recession and fiscal stress in 1973 – the year of the democratic breakdown – would bring the figure down to about 14 percent. See Chapter 1 for data sources and calculations.

[5] See Foxley and Arellano (1980, 151).

[6] Mesa Lago (1989, 105).

[7] Although the coup was organized by a military junta that acted as a collegial body, by 1974, Pinochet had marginalized the representatives of the other branches of the armed forces. He initially ruled as "Supreme Chief of the Nation." However, when a new constitution was adopted in 1980, he formally became President of the Republic.

to drastically alter Chile's economic model and radically transform its system of governance. Against the judgment of some government advisers, a radical program of structural adjustment, designed and implemented by a Pinochet-appointed group of Chilean economists trained at the University of Chicago, was imposed.[8] The program included a series of measures aimed at reducing trade and fiscal deficits, opening the economy to international-market competition, reducing the size and functions of the public administration, deregulating the financial sector, transforming social security legislation, and privatizing many state firms.[9] According to many observers, these economic measures led to a sharp reduction in social expenditures.[10]

However, the evidence presented herein suggests that although there was a drastic reduction in overall public expenditures that started almost immediately after Pinochet took over, the analysis of social expenditures has to be divided into two clearly different periods: a first period (1974–1982) characterized by a significant upward trend in social expenditures, and a second period (1983–1989) in which social spending did indeed go down dramatically.[11] To be sure, the pattern of upward/downward trends in social expenditures during the 1973–1989 period cannot be understood without giving closer attention to the radical transformation that the organization and delivery of social services experienced during those years.

This section describes the patterns of social spending during Pinochet's regime. To provide a pre-Pinochet benchmark, I also collected data for the eight years that preceded the military coup: namely, the presidencies of Eduardo Frei (1965–1970) and Salvador Allende (1970–1973).

---

[8] This group of economists would later be known as the "Chicago Boys." However, it is important to note that not all of the economists that played a prominent role during successive governments under Pinochet had graduated from the University of Chicago. For example, José Piñera, appointed by General Pinochet in 1978 to gain the junta's approval for the neoliberal proposal to reform pensions, had not graduated from Chicago.

[9] There is a vast literature on this topic; a good summary is Montecinos (1999).

[10] See, for example, Arellano (1985), Raczynski and Romaguera (1994), and Mesa-Lago (2000).

[11] Furthermore, as the next sections demonstrate, special attention must be devoted to the last two years of the Pinochet authoritarian regime (1988–1989). Although the aggregate levels of social spending as a percentage of GDP shown in Figure 5.1 still seem to show a decline in expenditures in 1988–1989, once we disaggregate social spending into different categories (i.e., social security versus health and education) and we focus on the fiscal priority of social expenditures (which governments can change relatively quickly), a different pattern emerges. As a result of the 1988 plebiscite and the 1989 presidential election, expenditures on health and education increased significantly when measured as a percentage of the overall public budget. However, this increase in 1988–1989 was relatively small when compared with the general downward trend of the 1980s.

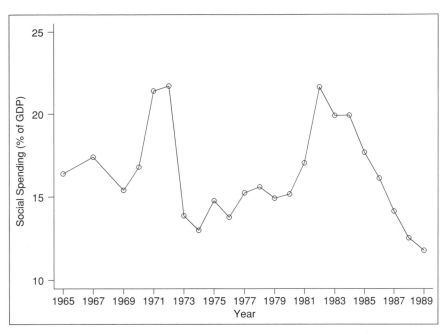

Figure 5.1. Evolution of Social Expenditures in Chile under the Democratic Presidencies of Frei (1965–1970) and Allende (1970–1973) and under Pinochet's Military Regime (1973–1989).

Note: As noted previously, because the military coup took place in September 1973, I considered this year to belong to the Allende administration for fiscal purposes. *Sources:* Data for 1965–1972 come from Arellano (1985); the 1973–1982 series was created with data from the *Government Finance Statistics* (IMF), various years. Although the two series are not strictly comparable, a comparative analysis of the years in which both series of data are available (1973–1982) indicates that there are only small differences in the levels of dynamic evolution of social expenditures in these two sources.

Figure 5.1 presents the evolution of social expenditures as a percentage of GDP during Pinochet's authoritarian regime (1973–1989) and during the last two democratic governments that preceded the September 1973 military coup.[12] The figure is based on a long historical time-series that

---

[12] The reference is to Presidents Eduardo Frei (1965–1970) and Salvador Allende (1971–1973). Before the September 11, 1973, coup, presidential elections in Chile took place in September, and the president-elect would assume office before the end of the year. Since the transition to democracy initiated with the presidential election of December 1989, presidential elections have always taken place in December, and the new president would take office in March of the following year. Hence, for fiscal purposes, an election year can be considered to belong to the old president and the year after the election to the new one. This decision rule provides the following division of presidential periods: Eduardo Frei (1965–1970), Salvador Allende (1971–1973), Augusto Pinochet (1974–1989), and Patricio Aywlin (1990–1993), after the 1989 transition to democracy. I thank Florencia Torche,

provides an interesting basis to compare patterns of spending under different governments and regimes in Chile.

President Eduardo Frei (1965–1970) left social expenditure levels at the end of his presidential term at about the same point as at the beginning. Frei was a Christian Democrat who had been elected at the end of 1964 with the support of a broad coalition of parties that included practically everyone except the supporters of the Communist and Socialist parties.[13] Social welfare was high on his agenda, which included a program to extend education at all levels, a reform of the highly fragmented and stratified social security system, and an expansion of health services to cover a greater proportion of the population. The program resulted in an increase in social expenditures during the first three years of his administration. However, as the budget was being prepared for 1967, it became apparently clear to the government that the need to control inflation, the impossibility of any further tax increases, and the drop in the international prices of copper would require lower budgets for the remaining years.

As Stallings noted, the 1968–1970 period was characterized by a complete absence of new reforms or even the maintenance of old ones. Social expenditure levels (see Figure 5.1) during the Frei administration reflect this underlying public-policy passivity. First, they go up to accommodate a relatively ambitious plan to improve health and education and reform the social security system. Then, because of economic imbalances, the government shifts to the right and social expenditures go back down to initial levels.

Under Salvador Allende (1971–1973),[14] expenditures skyrocketed during the first two years of his presidency (1971–1972) and then dropped dramatically in 1973.[15] The tremendous expansion of social expenditures during 1971–1972 corresponded to an overall strategy of using public spending as a

a sociology professor at the City University of New York, for clarifying some of these issues.

[13] See Stallings (1978, 99).

[14] As noted previously, Allende took office at the end of 1970. For fiscal purposes, it is therefore better to consider 1971 to be the first year of his administration. Pinochet's military coup took place on September 11, 1973. Because Allende was in power for three fourths of 1973, for fiscal purposes I am considering 1973 to be part of the Allende administration and 1974 to be the first year of Pinochet's military regime.

[15] As it is later explained in the text, however, it would be a mistake to assume that the reduction in expenditures in 1973 was due to the military coup of September 11. The reduction in expenditures in 1973 had been decided during the preparation of the budget at the end of 1972 and was also the ad hoc response of the Allende administration to a rapidly deteriorating situation in 1973. Although it is true that social expenditures continued to decline at an even faster rate after the September coup, it is also clear that the decline had been initiated much earlier in the year.

mechanism to fulfill several objectives, such as economic revival, urgent distribution, and the solution of social problems.[16] A number of mechanisms were put into place for redistributive purposes. First, there was a general tendency to increase wages and an expansion of public-sector employment. In 1971 alone, this strategy generated an increase in the public sector payroll of more than 3 percent of GDP. Similarly, central-government employment and public-sector enterprises rose by 50 and 35 percent, respectively, in 1971. Thus, a significant part of the increase in social expenditures during 1971–1972 did not correspond to a greater public provision of goods and services. Rather, it was mainly the result of tremendous real-wage increases awarded to teachers, doctors, and general staff in the health and education sectors.

Second, the government started to deliver massive handouts of specific goods to fight poverty. Patricio Meller, a well-known economist at the University of Chile, notes that during the first years of the Allende government, "half a liter of milk was distributed freely to every child in the country and 1,800,000 breakfasts and 560,000 lunches every day to school children, as well as 128,000 school overalls and aprons and 4,000,000 exercise books."[17] In 1973, however, negative economic growth, an inflationary surge that took the CPI index over 600 percent, and a budget deficit of more than 10 percent forced the government to reduce social expenditures drastically. Human capital expenditures (i.e., health and education) and social security transfers (e.g., pensions, family allowances, unemployment schemes, pro-poor programs) went down from 21.6 percent of GDP in 1972 to 13.8 percent in 1973 – a real reduction of about 36 percent. Real wages in the public sector (including those of staff in the health, education, and social-service delivery sectors), for example, went down to their original 1970 levels.

After Pinochet's coup in 1973, two totally different phases can be distinguished in the evolution of social expenditures. Figure 5.2 is useful to

---

[16] Allende came to power as the leader of the Socialist Party of Chile but with the support of a coalition of the Communist, Socialist, and Radical parties that came to be know as Unidad Popular (Popular Unity). The opening sentences of the economic program stated that "the central objective of the united popular forces is to replace the current economic structure, ending the power of national and foreign monopoly capitalists and large landowners, in order to initiate the construction of socialism" (cited in Stallings 1978, 126).

[17] Other measures taken by the Allende government did not have a direct impact on public expenditures but were also part of the redistributive policy mix. For example, during 1970–1972, the real price of electricity fell by 85 percent; the cost of mail and telephone services went down by 33 and 23 percent, respectively; and real prices of fuel declined by about 31 percent. For a thorough analysis of thes policies, see Meller (2000, 40–41).

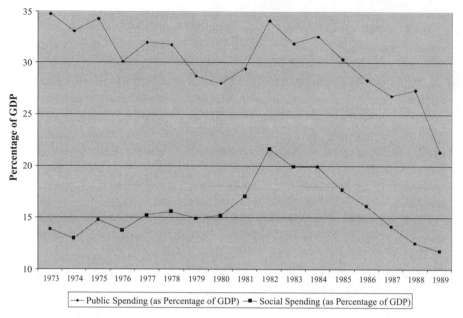

Figure 5.2. Evolution of Total Government Outlays and Social Expenditures in Chile under Pinochet's Authoritarian Regime (1973–1989).
Source: Created with data from the *Government Finance Statistics* (IMF), various years.

identify these two phases: a first phase (1973–1982) characterized by a clear upward trend that takes social expenditures back to the highest historical peaks reached during the Allende administration,[18] and a second phase of steady decline that would take social spending levels to an all-time historical low.[19] Hence, Figure 5.2 clearly demonstrates that the widespread perception that social expenditures were sharply reduced during Pinochet's regime has to be qualified. First, it has to be understood that although there was

[18] The sharp increase in social expenditures as a percentage of GDP in 1982 has to be taken with caution, however. As discussed herein, the increase was influenced by the tremendous decline of GDP in 1982 rather than by a deliberate political decision to raise social spending levels.

[19] As a percentage of GDP, social expenditures in 1989 were lower than in 1960. The next sections show that in 1989, health and education expenditures experienced a significant increase, especially as a percentage of the overall budget. As noted previously, this was connected to the plebiscite of late 1988 and the presidential election of 1989. But, as a percentage of GDP, social expenditures also declined in 1989. This is hardly surprising. Governments cannot change the macroeconomic priority of social spending quickly (because it depends on factors such as GDP growth, which are difficult to control), but they can move relatively fast to shift budget priorities from one year to the next.

a sharp decline in social expenditures in 1973, and the military coup took place in September of that year, the decision to cut down social spending had been taken during preparation of the budget in 1972; it was also the consequence of the erosion of the real value of pensions and real wages in the public sector provoked by high inflation levels. It should be clear, therefore, that 1973 must be considered an "Allende year" for fiscal purposes. This is an important point if we want to have a correct assessment of social spending patterns under Pinochet. Second, as discussed in the next section, after 1973 and until 1982, social security expenditures follow a markedly positive trend, and although health and education do not follow the same upward trend, they do not fall dramatically, as some researchers have suggested. After 1982, however, all types of expenditures started to drop very quickly. The only exception is 1989, in which social expenditures on health and education increased substantially. The next section explains how the 1988 constitutional plebiscite and the 1989 presidential election played a role in this outcome.

Finally, there is a certain tendency to evaluate the evolution of the Chilean welfare system by focusing on the overall size of the public sector, which was drastically reduced from the very beginning. Indeed, if we analyze the evolution of the public sector during the first years of the military regime, we do see a sharp decline in the ratio of public spending to GDP, consistent with the new market ideology and its main tenet: that the role of the state in the economy would have to be a subsidiary one.[20] However, Figure 5.2 clearly shows that this reduction of overall public expenditures did not translate, at least until 1982, into a reduction of social expenditures. The main conclusion we can draw from Figure 5.2 is that during the first phase of Pinochet's regime (1974–1982), the evolution of public expenditures and social expenditures follows rather different paths. Total government outlays fell at a steady pace until 1980, rose sharply during 1981–1982, and then continued to fall until the transition to democracy in 1989–1990. Conversely, social expenditures follow a significantly different path: a markedly upward trend until 1982 and then a sharp decline in line with the steep downward trend of public expenditures. How can we explain this pattern? The answer requires a careful examination of the program of economic adjustment and social-sector reform that was designed and initiated during the first half of

---

[20] The state, according to this model, would limit itself to providing a mechanism to correct market failures, but it would otherwise leave to the market alone the determination of the price of production factors.

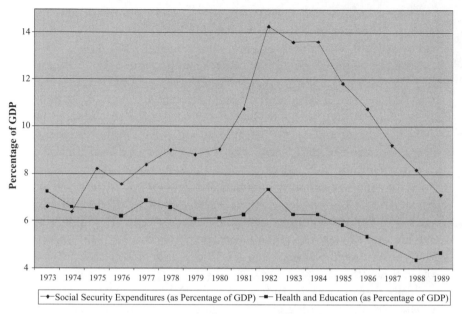

Figure 5.3. Evolution of Social Expenditures as a Percentage of GDP in Chile under Pinochet: Trends in Two Types of Social Expenditures, 1974–1989.
Source: Created with data from the *Government Finance Statistics* (IMF), various years.

Pinochet's regime (1974–1982) but whose effects were not fully felt until the second half of his authoritarian government (1983–1989). This is the purpose of the next section.

5.3 Within and beyond the Black Box of Aggregate Social Spending: Types of Social Expenditures and the Reorganization of the Welfare System under Pinochet

Decomposing Social Spending into Its Components

This subsection disaggregates social expenditures by different expenditure function (i.e., social security, health, and education) and considers not only the macroeconomic priority of social spending (i.e., social spending/GDP) but also its fiscal priority (i.e., social spending/total government expenditures). It also provides a detailed analysis of the transformations in the structure of the welfare system and the delivery of social services that underlie the different trends in expenditure levels described previously. Figure 5.3 shows the evolution of social security, health, and education expenditures as a percentage of GDP during Pinochet's military regime. The most important differences among these trends concern the dynamic behavior of social security expenditures vis-à-vis health and education. In 1973, social security expenditures were about 6.6 percent of GDP; by 1981,[21] they had increased to 10 percent of GDP – a relative increase of more than 60 percent. By contrast, the trend for health and education shows a moderate decline between 1973 and 1981.[22] In particular, public expenditures on health decreased from 2.78 percent of GDP in 1973 to 1.96 percent in 1981 – a relative decrease of about 30 percent. Education expenditures, in turn, started the series in 1973 at 4.44 percent of GDP and were at practically the same level (i.e., 4.32 percent of GDP) in 1981. Then, from 1982 to 1988, the behavior of the three trends became remarkably similar in that the three types of social spending followed a similarly pronounced decline. Finally, in 1989, the trends for social security and human capital expenditures followed different paths again. In 1988–1989, social security expenditures declined from 8.1 to 7.1 percent of GDP – a relative decline of 14 percent; whereas public expenditures on health and education – measured as a percentage of GDP – increased from 4.35 to 4.61 – a relative increase of 6 percent. The importance of the last two years of the Pinochet regime comes to the fore even further if we look at the fiscal priority of social expenditures – that is, the share of social expenditures within the overall composition of the budget. This is precisely the measure of social spending that governments can affect more rapidly, and it is therefore the one that is more sensitive to political pressures.[23] Figure 5.4 provides further evidence of the different behavior of social security vis-à-vis health and education expenditures and demonstrates

---

[21] I am taking 1981 and not 1982 as the point of reference to avoid the bias previously discussed.

[22] As discussed previously, in 1981–1982, all types of expenditures show a great increase when measured as a percentage of GDP. This occurred because of an economic recession that ended with a decline in GDP of 14.2 percent in 1982. Because expenditure commitments are stickier than business-cycle fluctuations, social spending usually fails to adjust downward with the same speed as GDP trends.

[23] To increase social expenditures as a percentage of GDP is usually more difficult than to increase social expenditures as a percentage of the budget. Whereas the former depends on tax revenues, economic growth, and so forth, which are, at least in part, beyond the control of the government, the latter depends only on how the government decides to allocate budget shares among different functions of government. Although a 10-point increase in social expenditures over GDP from one year to the next is not theoretically impossible, there are no cases in the Latin American sample that exhibit such an increase. By contrast, there are a number of instances in Latin America in which governments have decided to increase by 10 percentage points or more the budget share of social spending. Chile between 1989 and 1990 provides one of these examples.

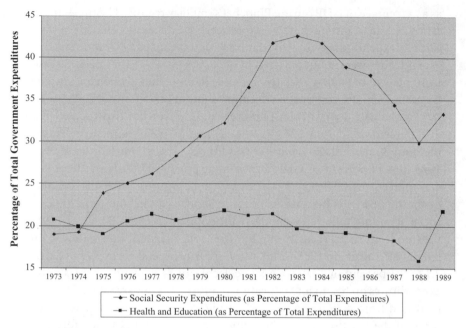

Figure 5.4. Evolution of Social Expenditures as a Percentage of Total Government Outlays in Chile under Pinochet: Trends in Social Security and Human Capital Spending, 1974–1989.

the enormous effect of electoral pressures on the fiscal priority of social spending (especially with respect to health and education) during 1988 and 1989.

As a result of the maturation of the public-pension system associated with population aging, during the 1970s, social security expenditures kept taking up a greater share of the budget. In contrast, health and education showed a much less important increase and even declined after 1977. In the 1980s, both lines follow similar downward trends up to 1988. From 1988 to 1989, social security expenditures as a percentage of the budget rose from 33.1 to 36.3 percent – a relative increase of almost 10 percent. During the same period, health and education expenditures increased from 17.6 to 23.7 percent of overall public expenditures – a relative increase of 35 percent! This increase is so large that in just one year, public spending on health and education returned to the level of 1977, which had the highest value in the series. Overall, if we combine social security, health, and education, the fiscal priority of social expenditures increased by more than 20 percent in just one year. What explains this huge increase in the fiscal priority of social spending in 1988–1989?

To understand this unprecedented increase in social spending as a percentage of public expenditures, we need to analyze one fundamental change that took place in 1988–1989, which sets these two years apart from the political environment of the previous fifteen years of military rule. From 1973 to 1987, Pinochet ruled without ever holding a significant election. However, in October 1988, Chilean citizens were called to participate in a plebiscite to decide whether Pinochet's rule would be extended for eight more years. The institutional foundation that made this possible was the 1980 Constitution, through which General Pinochet believed that his authority would be legitimized within a formal legal framework. The new 1980 Constitution established a new eight-year term for Pinochet and, as noted previously, called for a plebiscite in 1988 that would extend his tenure for eight more years if more than 50 percent of the popular vote was in favor of such an extension.

In "preparation" for the plebiscite, Pinochet began to stimulate aggregate demand through higher levels of public expenditures and to shift budget priorities toward the social sector. In particular, Pinochet's government authorized a one-time special increase in social expenditures, which was facilitated by the high international price of copper (i.e., the main export commodity in Chile). This was combined with a 20 percent cut in the value-added tax and significant reductions in import tariffs to stimulate consumption. Hence, Pinochet used a typical "populist" strategy of boosting domestic demand by increasing public expenditures. Although this went against the strict neoliberal model developed in Chile during the last decade, Pinochet realized that stimulating economic growth via higher levels of public expenditures might help him win the upcoming electoral battles. In 1988–1989, GDP growth was about 18 percent, almost twice as high as the level previously forecast by statistical agencies and international organizations. Aggregate demand rose by more than 22 percent of GDP. The real value of pensions, family allowances, and the real wages for doctors and teachers also went up during this period.[24] One does not need a sophisticated theory of the political business cycle to link all these policies with the 1988 plebiscite in which Pinochet could, for the first time since 1973, lose his power.

However, it is important to note that the large increase in social expenditures as a percentage of the budget did not occur in 1988 but rather in 1989. This is because of both economic and political factors. Economically, there is usually a lag between spending decisions and economic effects. It is therefore hardly surprising that the large increase in expenditures to influence

[24] See Olave Castillo (1997).

the 1988 October plebiscite appears most markedly between 1988 and 1989. Because of this "lag effect," some of the increases in spending levels in 1988 are not reflected until 1989. Furthermore, because Pinochet lost the 1988 plebiscite, in December 1989, a general presidential election was held. During 1989, the government continued to stimulate aggregate demand and maintained a high priority for social programs to enhance the chances of electoral success of the official candidate, Hernan Buchi – a former Minister of Finance under Pinochet and architect of Chile's economic recovery. Buchi would ultimately be defeated and Patricio Aylwin, supported by the parties who had backed the NO to Pinochet in the 1988 plebiscite, won the December 1989 election and was sworn in as the new democratic president in March 1990. The next sections study the evolution of social expenditures and social policy during the first decade after the restoration of democracy, including the Aylwin (1990–1994) and Frei (1995–2000) administrations. First, however, it is necessary to look beyond the black box of social expenditures and analyze briefly the enormous transformation in the architecture of the Chilean welfare state that took place under Pinochet.

The Restructuring of the Welfare System during Pinochet's Military Regime

The changes that took place in the Chilean welfare system under Pinochet's military government have to be understood within an all-encompassing strategy of structural reform that deeply transformed a great number of economic and social areas. The effect of these transformations would be felt in full during the 1983–1989 period and beyond. As noted previously, for analytical purposes it is, therefore, useful to distinguish two phases in Pinochet's military government: a first phase (1973–1982) in which the reforms were designed and began to be implemented, and a second phase (1983–1989), which started at the end of 1982 with a dramatic economic crisis in which GDP declined by more than 14 percent and would end in 1989 with the first democratic elections in sixteen years.

The program of economic reform under Pinochet proposed changes in seven policy areas: privatization, price system, the trade regime, the fiscal regime, the domestic capital market, the capital account, and the labor-market regime. From the end of 1973 to 1982, these changes led to a complete transformation of the structure of Chile's economy. In 1972–1973, just before the military coup, the state controlled more than four hundred companies and banks; there were generalized price controls, multiple exchange rates, import quotas, and average tariffs of about 94 percent; high public-employment and public-sector deficits; controls of credits, interest rates, and capital movements; and powerful unions with strong bargaining power, rigid labor markets, high nonwage labor costs (i.e., 40 percent of wages), and obligatory wage increases. The post-1973 period would gradually reverse this situation. During a period of about eight years, more than 350 public enterprises were privatized; prices were liberalized; a single exchange rate and a 10 percent uniform tariff were created (other trade barriers were eliminated); levels of employment in the public sector declined and the first budget surpluses emerged in 1979–1981; interest rates were freed, banks reprivatized, and capital markets liberalized; unions were crushed and lost all their bargaining power; real wages were drastically cut; employers gained the ability to fire workers with almost no justification; and nonwage costs were drastically reduced.[25] Welfare reform during this period has to be understood within the context of this overall strategy of structural reform just described. Raczynski, one of the leading scholars of Chilean social policy, summarizes the philosophy underlying the creation of the new welfare system as follows:

the military government tried to dismantle the old social policy system in order to build another. The policies that were implemented were viewed as opposite to and in conflict with those of the previous period. The military government, pressured by powerful international organizations, the neoliberal credo of its economic advisers, and the urgent need to control inflation and regain and maintain macroeconomic balance, reduced and narrowed the focus of public spending, privatized public companies and social services, deconcentrated ministries, and transferred the administration of primary health and education to the municipalities.[26]

The strategy had a number of parts. First, social expenditures would have to be redirected and, in some cases, reduced. Although a reduction of social expenditures was one of the declared objectives of the new military government, whether or not the reduction took effect depends on the measure, type, and period we focus on. Expenditures declined across the board from 1983 to 1989, but the story in the 1974–1982 period is more complex. As noted previously, as a percentage of GDP, health expenditures suffered a considerable decline, education expenditures remained at virtually the same level throughout the period, and social security expenditures followed a clear upward trend.

The most important characteristic of the new neoliberal social-policy model was not so much for the state to withdraw from social welfare areas but to profoundly transform the institutional environment in which social

---

[25] For a detailed description of these changes, see Meller (2000, 75–83). This discussion draws on his analysis.
[26] Raczynski (2000, 122).

policies took place. In this connection, focusing too much on the evolution of expenditures, albeit an important summary indicator of welfare effort, may be misleading. The real story lies behind and beyond social-expenditure figures, in the analysis of the ways in which the state decided to balance the attainment of individual versus collective goals.[27]

Welfare reforms took a number of forms. As Medlin argued, "in pensions, a system of individual retirement accounts administered by the private sector replaced a collectivized system of publicly-administered retirement funds. In health, a private insurance market was created to provide coverage to a growing number of clients seeking an alternative to the national health service. (...) In education, a school voucher system was introduced, spurring the growth of private sector schooling and forcing publicly-administered schools to compete for scarce resources."[28]

Second, social policy came to be seen as a poverty alleviation tool; expenditures on health and education were reoriented to primary and basic services. Funding was reduced for universities and hospitals, but it was maintained or even increased for primary education, health care, maternity programs, and infant nutrition. A new emphasis was placed on reaching geographically isolated areas that had previously received little or no social services from the state. In addition, a screening procedure was devised to separate groups in extreme poverty from the rest of the population, and a safety net – including emergency employment programs, family subsidies, and pensions for poor senior citizens – was created for these low- to very low-income families.[29]

Although targeting spending to low-income groups was deemed a more efficient form of social-service delivery, the screening system immediately received important criticisms.[30] The most important problem with the new system was that although it protected those in extreme poverty, middle- and low-income groups who were not extremely poor but nevertheless suffered a tremendous loss of real income with the new neoliberal policies, lost or saw a significant reduction in almost all types of state-sponsored social protection.

---

[27] The state can place its highest priority on individual freedom and the right for all citizens to exercise control over their own personal affairs, including how much to save for retirement, where to educate their children, and what kind of health services are desired. Conversely, the state can pursue collective goals giving "priority to securing a common social protection against the vicissitudes of life." See Heclo (1998).

[28] Medlin (1998).

[29] Raczynski (2000, 123)

[30] Raczynski (2000, 123) argues that the system was criticized for the following reasons: "stigmatization; social-structure polarization or dualization; suppression of initiatives for solving the problems of the poorest; and administrative costs."

As a result, despite generating high levels of economic growth (especially during 1983–1989), the new neoliberal model led to an increase in poverty levels and a more inequitable distribution of income.[31]

The Relationship between Trade Liberalization and Social Expenditures

As stated in the introduction to this chapter, one of the most important findings that emerged from the quantitative results presented in Chapter 4 was the strong relationship between increasing levels of trade openness and significant reductions in social spending levels, especially social security expenditures.[32] The Chilean case points to specific mechanisms that are useful in gaining a better understanding of this relationship.

Let us begin by describing the relationship between social spending and trade openness during Pinochet's military government. The next step is to study the probable causes for the association between these two trends.

Figure 5.5 unequivocally demonstrates that while there is no particularly strong relationship between trade openness and social spending during the 1973–1981 period, a strikingly strong negative correlation between both trends emerges from 1982 to 1989.[33] During this period, trade openness increased steadily from about 40 percent of GDP in 1981 to more than 65 percent of GDP in 1989. By contrast, social spending uninterruptedly declined from a peak of 22 percent of GDP in 1981 to a low of 12 percent in 1989. This pattern is consistent with the timing of trade liberalization – one of the top economic priorities of the economic reform package of the post-1973 military government.

---

[31] For example, the lower 40 percent of the population, which accounted for 1.7 percent of total income in 1969, by 1978 was receiving 9.7 percent, and by 1987, 7.5 percent of total income. Similarly, whereas the percentage of households living in poverty was about 6 percent in 1970, by 1987 it had increased to 13.5 percent. See Marcel and Solimano (1994).

[32] Chapter 4 argued that the statistical and substantive strength of this association withstood the inclusion of any control variable that may conceivably affect the behavior of public social spending – for example, fluctuations in the business cycle, changes in GDP per capita, population aging, tax revenues, shifts in the exchange rate, debt-service ratios, and democracy. In fact, the strength of this association was so powerful that it resisted the inclusion of every variable and the application of a wide variety of econometric methods.

[33] Pearson's correlation coefficient between trade openness and social spending is positive but substantively moderate between 1973 and 1981 (0.30) and strongly negative (−0.97) between 1982 and 1989. Because both variables seem heavily trended (in opposite directions), the question we need to address, to be sure, is whether or not the underlying trends are causally related.

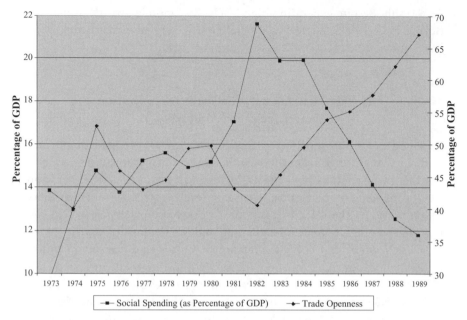

Figure 5.5. Long-Term Trends in Trade Openness and Social Expenditures as a Percentage of GDP under Pinochet's Military Government, 1973–1989.

Chile provides a paradigmatic example of a country that undertook a sharp switch away from ISI to an outward-oriented strategy of rapid trade liberalization. During a period of about six years, the government had eliminated all quotas, trade permits, and import restrictions; reduced average tariffs from 94 to 10 percent; eliminated all nontariff barriers; and unified the exchange rate.[34] Table 5.1 summarizes these changes. This process of trade liberalization had a tremendous impact on the degree of trade openness (i.e., [Imports + Exports]/GDP) of the Chilean economy. Total exports expanded by three to four times (in current dollars) between 1973 and 1981, reaching a record level in 1980.[35] Similarly, the annual real growth of imports during this period was about 27.5 percent.[36] As a result, whereas in 1973 the ratio of imports plus exports to GDP was about 30 percent, by 1981, it had increased to more than 49 percent. Although a deep economic crisis in 1982–1983 forced the government to reintroduce some moderate trade

[34] See Dornbusch and Edwards (1994).

[35] See Meller (1996).

[36] Different authors present different figures depending on whether nominal or real values are used. In any event, irrespective of the actual exact figures, all analysts concur that there was a tremendous expansion.

Table 5.1. *Trade Liberalization in Chile, 1974–1979*

	Pre-Reform Trade Policy (Before 1974)	Post-Reform Trade Policy (After 1979)
Maximum Tariff	220%	10%
Effective Rate of Protection	151.4%	13.6%
Non-Tariff Barriers	60% of imports required a prior deposit of 10,000%	Disappearance of all non-tariff barriers
Exchange-Rate Policy	Multiple exchange rates (the difference between the maximum and minimum exceeding 1,000%)	Unified exchange rate

Sources: Adapted from Meller (1996, 63) and Dornbusch and Edwards (1994).

restrictions,[37] by 1985, these restrictions had been lifted and the degree of trade openness experienced an unprecedented expansion, rising more than 67 percent by 1989, the last year of the military regime. Figure 5.6 presents a simple model of the relationships among structural reforms, trade openness, and reductions in social spending levels. Figure 5.6 unbundles the sequence of plausible causes associated with the reorganization of the Chilean welfare state and the reduction of social expenditures. Although the model is conceived to apply to the entire period of military rule (1973–1989), it is especially helpful for the 1980s (especially after 1982), a period in which, as noted previously, social expenditures suffered a tremendous decline. This is particularly useful to describe in a straightforward manner the sequence of links among structural reforms, trade openness, deindustrialization, and changes in social spending.

The Relationship among Structural Reforms, Trade Openness, and the Chilean Welfare System, 1973–1989

The military did not come to power with a clear intention to launch a drastic program of economic reform. Yet, prior to the coup, several retired generals

---

[37] Morley et al. (1999) created a summary indicator of the degree of trade openness of the Latin American economies. The indicator is standardized between 0 and 1, with 1 representing the lack of restrictions to trade, import quotas, tariff and non-tariff barriers, and so forth. In 1973, this indicator in Chile was 0.28, clearly pointing out the lack of openness of the Chilean economy to international trade. By 1979, it had reached 0.974. During the economic crisis of 1982–1983, some moderate trade restrictions were introduced. Morley et al. give an index of 0.88 for this period. By 1985–1986, the index had increased again up to 0.93.

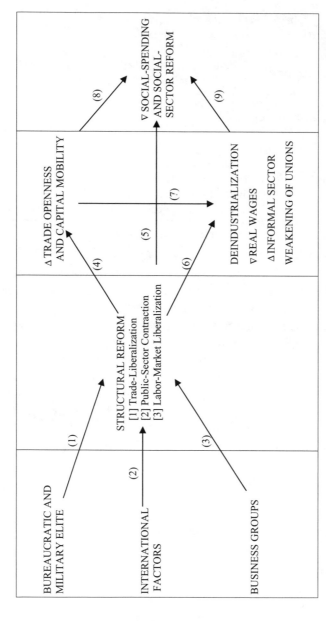

Figure 5.6. Relationship among Structural Reforms, Trade Openness, and the Chilean Welfare System, 1973–1989.

194

had been in close contact with a number of business groups and economists who had been meeting regularly to design an alternative to the state-centered policies of the Allende administration. A proposal known as "el ladrillo"[38] was drafted, and by the time the military had taken over, the economic plan described in el ladrillo began to receive serious attention by the military junta. The military government began to receive advice from a group of young Chilean economists who came to be known as the "Chicago Boys" because of their graduate studies at the University of Chicago's Department of Economics. These young economists came back to Chile with a strong commitment to the monetarist school of Milton Friedman and Arnold Harberger – two leading professors of economics at Chicago – and their philosophy of free markets and tight monetary policy.

Some of these economists immediately assumed key technocratic positions in the Ministries of Economics and Finance and in the central bank. The appointment of these economists to prominent positions coincided with the rise to power of General Pinochet and the demise of other members of the military junta – most notably General Leigh – who held more pro-state positions. Pinochet increasingly relied on the Chicago Boys because he liked their apolitical rhetoric and the promise of finding technical solutions to seemingly political problems. As one of the Chicago Boys confessed, "It wasn't hard to convince Pinochet, because he felt he was making history. He wanted to be ahead of both Reagan and Thatcher."[39] Although they all depended on the final authority of Pinochet, these economists acquired an increasingly greater degree of autonomy. Business groups, which had played a significant part in the preparation of the initial economic reform proposals, were no longer heard by government officials. Some of the policies of the military government did have a direct negative impact on entrepreneurs and upper-class groups. As Stepan suggested,

the persistence of fear within the upper bourgeoisie was an important element in the bourgeoisie's willingness to accept individual policies that hurt the upper class (there were numerous bankruptcies of domestic firms following the drastic tariff reductions and the decline of consumer purchasing power) but were seen to be the necessary cost of protecting its overall interests. It is impossible to understand the passivity of the industrial fraction of the bourgeoisie in Chile (a passivity that, of course, increased the policy autonomy of the state) outside the context of fear.[40]

[38] "El ladrillo" means "the brick" in Spanish. It was popularly known by this name because of the impressive thickness of the document.
[39] Cited in Medlin (1998, 18).
[40] Stepan (1985, 321).

We can safely conclude, therefore, that the decisions to initiate and follow structural reforms – and their impact on social welfare – was taken by a group of technocrats who had been influenced by the international ideas of Friedman and Harbeger at the University of Chicago – and managed to convince a military elite (especially Pinochet) of the possibility of finding technical solutions to Chile's economic (and social) problems. Although business groups were important in the design of the initial blueprint for economic reform (i.e., el ladrillo document), their influence became less important with the passing of time.

The second part of Figure 5.6 depicts the actual program of structural reform, which has already been analyzed with some detail herein. The key point to note is that this program of economic reform had direct and indirect effects on social expenditures. The direct effect was the reduction of social expenditures associated with the overall shrinking of the public sector. Because social expenditures are about two thirds of total public expenditures in Chile, it is hardly surprising that a reduction in the size of the public sector should be associated with a reduction in social spending levels as well. But, there are also important indirect effects concerning the relationship among trade liberalization, trade openness, and reductions in social spending.

In Chile, trade liberalization was, from the start, one of the most important components of the structural-reform package. The drastic reduction in tariffs, import quotas, and other restrictions to international trade led to an enormous increase in trade ratios (as measured by the ratio of imports plus exports to GDP). However, growing levels of trade openness had a strong negative impact on the domestic industrial sector. Many industries that had previously been sheltered from import competition lost all protection and found it hard to compete successfully. As a result, the size of the manufacturing sector went down from a 1974 peak of about 30 percent of GDP to a historical low of 18 percent of GDP in 1989 – a relative reduction of 40 percent. Figure 5.7 shows a relatively strong correlation between levels of trade openness and the size of the manufacturing sector in the Chilean economy. Figure 5.7 shows that increasing levels of trade openness were clearly associated with a steady decline in manufacturing production.[41] As Wisecarver noted, growing exposure to international competition in Chile led to a decline in industrial production in many sectors. In fact, Wisecarver's research shows that the impact of trade liberalization on industrial production was devastating. Some of his estimates of the losses in the importance of the industrial sector in the economy are as follows: nonmetallic mining

---

[41] The inclusion of other control variables such as GDP growth does not significantly affect the nature of this relationship.

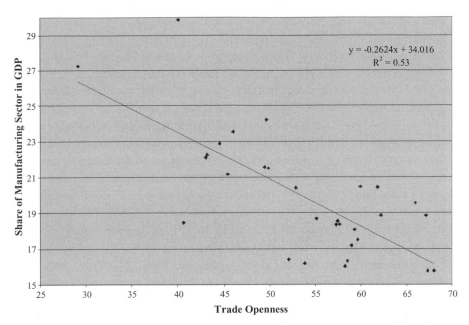

Figure 5.7. Relationship between Trade Openness and the Importance of the Manufacturing Sector in Chile, 1973–1989.
Note: The regression line (both the intercept and the slope coefficient) is statistically significant at the 95 or better confidence level, $R^2 = 0.53$.

industry (-25 percent), metallic mining industry (-33.7 percent), textiles (-22 percent), basic industries of iron and steel (-38.25 percent), chemical industry (-38.25 percent), nonelectrical machinery (-72 percent), and oil and petroleum (-64.4 percent).[42]

This process of "deindustrialization" was associated with a concurrent increase in the importance of the tertiary sector (i.e., services) and the primary sector (i.e., agriculture). The value added of agricultural production as a percentage of GDP also rose from 5.6 percent (1974) to 8.30 percent (1989) – a relative increase of about 48 percent. Similarly, the value added of the tertiary sector increased from 45 percent of GDP (1974) to 52 percent of GDP – a relative increase of about 18 percent. This reduction in the size of the manufacturing sector was associated with reductions in social spending for at least two reasons. First, in the Chilean welfare system, social protection against risk (e.g., unemployment, old age, sickness, maternity) is a function of a worker's contribution to the social security system. Hence,

---

[42] Some industrial sectors did see production increase. In particular, this was the case of sectors purely focused on exports: food and drink and wood-related products. See Wisecarver (1992).

when a worker loses his or her job for a long time, he or she moves into the unregulated informal sector or enters sectors (e.g., agriculture, services) where coverage tends to be lower, and his or her access to state-sponsored social policies is also likely to diminish. In the case of pensions, which are about half of social security expenditures, the Pinochet government deliberately decided in the 1980s to eliminate indexation and, during some years, the real growth of pension transfers was negative. It is in fact difficult to link these changes in pension transfers with transformations in the manufacturing industries. However, the other 50 percent of social security programs that a worker is entitled to as a result of his or her employment (e.g., family allowances, unemployment benefits, sick pay, maternity leave) are a function of (1) salary (the higher the salary, the higher the contribution and, hence, the subsequent benefits), and (2) the legal provisions under his or her contract. Although real wages declined in the 1980s, the decline was moderate (very different from the extreme case of Peru, which is analyzed later) so this cannot be considered the source of lower social spending.

By contrast, structural shifts in the economy, such as the increasingly smaller size of the manufacturing sector, did play a role in leaving a greater number of people without social security coverage. The percentage of the labor force covered by the social security system declined from a high of 76 percent in 1973 to a low of 57 percent in 1982. Coverage improved thereafter, but the conditions of the coverage were also far inferior than under the pre-reform period. The almost absolute flexibilization of the labor market weakened labor unions even further. Employers gained the ability to fire workers without justification, which led to a significant reduction in the type of fixed-term contracts usually required to accumulate welfare entitlements.

5.4 Patterns of Social Spending and Social Policy after the Transition to Democracy (1990–2000)

On March 11, 1990, Patricio Aylwin became the first democratic president of Chile after more than sixteen years of military rule. He was the leader of a coalition (i.e., Concertación) comprised of Christian Democrats and Socialists, as well as a number of additional parties and movements of much smaller size. As Mesa-Lago suggested, "with the return to democracy, the people had high expectations for a rapid response to unsatisfied social demands that had accumulated in the Pinochet years."[43] The new democratic government

---

[43] Mesa-Lago (2000, 105).

immediately put poverty and social equity on top of the agenda, reversing the trend of declining social expenditures that had occurred during the last seven years of military government. The new Minister of Finance, a prominent Chilean economist, called the new program a "social market economy." Behind this misleading phrase, there was a clear strategy that proved at the same time the limits of the possible and the impossible.

The impossible was to deviate too much from the free-market model inherited from the Pinochet military regime. The economic model had generated an average real growth of GDP of 7.5 percent during the last six years of the military government and had, therefore, generated significant support in the population. The possible was to increase state action in social and labor areas to reduce some of the excessive inequalities generated by the legacy of the Pinochet model. The Aylwin administration took a number of steps in this direction, using a leit motiv of "Growth with Equity." This is consistent with the theoretical framework presented in Chapter 3: namely, it can be argued that with the arrival of democracy, the increase in inequality during the 1980s increased the distance between the median voter and mean income, thus generating greater demands for redistribution. To this end, the new democratic government took a number of steps. First, a program of tax reform was initiated, with a view to increase revenues and therefore be able to finance substantial increases in social expenditures. In fact, close to 90 percent of the additional revenues was used to finance social spending. The plan to raise tax revenues involved a number of measures, including raising the corporate income tax from 10 to 15 percent, the value added tax (VAT) rate from 16 to 18 percent, and income tax rates for high-income groups.[44] The plan sought to increase tax revenues by 3 percent of GDP. This strategy of social spending financing was a radical departure from the last democratic attempt to raise social spending levels during the Allende presidency.[45] This tax-reform package was successful, managing to increase tax revenues in real terms by more than 40 percent between 1991 and 1993. As Foxley, Chilean Finance Minister at the time, suggested, the early success with tax reform proved crucial for later developments. The government had clearly indicated that all the new tax revenues would be used to finance programs to reduce poverty, increase health and education expenditures, and provide housing for poor people.[46]

---

[44] Foxley (2005, 134).

[45] During the years prior to the coup, the Allende administration (1970–1973) had financed rising levels of social spending through budget deficits and monetary expansions, which ended up in very high inflation levels.

[46] Foxley (2005, 135).

Second, the existing labor legislation was also reformed to restore some of the labor rights that had been severely reduced or suppressed during the military government. Under the new law, it became more difficult to fire workers, individual labor conditions and minimum wages were regulated, and unions improved their bargaining power vis-à-vis employers. As a result, during the first years of the Aylwin administration, the real minimum wage rose by 28 percent and family allowances were increased by 85 percent. There was also an expansion of house subsidies for workers, and a tripartite commission – business groups, workers, and the government – was created to devise ways to improve the education, health, and general labor conditions of workers.[47]

Third, there was a series of initiatives to improve the organization and service delivery in the areas of health, education, and social security pensions. In education, public expenditures per capita rose at an annual average rate of 17 percent. The key policy goal was to expand access and make the system as equitable as possible. A new program was designed to improve the quality and equity of the educational system. Under the Spanish acronym of MECE (i.e., Mejoramiento de la Calidad y Equidad de la Educación), the program's main objective was to improve the preschool and primary levels. International institutions, such as the World Bank and governments that had previously denied aid because of lack of democracy, would provide additional funds to finance some of these programs. Health expenditures per capita also rose at an average annual rate of 22 percent. These higher expenditure levels were used to open new emergency primary-care centers, increase resources to fight child care and infant malnultrition, expand health immunization programs, and even fight air pollution in Santiago. In addition, real salaries for doctors and medical staff rose by 43 percent during the 1991–1993 period. The Chilean government also received a significant amount of aid from international institutions to finance improvements in hospital infrastructure. Finally, the private-pension system established in 1981 was maintained, but the government tried to make the operations of the *Administradoras de Fondos de Pensiones* (AFP) more transparent, reduce evasion and payment delays, and improve the operation of capital markets upon which pension-fund investment depended.

Despite all these measures, the government was initially constrained by the fiscal situation inherited from the military regime. Social expenditures had risen sharply during the last year of the Pinochet administration. This forced Patricio Aylwin – the new democratic president – to use a nonexpansionary

---

[47] Mesa-Lago (2000, 114).

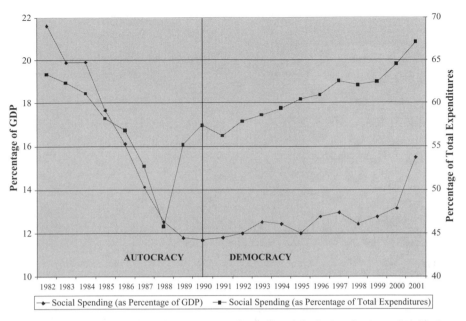

Figure 5.8. Evolution of Total Social Expenditures in Chile during the Second Half of Pinochet's Military Regime (1984–1989) and the First Democratic Decade (1991–2001). *Source: Government Finance Statistics.*

fiscal policy during 1990 and the first half of 1991 and provided justification for the tax-reform package described previously.

As Figure 5.8 clearly demonstrates, there is a clear shift in social spending trends after the transition to democracy in 1990. The greatest increases are in social expenditures per capita (not shown in the graph) and as a percentage of GDP. Social spending per capita, which is a direct measure of the resources each citizen receives on average from the state in social transfers or investments in health and education, grew from $349 to $476 during the 1990–1994 period. Although this measure of social spending increases as GDP per capita grows, the sharp increase observed after the transition to democracy cannot be attributed to a growing economy alone. During the last five years of the Pinochet regime (1985–1989), GDP growth had reached average annual levels of almost 7.5 percent; during the first democratic administration of Awlyin, the average rate of growth of GDP was practically the same: 7.3 percent.

Social spending as a percentage of GDP also experienced a significant increase from 11.7 percent in 1990 to 12.5 in 1994. Finally, social spending as a percentage of total government spending experienced a moderate decline

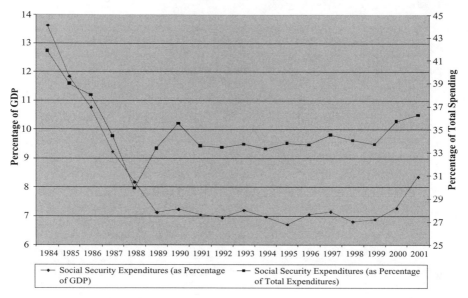

Figure 5.9. Evolution of Social Security Expenditures in Chile during the Second Half of Pinochet's Military Regime (1982–1989) and the First Democratic Decade (1991–2001).

from 63.4 to 62.3. The Aylwin administration was constrained by the large increase in the fiscal priority of social expenditures that had taken place between 1988 and 1989, in preparation for the 1988 plebiscite and 1989 presidential elections.

Finally, Figures 5.9 and 5.10 show that the new democratic government placed a higher emphasis on health and education than on social security programs. Social security expenditures per capita did go up from $215 in 1990 to $267 in 1994 – as a result of increases in the real value of pensions and the new antipoverty programs of FONASA – but their fiscal and macroeconomic priority remained practically the same. By contrast, health and education expenditures experienced a sharp upward trend irrespective of how we measure them: per capita health and education expenditures rose 57 percent during 1990–1994, whereas as a percentage of the budget and as a percentage of GDP, health and education rose by 13 and 22 percent, respectively.

These trends continued during the administration of President Eduardo Frei (1994–2000). Figures 5.9 and 5.10 clearly show that health and education continued to grow gradually from 5.5 to 6 percent of GDP and from 23 to 25 percent of total spending. When President Frei took office in 1994, he inherited a strong economic situation (the economy had averaged growth

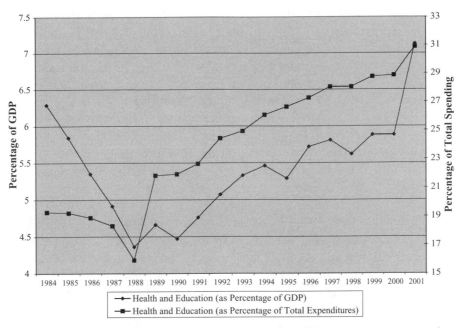

Figure 5.10. Evolution of Human Capital Expenditures in Chile during the Last Years of the Military Regime (1984–1989) and the First Democratic Decade (1991–2000).

rates of 7 percent between 1989 and 1993) and, despite the efforts to increase social spending during the Alwyn presidency, a number of analysts believed that Chile could still make a greater effort to improve education, health, and other social benefits, given the strong evidence that social returns to investment in these sectors would make an enormous contribution to Chile's stock of human capital.[48]

The greatest emphasis was placed on education reform and a redistributive agenda to carefully target social spending programs to the poorest segments of the population. The main purpose of the educational reform was to increase the quality and fairness of the educational system, and it included three key elements: extending school hours, increasing support for teachers, and improving management of the educational system. Each pillar of the reform had a clear objective. For example, extending school hours, in addition to having a significant educational benefit for the students, had a positive social effect on low-income groups by facilitating that both parents could work outside the household. In this regard, the number of weeks of classes increased from thirty-seven to forty a year; schedules in primary

[48] Aninat (2005, 306).

schools increased from thirty to thirty-eight hours a week and in secondary schools from thirty-six to forty-two hours. As a result, students beginning their education after the introduction of this reform would have two more years of education than under the previous system. The reform also included a system of bonuses to reward the best teachers.

These educational reforms were announced by President Frei to Congress in mid-1996, with an emphasis on their importance for increasing efficiency and equity. The reforms were then discussed in Congress and received broad public support. They were included in the 1998 government budget. Tax policy was a key element for the financing of the reforms. In this regard, maintaining the VAT rate at 18 percent (which had been raised from 16 percent during the Alwyn administration) was crucial. As Aninat points out, it is unlikely that Congress would have accepted the maintenance of the VAT at 18 percent if this had not been linked to the package of educational reforms.[49] Conversely, President Frei made the "war on poverty" the central theme of his presidential campaign. He expanded the Fund for Solidarity and Social Investment (FOSIS), which had been designed to promote productive employment in the poorest communities.

Despite these efforts on the social-policy front, the candidate of Concertación in the 2000 election (i.e., Ricardo Lagos) had a narrow victory with about 51 percent of the popular vote. It is not clear, however, whether this victory was the result of voters' perceptions that the "Growth with Equity" strategy had been insufficiently successful to better distribute the gains of economic growth or of other electoral factors such as the high personal appeal of the opposition candidate (i.e., Ricardo Lavín), who had earned a good reputation of solving citizen problems from his position as mayor of a Santiago suburb.

5.5 Summary and Conclusion

This chapter analyzed the evolution of the Chilean welfare system under Pinochet's military regime (1973–1989) and during the first democratic decade (1990–2000). First, the chapter showed that until the military coup of 1973, Chile had developed one of the most comprehensive welfare systems in Latin America, covering a wide variety of social risks and consolidating a relatively developed and universalistic educational and health system. A severe macroeconomic crisis put the system under serious fiscal stress in 1973, the year Pinochet led a military coup against President Allende. During

---

[49] Aninat (2005, 311).

the 1970s, Pinochet embarked on an all-out program of market-oriented reform in which public expenditures were dramatically reduced. However, until 1982, despite some declines in health and educational expenditures in which the government had more discretion, aggregate social spending levels did go up, driven by an aging population that required increasingly greater pension payments.

During the 1980s, however, social expenditures as a percentage of GDP declined dramatically by almost 50 percent. Two interrelated causal mechanisms lie at the heart of this phenomenon. On the one hand, reductions in social expenditures were the result of an overall strategy of gradual state retrenchment inspired by the neoliberal market philosophy. The reduction in social expenditures was accompanied by fundamental changes in the organization of social services: the pension system was privatized, thus replacing the pay-as-you-go system of publicly administered retirement funds; a system of vouchers was introduced in the educational system to force publicly administered schools to compete for scarce resources; and a private-insurance market was introduced to provide alternative health to the national health service. Within this context, reductions in social expenditures were the direct result of smaller overall budgets, rather than shifting government priorities to other areas. This strategy of welfare state retrenchment was made possible by the concentration of executive authority under Pinochet's military regime, the weakness of the labor movement that had been crushed by Pinochet, and the acquiescence of business groups that, despite opposing some of these measures, still remembered the threats to their property rights posed by the Socialist government of Allende and feared any alternative to military rule. On the other hand, the chapter also demonstrated that authoritarian regimes that face electoral pressures also have incentives to increase social expenditures to bolster their chances of electoral success. During 1973–1987, no major election for public office was allowed in Chile. In 1988, however, Pinochet subjected himself to a plebiscite in which citizens were asked whether they wanted him to be president for eight more years. In the months prior to the election and also during 1989 (in which there would be a presidential election), the fiscal priority of social spending increased by more than 20 percent. A similar phenomenon of autocrats using social expenditures to gain electoral support is observed in the case of Fujimori in Peru, which is analyzed in Chapter 7.

Second, the chapter also showed that there were indirect effects that link globalization with reductions in social expenditures. Indeed, one of the most important components of the overall program of market-oriented reform was trade liberalization. In fewer than five years, Chile eliminated practically all restrictions to international trade, thus subjecting ISI businesses to increasingly greater pressures from international competition. Having lost their previous levels of protection from international markets, many companies – especially in the manufacturing sector – lost their ability to compete and had to close down. As a result, the size of the manufacturing sector declined by almost 40 percent. The destruction of jobs in the manufacturing sector was not easily absorbed by other economic sectors; some of the workers became unemployed, others joined the rapidly expanding tertiary sector, and others joined the informal sector. Together with an almost total flexibilization of the labor market and the weakness of the labor movement, these workers found it increasingly difficult to accumulate welfare entitlements and lost most of the protection they had previously enjoyed in the manufacturing sector. In short, trade liberalization was part of a general strategy of market-oriented reform that put strong downward pressure on the budget and significantly affected social expenditures. However, increasingly greater degrees of trade openness also had an independent effect of their own: they put the domestic industrial sector under stress and, left to fend for themselves by the new flexible labor code and the weakness of labor unions, workers had to join other sectors of the economy where social protection was much smaller. Hence, Chile illustrates the fact that in the absence of strong trade unions, left-oriented parties, and executive accountability through regular elections, authoritarian governments face more limited pressures from civil society than democratic governments and have smaller incentives to use compensatory policies to benefit the potential losers of the process of globalization. This dynamic situates Chile at the opposite extreme of Costa Rica, a case that is analyzed in the next chapter.

Finally, this chapter also emphasized some of the ways in which democracy may affect the expansion of social welfare. After the transition to democracy in 1989–1990, political parties reemerged and membership in trade unions expanded dramatically. The new government of Patricio Alwyin realized that it could not depart too much from the general neoliberal strategy of the Pinochet regime, which had resulted in substantial economic growth over the last years of the decade. But, it could try to improve the distribution of income, reduce poverty levels, and gradually reinstate some labor rights. As part of this overall strategy, social expenditures, especially on health and education, experienced a significant increase and were financed by a reform in the tax system that successfully increased fiscal revenues.

6

Costa Rica

Globalization, Gradual Reform, and the Politics
of Compensation, 1973–2002

This chapter studies the evolution of the Costa Rican welfare system from
the early 1970s to the turn of the century. It pays special attention to the
process of economic reform and globalization that swept Latin America in
the 1980s and its particular impact on the Costa Rican welfare system – one
of the most advanced and comprehensive in the region. As with the previous
case studies, the purpose of this chapter is to illustrate some of the causal
mechanisms underlying the statistical relationships described in Chapters 3
and 4 and to take the analysis of the welfare state beyond the black box of
social expenditures.

What makes Costa Rica a particularly interesting case study is that unlike
most other countries in Latin America, in the 1980s and 1990s, Costa Rica
neither experienced a process of democratization[1] nor a *fast and radical* program of trade liberalization and market-oriented reform à la Chile. Costa
Rica has been continuously democratic for more than fifty years, and economic reforms took place within a context of constant negotiation and broad
participation by multiple interest groups, business associations, multilateral
organizations, and foreign governments. Furthermore, the case of Costa
Rica provides an opportunity to understand the conditions under which
the strong relationship between trade openness and reductions in social
expenditures (which emerged from the quantitative evidence presented in
Chapter 4 and was corroborated by the case of Chile) do not hold.

The remainder of the chapter is organized in four sections. The first section provides a historical overview of the emergence and development (up
to the 1970s) of the Costa Rican welfare system. The second section analyzes
patterns of social spending from the 1970s to the 1990s, describing trends

---

[1] Costa Rica has been uninterruptedly democratic since 1949 to the present. This is the
longest period of continuous political democracy of any country in Latin America.

in social expenditures and their relationship with substantive changes in the organization and delivery of public transfers and social services. The third section studies the relationships among globalization, economic reform, and social policies. The last section analyzes the interaction between international factors, as well as particular democratic institutions, on the type of economic reform (gradual and consensual) and the politics of social compensation that, unlike most other Latin American countries, developed in Costa Rica during the 1980s and 1990s.

6.1 Brief Historical Antecedents of the System (1940–1973)

In the 1930s, Costa Rica[2] was an agrarian country dependent almost exclusively on the export of coffee and bananas. Compared with Chile, Costa Rica had a much lower level of industrialization, and its labor force was consequently smaller and less mobilized than in Chile. Only unions in the banana plantations had a certain degree of power. As a result, unlike in Chile, the origins of the Costa Rican welfare system cannot be understood as the result of bottom-up pressures from an increasingly mobilized labor movement. The Costa Rican welfare system emerged in 1941 as an almost personal project of president Rafael Calderón Guardia, leader of the NRP – a conservative party shaped by the social doctrine of the Catholic Church. Calderón was a physician who had studied in Belgium and traveled extensively in Europe. He had been deeply influenced by the European welfare systems he had become acquainted with and by the social doctrine of the Catholic Church. Upon becoming president in 1941, he sought advice from the International Labour Organization (ILO) and promoted a law that established Costa Rica's Social Fund (i.e., Caja Costarricense de la Seguridad Social), an organization that became responsible for health-maternity and pension programs.[3] Costa Rica's welfare system expanded, however, under the auspices of the PLN, a Social Democratic party that would dominate Costa Rica's politics over the next three decades, in one of the longest periods of continuous democracy in Latin America.

From 1960 to 1982 (at the onset of the debt crisis), health coverage for the entire population grew from 15 to 77 percent of the population; infant

---

[2] For a more extensive analysis of the causes underlying the historical evolution of the Costa Rican welfare system, see Chapter 2. For the purposes of this chapter, this section is simply a brief characterization of the Costa Rican welfare system around the beginning of the 1970s.

[3] Mesa-Lago (1989, 45).

mortality declined from 74 to 19 per thousand; life expectancy increased from sixty-one to seventy-one years; illiteracy rates fell from 14 to about 7 percent; the percentage of the population receiving old-age pensions from the state rose from 6 to 50 percent; and the distribution of income became far more equitable.[4] This remarkable accomplishment in terms of social development cannot be understood outside the context of the enormous expansion of the Costa Rican welfare system from 1950 to 1980.

As Chapter 2 argued, the expansion of the welfare state in Costa Rica took place in the context of a long history of continuous democracy. However, it was not democracy per se that was associated with welfare state expansion in Costa Rica but rather the specific nature of electoral competition and democratic political institutions. Some of these democratic institutions include the dispersion of power between the Executive and other branches of government; the existence of a two-party system organized around a Social Democratic party (committed to social welfare) and a Christian Democratic party (claiming credit for the origins of the welfare state and unable to roll it back); the maintenance of high levels of electoral competition and voter turnout, which reduced ideological differences between parties and pushed them to compete for the median voter (usually in favor of the welfare state); and the existence of strong autonomous institutions (AIs), charged with specific responsibilities in the design and delivery of social policies, whose bureaucratic elite removed many "social questions" from the political agenda. Successive governments could attempt to introduce small changes in the welfare system, but both its scope and universalistic character continued to be considered a "Question of State."[5] The welfare state was, therefore, protected by the dispersion of power in the political system (which would make it difficult for conservative governments to reduce welfare entitlements); the existence of "stakeholders" who would not easily accept welfare retrenchment; and a highly competitive two-party system that, as discussed previously, pushed ideological positions toward the median voter. In the 1980s, however, Costa Rica was hit hard by the debt crisis and the new pressures from globalization. The following sections study how Costa Rica's democratic institutions and its welfare system faced up to these challenges.

---

[4] Whereas the top 20 percent of the population were receiving 60 percent of total national income in 1961, by 1983 their share of total income had declined to 51.8 percent.

[5] "Question of State" comes from the Spanish term "Cuestión de Estado" and refers to a fundamental issue whose general and widespread importance rises above the world of partisan politics.

Costa Rica

6.2 Patterns of Social Spending and the Restructuring of Costa Rica's Welfare System in the 1970s, 1980s, and 1990s

This section studies the evolution of social spending and the underlying changes in the Costa Rican welfare system from the mid-1970s to the mid-1990s. The analysis describes trends in social spending and their relationship with substantive social-policy changes, paying special attention to the relationship among globalization, Costa Rica's democratic institutions, and the evolution of its welfare system.

Phase I: Sustained Expansion (1972–1980) and Temporary Collapse (1980–1982)

The 1970s were characterized by a significant expansion of direct state intervention in the economy, both in the production and distribution of public goods and services and in the expansion of social welfare benefits. President José Figueres (1970–1974) initiated in March 1972 a process of tax reform aimed at increasing tax revenues[6] and making income-tax rates more progressive. Under the Figueres administration, the economy was stimulated by high levels of government consumption. Both Figueres (1970–1974) and his successor, Daniel Oduber (1974–1978), continued the PLN strategy of economic development through expansionary fiscal and credit policies and the use of public-sector agencies to directly increase or stimulate investments in infrastructure, industry, agriculture, and social development.[7]

The growth of state activity during the 1970s was facilitated by the expanding role and power of the AIs.[8] AIs in Costa Rica are semi-independent government agencies charged with responsibilities in specific policy areas. By the early 1980s, Costa Rica had more than two hundred AIs carrying out functions that in other countries would be undertaken by either the private sector or specific government departments. The most important AIs for our purposes are those that had social welfare functions, including the National Children Patronate (Patronato Nacional de la Infancia) set up in 1940 to provide assistance to mothers and children; The Costa Rican Social Fund (1941) (Caja Costarricense de la Seguridad Social), which administered the health and most of the public pension system; the Mixed Institute of Social Aid (1971) (Instituto Mixto de Ayuda Social), which administered

---

[6] This included a general tax rate of 5 percent and the introduction of consumption taxes that distinguished between essential and nonessential goods.
[7] Mesa-Lago (2000, 438).
[8] For an analysis of the importance of AIs in Costa Rica, see Ameringer (1982).

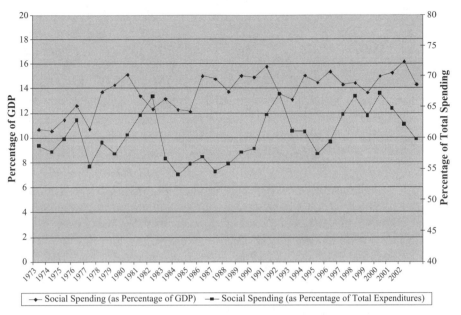

Figure 6.1. Evolution of Aggregate Social Expenditures in Costa Rica, 1973–2002.
Source: Created with data from the IMF's *Government Finance Statistics.*

a social-assistance program for poor families; and the Fund for Social Development and Family Allowances (Fondo de Desarrollo Social y Asignaciones Familiares, or FODESAF), established in 1971 to provide family allowances and fund welfare programs for low-income families. Other important AIs included the Costa Rican Development Corporation, or CODESA,[9] created in 1971 as a large holding of public enterprises through which the state planned to make investments that the private sector could not afford. Although most of these AIs had been created earlier, their economic role and power expanded substantially during the two PLN administrations of the 1970s. The evolution of social expenditures during this period also reflects this general pattern of state expansion.

As Figure 6.1 illustrates, after a short decline in 1976–1977, which was caused by the late impact of the 1973 oil crisis, social spending levels during the rest of the 1970s follow an upward trend. As noted previously, this growth of social expenditures took place in the context of two consecutive PLN administrations, which marked the first time since the end of the civil war in 1949 that a party had governed for two consecutive terms. This

[9] See Clark (2000).

continuation in government by the Social Democratic PLN party facilitated the expansion of the social agenda. Key social policies during those years included the universalization of social security, the creation of a national health plan, and the introduction of family allowances.

During this period, two new AIs – created in 1971 by president José Figueres – were particularly strengthened. On the one hand, The Institute of Social Assistance (Instituto Mixto de Ayuda Social) began to provide education, food, and housing subsidies to families without income. In 1975, this institute began to receive revenues from an increased sales tax and a 2 percent payroll tax. One of the main objectives of the institute was to raise the standard of living of the rural population by expanding access to electricity, roads, potable water, and basic food supplies. At the same time, the FODESAF became an important mechanism to promote preventive medicine, free school meals, pensions for poor people, and the supply of potable water in rural areas.[10] Seligson, Martínez, and Trejos calculate that during FODESAF's first twenty years, it distributed more than $1 billion in poverty-alleviation programs.[11] Finally, the growth of social expenditures during this period was also driven by a surge in public employment and substantial increases in the real wages of teachers and health workers.

During the next four years (1978–1982), Rodrigo Carazo and the anti-PLN conservative coalition he headed controlled the Executive and obtained a plurality in the Legislative Assembly. President Carazo, who had been elected through an unusual alliance of manufacturing interests with traditional coffee, sugar, and commercial groups, promised to initiate a program of economic reform to reduce the size of the state but failed to significantly reduce state activity.[12] As Wilson has noted, the Carazo administration (1978–1982), "although committed to significant economic reforms, ultimately found itself expanding rather than reducing the role of the state in response to the worsening economic conditions."[13] During the first two years of his administration (1978–1980), Carazo's fiscal policy was markedly expansionary, financed by heavy domestic and international borrowing. The fiscal deficit grew to 12 percent of GDP and inflation accelerated. By 1981–1982, the capacity of financing the deficit through external borrowing was reaching its limit,[14] and Carazo ended up declaring a moratorium on

[10] Wilson (1998, 102).
[11] Seligson, Martínez, and Trejos (1996, 24–25).
[12] See Nelson (1989).
[13] Wilson (1998, 113).
[14] About half of Costa Rica's external debt was with commercial banks that demanded higher interest rates and shorter maturities than loans by international agencies.

foreign debt service. International lending to Costa Rica immediately came to a complete halt.

Within this context, the sharp decline of social expenditures in 1981–1982 was more the result of a strong economic recession and the inability to finance fiscal deficits through external borrowing than the consequence of a deliberate attempt by the government to reduce the size of the social sector.[15] In fact, during the economic crisis of 1981–1982, the president faced the opposition of a wide variety of groups that had developed an interest in the welfare system and vehemently opposed any reductions in their subsidies and welfare entitlements. In fact, trade unions, business organizations, and bureaucratic agencies did not only oppose the state's attempt to reduce their benefits within the new context of economic recession and the pressures from international financial institutions but also began to demand the state to help them sail through these difficult economic times. As Eduardo Lizano noted, these groups began to demand higher wages, greater protection, and larger budgets for social programs.[16] Within this context, President Carazo felt unable to dismantle the extensive network of social protection in health care, education, family allowances, pensions, and food subsidies that were almost taken for granted by large numbers of citizens who had long benefited from these social policies and had therefore developed important stakes in the system. However, the Costa Rican welfare state was reaching the limits of its capacity to finance itself. At the same time, the ISI model of development predominant since the late 1960s was coming under increasing pressure. Government officials became increasingly convinced that trade protectionism was distorting the efficient distribution of resources, and it "impeded competition, fostered a dependence on imports, and did not stimulate investment in technological innovation that would have improved the comparative advantage of the country."[17]

Phase II: Gradual Economic Adjustment and Recovery of Social Spending Levels, 1982–1990

In 1982, Luis Alberto Monge (1982–1986) from the PLN party won the presidential election. Despite having campaigned on the traditional Social Democratic platform, once in office he initiated a program of economic reform that would introduce significant changes in the statist model of economic development that had been followed by successive Costa Rican governments

---

[15] Real GDP declined by about 2.2 percent in 1981 and by more than 7 percent in 1982.
[16] Lizano (1990).
[17] Mesa-Lago (2000, 451). For a more detailed analysis of this issue, see Andic (1983).

over the last three decades. The program of economic reform included a reduction of the role of the state in the economy, which included a comprehensive program of privatizations; a switch from ISI to an outward-oriented model based on the promotion of nontraditional exports; the reestablishment of relations with international financial organizations to renegotiate foreign public debt; and a process of social-policy reform aimed at restricting the scope and depth of the welfare state.

These policy measures were considered necessary by the new PLN government to take the country out of the severe economic recession.[18] Although it is clear that the government faced significant pressures from international financial institutions – that is, the World Bank, the Inter-American Development Bank, the IMF, and most especially, the U.S. Agency for International Development – to embark on a consistent process of economic reform, authors disagree as to the degree of influence exercised by these international organizations. Few analysts would deny that these organizations exerted significant pressures to push the Costa Rican government in the direction of fiscal discipline, trade liberalization, and privatization of public enterprises, but it also seems that most of the reforms would have taken place even in the absence of these international pressures.[19]

However, the economic reform package did not result in drastic cutbacks in social spending levels or in a substantial deterioration in social services. As Figure 6.1 illustrated, social spending levels began a substantial period of recovery after 1982–1983. This recovery was part of a general strategy aimed at rotating the costs of economic adjustment across many sectors of society.[20] For example, business groups had to bear an important share of the costs of adjustment through higher tax rates and increases in utility rates. Similarly, to moderate the potential social unrest associated with declining real wages and formal-sector employment, the government initiated a series of temporary public employment programs, unemployment assistance, food aid, and increases in the minimum wage.[21]

In 1986, Oscar Arias, candidate of the PLN, won the election by a comfortable majority. During the Arias administration (1986–1990), the program of

---

[18] These measures were rather successful. By mid-term, Monge had managed to reduce inflation from 90 to 32 percent, eliminated the trade imbalance, and reduced the fiscal deficit from 13.4 percent of GDP in 1981 to 3.4 percent. Unemployment and underemployment also declined and the trend in capital flight was also reversed.

[19] This is at least the perception of a number of PLN officials and academics that the author interviewed in February 2002 during a field trip to Costa Rica.

[20] Wilson (1998, 116).

[21] Huber (1996, 175).

gradual trade liberalization initiated under President Monge (1982–1986) continued. Social spending levels exhibited a clear upward trend during the Arias administration, which set Costa Rica apart from the general trend of declining social expenditures throughout the 1980s. One of the key social policies during his term included the expansion of the number and scope of the compensation schemes for the poor that President Monge had established. These programs included housing subsidies for low-income families and a targeted education program designed to improve the quality of basic education for poor children.[22]

The Arias administration established three priorities in the social-policy area. The first priority was the expansion of access to housing for low-income families through the construction of more than eighty thousand new units of accommodation. The second priority was in the area of education, in which the government attempted to reverse the decline in coverage and quality of the educational system associated with the debt crisis of the early 1980s.[23] Finally, in the area of health care, the Costa Rican Social Security Fund (CCSS) was strengthened and new forms of management to improve the efficiency of selected hospitals were successfully introduced.

Phase III: Continued Reform and Dilemmas of the Costa Rican Welfare State (1990–2002)

In 1990, Calderón Fournier, leader of the conservative PUSC party, began to introduce important changes in the organization and philosophy of social-service delivery as part of an overall strategy aimed at accelerating and deepening the process of structural reform. Calderón was a strong critic of what he called "excessive expenditures" from the previous two PLN administrations. His economic program focused on reducing the fiscal deficit and reestablishing the equilibrium in the balance of payments. His administration (1990–1994) implemented economic reform policies that had been proposed by the previous PLN administrations but had never been implemented. As Figure 6.1 shows, some of his reforms led to a significant reduction in social expenditures, especially in 1992–1993. The cuts in social expenditures were influenced by an agreement that Calderón signed with the IMF in 1991,

---

[22] Wilson (1998, 136).

[23] Some of the measures included the purchase of computers for an increasing number of schools. A private foundation – Fundación Omar Dengo – became responsible for the purchase and maintenance of computer equipment.

whereby the IMF would provide significant financial assistance in exchange for reductions in the fiscal deficit, mainly through cuts in public spending and public employment.

In addition, Calderón embarked on an attempt to initiate a means-tested system of *targeted* social expenditures. Through the Mixed Institute of Social Aid, the government established a screening system to identify who should be the beneficiaries of certain social policies.[24] In education, the coverage of the system improved but in health, the results during this period are mixed. However, the role of the state in the provision of health services was strengthened thanks to important international funding from the World Bank and the Inter-American Development Bank. Yet, the process of fiscal contraction during these years resulted in some deterioration in the programs of primary health care.[25]

In 1994, the Social Democratic PLN party captured the presidency again and the decline in social spending levels of the previous administration was reversed. During the administration of President Figueres Olsen (1994–1998), son of the legendary José "Pepe" Figueres, social policy received renewed importance. Social expenditures rose significantly during this period from about 13 percent to about 16 percent of GDP and from 68 to 75 percent of the budget. During his administration, Figueres also reversed the attempts made by the previous conservative government to introduce means-tested social assistance rather than universal coverage for social services. Although targeted programs to fight poverty continued (e.g., housing subsidies, family allowances, child care for single mothers), the general principle was to return to the Social Democratic philosophy of granting almost universal access to social services. Universal programs in the area of health and education were consequently strengthened. Finally, one of the most significant developments during this period was a 1997 constitutional amendment of Article 78 of the Constitution, which now mandates that public expenditures on education should not fall below 6 percent of GDP.

Some of these trends continued during the presidency of Miguel Angel Rodríguez (1998–2002) of the Christian Democratic party. But there were also important changes. Rodríguez was elected with an electoral campaign

---

[24] The new system was known as Sistema de Selección de Beneficiarios de la Política Social, or SISBEN, and was modeled after the Chilean targeting system, which had been developed during the Pinochet authoritarian period.

[25] Trejos argues that during these years, there was a significant deficit of more than five hundred doctors and medical staff in the primary sector and that some illnesses that had been eradicated reemerged because of a decline in vaccination rates.

that advocated "austeridad y trabajo las 24 horas del día" (i.e., austerity and work 24 hours a day). His government's plan included doubling economic growth to 6 percent (it had barely exceeded 3 percent in 1997), halving inflation to below 5 percent, while reducing poverty to no more than 16 percent. At the same time, Rodríguez also declared his support for a new program of privatizations, which he wanted to extend to the electricity and communication sectors. The purpose of these privatizations was to obtain resources to pay public debt at a faster pace. However, he also proposed a series of measures to increase the levels and efficiency of social spending. In particular, he showed preoccupation for the significant percentage of children and adolescents who were not receiving adequate schooling. This preoccupation for social issues, similar to that of previous leaders of the Christian Democracy, reflected his values as a devout Catholic and follower of the Christian Democratic tradition.

By 2000, the evaluation of the performance of his administration was mixed. On the one hand, the rate of economic growth had indeed exceeded 6 percent (in accordance with his electoral plans). However, inflation had barely decreased and the public deficit continued to be high (around 4 percent of GDP). Also, some difficulty began to emerge to maintain the levels of social spending and interest payments and the public debt began to increase at a faster rate than expected. President Rodriguez's public image also suffered a strong deterioration because of his privatization program, especially concerning the Costa Rican Institute of Electricity (Instituto Costarricense de Electricidad). Trade unions, teachers, and other social groups also mobilized to resist changes in social welfare and labor laws. As a result, most state services and the social safety net were kept in place. At the same time, tariffs continued to be lowered but policies designed to increase exports were simultaneously enacted. High-tech exports were boosted with the opening of a Motorola plant to make chips for cellular phones and an INTEL plant for computer microprocessors.[26]

Toward the end of his mandate, the Rodríguez administration accelerated its preoccupation for social issues in an effort to influence the upcoming election and ensure the victory of the Christian Democratic party. To this end, the president pushed through parliament new labor laws (e.g., Ley de protección del trabajador) and some educational reforms. These measures helped to substantially increase the president's popularity and facilitated the victory of his party in the 2002 presidential election.

[26] Vanden (2002, 170).

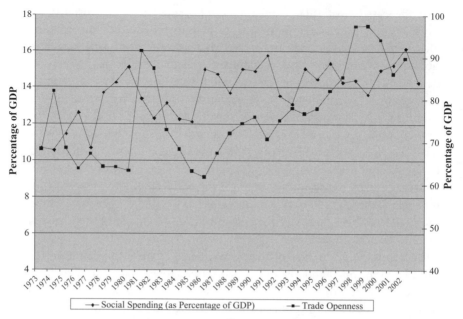

Figure 6.2. Relationship between Trade Openness and Social Spending in Costa Rica.

6.3 The Links among Economic Reform, Globalization, and Social Policies in Costa Rica

This section analyzes in more depth the relationship between trade liberalization – one of the key components in the economic reform package – and the evolution of the role of the state in the provision of public transfers and social services. Did trade liberalization in Costa Rica exert, as in Chile, substantial downward pressure on social spending? What was the position adopted by key business groups with respect to trade liberalization and welfare reform? What was the role played by Costa Rica's democratic institutions in shaping the welfare agenda? Figure 6.2 shows that in Costa Rica, there is no sustained negative relationship between increases in trade openness and social spending levels. Although trade liberalization clearly became one of the most important elements in the reform agenda, for reasons explored in this section, we do not find in Costa Rica the strong link between trade liberalization and significant reductions in social spending levels that Chapter 5 demonstrated was so important in the case of Chile. To understand why this is the case, it is necessary to review briefly how the process of trade liberalization took place in Costa Rica and how the government used certain economic policies, including social expenditures, to provide a "golden parachute" to those groups that would be negatively affected by growing exposure to international markets.

The main objective in the process of trade reform was to eliminate the anti-export bias that developed during the last two decades of ISI.[27] To this end, three fundamental reforms in the trade regime were put into place. The first was in the area of institutional development, with the creation (or strengthening) of three institutions, which included the creation of the Ministry of Exports and Investment (Ministerio de Inversiones y Exportaciones, or MINEX); the expansion and institutional strengthening of the Center for the Promotion of Exports (Centro de Promoción de las Exportaciones, or CENPRO), which had been created in 1972 to promote exports; and the establishment of the Costa Rican Coalition for Development Initiatives (Coalición Costarricense de Iniciativas de Desarrollo, or CINDE), which was created as a nonpartisan, not-for-profit organization devoted to promote exports and foreign investment. Also, in 1983, the government created a fund (FOPEX) to finance industrial and nontraditional agricultural products.

Second, export companies began to receive substantial tax subsidies and exemptions that in most cases eliminated the need to pay all direct and indirect taxes associated with export activities. The government also initiated a process of mini-devaluations, which reduced the real value of the exchange rate whenever inflation rates in Costa Rica exceeded those of the Unites States, thereby avoiding increases in domestic prices that would erode the competitiveness of Costa Rican exports. Finally, after 1985, the government initiated a process of gradual elimination of import tariffs. As Figure 6.2 illustrates, these measures had a direct impact on the level of trade openness of the Costa Rican economy. Imports plus exports increased from about 60 percent of GDP in 1986 to more than 90 percent in 1997.

Despite the fact that the process of trade liberalization was gradual, it did have a significant impact on the Costa Rican ISI manufacturing sector. The value added of manufacturing production declined from 22 to 18 percent of GDP – a relative decline of almost 20 percent – as a result of cheaper imports. Figure 6.3 illustrates this negative relationship between growing levels of trade openness and the importance of the manufacturing sector.

However, unlike in Chile, in Costa Rica the process of trade liberalization was gradual and negotiated, and the government used a number of mechanisms to allow those companies that were being affected by the new

---

[27] As noted previously, ISI was an inward-looking model of economic development based on restrictions to international trade to protect domestic producers from international-market competition.

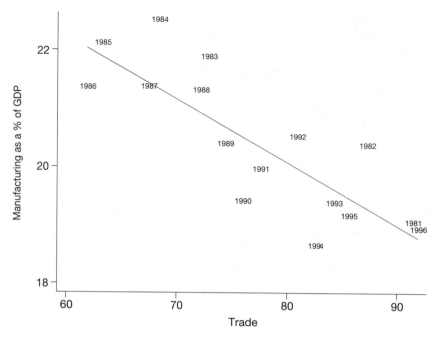

Figure 6.3. Relationship between Trade Openness and the Size of the Manufacturing Sector in Costa Rica, 1973–1997.

levels of international competition to adjust to the new competitive environment. Similarly, a number of compensatory mechanisms were put into place to facilitate the creation of new jobs for workers who were losing their jobs in the manufacturing and other economic sectors.

Business groups in the industrial sector, represented by the powerful Costa Rican Chamber of Industries (Cámara de Industrias de Costa Rica, or CICR), had a clear position with respect to structural adjustment policies and trade liberalization in particular. Initially, they pressed the government to keep its model of ISI within the common framework of the Central American Common Market.[28] However, since the early 1980s, some business groups in the export-oriented sectors began to demand greater trade openness and the elimination of the anti-export bias associated with ISI policies. Their power

[28] The Central American Common Market was created for the purposes of allowing free trade among the Central American Republics (i.e., Guatemala, El Salvador, Honduras, Nicaragua, and Costa Rica) and imposing a common external tariff for the rest of the countries.

and influence began to increase dramatically when Costa Rica started to receive significant flows of international aid in 1982–1983. This reflected one of the key demands from international institutions: namely, that along with privatization and the rationalization of the public sector, Costa Rica must encourage its export-oriented sector. The government became increasingly convinced that the export sector would become the new engine of economic growth, and practically every element in the economic reform agenda was analyzed in terms of its impact on the promotion of exports. The contraction of the public sector, the privatization of public enterprises, and the reduction of the effective rate of protection of the domestic industry became an intrinsic part of a new economic model in which the export sector, with its capacity to provide foreign exchange, would become predominant. Within this context, the government would favor the producers of tradable over nontradable goods, and there would have to be reductions in public expenditures that would inevitably affect the level of social benefits received by low-income groups.

To be sure, business groups were in favor of economic reforms aimed at reducing public expenditures and integrating the Costa Rican economy far more closely to international trade and capital markets. But, they expressed and successfully lobbied in favor of a slow and gradual reduction of tariffs, as opposed to the quick and sudden reduction that took place in many other Latin American countries. Business groups in Costa Rica – especially those in import-competing industries – therefore accepted the new model of "globalization" but strongly demanded (and managed to get) from the government a *slow and gradual* process of opening that would give them sufficient time to adapt their production technologies to the new competitive environment. Within this context, it immediately became clear to the government that the process of trade liberalization could only be successful if it was accompanied by a state-sponsored program of industrial transformation.[29] The government, therefore, introduced a new industrial policy that provided subsidies and incentives to help traditional industries adapt their production technologies and with a program of social compensation for the losers of the process of trade liberalization.

Hence, the reduction in the importance of the manufacturing sector associated with trade liberalization was cushioned by a series of compensatory policies aimed at ensuring a "soft landing" and facilitating the incorporation of workers into new sectors of the economy. In this sense, the Costa Rican

---

[29] For an excellent analysis of the relationship among the government, key business groups, and the process of structural reform, see Franco and Sojo (1992).

case is exceptional in Latin America because it approximates the political strategy of industrial adjustment combining international liberalization and domestic compensation followed by some European states such as Denmark, the Netherlands, Sweden, and Norway. As Katzenstein argued, these small European states kept themselves open to international trade and welcomed the inflow of foreign capital. For these countries, international liberalization was balanced against domestic compensation: "while each of the small European states has developed a distinctive capacity, a particular set of policies, these countries as a group are distinguished by the range and innovativeness of their policies of domestic compensation. These instruments include incomes policy, a large public sector, and generous social welfare expenditures."[30]

It is not surprising, given this gradual process of trade liberalization in Costa Rica, that the government's strategy to help companies adapt to the new competitive environment, the existence of European-type compensatory mechanisms, the strong link between reductions in the manufacturing sector, and declines in social spending that we had found in the case of Chile, is actually reversed in Costa Rica. As Figure 6.3 illustrates, social spending levels actually become higher as the size of the manufacturing sector decreases, which provides some support for the compensation hypothesis. In this respect, Costa Rica is more similar to some of the advanced capitalist economies of Western Europe described previously than to the rest of Latin America.[31] The next section analyzes the combination of international factors and domestic political institutions that make Costa Rica more similar to these European cases and make it so distinctive within the Latin American context.

6.4 The Essence of the Costa Rican Experience: International Factors, Domestic Political Institutions, and the Politics of Gradual Reform and Social Compensation

The gradual process of economic reform and the protection of social expenditures during the economic crisis of the 1980s cannot be understood without paying close attention to certain fundamental international factors and institutional aspects of the Costa Rican political system. In this section, I

---

[30] Katzenstein (1985, 57).
[31] For a detailed analysis of how the process of "deindustrialization" is theoretically and empirically linked with the expansion of the welfare state in Western European countries, see Iversen (2000) and Iversen and Cusack (2000).

analyze how these international and domestic political factors aligned to allow Costa Rica to respond to the economic crisis (and process of globalization) of the 1980s by keeping (and, in some areas, expanding) the welfare state, rather than significantly rolling it back as it occurred in Chile.

International Factors

It is not possible to understand how Costa Rica reacted to the pressures of globalization and the imperatives of economic reform without taking into account the enormous flow of international aid received by Costa Rica in the 1980s. By some estimates, during most of the 1980s, Costa Rica received an average of $1 million per day in international aid. Although some of this aid came from international financial institutions (i.e., the World Bank, Inter-American Development Bank, and IMF), the most important source of international aid was the U.S. Government. Through the U.S. Agency for International Development (USAID), between 1983 and 1990, Costa Rica received more than $1 billion. A major motivation of this enormous flow of aid was the attempt by the U.S. Government to induce democratic Costa Rica to facilitate the U.S.-sponsored contra rebels in their guerrilla fight against the Leftist undemocratic Sandinista government in Nicaragua. It is no small coincidence that during the administration of Costa Rican President Monge (1982–1986), who actively opposed the Sandinista government in Nicaragua and allowed contra rebels to build military airfields in northern Costa Rica, there was an unprecedented expansion of aid from USAID. In addition, while most international aid before 1983 had been in the form of conditional loans, after 1983 nearly all international aid became grants that could be used with much greater flexibility. This distinction is very important. Unlike loans, grants do not have to be repaid and are therefore not associated with future debt repayments that put strain on the fiscal budget. In addition, unlike international loans, grants did not need to be approved by the Legislative Assembly. According to Wilson, "the shift to grants removed a political bottleneck to the rapid application of neoliberal economic reforms while simultaneously giving USAID more freedom to allocate its money, effectively circumventing the Legislative Assembly, and facilitating the creation of organizations designed to undertake privatization and other programs favored by USAID."[32] When President Oscar Arias (1986–1990) started taking a less supportive position with regard to U.S. policy toward Nicaragua, the amount of aid began to decline. By 1990, Costa Rica

---

[32] Wilson (1998, 121).

was receiving about $100 million per year from USAID, about half the annual amount received during the Monge administration (1982–1986).

Democratic Political Institutions

Costa Rica has had a long history of continuous political democracy. However, democracy per se is not a sufficient explanation for the gradual process of economic reform and the wide range of compensatory social policies that emerged in the 1980s and 1990s. As Lijphart has argued, there are many ways in which a democracy can be organized and run: "modern democracies exhibit a variety of formal governmental institutions, like legislatures and courts, as well as political party and interest group systems."[33] Democracies differ in terms of the concentration of executive power; the nature of executive–legislative relations; the fragmentation, polarization, and institutionalization of the party system; the character of the electoral system; the degree of territorial and governmental centralization; and the forms in which interest groups and business organizations interact with the state. We cannot begin to understand the Costa Rican approach to gradual economic reform and the politics of social-policy compensation without paying close attention to the nature and causal effect of these different democratic institutional arrangements in Costa Rica. There are two interrelated institutional aspects of the Costa Rican democracy that deserve special mention: (1) the nature of the party system and electoral competition, and (2) the dispersion of power between the different branches of government and AIs.

First, Costa Rica has a two-party system modeled along Western European (especially German) lines, with a Social Democratic party (PLN) and a Christian Democratic party (PUSC). The PLN was founded in 1951 by José Figueres Ferrer and has always collected a minimum of 40 percent of the vote in every subsequent election.[34] The PUSC (United Social Christian Party) was formed in 1983 as the heir of a number of anti-PLN electoral alliances between the opposition parties. The PUSC (or the electoral coalitions that preceded it) has generally been able to call on the support of about 40 percent of the electorate as well.[35] It is also important to note that both parties have, since their inception, been committed to social welfare issues. The welfare state expanded under the leadership of the PLN, but the PUSC has also often claimed to be the heir of the NRP, the party that took Calderón

---

[33] Lijphart (1999, 1).
[34] Lehoucq (1998, 140).
[35] Yashar (1997, 88).

Guardia to power in the early 1940s when the most significant welfare legislation was introduced. Furthermore, anti-PLN parties had to form electoral coalitions to beat the Social Democratic PLN, but once in office, they lacked cohesion and were unable to dismantle the expansionary policies of the PLN. In addition, the coalitions that defeated the PLN at various times in the postwar period were diverse and covered a broad range of policy ideas. But, as noted previously, the most important party within this coalition was always the Christian Democratic party, which emphasized social programs and accepted (or found itself unable to challenge) the interventionist role of the state.

Another fundamental characteristic of Costa Rican democratic processes is the fact that elections in Costa Rica are characterized by high levels of voter turnout, which help to shape the preferences of the median voter in the direction of favoring social welfare. Since 1949, average voter turnout as a percentage of the voting-age population in Costa Rica has been 70 to 80 percent.[36] This means that most of the population actively participates in elections and that the difference in levels of political participation among groups with low income/education and high income/education is much smaller than in other countries.[37] High levels of voter turnout, coupled with the existence of a two-party system, favored the development and maintenance of the welfare state because political elites faced continuous pressure to compete for the votes of the economically disadvantaged groups. High levels of political participation in Costa Rica have therefore facilitated the emergence of public-policy patterns that incorporate the interests of most citizens, including the poorest and most disadvantaged groups. Hence, Costa Rica provides empirical support for the theoretical position that a two-party system in the context of high levels of voter turnout increases the chances that both parties will fight for the median voter, who is usually in favor of social welfare.

However, the protection of the Costa Rican welfare state during the process of economic reform and globalization of the 1980s was also facilitated by the broad dispersal of policy-making power across different branches of government and AIs. Presidents in Costa Rica are relatively weak[38]: they

---

[36] Voting in Costa Rica is compulsory, but this does not explain why Costa Rica enjoys this high level of voter turnout. Voting is also compulsory in other countries (e.g., Peru), where voter turnout is about 20 percentage points lower.

[37] In Guatemala, for example, where often less than 30 percent of the population participates in elections, the difference in voter-turnout rates between different levels of education and income is enormous.

[38] For a detailed description of the powers of the Costa Rican presidents, see Carey (1997).

have limited veto power over legislation, cannot legislate by decree, and may serve only one four-year term. In addition, the Costa Rican political system exhibits a significant degree of dispersion of political authority. Besides the Legislative Assembly, three other bodies play an influential role and may block, alter, or retard the policy-making process: the Supreme Court, the Comptroller, and the AIs. The Supreme Court has powerful rights that have often been applied to economic policy. The Comptroller has the right to void contracts when the rules of public finance have not been respected. The AIs control significant amounts of public resources and enjoy, as their name suggest, a high degree of autonomy from executive control. AIs such as the Costa Rican Social Fund (CCSS) – which administers health and pension programs – have developed strong technical bureaucracies that manage significant resources and strongly oppose any Executive attempt to reduce their power or capacity to implement their long-term objectives. This makes it difficult for any given government to break the built-in inertia in the system and introduce sweeping reforms in the welfare state.

The built-in inertia in the system facilitated by the bureaucratic processes of AIs reflects a more general argument developed by students of Western European welfare states: the importance of path dependence or, more simply put, the idea that history matters. As Pierson suggested,[39] certain courses of economic and political development generate feedback effects and, once initiated, are difficult to reverse. Actors adapt to the system of incentives and political opportunity structures, adjusting to the new environment. Although they may seek modifications to these policies, and their preferences may gradually shift over time, individual and organizational adaptations to previous arrangements may make a course reversal difficult and unappealing. Hence, social adaptation to certain institutional and organizational policy settings increases the costs of adopting alternatives that were previously available. Path-dependent processes are marked by incrementalism and irreversibility.[40] Within this context, "actors do not inherit a blank slate that they can remake at will when their preferences change or the balance of power shifts. Instead they find that the dead weight of previous institutional choices seriously limits their room to maneuver."[41] As Clark argued, in the particular case of a relatively comprehensive welfare state like the Costa Rican one, citizens begin to equate their democracy with the rights of social citizenship associated with widespread access to social services. Little

[39] See Pierson (1996).
[40] North (1990).
[41] Pierson (2000a, 810).

support for retrenchment can therefore be expected from either those who have vested interests in the system –that is, the workers who deliver social services and those who receive them – or from the broader public.[42]

6.5 Conclusion

This chapter studied how Costa Rica's welfare system – one of the most comprehensive and universalistic in Latin America – has evolved from the mid-1970s to the 1990s. The chapter showed that the combination of international and domestic institutional factors led to a very different relationship between globalization and social spending in Costa Rica than the one discovered in the case of Chile in the previous chapter. In Chile, a highly centralized Executive committed to far-reaching neoliberal reforms had little difficulty in rolling back the welfare state as a general strategy of market-oriented reform and state retrenchment. Also, the undemocratic character of the regime provided the military government with limited incentives either to design a new economic policy that could allow businesses in import-competing sectors to adapt to the new reality of international-market competition or to compensate workers that were losing their jobs because of the new economic model.

In Costa Rica, by contrast, Executive authority was dispersed among different branches of government and AIs; a strong two-party system in the context of high levels of voter turnout and electoral competition reduced ideological differences and pushed parties to compete for the median voter; and large groups of welfare state "stakeholders" both from the supply (i.e., workers in social sector delivery) and demand sides (i.e., beneficiaries) opposed any attempts to roll back the welfare state. In addition, business groups showed their support for economic reforms but pressed the government to liberalize trade gradually and to provide them with subsidies and other mechanisms that could facilitate the adaptation of their production technologies to the new competitive environment. Hence, unlike the general pattern in Latin America, the Costa Rican case resembles the small open economies of Western Europe (e.g., Belgium, Austria, the Netherlands, and the Scandinavian countries) in which trade liberalization was pursued in combination with a strategy of gradual industrial adjustment and a process of state intervention in the economy to protect the potential "losers" of international-market competition. The particular combination of international factors (i.e., substantial aid from international organizations and

---

[42] Clark (2000, 8).

the U.S. Government), a long history of continuous democracy with high levels of voter turnout, and a well-institutionalized two-party system (with both parties committed in different ways to social welfare) made this compensatory strategy possible in Costa Rica as well. Chapter 7 studies the case of Peru, a country at a relatively similar level of economic development in the early 1970s (measured in per capita GDP) as Costa Rica but in which almost all other political and institutional factors take different values. It is not surprising that the relationship among globalization, domestic politics, and social welfare in Peru is markedly different from the Costa Rican experience.

7

Peru

Political Instability, Regime Change, and Late
Economic Reform in a Non-Welfare State,
1973–2000

This chapter studies the evolution of the Peruvian welfare system from the
mid-1970s to the late 1990s. The case of Peru also provides further evidence
to identify some of the key causal mechanisms underlying the main statistical relationships analyzed in Chapter 4 through regression analysis and
studied in more detail through qualitative analysis in Chapters 5 and 6. First,
Peru reinforces two key insights developed in the case study of Chile. The
first is that fast and radical trade liberalization hurts domestic producers and
shifts the structure of employment toward sectors where workers typically
accumulate lower welfare entitlements (i.e., the informal sector and the service sector). This is one of the most important mechanisms through which
greater integration into international trade markets is associated with lower
levels of social spending – especially social security expenditures.[1] Unlike
in Costa Rica, where there is a much greater dispersion of political power,
Pinochet in Chile and Fujimori in Peru concentrated executive authority
to such an extent that they could overcome practically all resistance to their
policies of trade liberalization and labor market flexibilization.

Second, the Peruvian case also shows that a process of democratization in
the absence of a prior history of continuous democracy can have a weaker
effect on social welfare expansion than a process of democratization in a
country with a longer democratic tradition. This is not intuitively obvious.
At the theoretical level, one could also argue that in countries with a weaker
democratic history, citizen demands have been repressed to a greater extent

---

[1] However, unlike in Chile where trade liberalization started in the late 1970s, in Peru
the process of trade liberalization took place in the 1990s. In sharp contrast with Chile,
throughout the 1980s, a relatively appreciated real exchange rate and high import tariffs
led to a decline in trade openness. Hence, Peru is exceptional in the Latin American region
in that trade openness actually declined in the 1980s. Then it expanded quickly in the 1990s
as a result of trade liberalization.

than in countries with a longer previous history of democracy. Hence, the arrival of democracy could unleash greater pressures for social spending. Some of the empirical evidence presented in Chapter 4 provided some support for this hypothesis, even if the effect was not too large and the results insufficiently robust to draw a strong conclusion in this regard. The case of Peru actually shows that the opposite dynamic is also possible. In Peru, the transition to democracy in 1980 had a much weaker effect on social welfare expansion than the transition to democracy in Chile in 1990. Although the new democratic government in Chile inherited a more favorable economic environment than the Peruvian one, the economic situation at the time of the transition to democracy in Peru was relatively stable,[2] at least if we compare it with the performance that would take place during the rest of the decade. But, the limited expansion of the welfare state after the transition to democracy in 1980 cannot be explained by economic factors alone. Whereas in Chile there was a quick reemergence of civil and political society and an expansion of trade unions and interest groups that demanded "growth with equity," in Peru civil society was much more fragmented and political parties, in the absence of a prior continuous history of democratic practices, lacked the degree of institutionalization required to effectively channel citizen demands into the political system.

Third, the case of Peru also provides strong support for the argument that authoritarian governments that face electoral pressures are likely to expand social welfare as much or even more than their democratic counterparts. Using an even more radical strategy than the one pursued by Pinochet in Chile during 1988–1989, in Peru, Fujimori massively expanded social expenditures on health, education, and pro-poor programs with the clear goal of influencing electoral outcomes. Finally, the case of Peru illustrates the critical importance of the extractive capacity of the state to support social spending. The evidence presented in this chapter shows unequivocally that a bad macroeconomic policy is the worst type of social policy over the long term. Although certain populist measures (e.g., raise nominal wages, price controls, expansion of social transfers) may generate the illusion of better social welfare in the short term, in the end a strategy that does not respect economic fundamentals (e.g., moderate budget deficits, low inflation, limited current account deficits) such as the one pursued by Alan García (1985–1990)

---

[2] Economic growth during 1979 and 1980 averaged 4 percent, a relatively high level, but inflation exceeded 50 percent. Although this inflation level exceeds acceptable levels, it is low if compared with the inflation levels that would be observed during the rest of the decade.

in Peru ends up in macroeconomic chaos, devastates the capacity of the state to collect taxes, and makes it more difficult (if not impossible) for the government to provide even minimum levels of public services.

The remainder of this chapter is organized in three sections. The first section provides a historical review of the origins and evolution of the Peruvian welfare system since the mid-1930s. The second section analyzes social expenditures and the underlying changes in the welfare system during the last years of the military government (1973–1979) and during the two democratic governments of the 1980s (i.e., Fernando Belaúnde 1980–1985 and Alan García 1985–1990). Finally, the third section studies the evolution of the Peruvian welfare system under Fujimori during the 1990–2000 period.

7.1 Origins of the Peruvian Non-Welfare System

Following the general pattern in the region, the armed forces were the first group to obtain social security coverage through pension programs and hospitals for each of the four military branches (i.e., the army, navy, air force, and police). Some of these programs for the military and some senior civil servants started in the second half of the nineteenth century. However, until the 1930s, only a few and partial social security laws of limited scope were enacted. In 1924, the populist party APRA (Populist Revolutionary Alliance of the Americas) was founded by Victor Raúl Haya de la Torre.[3] Although the party would be banned for significant periods during the next four decades, it became the most influential and best organized political party in Peru until the 1990s. APRA appealed to the urban middle and working classes, and its program called for new social security legislation. But, APRA was never in power until 1985 and any development in the welfare system in Peru was actually carried out by anti-APRA governments or by governments that APRA was indirectly supporting.

The modern origins of the Peruvian welfare system can hardly be dated before the mid-1930s, during the presidency of Oscar Benavides, a military man who had banned APRA. In 1935, Benavides created the Ministry of Public Health, Labor, and Social Welfare, and in 1936 a new civil code expanded workers rights and mandated the establishment of a public system of health and maternity care, old age, and disability pensions. While passing this social legislation, President Oscar Benavides also decided to ban APRA and extend his presidential term until 1939. However, by 1946, APRA controlled the major trade union, the Confederation of Peruvian Workers

---

[3] For a comprehensive political history of APRA, see Wise (1992).

(Confederación de Trabajadores del Peru, or CTP), which demanded better labor rights and social protection for workers. APRA was later legalized but it could not use its name or nominate a candidate for the presidential elections.

In 1947, a worker's Social Fund law was passed with the goal of providing compulsory social insurance for white-collar workers in private enterprises and in the public sector. However, the new welfare laws were not implemented because of a military coup by General Manuel Odría (1948–1956). The new military president banned the operations of the major trade union – CTP – imposed strict controls on the operation of the other trade unions, and co-opted some of the union leaders to further undermine APRA's influence. Odría expanded the social security system but in an unequal manner: the new welfare programs benefited high- and middle-income groups only. Only powerful groups such as state teachers and railroad workers would later be incorporated; even then, the best pensions and hospitals continued to belong to the army, the navy, and the police. Health care for blue-collar workers was minimal at that time.[4]

In the 1956 election, Manuel Prado returned to power (1956–1962). APRA was legalized and the number of trade unions expanded dramatically. By 1961, the Confederation of Peruvian Workers (CTP) had a membership equivalent to 75 percent of all organized labor. Under pressure from APRA and the CTP, president Prado significantly expanded the welfare system. The expansion continued during the democratic presidency of Fernando Belaúnde Terry (1964–1968), who extended coverage to agricultural and indigenous groups.

In 1968, a new military coup ended the short democratic interlude. This time the military coup was headed by Velasco Alvarado, a left-oriented army general who initiated a program of land redistribution, nationalization of banks, and dramatic expansion of state activity. In 1969, Velasco also initiated a process of social security unification with a law that reorganized the Ministry of Labor, endowing it with supervision capacities over the social security system. Velasco's military government defined itself as the enemy of the oligarchic classes (i.e., large landholders and businessmen) who had historically dominated the country, but the government was more active in land reform, price controls, and the nationalization of key business sectors – which it argued would have a redistributive effect – than in the more direct expansion of the educational, health, and social security systems. By 1975, however, the statist model of development established by Velasco had run

[4] Mesa-Lago (1978, 118).

into severe macroeconomic difficulties and fiscal stress. General Morales Bermúdez replaced Velasco with a less reformist "phase" of military rule.

The history of social policy in Peru up to the 1970s is, therefore, characterized by lack of policy continuity, constant efforts to demobilize and fragment the working classes, and a series of mechanisms to impede access to power of the APRA, one of the best organized and influential left-oriented political parties in Latin America. The historical underdevelopment of the welfare state in Peru has to be understood, therefore, within the context of a short and troubled history with democracy, the continuous attempts by the military to control and weaken the Left – especially the dominant APRA party – and a relatively modest and unequal degree of economic development that until the late 1960s did not follow ISI policies.[5]

7.2 Economic and Social Policies in Peru from the Transition to Democracy to the Late 1980s: A Non-Welfare State under Increasing Economic Stress and Political Instability

Figure 7.1 presents the evolution of social expenditures both in percent of GDP and in percent of total spending over three decades. The evolution of expenditures in the graph can be divided into three broad periods: (1) the military governments of Velasco Alvarado (1967–1975)[6] and Morales Bermúdez (1976–1979); (2) the democratic governments of Fernando Belaúnde (1980–1985), Alan García (1985–1990), and Alberto Fujimori (1990–1991); and (3) the authoritarian regime of Alberto Fujimori (1992–2000). The following subsections analyze the evolution of social expenditures within each of these three periods. Special attention is given to the relationships among economic policy, social expenditures, and the underlying structure of social policies in the education, health, and social security sectors.

The Military Governments of Velasco Alvarado (1968–1975) and Morales Bermúdez (1976–1979)

In 1968, the military deposed President Fernando Belaúnde and proclaimed the so-called revolutionary government of the armed forces. Led by General

---

[5] For the importance of ISI for the development of the welfare state, see Chapter 2.
[6] Data in the figure start in 1973; hence, they only cover three years (1973–1975) of the Velasco regime. However, Velasco was in power from 1968 – after overthrowing the democratically elected government of Fernando Belaúnde Terry – to 1975, when Velasco himself would be overthrown by another military coup headed by Morales Bermúdez.

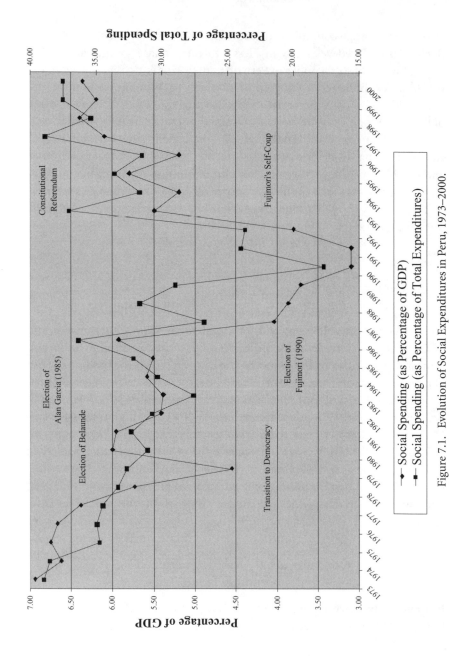

Figure 7.1. Evolution of Social Expenditures in Peru, 1973–2000.

234

Juan Velasco Alvarado, the military government embarked on a project of social reform that had been postponed since the 1930s. These reforms were aimed at eliminating the dominant oligarchic class and initiating a new model of state-led development. The military government "increased public expenditures, subsidized urban consumption, and promoted social rights and the organization of workers and peasants. Simultaneously, incentives were provided for the business community to encourage the development of an internal market."[7] In addition, in 1969 a radical program of land reform was approved by Executive decree. Although reliable sources of data for the period are scarce, one influential source reports that during the first years of the military government, total public sector outlays increased from 16 to 25 percent of GDP.[8] Public expenditures then stabilized during 1970–1973 and, as shown in Figure 7.1, so did social expenditures.

By 1976, the Peruvian economy was characterized by high fiscal deficits, growing trade imbalances, accelerating inflation levels, and substantial unemployment and underemployment. Within this context, on August 29, 1975, General Francisco Morales Bermúdez took power in a military coup that deposed General Velasco Alvarado. Morales Bermúdez, who had been Minister of Finance during the first years of the Velasco administration, initiated a modest program of economic reform to reduce inflation, correct the trade imbalance, and reduce the fiscal deficit. An important element in this strategy was the containment of public expenditures. However, as a military man, he was reluctant to cut down defense expenditures, and debt repayments could not be reduced quickly. Hence, the government decided to significantly cut down the amount of resources spent in social-sector activities (i.e., health, education, and social security). Social expenditures during this period declined from more than 5 to less than 3 percent of GDP.

Despite this attempt to stabilize the economy, the economic situation was even worse in 1978. Within this context, multilateral agencies and U.S. President Jimmy Carter urged Peru to implement further economic measures and to return to civilian rule.[9] At the end of 1977, Morales Bermúdez called a general election for a Constituent Assembly that would draft a new constitution. The elections took place on June 18, 1978, and the APRA obtained a plurality of the votes. Haya de la Torre, the historical leader of APRA, became President of the Constituent Assembly on July 28, 1978. The new constitution was approved on July 12, 1979. Then, on May 18, 1980, the first democratic election for president in more than sixteen years was held.

[7] Cotler (1995b, 333).
[8] Wise (1993, 5).
[9] Cotler (1995b, 334).

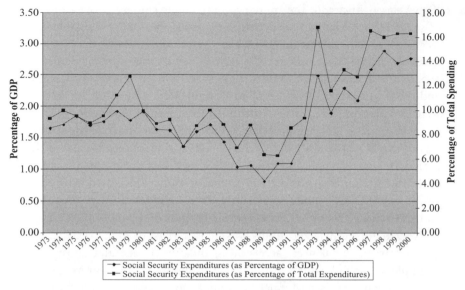

Figure 7.2.   Trends in Social Security Expenditures in Peru, 1973–2000.

The Democratic Governments of Fernando Belaúnde (1980–1985), Alan García (1985–1990), and Alberto Fujimori (1990–1991)

Fernando Belaúnde (1980–1985)

Fernando Belaúnde Terry, leader of Popular Action (Acción Popular, or AP) and previous president before the 1968 military coup, won the election and was sworn in as president on July 28, 1980. The transition to democracy in 1980 led to a sharp increase in health and education expenditures and had a more modest impact on social security expenditures (Figures 7.2 and 7.3). Health and education expenditures went up from 2.8 to 4.1 percent of GDP and from $76 to $113 per capita. By contrast, social security expenditures during the transition year declined from 2.9 to 1.7 percent of GDP and from $79 to $46 per capita.[10] Real GDP growth during 1980 – the transition year – was 3.1 percent, and this certainly may have helped the new democratic government increase social expenditures. However, economic growth alone is not a sufficient explanation. The year prior to the transition, the economy had grown at an even faster rate of 5.8 percent.

---

[10]   As a percentage of the budget, human capital expenditures remained relatively constant at around 26 percent of total government outlays. By contrast, the share of social security expenditures in the budget decline dramatically from 26 to 10 percent of total public expenditures.

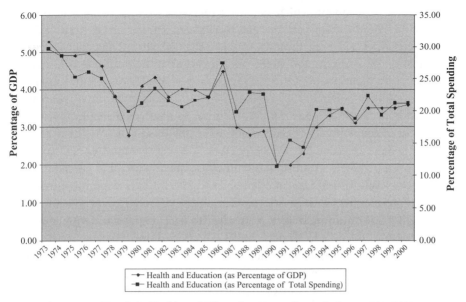

Figure 7.3. Trends in Health and Education Expenditures in Peru, 1973–2000.

Fernando Belaúnde turned health and education into an important part of his political campaign, and an effort was made during the first two years of the Belaúnde democratic administration to significantly increase the fiscal resources devoted to health and education. However, soon after the transition to democracy, social expenditures started to follow a moderately downward trend, which reflected the new reform ideas of Finance Minister Manuel Ulloa, a liberal technocrat with strong links to Peru's agro-export oligarchy.[11]

Ulloa had to face important economic difficulties, especially after the start of the debt crisis in 1982. Peru entered a program of debt rescheduling with the IMF in exchange for a commitment to economic reform. In collaboration with the Popular Christian Party (a conservative party), Ulloa implemented a series of economic reforms that included trade liberalization, new initiatives to attract foreign investment in mining and agriculture, and the privatization of firms that had previously been nationalized by Velasco.[12] As a result of this overall strategy, social expenditures during this period stagnated and in 1985 declined substantially. The inability to maintain fiscal expenditures on education was particularly damaging for the

[11] Haggard and Kaufman (1995, 186).
[12] Marcus-Delgado (1999, 105).

Belaúnde government, which saw itself incapable of improving very poor indicators of educational attainment. In 1981, only 58 percent of the population had access to basic education, and less than 10 percent had college-level education. In addition, the quality of education in the public sector, upon which most of the population depended, was very low. Fiscal constraints and lack of political will had left teachers with low salaries, and little investment in infrastructure was made. By 1982, illiteracy still affected an average of 18 percent of the population, with much worse figures in the case of women (26.1 percent) and rural areas (39.6 percent). To reverse this trend, it would have been necessary to substantially increase the quantity and efficiency of social expenditures. Yet, as noted previously, after the transition to democracy, the Belaúnde administration was unable to sustain high levels of public spending on education. In fact, from 1982 to 1985, expenditures on education declined from 3.2 to 2.7 percent of GDP. In addition, 90 percent of these expenditures were devoted to teachers' compensation, whereas only 10 percent was assigned to investments in infrastructure and academic materials. Finally, although the volume of expenditures did not decline substantially, average real wages for teachers did. In other words, whereas the number of teachers increased, their real wage was drastically cut. Some authors estimate that real wages for teachers during this period declined by almost 50 percent, 30 percent more than average declines in real wages in the rest of the economy.

In the health sector, expenditures during this period remained constant at around 1 percent of GDP. About 57 percent of the population was covered by the public-health system, which owned 35 percent of all hospitals and 73 percent of medical centers. However, Larrañaga estimates that public-health expenditures amounted to only 10 percent of total health expenditures in Peru.[13] The Peruvian capital, Lima, concentrated a disproportionate amount of health services: with about one fourth of the total population of Peru, Lima concentrated 66 percent of all doctors, 51 percent of nurses, and 49 percent of all available hospital beds.[14]

Regarding the social security system, the most important development during these years was the creation of the Peruvian Social Security Institute (Instituto Peruano de la Seguridad Social, or IPSS) as a decentralized, autonomous institution responsible for most work-related programs of social protection (e.g., old age and sickness pensions, family and maternity allowances, unemployment benefits). Trends in social security expenditures administered by the IPSS reflect rather closely economic fluctuations. When

[13] Larrañaga (1992, 180).
[14] Parodi (2000, 181).

the economy expanded, real wages went up, social security contributions increased, and the government decided to increase the budget of the IPSS. However, when the economy entered a recession (as in 1983–1985), real wages and social security contributions declined quickly, coverage deteriorated (as workers lost their jobs in the formal economy and joined the unregulated, unprotected informal sector), and under severe fiscal stress, the government failed to transfer previously committed resources to agencies administering social welfare programs.

Alan García (1985–1990)

In 1985, Alan García, the young leader of the left-oriented APRA, won the presidential election by a large margin.[15] García's policies were typically populist, appealing to a multiclass political constituency that included sectors of the working class, middle classes, and business groups oriented to domestic markets. His program used a nationalist, statist, and anti-imperialist discourse, and promised a mix of redistributive policies aimed at favoring the popular sector. President García responded to the economic crisis inherited from the previous government with a heterodox stabilization program that included increases in real wages, price freezes, tax cuts, and increases in government expenditures. He also declared that the government would limit foreign debt repayments to 10 percent of annual export earnings to free fiscal resources to redistribute income to the poorest groups. This strategy managed to boost domestic demand in 1985–1987, and real GDP grew by more than 18 percent in 1985–1986. By 1987, however, inflation was accelerating, real per capita income began to plummet (in 1987–1988, the economy contracted by 19 percent), and real wages initiated a virtual free fall. In short, as Table 7.1 demonstrates, García's policies led to total macroeconomic chaos. During his last two years in office, inflation levels averaged between 3,000 and 7,000 percent; real GDP growth declined by almost 12 percent in 1989 and more than 5 percent in 1990; and real wages declined by 56.9 percent in 1989 and 79.6 percent in 1990!

As Graham has argued, the García administration was typical of an old-style populist regime. The president did not allow other party members into his inner circle, used a heavily charged nationalistic rhethoric, relied on a vertical decision making structure, and ruled as if the government were a one-man show.[16]

---

[15] APRA won a majority of seats in both congressional chambers. It was the first time in history that APRA won an election. AP, the party of President Belaúnde, was severely punished at the polls and obtained only 6.3 percent of the popular vote.

[16] Graham (1990).

Table 7.1. *Evolution of Key Economic Indicators in Peru under Alan García, 1985–1990*

Year	Inflation (%)	GDP Growth (%)	% Variation in Real Wages
1985	163.39	2.26	2.5
1986	77.92	9.23	−5.7
1987	85.82	8.48	11.7
1988	667.01	−8.36	(*)
1989	3,389.67	−11.65	−56.9
1990	7,481.67	−5.40	−79.6

* Data not available.

Sources: World Bank, *World Development Indicators 2003*, and Verdera (1997a).

As Figure 7.4 shows, during his first two years in office (1985–1986), García increased social expenditures substantially: they rose from 3.7 to 4.4 as a percentage of GDP, while per capita and as a percentage of the budget, social expenditures rose by 26 and 24 percent, respectively.[17] However, after 1986, all types of expenditures followed a substantial downward trend. This decline in expenditures was the result of the rapid erosion of tax revenues associated with the economic recession (and macroeconomic chaos) that would follow in 1987–1990. Fiscal revenues during the García administration declined from 15 percent of GDP in 1985 to less than 7 percent in 1989. The García administration was not initially constrained by the fall in fiscal revenues and during 1985–1986, public expenditures were financed through fiscal deficits. But, this strategy was not sustainable over the long run and ended up in a devastating cycle of hyperinflation. Figures 7.1 through 7.3 show the overall negative evolution of social expenditures after 1986. During 1987–1988, when social expenditures per capita and as a percentage of GDP were declining fast, the government tried to slow down the fall of social spending by increasing the budget priority of social expenditures. However, during the last year of the García administration, even the budget priority of social expenditures suffered a dramatic reduction.

The strategy followed by García provides one of the best empirical examples of populism in Latin America. Populism involves a set of economic policies – including budget deficits, nominal wage increases, price and exchange-rate controls, et cetera – designed to achieve specific political goals

---

[17] Most of this increase was driven by the quick expansion of expenditures on education. In just one year, García managed to increase public spending on education by more than 25 percent. Health expenditures remained constant and social security expenditures actually experienced a moderate decline.

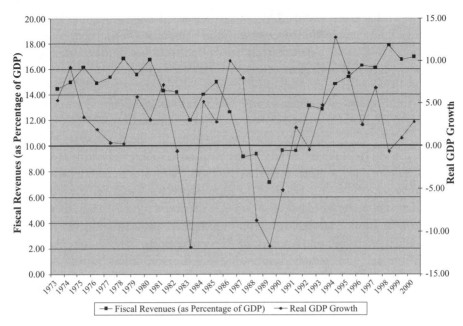

Figure 7.4. Economic Growth and Evolution of Fiscal Revenues in Peru, 1973–2000.

such as "(1) mobilizing support within organized labor and lower-middle class groups; (2) obtaining complementary backing from domestically oriented business; and (3) politically isolating the rural oligarchy, foreign enterprises, and large scale domestic industrial elites."[18]

However, we cannot understand García's appeals to the popular sector and his attempts at redistribution by looking at social expenditures alone. García's strategy was based on a set of policies aimed at favoring the popular sectors *indirectly:* gross manipulation of basic prices, astronomical increases in nominal wages, and price controls on key products such as fuel. The real price of gasoline and kerosene, for example, was frozen (even reduced in some cases). García argued that increases in oil prices had a regressive effect on the distribution of income because it was associated with relative increases in transport and food prices – two fundamental elements within the basic basket of poor families. This policy backfired and it soon became apparent that the government's deficit made these subsidies of public prices unsustainable. García then decided to increase fuel prices by 50 percent. He justified this change of strategy arguing that only a small proportion of Peruvians had a car and that the increase in the price of fuel was therefore

[18] Kaufman and Stallings (1991, 15–16).

not regressive. By the end of his term, García left the Peruvian economy with an inflation level of more than 7,000 percent, a profound economic recession, a huge fiscal deficit, and a level of political instability that put the country on the verge of civil war.

The 1980s: Anatomy of an Economic and Social Policy Failure

Before analyzing the evolution of social expenditures after the coup of April 5, 1992, it is useful to reflect on some of the causes associated with trends in social expenditures from the transition to democracy in 1980 to the breakdown of democracy in 1992. Figure 7.4 illustrates that a bad economic policy ends up having devastating effects for social policy. During the administration of Alan Garcia, total revenues declined from 15 percent of GDP to about 7 percent of GDP. This made it virtually impossible for the state to provide even the most basic social services. On the other hand, in light of some of the main findings from the quantitative chapters, do we find in the case of Peru a strong association between trade openness and reductions in social expenditures?

In the case of Peru, at least during the 1980–1991 period, we do not observe a link between rising levels of trade integration and declines in social expenditures. In fact, trade openness during the 1980s declined as a direct consequence of an overvalued exchange rate. The reductions in social spending during the 1980–1991 period were instead the direct result of increasingly greater fiscal stress that made it ever more difficult for the state to finance social programs, and the indirect result of a dramatic decline in real wages – the largest in Latin America – that reduced social security contributions and welfare entitlements. As Figure 7.5 shows, there is a high correlation between the decline in real wages and social spending levels in Peru in the 1980s. Real wages in the 1980s in Peru suffered the most pronounced and dramatic decline in all the sample of Latin American countries. Setting the index of real wages in the private sector at 100 in 1980, by 1991 they had declined to less than 50 percent. The decline of real wages in the public sector is even more dramatic: by 1991, real public-sector wages were about 11 percent of their 1980 levels!

In contrast, no causal relationship can be established between trade openness in the 1980s and social spending levels. As noted previously, trade openness in the 1980s actually declined. Hence, Peru did not join the widespread wave of globalization that swept Latin America during this period. In fact, the level of trade openness (i.e., the ratio of imports plus exports to GDP) in Peru during this period declined dramatically from 41 to 21 percent. This was the result of an unprecedented appreciation of the real exchange rate, the maintenance of relatively high levels of import protectionism, and the lack

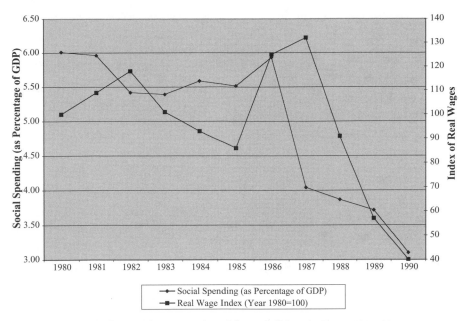

Figure 7.5.   Trends in Real Wages and Social Expenditures in Peru, 1980–1991.
Note: The index of real wages equals 100 in 1980, the base year. *Source:* Data on real wages from Verdera (1997a).

of incentives toward the export sector.[19] Figure 7.6 graphically represents the evolution of these trends.

The First Government of Alberto Fujimori (1990–1992)

Within this context of macroeconomic chaos, Alberto Fujimori, an engineer with no prior political experience, defeated world-renowned novelist Mario Vargas Llosa in the 1990 presidential election. Fujimori campaigned on a platform that promised no radical program of economic reform and severely criticized Vargas Llosa's electoral platform, which included a strong orthodox program of structural adjustment aimed at reducing the deficit and ending the devastating bout of hyperinflation. Once in office, however, Fujimori started an even more radical program of economic reform than

[19] The appreciation of the real exchange rate during this period was enormous. Whereas $1 was worth 6.4 soles (the Peruvian national currency) in 1980, by 1990 $1 was worth only 2.9 soles. This made it increasingly difficult for national producers of tradable goods to compete in international markets. At the same time, the appreciation of the real exchange rate did not result in substantial increases in imports because of the relatively high levels of tariff protections and other restrictions to free trade. Using an index that measures the degree of trade liberalization (1 = no restrictions to trade, 0 = maximum protectionism), Morley et al. (1999) estimate that the index of trade liberalization deteriorated in Peru in the 1980s, from 0.76 in 1980 to 0.56 in 1990.

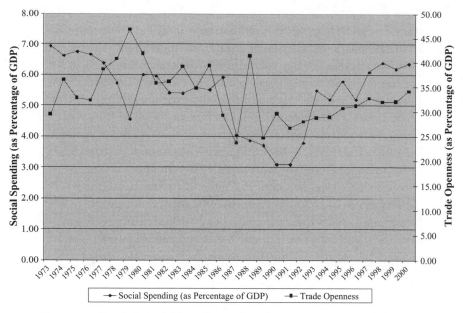

Figure 7.6. Trends in Social Spending and Trade Openness in Peru, 1973–2000.

the one Vargas Llosa had proposed during his campaign. This program also affected social expenditures, which hit an all-time low of 2.1 percent of GDP in 1991 – the lowest level in recorded history. Then, on April 5, 1992, Fujimori suspended the constitution, dissolved Congress and regional governments, and purged most of the judiciary in a military-backed *autogolpe* (i.e., self-coup).[20]

7.3 Social Policies under Fujimori's Authoritarian Rule (1991–2000)

Social expenditures after the April 1992 self-coup began a steep increase, especially after 1994. Overall, from 1991 (the year before the coup) to 2000 (the last full year of the Fujimori administration), social expenditures rose by almost 300 percent. How can we explain this tremendous, unprecedented increase in social expenditures in Peru during a period of authoritarian rule? According to our initial theoretical expectations and econometric results,

[20] This chapter focuses on the consequences of the *autogolpe* for the Peruvian welfare system rather than on the causes of the coup itself. For a comprehensive analysis of the economic and political environment that led to the 1992 self-coup, see Tanaka (1992). See also Kenney (1992) and McClintock (1996).

should we not expect democracies, rather than autocracies, to increase social spending levels? This subsection analyzes why a nondemocratic regime can also expand social welfare expenditures if it has certain (electoral) incentives to do so.

The explanation for this unprecedented expansion of social expenditures during Fujimori's presidency has both an economic and a political component. At the economic level, Fujimori reestablished economic growth, eliminated hyperinflation, and reformed the agency in charge of tax collection to limit tax evasion. At the political level, Fujimori used social welfare expenditures selectively to increase his chances of electoral success. As discussed herein, he expanded health, education, and pro-poor programs not in the provinces that most needed them given their social indicators but rather in those provinces of the country where surveys indicated that his chances of electoral success were more difficult. The following sections explore both the economic and political determinants of this unprecedented expansion of social expenditures in Peru.

The Economic Basis of the Expansion of Social Expenditures

After a period of international isolation and negative economic growth, by 1993 the economy began to exhibit important levels of economic growth. Average real GDP growth from 1993 to 1997 exceeded 7 percent, one of the highest in the region. Economic growth coupled with a comprehensive process of tax reform led to a substantial increase in fiscal revenues, which grew from 9 percent to more than 14 percent of GDP – a relative increase of more than 50 percent.

As Table 7.2 shows, the reorganization of the National Superintendency for Tax Administration (i.e., Superintendencia Nacional de Administración Tributaria, or SUNAT), the public agency in charge of collecting taxes, had a huge impact on the number of taxpayers and the total amount of tax revenue collected.

In addition to an increasingly greater flow of tax revenues, the government embarked on a process of privatization of public enterprises that led to a huge expansion of nontax revenues as well. The privatization of public enterprises began in June 1991 and expanded quickly. By 1997, the government had privatized 132 of a total of 186 public enterprises. As Table 7.3 shows, this generated a tremendous amount of additional resources available to the government. These higher levels of tax and nontax fiscal revenue provided the government with a significantly greater capacity to increase social spending levels.

Table 7.2. *Evolution of the Total Number of*
Taxpayers and Fiscal Revenue in Peru,
1990–1997

Year	Total Number of Taxpayers	Tax Revenues (in millions of U.S. dollars)
1990	287,075	2,850
1991	515,845	3,560
1992	545,196	4,053
1993	696,584	3,781
1994	890,008	5,468
1995	1,223,743	6,695
1996	1,748,899	8,139
1997	1,637,281	8,621

Source: Data provided to the author by the Ministry of Finance in Lima.

The growth of social expenditures was more moderate during 1991–1992, but it exploded after the 1992 self-coup. As Roberts argued, "during Fujimori's first years in office, few economic instruments were available to ameliorate the social costs of the stabilization plan and sustain his initial base of popular support. The shock program of August 1990 had a severe impact on popular living standards; it was administered largely without anesthesia, that is, with only a paltry compensation plan to cushion the impact of price increases, job losses, and wage cuts (...) although Fujimori promised to spend over $400 million in the months after the shock program to protect the poorest sectors, only $90 million was actually spent on programs to alleviate poverty, and other forms of spending were being cut."[21]

Fujimori established a new program called FONCODES in 1991 to administer poverty-relief programs, but the program was understaffed and lacked the administrative capacity to spend all the funds it was allocated. By 1994, the budget of FONCODES called for an expenditure in poverty-relief programs of more than $170 million, yet about half of the funds were never spent.[22] After 1994, however, social expenditures as percentage of GDP experienced the most spectacular relative growth in Latin America, increasing from 2.8 percent of GDP in 1994 to 8.2 percent in 1997. The sharp increase in social expenditures during this period cannot be understood

---

[21] Roberts (1997, 101–102).
[22] See the weekly political review *Caretas*, July 27, 1994.

Table 7.3. *The Privatization of Public Enterprises
in Peru, 1991–1997*

Year	Number of Privatized Public Enterprises	Revenue from Privatization (in millions of U.S. dollars)
1991	2	2.6
1992	10	219.9
1993	13	506.8
1994	25	2,983.6
1995	17	1,018.9
1996	36	2,272.2
1997	29	549.5

Source: Gonzales de Olarte, Efraín, 1998, *El Neoliberalismo
a la Peruana: Economía Política del Ajuste Estructural, 1990–
1997*; Lima: Instituto de Estudios Peruanos, p. 55.

as the sole result of a changing economic environment. Political factors, as the next section demonstrates, are crucial to understanding why social expenditures rose so dramatically in Peru after Fujimori's self-coup.

Figure 7.7 presents the evolution of public expenditures on health and education and those of social security programs (excluding pro-poor programs). The figure suggests that health and education expenditures experienced a huge increase after 1994, but at the same time social security expenditures began to decline relatively fast. However, for analytical purposes, it is necessary to distinguish two different types of social security expenditures that followed very different paths. On the one hand, pensions and other work-related programs of social protection (e.g., unemployment compensation, maternity allowances) declined significantly during this period. As explained in the next subsection, pressures from export-oriented business groups worried about international competition played an important role in the reduction of employer's payroll taxes and the almost absolute flexibilization of the labor market. On the other hand, however, pro-poor programs, also classified by the IMF within the social security-expenditures category, experienced tremendous growth.

The Decline of Pensions and Other Work-Related Social Benefits
As illustrated in Figure 7.4, after 1994 there was a significant expansion of trade openness and a concurrent reduction of social security expenditures. This reduction of social security expenditures affected primarily

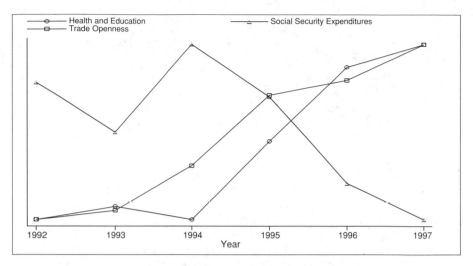

Figure 7.7. Trade Openness and Public Expenditures (Excluding Health, Education, and Pro-Poor Programs) under Fujimori's Authoritarian Regime.
Note: The scale on the y-axis is not shown because the graph has been rescaled to facilitate the analysis of the relative importance of the changes within the three variables at the same time. As a result, the different trends in the graph can therefore be compared. Each unit increase/decrease in the graph for every trend has the same relative magnitude with respect to the levels of the original variable.

work-related programs of social protection, which account for between two thirds and three fourths of all social security expenditures. There are two interrelated mechanisms through which greater levels of trade openness were associated with declining levels of social security expenditures. The first is a political–ideological mechanism; the second, an economic one. Let us begin with the political mechanism. Business groups liked the pragmatic character of President Fujimori, who was generally seen as responsible for the stabilization of the economy. Fujimori had inherited in 1990 a deep economic recession, one of the highest inflation levels ever recorded in Latin America, and a very low level of tax revenues. As Table 7.4 shows, by 1992–1993, he had managed to stabilize the economy.

Many prominent business figures even accompanied official delegations traveling around the country to explain why the 1992 coup was necessary. However, the radical program of structural adjustment implemented in 1992–1994 took many business leaders by surprise. The program implemented by Fujimori was actually very similar to the one the business community had helped to elaborate for Vargas Llosa, the defeated candidate in the 1990 elections. In the 1990 election, Fujimori had run on a platform

Table 7.4. *Economic Trends in Peru under Fujimori, 1990–2000*

Year	Tax Revenues (in percent of GDP)	Inflation	GDP Growth	Overall Fiscal Balance (in percent of GDP)
1990	9.64	7481.66	−5.14	−8.55
1991	9.62	409.53	2.17	−1.75
1992	13.14	73.53	−0.43	−3.05
1993	12.87	48.58	4.76	−3.23
1994	14.85	23.74	12.82	−2.79
1995	15.41	11.13	8.58	−3.07
1996	16.29	11.54	2.49	−1.15
1997	16.12	8.56	6.84	−0.61
1998	17.89	7.25	−0.65	−0.60
1999	16.76	3.47	0.91	−3.16
2000	16.97	3.76	2.82	−2.75

that promised a moderate and heterodox program of adjustment, and the business community had endorsed Vargas Llosa's more orthodox program of market-oriented reform. As Cotler suggested, this allowed Fujimori to keep business groups at a distance. The president felt he did not owe them anything and, hence, he did not seek their advice in the design and implementation of structural adjustment policies during his first two years in office. Rather, the president, much like Pinochet in Chile, sought the advice of a small group of "technocrats" and maintained links only with those sectors of the business community that were ready to accept without question the economic package approved by multilateral international organizations such as the IMF and the World Bank. Fujimori's strategy was to move decisively fast in its process of market-oriented reform, which included trade liberalization as one of the key reforms. Thus, he acted preemptively, in anticipation of the possible pressures from export-oriented business groups, who were in favor of trade liberalization, as well as those of businesses in import-competing sectors, which would seek continuing protectionism and therefore oppose trade liberalization.[23]

Within this context, Carlos Boloña – an Oxford-trained economist who became Finance Minister in 1991 – eliminated the system of multiple exchange rates, floated the "sol" (i.e., the national currency in Peru), and initiated a process of trade liberalization that standardized and reduced average

---

[23] See Cotler (1998a, 12).

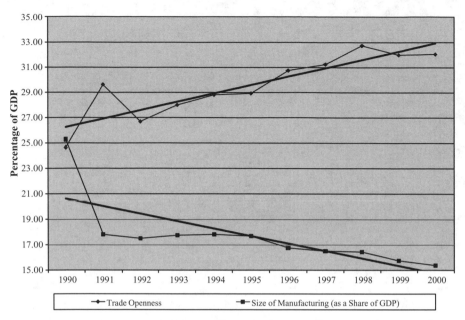

Figure 7.8. Trade Openness and the Size of the Manufacturing Sector in Peru, 1990–2000.

tariffs to 26 percent (the previous average tariff was close to 100 percent). The process of trade liberalization was fast and radical, following on the Chilean footsteps, and its impact on the domestic industrial sector was substantial. Many companies in import-competing sectors, previously protected by tariffs and import quotas from international-market competition, were unable to adapt to the new competitive environment once the trade barriers were eliminated. The size of the industrial sector (as measured by its share of GDP) declined from 43 to 34 percent in 1990–1995, and many workers previously employed in this sector lost their jobs and either became unemployed, moved to the service sector, or joined the informal sector; as a result, their level of social security coverage deteriorated. Figure 7.8 describes the relationship between trade openness and the size of the industrial sector. The increase in trade openness was the direct result of the process of fast trade liberalization (i.e., most of the restrictions to international trade were eliminated in 1991–1992). After 1991, trade liberalization had a significant impact on the degree of trade openness of the economy. Also, as a direct result of this increasing exposure to international-market competition, the size of the industrial sector declined quickly.

In addition, the program of trade liberalization took place in a context of labor-market deregulation, privatization of public enterprises, and fiscal reform aimed at reducing the size of the state and eliminating the fiscal

Table 7.5. *Labor-Market Conditions in Peru before and after the Reforms*

	Pre-Reform 1990–1991	Post-Reform 1994–1995
SOCIAL SECURITY CONTRIBUTIONS		
Employer Contributions		
• Pensions	6.0	0.0
• Health	6.0	6.0
• Unemployment[a]	8.3	9.7
Worker Contributions		
• Pensions	3.0	16.0
• Health	3.0	3.0
WAGES		
• Net Wage	100.0	88.0
• Minimum Wage	100.0	70.0
JOB SECURITY		
• Percentage of Indefinite Contracts	61.4	42.3
• Percentage of Temporary Contracts	38.6	57.7

[a] In Peru, there is no unemployment insurance per se. However, there is a program called CTS (Compensación por Tiempo de Servicios), whereby workers accumulate a percentage of their salary in a fund administered by the company. If the worker is dismissed or moves to another job, the company pays the worker the full amount accumulated in this fund.

Sources: Figures on social security contributions come from the ILO, based on official figures. Data on wages were calculated by the author on the basis of information provided by the Ministry of Labor and Social Development (Ministerio de Trabajo y Promoción Social). Data on labor-market conditions come from Verdera, Francisco, 1997a, *Mercados de trabajo, reforma laboral y creación de empleo: Perú, 1990–95*; Lima: Instituto de Estudios Peruanos, Documento de trabajo #87, p. 22.

deficit. Fujimori, with the support of his Finance Minister and the advice of multilateral organizations, regarded these economic measures as the only possible cure to restore the overall macroeconomic stability and efficiency of the economy. From this perspective, the president did not wait, for example, for the pressures of export-oriented business groups to reduce nonwage costs such as payroll taxes or deregulate the labor market. He acted preemptively, sure of the technical capacity of his finance minister and the recommendations from the IMF and the World Bank.

Table 7.5 summarizes the major changes in labor-market conditions in Peru. Regarding social security contributions, payroll taxes for health care of both workers and employers remained unchanged with the reform, but employers' contributions to the pension system were eliminated and those of workers' raised from 3 to 16 percent of their wage. As a result, the average net wage declined by about 12 percent. In addition, the minimum wage also declined by 30 percent. However, the most significant impact of the reform was the flexibilization of the labor market. In 1991, most restrictions that made it difficult for employers to dismiss workers were eliminated and by 1995, the law authorized employers to fire workers without the need to provide *any* justification.[24] As a result, the number of temporary contracts increased from 38.6 percent of all contracts in 1990 to 57.7 percent in 1995. The net result of the process of trade liberalization and labor-market flexibilization was a large increase in the supply of labor, which exerted downward pressure on real wages and forced workers to accept employment with lower-quality working conditions and worse social benefits.

The Political Determinants of the Expansion of Poverty-Relief Expenditures

Until 1993, Fujimori had relied on nonmaterial factors to sustain his popular support. He campaigned against the traditional political parties, accusing them of corruption, and he benefited from the rise in popular support associated with the capture in 1992 of Abimael Guzmán, the leader of the terrorist organization Shining Path. By 1993, economic conditions had improved and the links with international lending institutions had been reestablished. Government spending on poverty programs doubled in 1993. By the end of 1993, FONCODES had initiated ten thousand small-scale education, nutrition, sanitation, and health-care projects.[25] As Roberts noted, "between the April 1992 *autogolpe* and the November [sic] 1993 Constitutional referendum, Fujimori personally dedicated seventy-one schools, mostly in lower-class urban districts."[26]

Despite the economic recovery of 1993, in which the economy grew by more than 6 percent, and the increase in social spending levels, Fujimori won the October 1993 constitutional referendum by a small margin. Although he won in the capital (Lima), he lost in most other departments outside Lima. This reflected the fact that the benefits of economic stabilization had concentrated in Lima and that voters in rural areas had serious doubts about several aspects of Fujimori's economic and social policies. As Graham and Kane noted, "whatever the reasons for Fujimori's losses outside Lima, the national government seems to have taken the message seriously and

---

[24] The so-called arbitrary dismissal, whereby the employer decides to fire a worker without justification, only required the employer to pay one salary per every year the worker had been in the company, up to a maximum of twelve salaries.

[25] Interview with Arturo Woodman, former director of FONCODES, in *Caretas*, July 27, 1994.

[26] Roberts (1996, 101).

Table 7.6. *Annual Expenditures on Poverty Relief*
Programs in Peru, 1993–1996

Year	Expenditures on Poverty Relief Programs (in millions of U.S. dollars)
1993	318
1994	398
1995	1,007
1996	1,112

Source: Epstein, Edward. 1998. "Participation by the Poor in Government Anti-Poverty Programs: The Cases of Chile, Peru, and Argentina Compared"; Paper presented at the 1998 meeting of the Latin American Studies Association, Chicago, September 24–26, 1998.

responded with major increases in discretionary public expenditures outside the capital, particularly in some departments where the 'no' vote was high."[27]

In early 1994, the Fujimori regime received more than $2 billion from the sale of Peru's state-owned telephone and telecommunication industries to a Spanish-led consortium of investors. This sum represented more than half of Peru's annual export earnings. Although the IMF encouraged Peru to use this unexpected economic windfall for debt repayment, Fujimori insisted that most of the unexpected funds were invested in social programs to fight poverty. He managed to get IMF approval to double the amount devoted to social-emergency expenditures, announced a $400 million campaign to build thirty-one thousand homes, and promised to build two to three schools per day in 1995. Table 7.6 summarizes the enormous expansion of poverty-relief expenditures, which grew from $300 million to $400 million per year in 1993–1994 and to more than $1 billion in 1995–1996.

However, it is also important to note that the timing and manner in which these new social programs were implemented involved a great deal of political manipulation. In fact, as Roberts has argued, "the political manipulation was so blatant that the council which oversees national elections – a body not known at the time for its independence from the executive branch – proposed legislation in late 1994 that would prohibit an incumbent president from inaugurating public works, distributing goods, or even speaking of public works during a presidential campaign."[28]

---

[27] Graham and Kane (1998, 80).
[28] Roberts (1996, 104).

In short, the tremendous expansion of human capital and pro-poor expenditures in Peru during the 1995–1997 period was made possible by a positive economic environment and the improvement of fiscal revenues associated with international aid and the privatization of key public enterprises. With respect to expenditures on health and education, there is good evidence that the labor-market dynamics discussed previously did not apply. In fact, the available evidence suggests that business groups not only did not press the government to cut down public expenditures on health and education but also actually expressed to the government the need to expand the scope and improve the quality of the educational system. The widespread view of the business community was that higher levels of education were absolutely necessary to facilitate the adaptation of the labor force to technological change and the pressures of international-market competition.[29] Similarly, business groups also manifested their interest in improving the health of their workers, arguing that there can be "no healthy firms in a sick country."[30]

However, neither the improved economic situation after the process of structural reform nor the apparent agreement of business groups to expand human capital expenditures can explain on their own the huge increase in education, health, and pro-poor programs during those years. Political factors are a key part of the explanation, which is based on a relatively simple argument: Fujimori used social programs selectively to manipulate electoral results. Graham and Kane analyzed patterns in discretionary public expenditures (e.g., emergency social fund, municipal transfers, and school-building programs) and electoral data for a number of elections[31] in an attempt to determine the criteria for allocating expenditures across the different provinces (*departamentos*) of Peru. Using multivariate regression analysis, they concluded that high levels of social expenditures were associated with significant increases in support for Fujimori from 1993 to 1995. Fujimori increased expenditures the most in those provinces where his support in the 1993 constitutional referendum had been the lowest. As a result, in the 1995 elections, his level of support had increased substantially.

---

[29] This is the view of a number of key business leaders that the author interviewed in Lima between May and September 2001. A similar conclusion is reached by Cotler (1998a), who interviewed more than thirty of the most important business leaders in Peru.

[30] See the statement published by the main business organization of export groups (Sociedad Nacional de Exportadores, SNE 1997).

[31] The November 1992 constituent assembly election, the municipal elections of January 1993, the constitutional referendum in October 1993, national elections in April 1995, and municipal elections in November 1995.

Table 7.7. *Changes in Electoral Support for*
Fujimori in the Five Provinces
(Departamentos) *Where Discretionary Social*
Expenditures Increased the Most during
1993–1995

	Vote for Fujimori in 1993	Vote for Fujimori in 1995
Puno	17%	63%
Cuzco	32%	67%
Huancavelica	32%	64%
Amazonas	34%	61%
Ayacucho	39%	70%

Source: Graham and Kane (1995, 21).

As Table 7.7 shows, Fujimori was successful in his strategy of selectively using discretionary social expenditures. The five provinces where his electoral support had been the lowest saw the largest relative increases in social expenditures. As a result of these social programs, support for Fujimori in these provinces, which had averaged about one third of the vote in 1993, had increased to about two thirds of the vote by 1995. The most spectacular case is Puno (famous for Lake Titicaca – the highest navigable lake in the world), where the popular vote for Fujimori increased from 17 percent in 1993 to 63 percent in 1995!

However, these enormous increases in social expenditures also had consequences for the form and efficiency in which expenditures were used. On the one hand, there was a lack of coordination among the different agencies with social-policy responsibilities and a continuous erosion of intermediary social and political institutions. What is worse, social expenditures did not respond to actual social needs but rather to political imperatives to gain or maintain popularity levels. For example, the number of schools built by the Fujimori administration in different provinces of the country cannot be explained by differences in illiteracy rates. In fact, except in Huancavelica, many of the provinces with high illiteracy rates received relatively low investments in public education. In short, social expenditures experienced a tremendous growth, but they were often "allocated in a manner having little to do with relative levels of poverty or social indicators, with benefits going disproportionately to less-needy groups."[32]

[32] Graham and Kane (1998, 27–28).

Despite Fujimori's initial success in stabilizing the economy and the strategy just described of partisan use of social spending, a slower level of economic growth changed the economic and political dynamics of Fujimori's second term. Approval for his economic program began to fall in 1996. As of mid-1996, his approval rating began to fall behind his disapproval rating, and it continued to fall steadily through 1999. His legitimacy was particularly eroded by his continuous efforts to concentrate authority in the Executive and eliminate all mechanisms of horizontal accountability. Because Fujimori's reelection in 2000 was unconstitutional (given that the Constitution only allowed one reelection), the entire institutional order had to be changed to give his reelection an appearance of legality. To this end, the Constitutional Court was purged with the removal of three of its seven members, and Congress (dominated by the president's supporters) stopped a referendum on Fujimori's reelection. In the end, Fujimori's policies, including his politically driven social programs, had focused only on the short term and, once economic growth began to slow down, were unable to offset the president's continuous attacks on the institutional order (Tanaka, 2003, 226).

7.4 Conclusion

We can draw three broad conclusions from the Peruvian case, which illustrates a number of causal mechanisms underlying the statistical associations described in Chapters 3 and 4 and have broader theoretical implications for the analysis of welfare systems. The first conclusion is that although a sound and balanced macroeconomic policy is not necessarily a good social policy in itself, a bad macroeconomic policy is always a bad social policy in the intermediate to long term. Chile in the 1970s and 1980s tried to reestablish basic economic equilibria and gave only secondary importance to social policy; as a result, some social indicators like inequality deteriorated. In Peru, by contrast, the inability (or unwillingness) of the democratic governments in the 1980s to maintain a minimum equilibrium in the most basic macroeconomic indicators (e.g., inflation, fiscal deficit) ended in total macroeconomic chaos, a sharp drop in output, a dramatic erosion of fiscal revenues, and the inability of the state to provide even the most basic social services.

The second lesson we can draw from the Peruvian case is similar to one that was also observed in the case of Chile: a process of fast and radical economic reform, facilitated by an extreme concentration of power in the Executive and the virtual elimination of all resistance from civil and political society, has a strong negative effect on employment-based social protection.

The fast process of trade liberalization and the radical flexibilization of the labor market in the 1990s led to a significant decline in the size of the industrial sector, a huge increase in the percentage of temporary contracts, and an expanding flow of workers into the service and informal sector – where social protection is usually lower. Business groups lobbied in favor of a reduction of labor costs, but the insulation of the Executive (which, after the 1992 coup, began to rule by decree) makes it difficult to determine whether the reductions in employer-based labor taxes[33] (used to finance social security expenditures) and the flexibilization of the labor market were the consequence of these pressures or rather the result of an ideological conviction of key policymakers, and Fujimori himself, that lower wage and nonwage labor costs and a flexible labor market were necessary to ensure greater efficiency and capacity to compete in international markets.

Finally, the Peruvian case also illustrates why we should not expect a direct relationship between democracy and social expenditures. Authoritarian regimes may in fact increase social spending as much or even more than democratic regimes if they have political incentives to do so. In Chile, there were no presidential or congressional elections between the 1973 coup and the 1988 plebiscite to decide whether Pinochet would continue in power for eight more years. Hence, until 1988, Pinochet felt no electoral pressures to use social expenditures to his advantage. In fact, as Chapter 5 demonstrated, the first time he felt that he might lose his personal power grip (i.e., right before the plebiscite to decide whether he could continue as president after 1988) and during the 1989 presidential election in which he wanted to favor his former Finance Minister (i.e., Hernan Buchi), social expenditures rose dramatically. Similarly, in Peru after the process of economic reform of the early 1990s, Fujimori saw that his support among low-income groups was declining. In the 1993 constitutional referendum, which he almost lost, low-income groups (who had been hit the hardest by structural-reform programs) voted against him. Fujimori immediately moved to "remedy" this problem. Taking advantage of a better economic environment and the expansion of fiscal revenues associated with tax reforms and privatizations, he immediately began to expand social expenditures on education, health, and pro-poor programs. The evidence clearly demonstrates that the expansion of these expenditures was not based on need but rather on political

---

[33] In fact, the nonwage costs paid by employers followed a highly volatile pattern. The effective rate of taxation increased from about 52 percent in July 1990 to 56 percent in July 1991. Then they dropped dramatically to 40 percent in January 1993, but by the end of the year, they increased to 46 percent. They then increased again to 53 percent in July 1995, to be reduced again to 50 percent in July 1997 (Saavedra and Torero 2004, 143).

opportunity. Schools, hospitals, and pro-poor programs were not higher in the provinces that most needed them but rather in those in which Fujimori had seen his electoral basis of support decline the most. This dynamic would never have been possible in Costa Rica, where the legislature and its strong two-party system are capable of holding the government accountable for its actions in the public realm, and where relatively autonomous institutions have the bureaucratic capacity to implement key social programs (and, hence, the government had much less freedom to manipulate social policies at its convenience).

8

Conclusion

Summary and Final Reflections on
the Sustainability and Effectiveness of
Latin American Welfare Systems

This book has studied the reasons why some Latin American countries have historically constructed more developed welfare systems than others during the preglobalization period (i.e., 1920s–1970s) and how these welfare systems have been transformed by the more recent processes of globalization and democratization that have swept Latin America during the last three decades. This concluding chapter recapitulates the main findings, highlights some limitations of the study, and suggests a number of areas for future research. The chapter is divided in two sections. The first section provides an overview of the main findings regarding (1) the historical development of welfare systems in Latin America, (2) the determinants of changes in social spending in the 1973–2003 period, and (3) the in-depth case studies of Chile, Costa Rica, and Peru.

The second section briefly analyzes two of the most important challenges facing Latin American welfare systems in the future and suggests a number of issues for future research. The first challenge is how to reconcile current levels of welfare effort, or even expand them, within existing macroeconomic (especially fiscal) constraints. As the cases of Chile under Allende (1970–1973) and Peru under García (1980–1985) demonstrated, to expand social welfare without paying attention to basic macroeconomic fundamentals has devastating consequences for the economy at large and the welfare state in particular. The second challenge is how to increase the effectiveness of Latin American welfare systems. Although this book has taken the welfare state as a dependent variable, and looking at the effects of the welfare state as an independent variable is, in fact, beyond the scope of this study, this section briefly compares the effect of the welfare state on one of its most studied effects: income inequality. To this end, a brief comparison of the tentative impact of different types of expenditures on income inequality in advanced industrial democracies and in Latin America is presented. Both the long-term

259

expansion and sustainability of the welfare state and its effects on social welfare outcomes are important areas that deserve future research. If the chapter cannot provide sufficiently convincing answers to all the questions raised, it at least points to some directions that are clearly worth pursuing in future research endeavors.

8.1 Overview of Main Findings

Historical Origins and Development of Latin American Welfare Systems 1920s –1970s

As shown in Chapter 2, although the emergence of welfare systems in Latin America was influenced by pressures from powerful groups (e.g., the military, senior civil servants, white-collar workers), we cannot simply assume that initial social legislation was an automatic governmental response to group pressures. In fact, in many Latin American countries, states introduced social legislation as a mechanism to control increasingly mobilized labor movements and urban middle classes. In Chile and Argentina, for example, bottom-up pressures from a rapidly expanding critical mass of workers in the industrial sector played a critical role. However, political elites often acted preemptively, not in response to specific class demands but rather in a deliberate effort to co-opt, control, and hence demobilize key groups. The origins of the welfare state in Latin America – like in many of its Western European counterparts – is therefore best understood as a top-down reform project aimed at achieving two simultaneous objectives. The first was to consolidate divisions among different economic and social groups in order to prevent possible challenges to state power. This was typically accomplished through particular social legislation for different economic classes and status groups. Each program had its own legally embedded set of rights and privileges, and its timing and scope tended to reflect the top-down, rigidly stratified structure of Latin American societies. It is, therefore, no coincidence that social security coverage (e.g., pensions, health insurance) started with the military, civil servants, and judiciary and later extended to the liberal professions and workers in the best organized and strategically located sectors of the middle and working classes. In most cases, coverage never extended to the self-employed and those working in the informal sector, whose size in Latin America ranges between one and two thirds of the economically active working population. The second objective was to tie the loyalty of key social groups (i.e., the military, senior civil servants, and an increasingly mobilized industrial class) directly to the central authority of the state. This had also been Bismarck's main motivation when he introduced in the 1880s the first comprehensive social legislation in Germany, which would become a model for many Western European nations (especially Austria, Italy, and France) and elsewhere. Batlle in Uruguay, Vargas in Brazil, Ibáñez in Chile, Perón in Argentina, and Calderón Guardia in Costa Rica were driven by similar motivations when they introduced or effectively enforced new social legislation in their countries.

However, whereas it is true that the emergence of welfare systems in Western Europe and in Latin America cannot be understood without specifically acknowledging the fundamental role played by the state, it is also true that we can hardly understand its expansion and development in subsequent decades without paying attention to other economic and political factors. After all, the same motivation for top-down social control led Oscar Benavides in Peru and Avila-Camacho in Mexico to introduce the first relatively comprehensive social legislation in 1936 and 1941, respectively. However, neither Mexico nor Peru (or any other country in Latin America,[1] for that matter) was able to construct, during subsequent decades, welfare systems of the same depth and scope as those in Argentina, Brazil, Chile, Costa Rica, and Uruguay.

Chapter 2 analyzed four economic and political variables in an attempt to explain these divergent outcomes, and used QCA to specify two alternative paths to the welfare state in Latin America. The first path – with favorable economic conditions – combined economic development *and* a protected economy from international markets (i.e., limited trade openness) with *either* democracy (Brazil) *or* left-labor power (Argentina), or both (Chile and Uruguay). The second path – with unfavorable economic conditions – combined democracy and left-labor power with trade openness in the absence of substantial economic development (Costa Rica). The specific contributions of each variable are discussed in detail in Chapter 2. However, for scholars interested in the comparative analysis of the welfare state, there is one striking finding in this chapter that deserves some additional reflection: unlike in Western Europe, welfare systems in Latin America developed in the context of ISI – an inward-looking model of development that rested on a mix of policies regarding tariffs, licenses, quotas, and exchange rates that shielded domestic producers (especially in manufacturing) from

---

[1] The reference is to the following countries for which Chapter 2 systematically presented data: Venezuela, Bolivia, Dominican Republic, El Salvador, Ecuador, Guatemala, and Paraguay, in addition to the cases of Mexico and Peru noted previously. The only country that is not in the sample and developed a rather comprehensive system of public health and education is Cuba.

international-market competition. Four of the five Latin American welfare states (i.e., Argentina, Brazil, Chile, and Uruguay) developed under ISI, and even Costa Rica (the other welfare state), which always maintained a relatively more open economy, turned to ISI in the 1960s. The only relatively closed economy before the 1980s that did not become a welfare state in Latin America was Mexico, and Chapter 2 explains some of the reasons why this might have been the case. In contrast, with the noted exception of Costa Rica, all other Latin American countries under study that remained significantly open to trade during the preglobalization period (1920s–1970s) failed to construct relatively developed welfare systems. How can we explain this outcome in light of the evidence from advanced industrial countries that the most significant expansion of the welfare state occurred in small trade-dependent economies such as Austria, Belgium, Denmark, the Netherlands, and Sweden?

One possible answer is that in these European countries, the welfare state developed after 1945 within a context of continuous democracy and the existence of relatively powerful labor unions organically tied to left-oriented parties, which enjoyed significant levels of electoral success. Trade openness in these countries did not curtail significantly the ability of governments to manage aggregate demand and control the levels of unemployment and capital formation, because with a relatively closed capital account, fiscal policy could still be used for domestic-policy purposes. At the same time, trade openness in a number of countries was associated with higher levels of industrial concentration. In those countries in which industrialization was based on exports (because of the limited size of their domestic markets), a few large firms had an unusually large share of production and employment. The labor force was, therefore, less differentiated in terms of occupation and less fragmented, which facilitated high levels of worker unionization. At the same time, industrial concentration was associated with systems of centralized collective bargaining. In such systems, wages and labor standards are negotiated for the whole economy among the state, labor unions, and employer confederations. Because union leaders represent most of the working class, employer confederations know that the agreements they reach are more likely to be respected and their resistance to unions is therefore reduced. This combination of factors made labor unions strong and homogeneous, representing most of the working class, and provided the critical basis of electoral support for Labor and Social Democratic parties that, once in power, expanded social welfare. Furthermore, in some cases (e.g., Austria, Belgium, and the Netherlands) when parties of the Left were not in power, the other dominant party (usually Christian Democratic) either did not wish to roll back social expenditures because it also shared a commitment to the welfare state as an instrument of social solidarity or was unable to do so because the system had already generated a large group of stakeholders that would critically oppose such strategy.

In contrast, as noted previously, welfare systems in Latin America developed in the context of limited trade openness associated with ISI. ISI fostered the consolidation of the domestic industrial sector and facilitated the expansion of a critical mass of workers who, depending on other labor-market and political conditions, gained the capacity to act collectively in the pursuit of state-sponsored social programs. However, because of the nature of late, capital-intensive, dependent development, ISI did not manage to expand the size of the industrial class to the same extent as in Western Europe. There was never the degree of industrial concentration that facilitated labor unionization and the establishment of a centralized system of collective bargaining. To the contrary, there was a predominance of small enterprises characterized by paternalistic relations, many of which tended to operate in the informal sector beyond the regulation of labor and social security legislation. As a result, large sectors of the urban population never received significant levels of social protection, which was even more limited if not totally absent in most rural areas. The main difference between Latin American and Western European welfare systems lies, therefore, in the much more fragmented and limited effective coverage of the former. The most developed welfare states in Latin America (i.e., probably Costa Rica and Uruguay) still would lag behind in terms of the quality, scope, and coverage of their systems of social protection when compared to Western European standards.

Yet, this is only part of the story. What happened with the highly trade-dependent countries in Latin America (especially in Central America and in the Andean region)? Why did trade openness in these cases not lead to demands for compensation as in Western Europe? First, unlike their Western European counterparts, these countries were relatively poor and had a comparative advantage in the production and export of agricultural and mineral products rather than in export-oriented manufacturing industries. Limited levels of industrialization and economic development never created a sufficiently large critical mass of workers that could press the state for significant welfare reform. Furthermore, except in the rather exceptional case of Costa Rica, none of these countries remained continuously democratic for a significant period.

Finally, in most cases, parties of the Left did either not have a sufficiently large constituency or, when they did, they were often banned from participating in national elections (as in the case of APRA in Peru). Hence, in the

Latin American case, trade openness did not lead to industrial concentration; it did not foster higher levels of unionization; and, in the absence of democracy, demands for compensation were either not voiced by groups that may have suffered the consequences of trade openness or not heard because governments were not accountable to citizens for their actions in the public realm through regular elections.

The Evolution of Latin American Welfare Systems in the Era of Globalization and "Third Wave" Democratization, 1973–2003

Chapter 3 presented the main economic and political hypotheses that provided the basic theoretical framework to study the evolution of Latin American welfare systems from the early 1970s onward. Chapter 4 tested these hypotheses using a TSCS data set of fourteen Latin American countries from 1973 to 2003. These two chapters analyzed why the relationship between globalization and welfare state development in Latin American has been affected by different forces than the ones observed in Western European countries. The results suggested that growing levels of trade integration had a substantial negative effect on aggregate social expenditures, with the effect being driven entirely by the social security-spending category. In addition, the effect was much larger for the group of welfare states (which had embraced ISI for significant periods before the mid-1970s) than for the group of non-welfare states that had, on average, been historically much more open to international markets. Integration into global capital markets affected social spending only to the extent that markets perceived the fiscal deficit to be unsustainable.

The importance of these findings can hardly be overstated. It could not contrast more starkly with the experience of advanced capitalist democracies, especially in Western Europe. Globalization in Latin America was not associated with an expansion of welfare effort as a state-led policy to compensate the losers from international economic integration. Instead, it unleashed a series of forces that put downward pressure on Latin America's beleaguered welfare systems. First, economic openness increased the social value that key actors attached to economic stability. In a number of countries, high social spending levels had contributed to chronic fiscal deficits that were associated with unsustainable public-debt levels, high inflation, overvalued exchange rates, and a loss of international reserves leading in some cases to a currency crisis. In a more open economic environment, the need to be competitive in international markets placed a particular premium on macroeconomic stability. Within this context, the need to reduce fiscal deficits put downward pressures on public-spending levels and extended to social expenditures, which account for between one and two thirds of Latin America's public budgets.

Second, globalization also introduced other changes in the economy and in labor markets that affected the structure of previously dominant companies in import-competing sectors, characteristic of the ISI model described in Chapter 2. Trade liberalization eliminated the previous system of protection, led to the destruction of firms that were no longer able to compete, and forced surviving firms in import-competing sectors to be more efficient. As a result, in a number of countries, employment in the manufacturing sector declined, the service sector expanded, greater labor-market flexibility was introduced, and real wages fell. This was also accompanied by a relative increase in the size of the informal economy. All these changes weakened the link between employment and social protection (i.e., social security benefits) as many workers saw their welfare entitlements reduced or eliminated. At the same time, trade unions were weakened, with affiliation rates declining in practically all countries in the region,[2] and the low level of institutionalization of the party system implied that the traditional Western European "organic" link between trade unions and left-oriented parties that can push demands for compensation did not exist. This is the second channel through which globalization put downward pressure on social spending and social security expenditures in particular. These forces did not lead to declines in public spending on health and education, but there was at the same time no evidence that Latin American governments increased expenditures on health and education to raise skill levels, enhance productivity, and be better able to compete in international markets.[3]

Although these economic variables are key to understanding the recent evolution of welfare systems in Latin America, no serious student of the welfare state can obviate political factors. The book has focused on two critical political dimensions likely to affect social welfare in several ways: political regime type and the popular basis of support for Latin American presidents.[4] A fundamental question for students of comparative political economy is whether the wave of democratization that swept Latin America

---

[2] In fact, a recent study by Dumont, Rayp, and Willeme (2005) has shown that globalization is also reducing union bargaining power in some EU countries.

[3] The challenges that this poses for Latin America are discussed in Garrett (2004).

[4] An explanation was also provided about why other critical political–institutional variables (e.g., federalism, voter turnout, and constitutional structures) could not be easily incorporated in the quantitative analysis. Statistical techniques called for the use of "fixed effects" to control for "omitted variable" biases. Fixed effects remove the influence of time-invariant variables, thus making it impossible to investigate the effects of unchanged or very slowly moving variables. This did not mean that these variables are unimportant, but it means that their effect had to be captured by other means (e.g., case studies).

in the late 1970s and 1980s was associated with an increase in the fiscal commitment of the state to social welfare. The results show that, given the regressive character of social security systems in Latin America, it is difficult to believe that the poor, who would presumably be more empowered in a democracy, would mobilize for a type of expenditure (e.g., social security expenditures) that hardly benefits them.

Likewise, although democratic governments may attempt to increase the share of social security expenditures that goes to the poor, they have to keep current transfers in line with prior contributions to the system. The poor, who typically belong to the informal sector, cannot afford to pay social security contributions and are, therefore, excluded from the system in most cases. In addition, elites in the military, civil administration, and business sectors, who are usually the recipients of large pension transfers, exert a disproportionate amount of influence on the state, and their privileges cannot be reduced easily. In contrast, health and education expenditures reach a much larger proportion of the population and tend to have a much less regressive effect or even a progressive effect, in some cases (i.e., primary education and basic health services). Hence, we might expect democracy to be associated with an expansion of these types of expenditures. The empirical evidence was consistent with this. This is also in line with in-depth country studies of Argentina, Brazil, and Chile, which show that spending on health and education constitutes about 75 percent of the total social expenditures received by families in the lowest income quintile and has a positive impact on the overall distribution of income.

Finally, popularly based presidents had a positive impact on the fiscal priority of social security expenditures. The bulk of social security expenditures (e.g., pensions, unemployment benefits) is tied to labor-market relations, precisely where labor unions – which comprise the core constituency of popularly based presidents – tend to be stronger. A second important component of social security expenditures is pro-poor programs. Although far less significant in size than pensions, this has also been an important component in the repertoire of electoral appeals of popularly based presidents.

Country Experiences: Beyond the Black Box of Social Expenditures

The country studies of Chile, Costa Rica, and Peru were useful complements to the historical and statistical analysis of previous chapters. They served two interrelated objectives. First, they allowed a better specification of some of the key causal mechanisms underlying the main statistical associations among globalization, domestic political institutions, and social expenditures presented in Chapter 3. Second, they took the analysis of welfare systems beyond the black box of social expenditures, going deeper into how, for example, social spending patterns are associated with changes in the organization and delivery of social services.

Three general conclusions can be drawn from these three case studies. The first conclusion, by now widely recognized among most students of the welfare state, is that history matters. The TSCS data set used in this book extends from the early 1970s to 2003 and, at times, the analyst may be tempted to assume that causal processes and relationships among variables could be restricted to this period. Yet, the case studies show that this is not appropriate. The effect of democracy was not the same in Chile, which had had a long history of continuous democracy before the 1970s, than in Peru, which has never been continuously democratic for more than ten years since independence from Spain. The effect of trade liberalization was also not the same in Chile, which had a relatively large industrial sector and opened up its economy very quickly, as in Costa Rica, which had a smaller industrial sector, had maintained a historically more open economy to international markets, and took a more gradual approach to trade liberalization. Similarly, the historical size of the welfare state prior to the 1970s also matters. Highly developed welfare states generate certain expectations from citizens, who come to regard social policies as a social right of citizenship. Citizens become stakeholders in the system and will oppose any attempt to roll back the welfare state. This is why it was not easy for successive Costa Rican governments to cut down, even marginally, most levels of welfare benefits. In Chile, by contrast, where citizens would probably also have opposed the quick process of state retrenchment in the social-policy domain that took place in the 1980s, a highly centralized executive authority under the military leadership of General Pinochet inhibited any significant opposition to the reform agenda. In Peru, where the welfare state had never been very well developed, only certain sectors of the population (i.e., workers in the public sector and in strategically located sectors of the economy) had expectations about the role of the state for social policy. Most workers in the informal economy (i.e., more than 50 percent of the economically active population) have never received welfare benefits and, therefore, unlike in Costa Rica, never became a strong force against social-policy reforms.

The second conclusion has to do with the way in which trade openness is connected with reductions in social expenditures. The three case studies point in the same direction, although the results are markedly different in Costa Rica when compared with Chile and/or Peru. We can generally distinguish two mechanisms through which trade integration has exerted downward pressure on social expenditures: an economic effect and a political effect. At the economic level, trade liberalization ended the inward-looking model of development associated with ISI. Domestic producers in import-substituting sectors found it increasingly more difficult to compete once import tariffs were removed. As the cases of Chile and Peru vividly demonstrated, this had a negative effect on the domestic industrial sector. Unable to compete once their protective screens were lifted, a significant number of industrial firms had to close down, and their workers either joined the service sector or flowed into the informal sector. Combined with an increasingly greater flexibilization of the labor market, labor contracts in nonindustrial sectors of the economy tended to become temporary and did not allow workers to accumulate welfare entitlements to the same extent as in, for example, the manufacturing sector.

At the same time, those who joined the informal sector stopped contributing to the social security systems and no longer qualified for most types of social security expenditures. In contrast, in Costa Rica – although the pressures to be competitive in international markets were equally large – business groups pressed the government to embark on a gradual process of liberalization and to provide them with subsidies that would allow them to adapt to the new competitive environment. As a result, despite the fact that trade openness led to some deindustrialization, the magnitude of this effect was smaller than in Chile or Peru. More important, the link between deindustrialization and reductions in social spending did not operate in Costa Rica because the government embarked on a comprehensive campaign to provide subsidies to economic sectors affected by trade liberalization and expanded its social safety net to protect low-income groups.

However, there was also a second (political) mechanism in which trade openness affected social expenditures. Governments in these three countries were increasingly concerned about competitiveness. Trade liberalization was one of the key components of the overall neoliberal platform of economic reform. Although it is not totally obvious from the case studies whether governments decided to cut down social security expenditures preemptively anticipating pressures from business groups worried about international competition, or whether they actually reacted to these pressures, it is clear that competitiveness became one of the main preoccupations of governments as they embarked in their programs of economic adjustment.

The third fundamental lesson we can draw from the case studies is that although the regime-type distinction is useful to identify general trends in social policy (e.g., democracies spending more on health and education than autocracies), the study of different types of institutional arrangements *within* democratic and *within* authoritarian systems is equally if not even more important. The cases of Chile in 1988–1989 and Peru after 1992 vividly illustrated that authoritarian regimes that face electoral pressures are also likely to increase social expenditures, especially prior to each major popular vote. Although theories of the political business cycle have long predicted that democratic incumbents tend to stimulate aggregate demand and increase social expenditures prior to elections,[5] these cases show that this phenomenon can also take place when authoritarian leaders link their political survival to some form of electoral process. In particular, Pinochet increased expenditures dramatically during 1988–1989 in preparation for the 1988 plebiscite that would decide if he would continue in power as president for eight more years, and then in support of "his" candidate in the 1989 presidential election. Similarly, after almost losing the 1993 constitutional referendum, Fujimori began to massively expand social expenditures in Peru. He did not do so as part of a well-designed plan to increase overall levels of education and health and to reduce poverty. Rather, he astutely increased expenditures in those electoral districts in which his basis of popular support had eroded the most. The strategy was successful and he was able to win the 1995 election by a wide margin.

Furthermore, the institutional arrangements within a democracy also make a difference. Unlike in Peru, where the party system lacks institutionalization, both Chile and Costa Rica have a two-party system dominated by a Social Democratic party and a Christian Democratic party that have historically structured political competition along well-defined lines. In a two-party system, parties compete for the median voter who in relatively unequal societies is in favor of social welfare. At the same time, both Social Democratic and Christian Democratic parties are somehow committed to the welfare state. Social Democrats see the welfare state as an agent of redistribution, Christian Democrats as a mechanism to support a system of social solidarity. As studies of advanced capitalist democracies have demonstrated, the type of welfare state that is likely to emerge varies depending on which of the two parties is hegemonic, but in countries like Germany, Belgium, and Austria, the commitment of these two parties to social welfare has been quite substantial. This mechanism clearly operated in the case of Costa Rica and in Chile after the transition to democracy in 1990 (where Christian Democrats and Social Democrats actually formed an alliance called Concertación, which won the 1989 elections).

Another important dimension within a democratic system that is of special importance for social policy is voter turnout. Both Costa Rica and Chile (when democratic) have maintained average levels of voter turnout

[5] See Alesina, Roubini, and Cohen (1997).

significantly higher than in Peru. This means that in Peru, the poor, who would actually stand to benefit the most from social policies, had been voting to a lesser extent than in Costa Rica and Chile. This is the case because the poor have lower levels of income and education – perhaps the two most important predictors of voter turnout.

Finally, democracies vary widely in terms of the number of veto points in the system. Veto points are institutional mechanisms that allow certain key actors to block reform, making it difficult for the welfare state to expand, but also making it more difficult to roll back a welfare state once it is already in place. In Chile, Pinochet concentrated all effective policy-making power in the Executive and eliminated any sort of institutional mechanisms that would have allowed organized groups to stall the process of welfare state retrenchment. A similar story can be seen in Peru under the authoritarian period of Fujimori after 1992 – although Fujimori faced electoral pressures that Pinochet never faced between 1973 and 1987. In contrast, in Costa Rica, political power in the social-policy domain remained dispersed among the different branches of government (i.e., Executive, Legislative, and Judiciary) and some AIs that had developed their own policy inertia and were controlled by bureaucratic elites committed to social welfare. This made it difficult for the government to change the status quo and scale back social expenditures drastically.

The fourth lesson that we can draw from these case studies is that social policies that are not based on a sustainable fiscal and macroeconomic position are bound to collapse. The experience of the populist governments of Allende in Chile (1970–1973) and García (1985–1990) in Peru clearly demonstrate that a bad economic policy is the worse kind of social policy. The case of Chile under Pinochet suggests that this does not mean that a government that is fiscally responsible and reestablishes fundamental macroeconomic equilibria is going to do well in the area of social policy. But, it clearly points to the fact that populism has a devastating effect on the welfare state over the long term – an effect that is, in fact, greater than an austere economic policy that pays limited attention to social issues. Both Chile during the last year of the Allende government and Peru during the last two or three years of the García administration ran into huge budget deficits and hyperinflation. In both cases, not only did social expenditures fall below the initial levels prior to the start of their administrations, but also real wages across the economy deteriorated to unprecedented levels. In Peru, for example, the average wage of a teacher in the public sector fell from $300 to less than $30. This is the worst of all worlds: a state that has falling resources to support its social programs and a private sector that puts tremendous downward pressure on real wages.

8.2 Future Challenges for the Welfare State in Latin America: Long-Term Sustainability and Greater Efficiency

The Long-Term Sustainability of Social Expenditures

One of the main challenges for the welfare state in advanced capitalist democracies is to reconcile fiscal discipline, employment growth, and limited economic inequality.[6] The challenge for the welfare state in Latin America, and probably in other parts of the developing world as well, is a related but somewhat different one. The main question can be posed as follows: How can the welfare state be more equitable and effective (i.e., be more progressive, reach a larger segment of the population, and contribute to improve social welfare)? It is a well-known fact that social expenditures in Latin America are markedly regressive and generally reach workers in the formal sector only. When the informal economy accounts, in many cases, for more than half of the economically active population, how to expand social protection to these sectors becomes a crucial concern.

The second challenge is for the state to devise long-term sustainable social policies that do not endanger macroeconomic stability and minimize microeconomic distortions. This begins with levels of social spending that are compatible with a minimum degree of fiscal discipline and are financed through a system of taxation that is simple and broad-based and minimizes distortions. There are no other magic formulas to generate economic growth and improve welfare outcomes. The experiences of one Latin American country after another attest to this simple fact. As noted previously, a bad economic policy always ends up having devastating effects for social policy, even if the initial social policy itself was successful in achieving certain positive welfare outcomes. If governments do not respect basic macroeconomic equilibria, social policies will almost without exception collapse. At the same time, if the tax base is narrow, and tax policy is complex and introduces large microeconomic distortions, this is likely to drag down economic growth and limit further fiscal revenues needed to expand social spending.

The analysis of these questions is beyond the scope of this study, but we can use a simple framework to set some tentative bounds beyond which welfare systems in Latin America are likely to lead to serious macroeconomic imbalances. The framework suggests that political leaders in Latin American countries still enjoy a considerable degree of flexibility to modify current levels of welfare effort without endangering hard-won macroeconomic

---

[6] See Iversen and Wren (1998) and, more recently, Thakur et al. (2003).

stability. In other words, there is hope that social welfare spending can expand in many countries without "magic" populist formulas that tend to end in macroeconomic chaos.

The framework is based on a relatively simple idea: whereas the fiscal priority of social spending (i.e., social spending as a share of total government spending) may vary widely among countries (it can range from about one third to about two thirds of the budget), the macroeconomic priority of social spending (i.e., the share of social spending in GDP) is heavily constrained by the capacity of the state to collect taxes.

Over the long term, a state can only have higher levels of social spending in two ways: by collecting more taxes or by increasing the fiscal priority of social expenditures. There is a third way to increase social expenditures: namely, running a budget deficit. However, this third option is not sustainable over the long term. Budget deficits may be used as a mechanism to finance higher social spending levels in the short term but, if unchecked, they are likely to generate severe macroeconomic imbalances.

In advanced industrial democracies, raising taxes is politically difficult, and although tax evasion is not uncommon in some countries, the ratio of taxpayers to the economically active population is rather high. By contrast, in Latin America, between one and two thirds of the population belong to the unregulated informal sector. Workers in the informal sector do not pay social security contributions nor, to be sure, do they receive in most cases any significant social benefits from the state. This poses one of the key challenges for Latin American welfare systems. Unless the size of the informal sector declines, expansions in the tax base necessary to finance higher social spending are likely to be limited. States can reform their tax code to increase revenues (as in Chile with President Alwyin or in Peru with President Fujimori), but if the size of the informal sector does not shrink, the expansion of fiscal revenues as a percentage of GDP is not likely to be very large over the long term.

The second way in which states can increase social expenditures is by shifting budget priorities. Latin American countries differ widely in terms of the priority that social expenditures receive within the overall public budget. In some countries (e.g., Costa Rica, Chile, and Uruguay), public expenditures on health, education, and social security take up almost two thirds of the budget.[7] In other countries, states commit a more modest amount, slightly

---

[7] As Chapter 1 showed, no country in the OECD or Eastern Europe has ever assigned less than one third of the budget to the social sector (see Table 1.2). In contrast, East Asian countries have traditionally allocated between 20 and 30 percent of the budget to the social sector.

more than one third of the budget. There are cases in which social expenditures do not even reach one third of the budget (e.g., Peru in the 1980s). Shifting priorities is not always an easy task, however, because there are a number of institutional rigidities that sometimes make this difficult: pervasive revenue-earmarking, legally mandated minimum expenditure levels for certain spending categories, and simply political opposition for changing the status quo.

Although the optimal level of social spending cannot be established by economic criteria alone, it seems reasonable to assume that appropriate levels are likely to fall within these lower and upper bounds of one third and two thirds of the budget, respectively. To be sure, the "optimal" fiscal priority for each country may depend on a number of variables, including public preferences for the overall size of the public sector, the efficiency of social spending, the percentage of the population older than sixty-five, the size of interest repayments on the public debt, the degree to which the tax system is distortionary, and many other factors. Hence, no general rules can be set a priori to decide what the optimal level of social spending should be. However, as a simple rule of thumb, it seems reasonable to assume that when social spending declines below one third of the budget, public funds for the social sector are likely to be inadequate. However, when social expenditures exceed two thirds of the budget, other important categories of spending (e.g., public transportation, infrastructure, and the judicial system) are likely to be compressed below critical levels.[8]

In this context, Table 8.1 develops the notion of lower and upper "fiscal bounds" for social spending. The lower bound is calculated by multiplying fiscal revenues (in percent of GDP) by one third; the upper bound is obtained after multiplying fiscal revenues by two thirds. We can then ask: How much scope do countries have to increase social expenditures beyond their current levels?[9] To answer this question, we can construct a measure of the fiscal space for social spending. *Fiscal space* can be defined simply as the difference between the average level of social expenditures within each period and the upper fiscal bound. If positive, it tells us that countries have some flexibility to reallocate expenditures toward the social sectors without necessarily having to expand their tax base or running into budget deficits.

---

[8] This assumes a balanced budget. To be sure, other categories of spending would not have to be crowded out if the state runs a fiscal deficit. This strategy is, however, not feasible in the intermediate term in most cases because of debt-sustainability concerns.

[9] The framework is presented for illustration purposes only. It is not supposed to provide an exact calculation of the fiscal space currently available in each case. Such an exercise would require the use of the most recent data (i.e., 2005–2006), which at the time of this writing were not available in any of the cases under study.

Table 8.1. *Sustainability of the Welfare State in Latin America I: Potential Fiscal Bounds and the Sustainability of Social Expenditures, 1973–2000*

	1973–1981				1982–1989				1990–2000			
	Fiscal Revenues	Fiscal Bounds	Welfare Effort	Fiscal Space	Fiscal Revenues	Fiscal Bounds	Welfare Effort	Fiscal Space	Fiscal Revenues	Fiscal Bounds	Welfare Effort	Fiscal Space
Welfare States												
Chile	31.9	10.5–21.1	15.5	+5.6	26.4	8.7–17.4	16.0	+1.4	20.6	6.8–13.6	12.3	+1.3
Uruguay	21.6	7.1–14.2	14.6	−0.4	23.2	7.7–15.3	14.7	+0.6	30.0	9.9–19.8	21.7	−1.9
Brazil	20.3	6.7–13.4	13.1	+0.2	36.3	14.2–23.9	14.2	+9.7	38.4	12.7–25.4	17.8	+7.5
Costa Rica	17.7	5.8–11.7	12.5	−0.8	13.7	7.6–15.2	13.7	+1.4	22.1	7.2–14.5	14.5	−0.1
Argentina	9.6	3.1–6.3	10.5	−4.2	10.0	3.3–6.6	9.1	−2.5	14.4	4.7–9.5	12.2	−2.7
Non-Welfare States												
Venezuela	29.5	9.7–19.5	7.6	+11.9	23.1	7.6–15.3	7.7	+9.2	20.1	6.6–13.2	8.1	+5.1
El Salvador	15.6	5.1–10.3	5.1	+5.5	13.0	4.2–8.6	3.8	+4.7	11.6	3.8–7.7	3.6	+4.0
Peru	15.3	5.1–10.1	4.3	+5.8	11.3	3.7–7.4	4.1	+4.7	11.9	3.9–7.8	4.3	+3.5
Dom. Republic	15.1	4.9–9.9	4.7	+5.2	12.8	4.2–8.5	3.9	+4.5	15.4	5.1–10.2	4.0	+6.2
Mexico	13.2	4.3–8.7	6.7	+1.9	16.8	5.5–11.1	5.2	+5.8	14.8	4.8–9.8	6.9	+2.8
Paraguay	11.3	3.7–7.4	3.8	+3.7	10.1	3.3–6.6	4.1	+2.6	13.1	4.3–8.7	4.4	+4.2
Ecuador	11.2	3.7–7.4	4.6	+2.7	13.8	4.5–9.1	5.1	+4.0	16.2	5.4–10.7	4.7	+6.0
Bolivia	10.0	3.3–6.6	4.5	+2.1	5.4	3.5–7.0	5.4	+1.6	17.7	5.9–11.7	8.6	+3.1
Guatemala	9.8	3.2–6.5	3.0	+3.5	9.3	3.1–6.1	2.9	+3.2	8.8	2.9–5.8	3.3	+2.5

Notes: "Revenues" measure the total amount of tax and nontax revenues as a percentage of GDP. "Fiscal Bounds" provide the minimum and maximum level of welfare effort (social expenditures/GDP) assuming a balanced budget and setting minimum (lower bound) and maximum (upper bound) priorities for social spending. The lower bound (first figure in the "Fiscal Bounds" column) assumes a fiscal priority of social spending of about one third of the budget; the upper bound (second figure) assumes a fiscal priority of social spending of about two thirds of the budget. Thus, the figures provide the margins within which governments can increase or decrease social spending levels without placing them under severe fiscal stress. Although the fiscal priority of social spending can certainly fall below one third of total expenditures (as it did, for example, in Peru in the 1980s), most countries tend to devote at least 30 percent of their budgets to social security programs and public health and education. On the other hand, although governments can raise the fiscal priority of social spending over two thirds of the budget (as it has sometimes happened in Costa Rica and Uruguay), they can hardly do so without significantly cutting down other types of expenditures (e.g., investment in infrastructure, police, the judiciary) below a minimum floor of reasonable standards or running a large fiscal deficit. The "fiscal space" is the difference between the upper fiscal bound and the real recorded level of welfare effort (social expenditures/GDP). A positive fiscal space indicates that even without expanding the tax base or running necessarily into a fiscal deficit, the state can shift resources toward the social sector. A negative fiscal space indicates that current levels of social welfare are not likely to be sustainable unless tax revenues are increased.

274

Table 8.2. *Sustainability of the Welfare State in Latin America II: Effective Fiscal Bounds and the Sustainability of Social Expenditures, 1973–2000*

	1973–1981		1982–1989		1990–2000	
	Net Fiscal Bounds	Net Fiscal Space	Net Fiscal Space	Net Fiscal Space	Net Fiscal Bounds	Net Fiscal Space
Welfare States						
Chile	10.06–20.12	+4.61	8.12–16.25	+0.24	6.41–12.83	+0.55
Uruguay	6.96–13.93	−0.68	7.04–14.09	−0.63	9.33–18.66	−3.04
Brazil	6.10–12.21	+0.92	7.93–15.86	+1.57	7.18–14.36	−3.48
Costa Rica	5.45–10.90	−1.57	6.85–13.71	−0.01	6.05–12.11	−2.48
Argentina	2.68–5.36	−5.16	2.87–5.75	−3.39	4.33–8.67	−3.58
Non-Welfare States						
Venezuela	9.40–18.81	+11.19	6.74–13.49	+7.68	5.45–10.90	+1.5
El Salvador	4.97–9.95	+5.11	3.89–7.79	+3.94	3.34–6.69	+3.03
Peru	4.20–8.41	+4.04	2.70–5.41	+2.15	2.81–5.63	−1.33
Dominican Republic	4.82–9.64	+4.90	4.08–8.16	+4.17	4.83–9.67	+5.68
Mexico	3.72–7.44	+0.69	1.49–2.99	−2.23	4.19–8.39	+1.42
Paraguay	3.65–7.30	+3.49	3.12–6.25	+2.22	4.04–8.09	+3.62
Ecuador	3.62–7.25	+2.62	4.39–8.79	+3.70	4.22–8.44	+3.70
Bolivia	2.73–5.47	+0.92	3.29–6.59	+1.10	5.30–10.60	+2.00
Guatemala	3.04–6.08	+3.08	2.70–5.41	+2.48	2.58–5.17	+1.84

Note: The net fiscal bounds provide the minimum and maximum levels of sustainable social expenditures (in percent of GDP) after interest repayments, assuming a balanced budget. The lower bound is estimated by assigning one third of public expenditures to the social sector, whereas the upper bound is estimated by allocating two thirds of public expenditures to the social sector.

If negative, it suggests that social spending is probably "too high," given the existing fiscal constraints and the need to provide adequate funding for other categories of spending.

The figures in Table 8.1 are useful to illustrate a clear difference between the group of welfare and non-welfare states. In the 1990s, welfare states seem to have approached (i.e., Chile) or exceeded (i.e., Argentina, Costa Rica, and Uruguay) the upper fiscal bound. The only exception is Brazil, but as Table 8.2[10] makes clear, Brazil also seems to have exceeded the upper fiscal bound once we take into account the effect of interest repayments. Within this group of countries, levels of welfare effort cannot expand easily by shifting budget priorities toward the social sector. Hence, unless these countries

---

[10] Table 8.2 is the same as Table 8.1 but takes into account interest payments on public debt in the calculations of fiscal space.

increase their tax-collection levels, they will not be able to expand social spending levels.[11] In the case of Argentina, which has recently experienced a major economic crisis, it becomes immediately clear that the long-term unsustainability of the welfare state may have contributed to the most recent economic crisis. In particular, Argentina exceeds by between 2.5 and 4 percent of GDP the upper fiscal bound. In other words, in the 1990s, for example, social expenditures were about 30 percent higher than the maximum level suggested by the upper fiscal bound.[12] To maintain a balanced fiscal position with its ratio of social spending to GDP, Argentina would have needed to allocate 85 percent of the budget to the social sector, crowding out many other categories of spending, including public investment, which could be seen as equally important. Obviously, history tells us that this level of spending was maintained not by cutting all other expenditure below 15 percent of the budget but rather by running persistently large fiscal deficits, which was a contributing factor to the crisis that devastated its economy in 2001–2002.

The other message that emerges from Table 8.1 is that non-welfare states in Latin America could, in principle, increase the size of the welfare state considerably by shifting priorities within the budget. Although the margin to do so seems to have changed over time, in the 1990s some countries like El Salvador, Guatemala, the Dominican Republic, Paraguay, and Ecuador could have increased social spending levels substantially by shifting budget priorities toward the social sector. What is interesting is that even if we take into account the weight of interest repayments associated with current debt levels in the public sector (Table 8.2), most non-welfare states are still too close to the lower fiscal bound. Hence, they still have substantial margin to shift public resources toward the social sector without endangering fiscal discipline and even without expanding their tax base.

The Effectiveness of the Welfare State

A second important area for future research would be to study the effects of the welfare state as an independent variable. This can lead to a number of

---

[11] It is true, however, that as long as economic growth is positive and fiscal revenues are buoyant, social expenditures per capita are likely to increase. But, if we are interested in analyzing the ways in which the welfare state in Latin America can be deepened to approach Western European standards (where social spending levels as a percent of GDP are typically much higher), the focus should be on social spending as a percentage of GDP.

[12] If we take into account interest repayments, then expenditures were 40 percent higher than the level suggested by the upper fiscal bound.

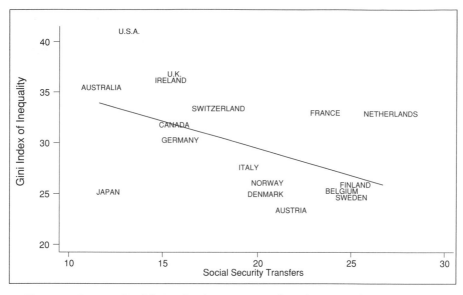

Figure 8.1. Impact of Social Transfers (as Percentage of GDP) on Inequality in the OECD, 1973–2000 Averages.
Notes: Regression equation is as follows: GINI = 40.1 – 0.53* (Soc. Security Transfers). The slope coefficient is statistically significant at a 95 percent or better level of confidence, and the model explains about 25 percent of variation in the dependent variable. The regression is presented for illustration purposes only. With such small-n regression, estimates are only tentative.

research questions that have long been studied in advanced countries, such as the impact of the welfare state on labor markets, social development, or economic inequality. Although a full discussion of these issues is also beyond the scope of this book, a brief discussion of the relationship between the welfare state and economic inequality can suggest a critical new area for further research. Students of the welfare state have long recognized the importance of social spending in reducing income disparities and equalizing economic opportunities. As Figure 8.1 shows, in advanced industrial democracies, there seems to be a relationship between levels of social security transfers and income inequality. Although there are clearly other factors that affect income inequality, and there are countries that deviate significantly from the regression line (e.g., Japan and the United States), this simple relationship is statistically significant. For every 1-point increase in social security transfers as a percentage of GDP, the gini index of economic inequality decreases by about 0.5 percentage points. This effect can be considered rather large. If, for example, the United States increased social security expenditures to the level of France (i.e., an increase of 10 points of GDP), its gini index would decline by 5.3 percentage points, thus reducing the difference in terms of inequality between both countries by more than half.[13]

Students of Latin American political economy have long argued that, unlike in advanced industrial democracies, social security expenditures in Latin America are markedly regressive. If this is true, one would expect a regression line with a positive slope in the Latin American case. The empirical evidence, however, does not support this hypothesis, at least in the context of the simple bivariate relationship presented herein. Although it is true that social security transfers in Latin America do not have the redistributive effect that they generate in advanced industrial democracies, the evidence does not suggest that they have necessarily a negative effect on inequality. Figure 8.2 shows that there is neither a positive nor a negative relationship between higher and lower levels of social security expenditures and economic inequality. In some countries like Uruguay, high levels of social security transfers correspond with low levels of economic inequality. But, in other countries such as Chile and Brazil, they do not.

Conversely, both the ECLAC and many other studies have stressed the potentially redistributive effect of public expenditures on health and education, which reach a much larger segment of the population. Figure 8.3 provides some tentative evidence in this direction, but there is, in fact, too much dispersion around the regression line and the relationship is not statistically significant.

Higher expenditures on health and education do seem to be associated with reductions in income inequality, but we should be cautious about this conclusion because of the lack of statistical significance of the association, the small sample size, and the lack of statistical controls. Without further analysis and perhaps additional indicators of economic inequality, we cannot have a sufficient degree of confidence on the substantial effects of health and education on actual levels of income inequality. In any event, this brief discussion is not provided to make any bold claims but rather simply to suggest an area where more research is clearly needed.

---

[13] According to the World Bank, in 2000, the United States had a gini index of economic inequality of about 40.8, while in France it was 32.7. Although an increase in 10 points of GDP for the United States is a large one, the reduction of inequality associated with this increase would also be large. The gini index in the United States would become 35.5, reducing by more than half the difference in inequality between the United States and France. The equation has also been estimated controlling for other factors, such as GDP per capita and trade openness, and the slope coefficient never suffered a large change in either size or levels of statistical significance.

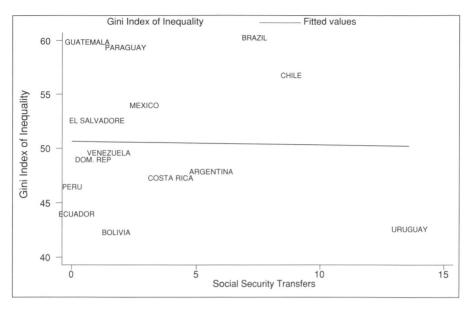

Figure 8.2. Impact of Social Transfers on Inequality in Latin America, 1973–2000 Averages.

Notes: Neither the constant nor the slope coefficient is statistically significant. Furthermore, the model explains less than 1 percent of the variation in the dependent variable. Some Latin American experts may find it hard to believe that Costa Rica has worse levels of income inequality than the Andean countries (i.e., Ecuador, Bolivia, and Peru). Patterns of land distribution in the Andes have been historically more unequal than in Costa Rica, and there is also a general consensus that Costa Rica is one of the few countries where inequality did not deteriorate substantially during the debt crisis of the 1980s. Although it might be possible that the World Bank is using different criteria in these countries, or that it focuses on urban areas only, what is important for our purposes here is that even if Peru, Ecuador, and Bolivia had worse levels of inequality, the line would still remain flat (unless they reached the levels of inequality of Brazil, which is clearly not the case). *Source:* World Bank, *World Development Report*, various issues.

So far, there has been a surprising lack of research on how states in the developing world have constructed their welfare systems and how these systems have been transformed by the recent processes of globalization and democratization. This book has been an attempt to advance our knowledge in this direction, hoping that other researchers will modify or improve the analysis presented herein and perhaps expand it to other areas. There are many other directions where further research is also needed, including two that have been only briefly discussed: how to expand the welfare state respecting basic macroeconomic equilibria, and how to make it more progressive

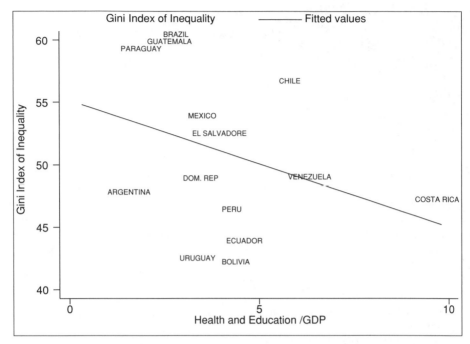

Figure 8.3. Impact of Health and Education on Inequality in Latin America, 1973–2000 Averages.
Source: World Bank, *World Development Report*, various issues.

and efficient.[14] These are two of the most important challenges for the welfare state in Latin America. Other avenues for further research also include the exploration of how decentralization may have affected patterns of social spending (an area that has not been addressed adequately in this book because of lack of data); and how other political institutions (including political parties, constitutional structures, and voter turnout) may have shaped and will continue to shape how governments in the developing world decide to become or cease to be welfare states. It is hoped that some of the thoughts presented in this book will encourage other researchers to pursue these questions in the future.

---

[14] For recent research in the area of the efficiency of public spending, see Greene (2004), Murillo-Zamorano (2004), Afonso and Aubyn (2005), and Van der Ploeg (2006).

Bibliography

Abel, Christopher, and Colin M. Lewis, eds. 1993. *Welfare, Poverty and Development in Latin America.* London: The Macmillan Press.

Abugattás, Luis. 1996. "Estabilización, reforma estructural e industria en el Perú: 1990–1995. Lineamientos para una política de desarrollo industrial." *Socialismo y Participación* #74, pp. 9–40.

Acemoglu, Daron. 2003. "Why Not a Political Case Theorem? Social Conflict, Commitment and Politics." *Journal of Comparative Economics* 31(December): 620–652.

Acemoglu, Daron. 2005. "Politics and Economics in Weak and Strong States." *Journal of Monetary Economics* 52(December): 1199–1226.

Acemoglu, Daron, and Simon Johnson. 2005. "Unbundling Institutions." *Journal of Political Economy* 113(October): 949–995.

Acemoglu, Daron, and James Robinson. 2000. "Why Did the West Extend the Franchise? Democracy, Inequality, and Growth in Historical Perspective." *Quarterly Journal of Economics* 115(November): 1167–1199.

Acemoglu, Daron, and James Robinson. 2001. "Inefficient Redistribution." *American Political Science Review* 95(3): 649–661.

Acemoglu, Daron, and James Robinson. 2006. *Economic Origins of Dictatorship and Democracy.* New York: Cambridge University Press.

Adcock, Robert, and David Collier. 1999. "Measurement Validity: A Shared Standard for Qualitative and Quantitative Research." *American Political Science Review* 95(3): 529–546.

Adsera, Alicia, and Carles Boix. 2002. "Trade, Democracy, and the Size of the Public Sector: The Political Underpinnings of Openness." *International Organization* 56(2): 229–262.

Afonso, Antonio, and Miguel St. Aubyn. 2005. "Cross-Country Efficiency of Secondary Education Provision; A Semi-Parametric Analysis with Non-Discretionary Inputs." Working Paper no. 49, European Central Bank.

Aggarwal, Vinod K., Ralph Espach, and Joseph Tulchin, eds. 2004. *The Strategic Dynamics of Latin American Trade.* Stanford, CA: Stanford University Press.

Aghion, Philippe, Alberto Alesina, and Francesco Trebbi. 2004. "Endogenous Political Institutions." *Quarterly Journal of Economics* 119(May): 565–612.

Alcala, Francisco, and Antonio Ciccone. 2004. "Trade and Productivity." *Quarterly Journal of Economics* 119(May): 613–646.

Alesina, Alberto, and George-Marios Angeletos. 2005. "Fairness and Redistribution: US vs. Europe." *American Economic Review* 95 (September): 913–935.

Alesina, Alberto, Edward Glaeser, and Bruce Sacerdote. 2001. "Why Doesn't the U.S. Have a European Style Welfare State." *Brookings Paper on Economics Activity* (Fall): 187–278.

Alesina, Alberto, Ricardo Hausman, Rudolf Hommes, and Ernesto Stein. 1999. "Budget Institutions and Fiscal Performance in Latin America." *Journal of Development Economics* 59: 253–273.

Alesina, Alberto, and Roberto Perotti. 1997. "The Welfare State and Competitiveness." *American Economic Review* 87(5): 921–939.

Alesina, Alberto, Nouriel Roubini, and Gerald Cohen. 1997. *Political Cycles and the Macroeconomy.* Cambridge, MA: The MIT Press.

Alesina, Alberto, and Enrico Spolaore. 1997. "On the Number and Size of Nations." *Quarterly Journal of Economics* 112(November): 1027–1056.

Alesina, Alberto, Rafael di Tella, and Robert McCulloch. 2004. "Inequality and Happiness: Are Americans and Europeans Different?" *Journal of Public Economics* 88(August): 2009–2042.

Alesina, Alberto, and Romain Wacziarg. 1998. "Openness, Country Size and the Government." *Journal of Public Economics* 69(September): 305–322.

Alvarez, Michael, Jose Antonio Cheibub, Fernando Limongi, and Adam Przeworski. 1996. "Classifying Political Regimes." *Studies in Comparative International Development* 31: 3–36.

Ameringer, Charles D. 1982. *Democracy in Costa Rica.* New York: Praeger.

Ames, Barry. 1987. *Political Survival; Politicians and Public Policy in Latin America.* Berkeley: University of California Press.

Andic, Fuat M. 1983. *What Price Equity? A Macroeconomic Evaluation of Government Policies in Costa Rica.* Rio Piedras: Institute of Caribbean Studies, University of Puerto Rico.

Andrews, David. 1994. "Capital Mobility and State Autonomy: Toward a Structural Theory of International Monetary Relations." *International Studies Quarterly* (Fall): 193–218.

Aninat, Eduardo. 2005. "Options and Outcomes of Chile's Education Reforms, 1990–2000," in Roberto Zagha and Tim Besley, eds., *Development Challenges in the 1990s: Leading Policy Makers Speak from Experience.* Washington, DC: World Bank.

Arellano, José Pablo. 1985. *Políticas Sociales y Desarrollo: Chile, 1924–1984.* Santiago: CIEPLAN.

Arellano, Manuel, and Stephen Bond. 1991. "Some Tests of Specification for Panel Data: Monte Carlo Evidence and an Application to Employment Equations." *Review of Economic Studies* 58(2): 277–297.

Atkinson, Anthony. 1996. *Incomes and the Welfare State.* Cambridge, UK: Cambridge University Press.

Atkinson, Anthony, ed. 1999. *The Economic Consequences of Rolling Back the Welfare State.* Cambridge, MA: The MIT Press.

Auriol, Emmanuelle, and Michael Warlters. 2005. "Taxation Base in Developing Countries." *Journal of Public Economics* 89: 625–646.

Auster, Richard, and Morris Silver. 1979. *The State as a Firm.* Boston: Martinus Nijhoff.

Avelino, George. 2000. "Democratization and Social Expenditures in Latin America, 1980–1994." Ph.D. Dissertation, Stanford University.

Avelino, George, David Brown, and Wendy Hunter. 2005. "The Effects of Capital Mobility, Trade Openness and Democracy on Social Spending in Latin America 1980–1999." *American Journal of Political Science* 49(3): 625–641.

Baldassarri, Mario, Luigi Paganetto, and Edmund S. Phelps, eds. 1994. *Equity, Efficiency and Growth: The Future of the Welfare State.* London: Macmillan Press Ltd.

Banerjee, Anindya, Juan Dolado, John Galbraith, and David Henry. 1993. *Co-Integration, Error Correction, and the Econometric Analysis of Non-Stationary Data.* Oxford: Oxford University Press.

Barr, Nicholas. 1992. "Economic Theory and the Welfare State: A Survey and Interpretation." *Journal of Economic Literature* 30(2): 741–803.

Barr, Nicholas. 2004 (fouth edition). *The Economics of the Welfare State.* Oxford: Oxford University Press.

Barro, Robert J. 1990. "Government Spending in a Simple Model of Endogenous Growth." *Journal of Political Economy* 98(5): 103–126.

Barro, Robert J. 2001. "Human Capital and Growth." *American Economic Review* 91(2): 12–17.

Barry, Brian. 1989. *Democracy, Power and Justice: Essays in Political Theory.* Oxford: Oxford University Press.

Baumol, William. 1967. "Macroeconomics of Unbalanced Growth: The Anatomy of the Urban Crisis." *American Economic Review* 57: 415–426.

Beck, Hermann. 1995. *The Origins of the Authoritarian Welfare State in Prussia: Conservatives, Bureaucracy and the Social Question, 1815–70.* Ann Arbor: University of Michigan Press.

Beck, Nathaniel. 1991. "Comparing Dynamic Specifications: The Case of Presidential Approval." *Political Analysis* 3: 51–87.

Beck, Nathaniel. 1992. "The Methodology of Cointegration." *Political Analysis* 4: 237–254.

Beck, Nathaniel. 2000. "Time-Series Cross-Section Data: What Have We Learned in the Last Few Years?" *Annual Review of Political Science* 4: 271–293.

Beck, Nathaniel, and Jonathan Katz. 1995. "What to Do (and Not to Do) with Time-Series Cross-Section Data." *American Political Science Review* 89(3): 634–647.

Beck, Nathaniel, and Jonathan Katz. 1996. "Nuisance versus Substance: Specifying and Estimating Time-Series Cross-Section Models." *Political Analysis* 6(July): 1–37.

Beck, Nathaniel, and Jonathan Katz. 2001. "Throwing Out the Baby with the Bath Water: A Comment on Green, Kim, and Yoon." *International Organization* 55(2): 487–496.

Benabou, Roland, and Efe A. Ok. 2001. "Social Mobility and the Demand for Redistribution: The Poum Hypothesis." *Quarterly Journal of Economics* 2(May): 447–487.

Berry, Albert, ed. 2000. *Labor Market Policies in Canada and Latin America: Challenges of the New Millennium.* Boston: Kluwer Academic Publishers.

Bhagwati, Jagdish. 2001. "Targeting Rich-Country Protectionism." *Finance and Development* 38(3): 14–15. Washington, DC: International Monetary Fund.

Bhagwati, Jagdish. 2002. *Free Trade Today.* Princeton, NJ: Princeton University Press.

Bhagwati, Jagdish. 2004. *In Defense of Globalization.* Oxford: Oxford University Press.

Birdsall, Nancy, and Carol Graham, eds. 1999. *New Markets, New Opportunities?: Economic and Social Mobility in a Changing World.* Washington, DC: The Brookings Institution and Carnegie Endowment for International Peace.

Birdsall, Nancy, Carol Graham, and Richard Sabot, eds. 1998. *Beyond Trade-Offs: Market Reforms and Equitable Growth in Latin America.* Washington, DC: The Brookings Institution and Inter-American Development Bank.

Blanchard, Olivier. 2000. *Macroeconomics.* Upper Saddle River, NJ: Prentice Hall.

Boix, Carles. 1998. *Political Parties, Growth and Equality: Conservative and Social Democratic Economic Strategies in the World Economy.* New York: Cambridge University Press.

Boix, Carles. 2000. "Partisan Governments, the International Economy, and Macroeconomic Policies in Advanced Nations, 1960–93." *World Politics* 53(October): 38–73.

Boix, Carles. 2001. "Democracy, Development and the Public Sector." *American Journal of Political Science* 45(1): 1–17.

Boix, Carles. 2003. *Democracy and Redistribution.* Cambridge, UK: Cambridge University Press.

Bollen, Kenneth, and Robert Jackman. 1989. "Democracy, Stability and Dichotomies." *American Sociological Review* 54(4): 612–621.

Borchardt, Michael, Isabel Rial, and Adolfo Sarmiento. 1998. "Sostenibilidad de la política fiscal en Uruguay." Inter-American Development Bank, Office of the Chief Economist, Working Paper no. 320.

Bosworth, Barry P., Rudiger Dornbusch, and Raúl Labán, eds. 1994. *The Chilean Economy: Policy Lessons and Challenges.* Washington, DC: The Brookings Institution.

Brambor, Thomas, William Roberts Clark, and Matt Golder. 2006. "Understanding Interaction Models: Improving Empirical Analyses." *Political Analysis* 14: 63–82.

Bresser, Pereira, Luis Carlos, José María Maravall, and Adam Przeworski. 1993. *Economic Reforms in New Democracies: A Social Democratic Approach.* Cambridge, UK: Cambridge University Press.

Brooks, Sarah. 2002. "Social Protection and Economic Integration: The Politics of Pension Reform in an Era of Capital Mobility." *Comparative Political Studies* 35(5): 491–523.

Brooks, Sarah. 2004. "Explaining Capital Account Liberalization in Latin America: A Transitional Cost Approach." *World Politics* 56(3): 389–430.

Brown, David, and Wendy Hunter. 1999. "Democracy and Social Spending in Latin America, 1980–92." *American Political Science Review* 93(4): 779–790.

Buchanan, James. 1980. *Toward a Theory of the Rent-Seeking Society.* College Station: Texas A&M Press.

Bueno de Mesquita, Bruce, Alastair Smith, Randolph M. Siverson, and James D. Morrow. 2003. *The Logic of Political Survival.* Cambridge, MA: The MIT Press.

Bulmer-Thomas, Victor. 1994. *The Economic History of Latin America Since Independence.* Cambridge, UK: Cambridge University Press.

Buvinic, Mayra, and Jacqueline Mazza, with Ruthanne Deutsch. 2004. *Social Inclusion and Economic Development in Latin America.* Baltimore: Johns Hopkins University Press.

Caballero, Ricardo J., Eduardo Engel, and Alejandro Micco. 2004. "Microeconomic Flexibility in Latin America." NBER Working Paper Series no. 10398.

Cameron, David. 1978. "The Expansion of the Public Economy: A Comparative Analysis." *American Political Science Review* 72: 1243–1261.

Carey, John. 1997. "Strong Candidates for a Limited Office: Presidentialism and Political Parties in Costa Rica," in Scott Mainwaring and Matthew Soberg Shugart, eds., *Presidentialism and Democracy in Latin America.* Cambridge, UK: Cambridge University Press.

Casacuberta, Carlos, Gabriela Fachola, and Nestor Gandelman. 2004. "The Impact of Trade Liberalization on Employment, Capital, and Productivity Dynamics: Evidence from the Uruguayan Manufacturing Sector." *Policy Reform* 7(4): 225–248.

Castiglioni, Rossana. 2000. "Welfare State Reform in Chile and Uruguay: Cross-Class Coalitions, Elite Ideology, and Veto Players." Paper presented at the Annual Meeting of the Latin American Studies Association, Miami, March 16–18.

Castles, Francis, ed. 1982. *The Impact of Parties*. Beverly Hills, CA: Sage Publications.

Castles, Francis. 1985. *The Working Class and Welfare*. Sydney: Allen and Unwin.

Castles, Francis. 1998a. *Comparative Public Policy*. Northampton, MA: Edward Elgar Publishing, Inc.

Castles, Francis. 1998b. *Comparative Public Policy: Patterns of Post-War Transformation*. Cheltenham: Edward Elgar Publishing, Inc.

Castles, Francis, and R. D. McKinlay. 1979. "Does Politics Matter? An Analysis of the Public Welfare Commitment in Advanced Democratic States." *European Journal of Political Research* 7: 169–186.

Chalmers, Douglas A. 1977. "The Politicized State in Latin America," in James Malloy, ed., *Authoritarianism and Corporatism in Latin America*. Pittsburgh: University of Pittsburgh Press.

Cheibub, José Antonio. 1998. "Political Regimes and the Extractive Capacity of Governments: Taxation in Democracies and Dictatorships." *World Politics* 50(3): 349–376.

Chong, Alberto, and Mauricio Olivera. 2005. "On Compulsory Voting and Income Inequality in a Cross-Section of Countries." Inter-American Development Bank, Working Paper no. 533.

Clark, Mary. 2001. *Gradual Economic Reform in Latin America. The Costa Rican Experience*. New York: State University of New York Press.

Clayton, Richard, and Jonas Pontusson. 1998. "Welfare-State Retrenchment Revisited: Entitlement Cuts, Public Sector Restructuring, and Inegalitarian Trends in Advanced Capitalist Societies." *World Politics* 51(1): 67–98.

Collier, David, and Richard Messick. 1975. "Prerequisites Versus Diffusion: Testing Alternative Explanations of Social Security Adoption." *American Political Science Review* 69(4): 1299–1315.

Collier, Ruth Berins. 1999. *Paths Towards Democracy: The Working Class and Elites in Western Europe and South America*. Cambridge, UK: Cambridge University Press.

Collier, Ruth Berins, and David Collier. 1992. *Shaping the Political Arena*. Princeton, NJ: Princeton University Press.

Cominetti, Rosella, and Gonzalo Ruiz. 1998. "Evolución del Gasto Público Social en América Latina: 1980–1995." Santiago: CEPAL.

"Comisión Económica para América Latina y el Caribe (CEPAL)," several years, *Panorama Social de América Latina*. Santiago: CEPAL.

Conaghan, Catherine. 1995. "Polls, Political Discourse, and the Public Sphere: The Spin on Peru's Fuji-golpe," in Peter Smith, ed., *Latin America in Comparative Perspective*. Boulder, CO: Westview Press.

Coppedge, Michael. 1998. "The Dynamic Diversity of Latin American Party Systems." *Party Politics* 4(4): 547–568.

Cortázar, René. 2001. "Unemployment Insurance Systems for Latin America," in Albert Berry, ed., *Labor Market Policies in Canada and Latin America: Challenges of the New Millennium*. Boston: Kluwer Academic Publishers.

Cotler, Julio. 1995a. "Political Parties and the Problem of Democratic Consolidation in Peru," in Scott Mainwaring and Timothy Scully, eds., *Building Democratic Institutions: Party Systems in Latin America.* Stanford, CA: Stanford University Press.

Cotler, Julio, ed. 1995b. *Perú 1964–1994: Economía, Sociedad y Política.* Lima: Instituto de Estudios Peruanos.

Cotler, Julio. 1998a. "Los empresarios y las reformas económicas en el Perú." Documento de trabajo #91. Lima: Instituto de Estudios Peruanos.

Cotler, Julio. 1998b. "La articulación y los mecanismos de representación de las organizaciones empresariales." Documento de trabajo #97. Lima: Instituto de Estudios Peruanos.

Cox, Robert. 1996. "A Perspective on Globalization," in James Mittleman, ed., *Globalization: Critical Reflections.* Boulder, CO: Lynne Rienner Publishers.

Crabtree, John, and Jim Thomas. 1999. *El Peru de Fujimori.* Lima: Instituto de Estudios Peruanos.

Craig, Ann L., and Wayne Cornelius. 1995. "Houses Divided: Parties and Political Reform in Mexico," in Scott Mainwaring and Timothy Scully, eds., *Building Democratic Institutions: Party Systems in Latin America.* Stanford, CA: Stanford University Press.

Crepaz, Markus M. L. 1998. "Inclusion versus Exclusion: Political Institutions and Welfare Expenditures." *Comparative Politics* 31(October): 61–77.

Crew, David. 1996. "The Ambiguities of Modernity: Welfare and the German State from Wilhelm to Hitler," in Geoff Eley, ed., *Society, Culture, and the State in Germany, 1870–1930.* Ann Arbor: University of Michigan Press.

Cunha Fernandez, Maria Alice, Denise Correa da Rocha, Margarida Maria Sousa de Oliveira, José Aparecido Carlos Ribeiro, and Luseni Maria Cordeiro de Aquino. 1998. "Gasto Social das Tres Esferas de Governo – 1995." Texto para Discussao #598. Rio de Janeiro: Instituto de Pesquisa Economica Aplicada (IPEA).

Dahl, Robert. 1971. *Polyarchy: Participation and Opposition.* New Haven: Yale University Press.

Dahl, Robert. 1989. *Democracy and Its Critics.* New Haven: Yale University Press.

Dahl, Robert. 1998. *On Democracy.* New Haven: Yale University Press.

Dalton, Russell, Scott Flanagan, and Paul Allen Beck, eds. 1984. *Electoral Change in Advanced Industrial Democracies.* Princeton, NJ: Princeton University Press.

De Mesquita, Bueno, Alastair Smith, Randolph M. Siverson, and James D. Morrow. 2003. *The Logic of Political Survival.* Cambridge, MA: MIT Press.

Diamond, Larry, Juan Linz, and Seymour Martin Lipset. 1995. "Introduction: What Makes for Democracy?," in Larry Diamond, Juan Linz, and Seymour Martin Lipset, eds., *Politics in Developing Countries: Comparing Experiences with Democracy* (second edition). Boulder, CO: Lynne Rienner Publishers.

Diamond, Peter. 2005. "Pensions for an Ageing Population." Manuscript (available at http://econ-www.mit.edu/faculty/download_pdf.php?id=1255).

Dollar, David, and Aart Kray. 2001. "Trade, Growth and Poverty." *Finance and Development* 38(3): 16–19. Washington, DC: International Monetary Fund.

Dornbusch, Rudiger, and Sebastian Edwards. 1994. "Exchange Rate Policy and Trade Strategy," in Barry P. Bosworth, Rudiger Dornbusch, and Raúl Labán, eds., *The Chilean Economy: Policy Lessons and Challenges.* Washington, DC: The Brookings Institution.

Downs, Anthony. 1957. *An Economic Theory of Democracy.* New York: Harper.

Draibe, Sonia Miriam, Maria Elena Guimaraes de Castro, and Beatriz Azeredo. 1995. "The System of Social Protection in Brazil." Kellogg Institute, University of Notre Dame, Democracy and Social Policy Series. Working Paper no. 3.

Dumont, Michael, Glenn Rayp, and Peter Willemé. 2005. "Does Internationalization Affect Union Bargaining Power: An Empirical Study for Five EU Countries." *Oxford Economic Papers* 58: 77–102.

Durr, Robert H. 1992. "An Essay on Cointegration and Error Correction Models," in John R. Freeman, ed., *Political Analysis*, Vol 4. Ann Arbor: University of Michigan Press.

Easterly, William, Carlos Alfredo Rodríguez, and Klaus Schmidt-Hebbel, eds. 1994. *Public Sector Deficits and Macroeconomic Performance.* New York: Oxford University Press.

Easterly, William, and Klaus Schmidt-Hebbel. 1993. "Fiscal Deficits and Macroeconomic Performance in Developing Countries." *The World Bank Research Observer* 8(2): 211–237.

Economic and Social Commission on Latin America and the Caribbean (ECLAC), various years, *Social Panorama of Latin America.*

Edwards, Sebastian. 1997. "Trade Liberalization Reforms and the World Bank." *The American Economic Review* 87(2): 43–48.

Edwards, Sebastian, and Nora Claudia Lustig, eds. 1997. *Labor Markets in Latin America. Combining Social Protection with Market Flexibility.* Washington, DC: Brookings Institution Press.

Eloy Aguilar, Edwin, and Alexander Pacek. 2000. "Macroeconomic Conditions, Voter Turnout, and the Working-Class/Economically Disadvantaged Party Vote in Developing Countries." *Comparative Political Studies* 33(8): 995–1017.

Epstein, Edward. 1998. "Participation by the Poor in Government Anti-Poverty Programs: The Cases of Chile, Peru, and Argentina Compared." Paper presented at the 1998 meeting of the Latin American Studies Association, Chicago, September 24–26.

Esping-Andersen, Gøsta. 1985. *Politics Against Markets.* Princeton, NJ: Princeton University Press.

Esping-Andersen, Gøsta. 1990. *The Three Worlds of Welfare Capitalism.* Princeton, NJ: Princeton University Press.

Esping-Andersen, Gøsta, ed. 1996. *Welfare States in Transition: National Adaptations in Global Economies.* London: Sage Publications.

Esping-Andersen, Gøsta. 1999. *Social Foundations of Postindustrial Economies.* Oxford: Oxford University Press.

Esping-Andersen, Gøsta, ed. 1999. *Why We Need a New Welfare State.* Oxford: Oxford University Press.

Estevez-Abe, Margarita, Torben Iversen, and David Soskice. 2001. "Social Protection and the Formation of Skills: A Reinterpretation of the Welfare State," in Peter Hall and David Soskice, eds., *Varieties of Capitalism: The Institutional Foundations of Comparative Advantage.* London: Oxford University Press.

Evans, Peter. 1997. "The Eclipse of the State? Reflections on Stateness in an Era of Globalization." *World Politics* 50(1): 62–87.

Feldstein, Martin. 1987. "Should Social Security be Means Tested?" *Journal of Political Economy* 95(3): 468–485.

Feldstein, Martin. 2001. "The Future of Social Security Pensions in Europe." NBER Working Paper no. 8487.

Feldstein, Martin. 2005. "Structural Reform of Social Security." *Journal of Economic Perspectives* 19(2): 33–55.

Feldstein, Martin, and Jeffrey Liebman, eds. 2002. *Distributional Aspects of Social Security and Social Security Reform*. Chicago: University of Chicago Press.

Figueroa, Adolfo. 1994. "La cuestión distributiva en Peru," in Julio Cotler, ed., *Peru 1964–1994*. Lima: Instituto de Estudios Peruanos.

Filgueira, Fernando. 1995. "A Century of Social Welfare in Uruguay: Growth to the Limit of the Batllista Social State." Kellogg Institute, University of Notre Dame: Democracy and Social Policy Series. Working Paper no. 5.

Fishlow, Albert. 1991. "Liberalization in Latin America," in Tariq Banuri, ed., *Liberalization: No Panacea*. Oxford: Oxford University Press.

Fishlow, Albert. 1995a. "Future Sustainable Latin American Growth: A Need for Savings." *Review of Black Political Economy* 24(1).

Fishlow, Albert. 1995b. "Inequality, Poverty and Growth: Where Do We Stand?" *The World Bank Research Observer*. Washington, DC: Annual Conference Supplement.

Fishlow, Albert. 2000. "Brazil and Economic Realities." *Daedalus* 129(2): 339–357.

Foxley, Alejandro. 2005. "Lessons from Chile's Development in the 1990s," in Roberto Zagha and Tim Besley, eds., *Development Challenges in the 1990s: Leading Policy Makers Speak from Experience*. Washington, DC: World Bank.

Foxley, Alejandro, E. Aninat, and J. P. Arellano. 1980. *Las desigualdades económicas y la acción del Estado*. Mexico: FCE.

Franco, Eliana, and Carlos Sojo. 1992. *Gobierno, empresarios y políticas de ajuste*. San José, Costa Rica: FLACSO.

Freeman, John R. 1992. *Political Analysis: An Annual Publication of the Methodology Section of the American Political Science Association*. Ann Arbor: University of Michigan Press.

Frieden, Jeffry. 1991. *Debt, Development, and Democracy*. Princeton, NJ: Princeton University Press.

Frieden, Jeffry, and Ronald Rogowski. 1996. "The Impact of the International Economy on National Policies: An Analytical Overview," in Robert Keohane and Helen Milner (eds.), *Internationalization and Domestic Politics*. New York: Cambridge University Press.

Froot, Kenneth, and Kenneth Rogoff. 1996. "Perspectives on PPP and Long-Run Real Exchange Rates." National Bureau of Economic Research Working Paper 4952. Cambridge, MA.

Funkhouser, Edward, and Juan Pablo Pérez Sáinz. 1998. *Centroamérica en reestructuración. Mercado laboral y pobreza en Centroamérica*. San José, Costa Rica: FLACSO.

Gamarra, Eduardo, and James Malloy. 1995. "The Patrimonial Dynamics of Party Politics in Bolivia," in Scott Mainwaring and Timothy Scully, eds., *Building Democratic Institutions: Party Systems in Latin America*. Stanford, CA: Stanford University Press.

Ganuza, Enrique, Ricardo Paes de Barros, Lance Taylor, and Rob Vos, eds. 2001. *Liberalización, desigualdad y pobreza: América Latina y el Caribe en los 90*. Buenos Aires: Editorial Universitaria de Buenos Aires.

Garrett, Geoffrey. 1995. "Capital Mobility, Trade, and the Domestic Politics of Economic Policy." *International Organization* 49(4): 657–687.

Garrett, Geoffrey. 1998. *Partisan Politics in the Global Economy*. New York: Cambridge University Press.

Garrett, Geoffrey. 2000a. "The Causes of Globalization." *Comparative Political Studies* 33(6/7): 941–991.

Garrett, Geoffrey. 2000b. "Capital Mobility, Exchange Rates and Fiscal Policy in the Global Economy." *Review of International Political Economy* 7(1): 153–170.

Garrett, Geoffrey. 2001. "Globalization and Government Spending Around the World." *Studies in Comparative International Development* 35(4): 3–29.

Garrett, Geoffrey. 2004. "Globalization's Missing Middle." *Foreign Affairs* 83(6).

Garrett, Geoffrey, and Nancy Brune. 2005. "The Globalization Rorschach Test." *Annual Review of Political Science* 8(June): 399–423.

Garrett, Geoffrey, and Deborah Mitchell. 2001. "Globalization, Government Spending and Taxation in the OECD." *European Journal of Political Research* 39(2): 145–177.

Gasiorowski, Mark. 2000. "Democracy and Macroeconomic Performance in Underdeveloped Countries." *Comparative Political Studies* 33(3): 319–349.

Gavin, Michael, Ricard Hausmann, Roberto Perotti, and Ernesto Talvi. 1996. "Managing Fiscal Policy in Latin America and the Caribbean: Volatility, Procyclicality, and Limited Creditworthiness." Working Paper no. 326. Washington, DC: Inter-American Development Bank.

Geddes, Barbara. 1999. "What Do We Know about Democratization after 20 Years?" *Annual Review of Political Science* 2: 115–144.

Genschel, Philipp. 2000. "Tax Competition and the Welfare State." Paper presented to the American Political Science Association's Annual Meeting, Washington, DC, August 31–September 3.

Gereffy, Gary, and Donald L. Wyman, eds. 1990. *Manufacturing Miracles: Paths of Industrialization in Latin America and East Asia.* Princeton, NJ: Princeton University Press.

Ghai, Dharam. 1996. "Foreword," in Gøsta Esping-Andersen, ed., *Welfare States in Transition: National Adaptations in Global Economies.* London: Sage Publications.

Gill, Indermit S., Truman Packard, and Juan Yermo. 2005. *Keeping the Promise of Social Security in Latin America.* Stanford, CA: Stanford University Press.

Gonzales de Olarte, Efraín. 1998. *El Neoliberalismo a la Peruana: Economía Política del Ajuste Estructural, 1990–1997.* Lima: Instituto de Estudios Peruanos.

Goodman, Roger, and Ito Peng. 1996. "The East Asian Welfare States: Peripatetic Learning, Adaptive Change, and Nation-Building," in Gøsta Esping-Andersen, ed., *Welfare States in Transition: National Adaptations in Global Economies.* London: Sage Publications.

Gough, Ian. 2004. *Insecurity and Welfare Regimes in Asia, Africa and Latin America.* Cambridge, UK: Cambridge University Press.

Gourevitch, P. 1986. *Politics in Hard Times: Comparative Responses to International Economic Crises.* Ithaca, NY: Cornell University Press.

Graham, Carol. 1990. "Peru's APRA in Power: Impossible Revolution, Relinquished Reform." *Journal of Interamerican Studies and World Affairs* 23(3): 75–115.

Graham, Carol. 1992. *Peru's APRA: Parties, Politics and the Elusive Quest for Democracy.* Boulder, CO: Lynne Rienner Publishers.

Graham, Carol, and Cheikh Kane. 1998. "Opportunistic Government Spending or Sustaining Reform?" *Latin American Research Review* 33(1): 67–104.

Granato, Jim. 1991. "An Agenda for Econometric Model Building." *Political Analysis* 3: 123–154.

Green, Donald P., Soo Yeon Kim, and David H. Yoon. 2001. "Dirty Pool." *International Organization* 55(2): 441–468.

Greene, William. 2000. *Econometric Analysis*. Upper Saddle River, NJ: Prentice Hall.

Greene, William. 2004. "Distinguishing between Heterogeneity and Inefficiency: Stochastic Frontier Analysis of the World Health Organization's Panel Data on National Health Care Systems." *Health Economics* 13: 959–980.

Greve, Bent. 1996. *Comparative Welfare Systems*. London: Macmillan Press Limited.

Gupta, Sanjeev, Benedict Clemens, Maria Teresa Guin-Siu, and Luc Leruth. 2001. "Debt Relief and Public Health Spending in Heavily Indebted Poor Countries." *Finance and Development* 38(3): 10–13. Washington, DC: International Monetary Fund.

Haggard, Stephan. 1990. *Pathways from the Periphery: The Politics of Growth in the Newly Industrializing Countries*. Ithaca, NY: Cornell University Press.

Haggard, Stephan, and Robert R. Kaufman, eds. 1992. *The Politics of Economic Adjustment*. Princeton, NJ: Princeton University Press.

Haggard, Stephan, and Robert R. Kaufman. 1995. *The Political Economy of Democratic Transitions*. Princeton, NJ: Princeton University Press.

Haggard, Stephan, and Robert R. Kaufman. 2004. "Revising Social Contracts: Social Spending in Latin America, East Asia and the Former Socialist Countries, 1980–2000." *Revista de Ciencia Politica* XXIV(1): 3–37.

Haggard, Stephan, and Nita Rudra. 2005. "Globalization, Democracy, and Effective Welfare Spending in the Developing World." *Comparative Political Studies* 38(9): 1015–1049.

Hagopian, Frances, and Scott P. Mainwaring, eds. 2005. *The Third Wave of Democratization in Latin America: Advances and Setbacks*. Cambridge, UK: Cambridge University Press.

Haltiwanger, John, Adriana Kugler, Maurice Kugler, Alejandro Micco, and Carmen Pages. 2004. "Effects of Tariffs and Real Exchange Rates on Job Reallocation: Evidence from Latin America." *Policy Reform* 7(4): 191–208.

Haque, Nadeem, M. Hashem Pesaran, and Sunil Sharma. 2000. "Neglected Heterogeneity and Dynamics in Cross-Country Savings Regressions," in J. Krishnamukar and E. Ronchetti, eds., *Panel Data Econometrics: Future Directions*. Amsterdam: Elsevier Science B.V.

Heckman, James, and Carmen Pages, eds. 2004. *Law and Employment: Lessons from Latin America and the Caribbean*. Chicago: University of Chicago Press.

Heclo, Hugh. 1974. *Modern Social Politics in Britain and Sweden*. New Haven, CT: Yale University Press.

Heclo, Hugh. 1998. "A Political Science Perspective in Social Security Reform," in R. D. Arnold, M. Graetz, and A. Munnel, eds., *Framing the Social Security Debate*. Washington, DC: National Academy of Social Insurance.

Held, David. 1996. *Models of Democracy*. Stanford: University of California Press.

Heller, Peter S. 2003. *Who Will Pay? Coping with Aging Societies, Climate Change, and Other Long-Term Fiscal Challenges*. Washington, DC: International Monetary Fund.

Hellinger, Daniel, and Dorothea Melcher. 1998. "Venezuela: A Welfare State Out of Gas?" Paper presented at the Annual Meeting of the Latin American Studies Association, Chicago, September 24–26.

Heston, Alan, and Robert Summers. 1991. "The Penn World Table (Mark 5): An Expanded Set of International Comparisons, 1950–1988." *Quarterly Journal of Economics* 2(May): 327–368.

Hicks, Alexander. 1999. *Social Democracy and Welfare Capitalism: A Century of Income Security Politics.* Ithaca, NY: Cornell University Press.

Hicks, Alexander, and Joya Misra. 1993. "Political Resources and the Growth of Welfare in Affluent Capitalist Democracies, 1960–82." *American Journal of Sociology* 99: 668–710.

Hicks, Alexander, and Duane Swank. 1984. "On the Political Economy of Welfare Expansion: A Comparative Analysis of 18 Advanced Capitalist Democracies, 1960–1971." *Comparative Political Studies* 17: 81–118.

Hicks, Alexander, and Duane Swank. 1992. "Politics, Institutions, and Welfare Spending in Industrialized Democracies, 1960–1982." *American Political Science Review* 86: 658–674.

Hiscox, Michael. 2001. "Class Versus Industry Cleavages: Inter-Industry Factor Mobility and the Politics of Trade." *International Organization* 55(1): 1–46.

Hollingsworth, Rogers, Philippe Schmitter, and Wolfgang Streeck, eds. 1994. *Governing Capitalist Economies.* New York: Oxford University Press.

Holsey, Cheryl, and Thomas Bordering. 1997. "Why Does Government's Share of National Income Grow? An Assessment of Recent Literature on the US Experience," in Dennis Mueller, ed., *Perspectives on Public Choice: A Handbook.* New York: Cambridge University Press.

Hsiao, Cheng, and Baohong Sun. 2000. "To Pool or Not Pool Panel Data," in J. Krishnamukar and E. Ronchetti, eds., *Panel Data Econometrics: Future Directions.* Amsterdam: Elsevier Science B.V.

Huber, Evelyne. 1996. "Options for Social Policy in Latin America: Neoliberal versus Social Democratic Models," in Gøsta Esping-Andersen, ed., *Welfare States in Transition: National Adaptations in Global Economies.* London: Sage Publications.

Huber, Evelyne, Francois Nielsen, Jenny Pribble, and John Stephens. 2004. "Social Spending and Inequality in Latin America and the Caribbean." Paper prepared for the Meeting of the Society for the Advancement of Socio-Economics, Washington, DC.

Huber, Evelyne, Charles Ragin, and John Stephens. 1993. "Social Democracy, Christian Democracy, Constitutional Structure and the Welfare State: Towards a Resolution of Quantitative Studies." *American Journal of Sociology* 99(3): 711–749.

Huber, Evelyne, and John Stephens. 2001. *Development and Crisis of the Welfare State: Parties and Policies in Global Markets.* Chicago: University of Chicago Press.

Huber, John. 1998. "How Does Party Instability Affect Political Performance? Portfolio Volatility and Health Care Cost Containment in Parliamentary Democracies." *American Political Science Review* 92(3): 577–591.

Hunter, Wendy, and David Brown. 2000. "World Bank Directives, Domestic Interests, and the Politics of Human Capital Investment in Latin America." *Comparative Political Studies* 33(1): 113–143.

Huntington, Samuel. 1991. *The Third Wave: Democratization in the Late Twentieth Century.* Norman: University of Oklahoma Press.

Ikenberry, G. John, and Theda Skocpol. 1987. "Expanding Social Benefits: The Role of Social Security." *Political Science Quarterly* 102(3): 389–416.

Immergut, Ellen. 1992. *The Political Construction of Interests: National Health Insurance Politics in Switzerland, France and Sweden, 1930–1970.* New York: Cambridge University Press.

Inter-American Development Bank. 2004. *Good Jobs Wanted: Labor Markets in Latin America.* Baltimore: Johns Hopkins University Press.

International Monetary Fund (Various Years). *Government Finance Statistics.* Washington, DC.

International Monetary Fund (Various Years). *International Financial Statistics.* Washington, DC.

International Monetary Fund. 1986. *A Manual on Government Finance Statistics.* Washington, DC.

International Monetary Fund. 2001. *A Manual on Government Finance Statistics.* Washington, DC.

Institute for Democracy and Electoral Assistance (IDEA). 2005. *Voter Turnout from 1945 to 1997: A Global Report on Political Participation.* Stockholm: International Institute for Democracy and Electoral Assistance.

Iversen, Torben. 2000. "The Dynamics of Welfare State Expansion: Trade Openness, Deindustrialization, and Partisan Politics," in Paul Pierson, ed., *The New Politics of the Welfare State.* New York: Oxford University Press.

Iversen, Torben. 2001. "An Asset Theory of Social Policy Preferences." *American Political Science Review* 95(4): 875–893.

Iversen, Torben, and Thomas Cusack. 2000. "The Causes of Welfare State Expansion: Deindustrialization or Globalization?" *World Politics* 52: 313–349.

Iversen, Torben, and Anne Wren. 1998. "Equality, Employment, and Budgetary Restraint: The Trilemma of the Service Economy." *World Politics* 50(4): 507–546.

Janoski, Thomas, and Alexander Hicks. 1994. "Methodological Innovations in Comparative Political Economy: An Introduction," in Thomas Janoski and Alexander Hicks, eds., *The Comparative Political Economy of the Welfare State.* Cambridge, UK: Cambridge University Press.

Johnston, J. 1972. *Econometric Methods.* New York: McGraw-Hill.

Kam, Cindy D., and Robert J. Franzese. 2005. *Modeling and Interpreting Interactive Hypotheses in Regression Analysis: A Refresher and Some Practical Advice.* Unpublished manuscript.

Karl, Terry Lynn. 1997. *The Paradox of Plenty: Oil Booms and Petro-States.* Berkeley and Los Angeles: University of California Press

Katzenstein, Peter. 1985. *Small States in World Markets.* Ithaca, NY: Cornell University Press.

Kaufman, Robert. 1977. "Corporatism, Clientelism, and Partisan Conflict: A Study of Seven Latin American Countries," in James Malloy, ed., *Authoritarianism and Corporatism in Latin America.* Pittsburgh, PA: University of Pittsburgh Press.

Kaufman, Robert. 1997. "Moving Ahead: The Coming Challenges for South America." *Harvard International Review* 19(4).

Kaufman, Robert. 2000. "The Origins and Evolution of Social Security in Latin America, 1900–1980." New York: Columbia University, manuscript.

Kaufman, Robert, and Joan Nelson. 2004. *Crucial Needs, Weak Incentives: Social Sector Reform, Democratization, and Globalization in Latin America.* Baltimore: Johns Hopkins University Press.

Kaufman, Robert, and Alex Segura-Ubiergo. 2001. "Globalization, Domestic Politics and Social Spending in Latin America: A Time-Series Cross-Section Analysis." *World Politics* 53(4): 553–587.

Kaufman, Robert, and Barbara Stallings. 1991. "The Political Economy of Latin American Populism," in Rudiger Dornbusch and Sebastian Edwards, eds., *The Macroeconomics of Populism in Latin America.* Chicago: University of Chicago Press.

Kenney, Charles. 1992. "Por qué el autogolpe? Fujimori y el Congreso, 1990–92," in Fernando Tuesta Soldevila, ed., *Los Enigmas del Poder*. Lima: Fundación Friedrich Ebert.

Keohane, Robert, and Helen Milner, eds. 1996. *Internationalization and Domestic Politics*. New York: Cambridge University Press.

Key, V. O. 1949. *Southern Politics in State and Nation*. New York: Knopf.

Kitschelt, Herbert, Peter Lange, Gary Marks, and John Stephens, eds. 1999. *Continuity and Change in Contemporary Capitalism*. New York: Cambridge University Press.

Kitschelt, Herbert, Zdenka Mansfeldova, Radoslaw Markowski, and Gábor Tóka. 1999. *Post-Communist Party Systems: Competition, Representation, and Inter-Party Cooperation*. New York: Cambridge University Press.

Kmenta, J. 1971. *Elements of Econometrics*. New York: Macmillan Co.

Korpi, Walter. 1978. *The Working Class in Welfare Capitalism*. London: Routledge and Kegan Paul.

Korpi, Walter. 1983. *The Democratic Class Struggle*. London: Routledge and Kegan Paul.

Korpi, Walter. 1989. "Power, Politics, and State Autonomy in the Development of Social Citizenship: Social Rights during Sickness in Eighteen OECD Countries since 1930." *American Sociological Review* 54: 309–329.

Korpi, Walter, and Joakim Palme. 1998. "The Strategy of Equality and the Paradox of Redistribution." *American Sociological Review* 63: 661–687.

Korpi, Walter, and Joakim Palme. 2003. "New Politics and Class Politics in the Context of Austerity and Globalization: Welfare State Regress in 18 Countries, 1975–95." *American Political Science Review* 97(3): 425–446.

Krishnakumar, Jaya, and Elvezio Ronchetti, eds. 2000. *Panel Data Econometrics: Future Directions*. Amsterdam: Elsevier.

Krugman, Paul. 1999. *International Economics*. New York: Addison-Wesley Longman.

Kurtz, Marcus. 2004. "The Dilemmas of Democracy in the Open Economy: Lessons from Latin America." *World Politics* 56(2): 262–302.

Lake, David, and Matthew Baum. 2000. "The Invisible Hand of Democracy: Political Control and the Provision of Public Services." Los Angeles: University of California, Mimeo.

Lamounier, Bolivar. 1999. "Brazil: Inequality against Democracy," in Larry Diamond, Jonathan Hartlyn, Seymour Martin Lipset, and Juan J. Linz, eds., *Democracy in Developing Countries: Latin America*. Boulder, CO: Lynne Rienner Publishers.

Lara, Silvia. 1995. *Inside Costa Rica*. Albuquerque, NM: Resource Center.

Larrañaga, Osvaldo. 1992. *Macroeconomics, Income Distribution and Social Services: Peru during the 1980s*. Santiago de Chile: ILADES-Georgetown University.

Lehoucq, Fabrice. 1997. *Lucha electoral y sistema político en Costa Rica, 1948–1998*. San José, Costa Rica: Editorial Porvenir.

Lehoucq, Fabrice. 1998. *Instituciones democráticas y conflictos políticos en Costa Rica*. San José, Costa Rica: Euna.

Lengyel, Miguel, and Vivianne Ventura-Dias, eds. 2004. *Trade Policy Reforms in Latin America*. New York: Palgrave MacMillan.

Levin, Andrew, and C. F. Lin. 1993. "Unit Root Tests in Panel Data: Asymptotic and Finite-Sample Properties." Discussion Paper 92–93, Department of Economics, University of California, San Diego.

Levy, Daniel C., and Kathleen Bruhn. 1995. "Mexico: Sustained Civilian Rule Without Democracy," in Larry Diamond, Juan Linz, and Seymour Martin Lipset, eds., *Politics in Developing Countries: Comparing Experiences with Democracy*. Boulder, CO: Lynne Rienner Publishers.

Lijphart, Arend. 1999. *Patterns of Democracy. Government Forms and Performance in Thirty-Six Countries*. New Haven: Yale University Press.

Lindert, Peter. 1994. "The Rise of Social Spending 1880–1930." *Explorations in Economic History* 31(1): 1–37.

Linz, Juan J. 1975. "Totalitarian and Authoritarian Regimes," in Fred I. Greenstein and Nelson W. Polsby, eds., *Handbook of Political Science*, Vol. 3. Reading, MA: Addison Wesley.

Linz, Juan J. 1994. "Presidential or Parliamentary Democracy: Does It Make a Difference?," in Juan J. Linz and Arturo Valenzuela, eds., *The Failure of Presidential Democracy: The Case of Latin America*. Baltimore: Johns Hopkins University Press.

Linz, Juan J., and Alfred Stepan. 1996. *Problems of Democratic Transition and Consolidation*. Baltimore: Johns Hopkins University Press.

Linz, Juan J., and Arturo Valenzuela, eds. 1994. *The Failure of Presidential Democracy*. Vol. II. Baltimore: Johns Hopkins University Press.

Lipset, Seymour, and Martin Rokkan, eds. 1967. *Party System and Voter Alignments*. New York: Free Press.

Lizano, Eduardo. 1990. *Programa de ajuste estructural en Costa Rica*. San José: Academia de Centroamérica.

Lizzeri, Alessandro, and Nicola Persico. 2004. "Why Did the Elites Extend the Suffrage? Democracy and the Scope of Government, with an Application to Britain's 'Age of Reform.'" *Quarterly Journal of Economics* 119(May): 705–765.

Lloyd-Sherlock, Peter. 2000. "Failing the Needy: Public Social Spending in Latin America." *Journal of International Development* 12: 101–119.

Lora, Eduardo, Carmen Pages, Ugo Panizza, and Ernesto Stein. 2004. *A Decade of Development Thinking*. Washington, DC: Inter-American Development Bank.

Lynch, Nicolás. 1999. *Una tragedia sin héroes: La derrota de los partidos y el orígen de los independientes en el Perú 1980–1992*. Lima: Fondo editorial de la Universidad Mayor de San Marcos.

Maddala, G. S. 1971. *Econometrics*. New York: McGraw-Hill.

Maddala, G. S. 1998. "Recent Developments in Dynamic Econometric Modelling: A Personal Viewpoint." *Political Analysis* 7: 59–87.

Maddala, G. S., Shaowen Wu, and Peter C. Liu. 2000. "Do Panel Data Rescue the Purchasing Power Parity (PPP) Theory?," in J. Krishnamukar and E. Ronchetti, eds., *Panel Data Econometrics: Future Directions*. Amsterdam: Elsevier Science B.V.

Mainwaring, Scott. 1999. *Rethinking Party Systems in the Third Wave of Democratization, The Case of Brazil*. Stanford, CA: Stanford University Press.

Mainwaring, Scott, Daniel Brick, and Aníbal Pérez-Liñán. 2001. "Classifying Political Regimes in Latin America, 1945–1999." *Studies in International Comparative Development* 36(1): 37–65.

Mainwaring, Scott, and Aníbal Pérez-Liñán. 2005. "Latin American Democratization since 1978: Regime Transitions, Breakdowns, and Erosions," in F. Hagopian and S. Mainwaring, eds., *The Third Wave of Democratization in Latin America – Advances and Setbacks*. New York: Cambridge University Press.

Mainwaring, Scott, and Timothy Scully, eds. 1995. *Building Democratic Institutions: Party Systems in Latin America*. Stanford, CA: Stanford University Press.

Mainwaring, Scott, and Timothy Scully. 1995. "Introduction," in Mainwaring and Scully, eds., *Parties and Party Systems in Latin America*. Stanford, CA: Stanford University Press.

Malloy, James M. 1979. *The Politics of Social Security in Brazil*. Pittsburgh, PA: University of Pittsburgh Press.

Maravall, José María. 1997. *Regime Politics and Markets: Democratization and Economic Change in Southern Europe and Eastern Europe*. New York: Oxford University Press.

Marcel, Mario, and Andrés Solimano. 1994. "The Distribution of Income and Economic Adjustment," in Barry Bosworth, Rudiger Dornbusch, and Raúl Labán, eds., *The Chilean Economy: Policy Lessons and Challenges*. Washington, DC: The Brookings Institution.

Marcus-Delgado, Jane. 1999. *The Logic of Presidential Legitimacy and Neoliberal Reform in Argentina and Peru*. Johns Hopkins University, Unpublished Ph.D. Dissertation.

Mares, Isabela. 2004. "Economic Insecurity and Social Policy Expansion: Evidence from Interwar Europe." *International Organization* 58(Fall): 745–774.

Marshall, Monty, Keith Jaggers, and Ted Robert Gurr. 2005. *Polity IV, Political Regime Characteristics and Transitions, 1800–2003*. Available at http://www.cidcm.umd.edu/inscr/polity/.

Marshall, T. H. 1963. *Class, Citizenship and Social Development*. Chicago: University of Chicago Press.

Martin, Cathie Jo, and Duane Swank. 2004. "Does the Organization of Capital Matter? Employers and Active Labor Market Policy at the National and Firm Levels." *American Political Science Review* 98(4): 593–611.

Martínez, Juliana. 2000. "Luces y sombras: formación y transformación de las políticas sociales en América Latina." *Cuaderno de Ciencias Sociales 117*. San José, Costa Rica: CLACSO.

Mazza, Jacqueline. 2004. "Social Inclusion, Labor Markets and Human Capital in Latin America," in Mayra Buvinic and Jacqueline Mazza, eds., *Social Inclusion and Economic Development in Latin America*. Baltimore: Johns Hopkins University Press.

McClintock, Cynthia. 1996. "La voluntad política presidencial y la ruptura constitucional de 1992 en el Perú," in Fernando Tuesta Soldevila, ed., *Los Enigmas del Poder*. Lima: Fundación Friedrich Ebert.

McGuire, James W. 1995. "Political Parties and Democracy in Argentina," in Scott Mainwaring and Timothy Scully, eds., *Building Democratic Institutions: Party Systems in Latin America*. Stanford, CA: Stanford University Press.

McNutt, P. A. 1996. *The Economics of Public Choice*. Cheltenham, UK: Edward Elgar.

Medlin, Carol Ann. 1998. *Limits to Reform: Neoliberal Social Policy in Chile (1973–89)*. University of California, Berkeley: Ph.D. Dissertation.

Meller, Patricio, ed. 1996. *El modelo exportador chileno. Crecimiento y equidad*. Santiago de Chile: CIEPLAN.

Meller, Patricio. 2000. *The Unidad Popular and the Pinochet Dictatorship: A Political Economy Analysis*. London: Macmillan Press Limited.

Meltzer, A. H., and S. F. Richards. 1981. "A Rational Theory of the Size of Government." *Journal of Political Economy* 89: 914–927.

Mesa-Lago, Carmelo. 1978. *Social Security in Latin America: Pressure Groups, Stratification, and Inequality*. Pittsburgh, PA: University of Pittsburgh Press.

Mesa-Lago, Carmelo. 1989. *Ascent to Bankruptcy: Financing Social Security in Latin America*. Pittsburgh, PA: University of Pittsburgh Press.

Mesa-Lago, Carmelo. 2000. *Market, Socialist, and Mixed Economies: Comparative Policy Performance: Chile, Cuba, Costa Rica*. Baltimore: Johns Hopkins University Press.

Milanovic, Branko. 1999. "Do More Unequal Countries Redistribute More? Does the Median Voter Hypothesis Hold?" World Bank, Policy Research Working Paper no. 2264.

Milesi-Ferretti, Gian Maria, and Roberto Perotti (with Massimo Rostagno). 2001. "Electoral Systems and Public Spending." IMF Working Paper WP/01/22.

Mittleman, James. 1996. "The Dynamics of Globalization," in James Mittleman, ed., *Globalization: Critical Reflections*. Boulder, CO: Lynne Rienner Publishers.

Modigliani, Franco, and Arun Muralidhar. 2005. *Rethinking Pension Reform*. New York: Cambridge University Press.

Moene, Karl Ove, and Michael Wallerstein. 2001. "Inequality, Social Insurance, and Redistribution." *American Political Science Review* 95(4): 859–874.

Montecinos, Veronica. 1999. *Economists, Politics and the State: Chile 1958–1994*. Amsterdam: Center for Latin American Research and Documentation.

Moon, Bruce E. 1991. *The Political Economy of Basic Human Needs*. Ithaca, NY: Cornell University Press.

Morales-Gómez, Daniel, ed. 1999. *Transnational Social Policies: The New Development Challenges of Globalization*. London: Earthscan Publications Ltd.

Morley, Samuel. 2001. *The Income Distribution Problem in Latin America and the Caribbean*. Santiago de Chile: Economic Commission for Latin America and the Caribbean (ECLAC).

Morley, Samuel, Roberto Machado, and Stefano Pettinato. 1999. "Indexes of Structural Reform in Latin America," *ECLAC Economic Development Division*, LC/L.1166, January.

Mosley, Layna. 1998. "Strong but Narrow: International Financial Market Pressures and Welfare State Policies." Paper presented at the Eleventh Annual Conference of Europeanists, Baltimore, MD, February 26–28.

Mosley, Layna. 2003. *Global Capital and National Governments*. New York: Cambridge University Press.

Mostajo, Rossana. 2000. "Gasto Social y Distribución del Ingreso: Caracterización e Impacto Redistributivo en Países Seleccionados de América Latina y el Caribe." *Serie Reformas Económicas #69*. Santiago: CEPAL.

Mulas-Granados, Carlos. 2006. *Economics, Politics and Budgets: The Political Economy of Fiscal Consolidations in Europe*. New York: Palgrave Macmillan.

Mulligan, Casey, and Ricard Gil. 2002. "Social Spending and Democracy: Some Evidence from South America." *Estudios de Economia* 29(1): 5–33.

Mulligan, Casey, and Xavier Sala-i-Martin. 2003. "Social Security, Retirement, and the Single-Mindedness of the Electorate"; NBER Working Paper Series no. 9691. Cambridge, MA: National Bureau of Economic Research.

Muñoz, Oscar. 1968. *Crecimiento Industrial de Chile 1914–1965*. Santiago: Universidad de Chile.

Murillo, M. Victoria. 2000. "From Populism to Neoliberalism: Labor Unions and Market Reforms in Latin America." *World Politics* 52(2): 135–174.

Murillo-Zamorano, Luis. 2004. "Economic Efficiency and Frontier Techniques." *Journal of Economic Surveys* 18(1): 33–77.

Nelson, Joan M. 1989. "Crisis Management, Economic Reform and Costa Rican Democracy," in Barbara Stallings and Robert Kaufman, eds., *Debt and Democracy in Latin America*. Boulder, CO: Westview Press.

Nelson, Joan M. 1997. "Social Costs, Social-Sector Reforms, and Politics in Post-Communist Transformations," in Joan M. Nelson, Charles Tilly, and Lee Walker, eds., *Transforming Post-Communist Political Economies*. Washington, DC: National Academy Press.

Nelson, Joan M. 2000. "The Politics of Pension and Health-Care Delivery: Reforms in Hungary and Poland," in Janos Kornai, Stephan Haggard, and Robert R. Kaufman, eds., *Reforming the State: Fiscal and Welfare Reform in Post-Socialist Countries*. Cambridge, UK: Cambridge University Press.

Nickell, S. 1981. "Biases in Dynamic Models with Fixed Effects." *Econometrica* 49(6): 1417–1426.

Niskanen, W. 1987. *Bureaucracy and Representative Government*. Chicago: Aldine Atherton.

North, Douglas. 1990. *Institutions, Institutional Change and Economic Performance*. Cambridge, UK: Cambridge University Press.

Oatley, Thomas. 1999. "How Constraining Is Capital Mobility? The Partisan Hypothesis in an Open Economy." *American Journal of Political Science* 43(4): 1003–1027.

Ocampo, José Antonio, and Juan Martin, eds. 2003. *Globalization and Development*. Stanford, CA: Stanford University Press.

O'Donnell, Guillermo. 1994. "Delegative Democracy." *Journal of Democracy* 5(1): 55–69.

O'Donnell, Guillermo, and Philippe Schmitter. 1986. *Tentative Conclusions about Uncertain Democracies*. Baltimore: Johns Hopkins University Press.

Offe, Claus. 1984. *Contradictions of the Welfare State*. Cambridge, MA: The MIT Press.

Olave Castillo, Patricia. 1997. *El Proyecto Neoliberal en Chile y la Construcción de una Nueva Economía*. Mexico City: Instituto de Inverstigaciones Económicas, Universidad Nacional Autónoma de Mexico.

Olson, Mancur. 1993. "Dictatorship, Democracy, and Development." *American Political Science Review* 87(3): 567–576.

Olson, Mancur, and Martin McGuire. 1996. "The Economics of Autocracy and Majority Rule: The Invisible Hand and the Use of Force." *Journal of Economic Literature* 34(1): 72–97.

Orloff, Ann S. 1992. *The Politics of Pensions*. Madison: University of Wisconsin Press.

Orloff, Ann S. 1993. *The Politics of Pensions: A Comparative Analysis of Britain, Canada, and the United States, 1880–1940*. Madison: University of Wisconsin Press.

Ostrom, Charles, and Reneé Smith. 1992. "Error Correction, Attitude Persistence, and Executive Rewards and Punishments: A Behavioral Theory of Presidential Approval." *Political Analysis* 4: 127–181.

Palacios, Robert, and Montserrat Pallares-Miralles. 2000. "International Patterns of Pension Provision," World Bank, Manuscript.

Pampel, Fred, and John Williamson. 1989. *Age, Class, Politics and the Welfare State*. New York: Cambridge University Press.

Parodi, Carlos. 2000. "Perú 1960–2000." *Políticas Económicas y Sociales en Entornos Cambiantes*. Lima: Universidad del Pacífico.

Paus, Eva Reinhardt, and Michael Robinson. 2003. "Trade Liberalization and Productivity Growth in Latin American Manufacturing, 1970–98." *Policy Reform* 6(1): 1–15.

Pesaran, M. Hashem, and Ron Smith. 1995. "Estimating Long-Run Relationships from Dynamic Heterogeneous Panels." *Journal of Econometrics* 68: 79–113.

Pfeffermann, Guy. 1998. "The Way Ahead: Economic Reform in Latin America." Paper presented at the Second Latin American Conference, Center for Global Energy Studies, Miami, March 4.

Phelps, Edmund S. 1996. "On the Damaging Side Effects of the Welfare System: How, Why and What to Do," in Mario Baldassarri, Luigi Paganetto, and Edmund S. Phelps, eds., *Equity, Efficiency and Growth: The Future of the Welfare State*. London: Macmillan Press Ltd.

Pierson, Paul. 1991. *Beyond the Welfare State?* Cambridge, MA: Polity Press.

Pierson, Paul. 1995. "Fragmented Welfare States: Federal Institutions and the Development of Social Policy." *Governance: An International Journal of Policy and Administration* 8(4): 449–478.

Pierson, Paul. 1996. "The New Politics of the Welfare State." *World Politics* 48(2): 143–179.

Pierson, Paul. 2000a. "Three Worlds of Welfare State Research." *Comparative Political Studies* 33(6/7): 791–821.

Pierson, Paul, ed. 2000b. *The New Politics of the Welfare State*. New York: Oxford University Press.

Polanyi, Karl. 1944. *The Great Transformation: The Political and Economic Origins of Our Time*. Boston: Beacon Press.

Pontual Ribeiro, Eduardo, Carlos Corseuil, Daniel Santos, Paulo Furtado, Brunu Amorim, Luciana Servo, and Andre Souza. 2004. "Trade Liberalization, the Exchange Rate and Job Flows in Brazil." *Policy Reform* 7(4): 209–223.

Portes, Alejandro, Manuel Castells, and Lauren A. Benton. 1989. *The Informal Economy*. Baltimore: Johns Hopkins University Press.

Porzecanski, Arturo. 1978. "The Case of Uruguay," in Carmelo Mesa-Lago, *Social Security in Latin America: Pressure Groups, Stratification, and Inequality*. Pittsburgh, PA: University of Pittsburgh Press.

Przeworki, Adam. 1985. *Capitalism and Social Democracy*. New York: Cambridge University Press.

Przeworski, Adam. 1991. *Democracy and the Market*. Cambridge, UK: Cambridge University Press.

Przeworski, Adam. 1993. "The Neoliberal Fallacy," in Diamond and Plattnet, eds., *Capitalism, Socialism and Democracy Revisited*. Baltimore: Johns Hopkins University Press.

Przeworski, Adam. 1995. *Sustainable Democracy*. Cambridge, UK: Cambridge University Press.

Przeworski, Adam, Fernando Limongi, Michael Alvarez, and José Antonio Cheibub. 2000. *Democracy and Development: Political Institutions and Well-Being in the World, 1950–1990*. New York: Cambridge University Press.

Quinn, Dennis. 1997. "The Correlates of Change in International Financial Regulation." *American Political Science Review* 91: 531–552.

Raczynski, Dagmar. 1994. "Social Policies in Chile: Origin, Transformation, and Perspectives." Kellogg Institute, University of Notre Dame, Democracy and Social Policy Series, Working Paper no. 4.

Raczynski, Dagmar. 2000. "Overcoming Poverty in Chile," in Joseph S. Tulchin and Allison M. Garland, eds., *Social Development in Latin America: The Politics of Reform*. Boulder, CO, and London: Lynne Rienner Publishers.

Raczynski, Dagmar, and Pilar Romaguera. 1994. "Chile: Poverty, Adjustment, and Social Policies in the 1980s," in Nora Lustig, ed., *Coping with Austerity: Poverty and Inequality in Latin America*. Washington, DC: The Brookings Institution.

Ragin, Charles. 1987. *The Comparative Method: Moving Beyond Quantitative and Qualitative Strategies*. Berkeley: University of California Press.

Ragin, Charles. 1994. "A Qualitative Comparative Analysis of Pension Systems," in Thomas Janoski and Alexander M. Hicks, eds., *The Comparative Political Economy of the Welfare State*. New York: Cambridge University Press.

Ram, Rati. 1987. "Wagner's Hypothesis in Time-Series and Cross-Section Perspectives: Evidence from Real Data for 115 Countries." *Review of Economics and Statistics* 69: 194–204.

Reinecke, Gerhard, and Raymond Torres. 2001. "Chile." *Studies on the Social Dimensions of Globalization*. Geneva: International Labor Office.

Rhodes, Martin, ed. 1997. *Southern European Welfare States: Between Crisis and Reform*. London: Frank Cass.

Roberts, Kevin. 1977. "Voting over Income Tax Schedules." *Journal of Public Economics* 8: 329–347.

Roberts, Kenneth. 1996. "Neoliberalism and the Transformation of Populism in Latin America: The Peruvian Case." *World Politics* 48(1): 82–116.

Roberts, Kenneth. 1997. *Deepening Democracy? The Modern Left and Social Movements in Chile and Peru*. Stanford, CA: Stanford University Press.

Roberts, Kenneth, and Moises Arce. 1998. "Neoliberalism and Lower-Class Voting Behavior in Peru." *Comparative Political Studies* 31(2): 217–246.

Roberts, Kenneth, and Erik Wibbels. 1999. "Party Systems and Electoral Volatility in Latin America: A Test of Economic, Institutional, and Structural Explanations." *American Political Science Review* 93(3): 575–590.

Rodden, Jonathan. 2000. "Reviving Leviathan: Fiscal Federalism and the Growth of Government." Paper prepared for delivery at the 2000 Annual Meeting of the American Political Science Association, August 31–September 3.

Rodrik, Dani. 1997. *Has Globalization Gone Too Far?* Washington, DC: Institute for International Economics.

Rodrik, Dani. 1998. "Why Do More Open Economies Have Bigger Governments?" *Journal of Political Economy* 106(5): 997–1032.

Rodrik, Dani. 1999a. "The New Global Economy and Developing Countries: Making Openness Work." Policy Essay no. 24. Washington, DC: Overseas Development Council.

Rodrik, Dani. 1999b. "Why Is There So Much Economic Insecurity in Latin America?" Harvard University, manuscript.

Rogowski, Ronald. 1989. *Commerce and Coalitions.* Princeton, NJ: Princeton University Press.

Rojas Bolaños, Manuel, and Carlos Sojo. 1995. *El malestar con la política: Partidos y élites en Costa Rica.* San José, Costa Rica: FLACSO.

Romer, Thomas. 1975. "Individual Welfare, Majority Voting, and the Properties of a Linear Income Tax." *Journal of Public Economics* 4: 163–185.

Rudra, Nita. 2002. "The Decline of the Welfare State in Less Developed Countries." *International Organization* 56(2): 411–445.

Rudra, Nita. 2005. "Globalization and the Strengthening of Democracy in the Developing World." *American Journal of Political Science* 49(4): 704–730.

Rueda, David. 2005. "Insider-Outsider Politics in Industrialized Democracies: The Challenge to Social Democratic Parties." *American Political Science Review* 99(1): 61–74.

Rueda, David, and Jonas Pontusson. 2000. "Wage Inequality and Varieties of Capitalism." *World Politics* 52(July): 350–383.

Rueschemeyer, Dietrich, Evelyne Huber Stephens, and John D. Stephens. 1992. *Capitalist Development and Democracy.* Chicago: University of Chicago Press.

Ruggie, John Gerard. 1983. "International Regimes, Transactions, and Change: Embedded Liberalism in the Postwar Economic Order," in Stephen D. Krasner, *International Regimes.* Ithaca, NY: Cornell University Press.

Saavedra, Jaime, and Maximo Torero. 2004. "Labor Market Reforms and Their Impact over Formal Labor Demand and Job Market Turnover," in James Heckman and Carmen Pages, eds., *Law and Employment. Lessons from Latin America and the Caribbean.* Chicago: University of Chicago Press.

Sala-i-Martin, Xavier. 1997. "Transfers, Social Safety Nets, and Economic Growth." *International Monetary Fund Staff Papers* 44(1): 81–102.

Sala-i-Martin, Xavier. 1999. "*Social Security in Theory and Practice (I): Facts and Political Theories.*" Working Paper no. 7118. Cambridge, MA: National Bureau of Economic Research.

Sala-i-Martin, Xavier. 2004. "Do Democracies Have Different Public Policies than Non-Democracies?" *Journal of Economic Perspectives* 18(1): 51–74.

Samuelson, Paul. 1975. "Optimum Social Security in a Life-Cycle Growth Model." *International Economic Review* 16(3): 539–544.

Sanchez, Gabriel, and Ines Butler. 2004. "Market Institutions, Labor Market Dynamics, and Productivity in Argentina during the 1990s." *Policy Reform* 7(4): 249–278.

Sartori, Giovanni, ed. 1984. *Social Science Concepts: A Systematic Analysis.* Beverly Hills, CA: Sage Publications.

Sayrs, Lois. 1989. *Pooled Time-Series Analysis.* London: Sage Publications.

Schamis, Hector E. 1999. "Distributional Coalitions and the Politics of Economic Reform in Latin America." *World Politics* 51(2): 236–268.

Scharpf, Fritz. "Welfare and Work in the Open Economy: Constraints, Challenges and Vulnerabilities." Paper prepared for delivery at the 2000 Annual Meeting of the American Political Science Association, Washington, DC, August 31–September 3.

Schmitter, Philippe. 1992. "The Consolidation of Democracy and the Representation of Social Groups." *American Behavioral Scientist* 35(March–June): 422–449.

Schneider, Ben Ross. 2004a. *Business Politics and the State in Twentieth-Century Latin America.* Cambridge, UK: Cambridge University Press.

Schneider, Ben Ross. 2004b. "Organizing Interests and Coalitions in the Politics of Market Reform in Latin America." *World Politics* 56(3): 456–479.

Schumpeter, Joseph. 1950. *Capitalism, Socialism and Democracy.* New York: Harper & Row.

Scully, Timothy. 1995. "Reconstituting Party Politics in Chile," in Scott Mainwaring and Timothy Scully, eds., *Building Democratic Institutions: Party Systems in Latin America.* Stanford, CA: Stanford University Press.

Seligson, M. A., J. Martínez, and J. D. Trejos. 1996. "Reducción de la pobreza en Costa Rica: el impacto de las políticas públicas." *Serie Divulgación Económica #51.* San José, Costa Rica: Instituto de Investigaciones en Ciencias Económicas de la Universidad de Costa Rica.

Selowsky, Marcelo. 1979. *Who Benefits from Government Expenditure?* New York: Oxford University Press.

Shack, Nelson. 1999. "Ensayando una nueva taxonomía del Gasto Público en el Perú." Documento de trabajo, Ministerio de Economía y Finanzas. Lima: MEF.

Sheahan, John. 2001. *La economía Peruana desde 1950. Buscando una sociedad mejor.* Lima: Instituto de Estudios Peruanos.

Silva, Eduardo. 1998. "Organized Business, Neoliberal Economic Restructuring, and Redemocratization in Chile," in Francisco Durand and Eduardo Silva, *Organized Business, Economic Change, and Democracy in Latin America.* Miami: North-South Center Press, University of Miami.

Skocpol, Theda. 1986. "States and Social Policies." *Annual Review of Sociology* 12: 131–157.

Skocpol, Theda. 1988. "The Limits of the New Deal System and the Roots of Contemporary Welfare Dilemmas," in Margaret Wier, Ann Shola Orloff, and Theda Skocpol, eds., *The Politics of Social Policy in the United States.* Princeton, NJ: Princeton University Press.

Sloan, John, and Kent Tedin. 1987. "The Consequences of Regime Type for Public Policy Outcomes." *Comparative Political Studies* 20(April): 98–124.

Snower, Dennis. 1996. "What Is the Domain of the Welfare State?" in Mario Baldassarri, Luigi Paganetto, and Edmund S. Phelps, eds., *Equity, Efficiency and Growth: The Future of the Welfare State.* London: Macmillan Press Ltd.

Sociedad Nacional de Exportadores. 1997. *Empresa, Sociedad y Estado. Por qué y cómo la responsabilidad social deber ser compartida entre el sector privado y el Estado.* Lima: Sociedad Nacional de Exportadores.

Sojo, Carlos. 1997. *Los de en medio. La nueva pobreza en Costa Rica.* San José, Costa Rica: FLACSO.

Sojo, Carlos. 1999. *Democracias con fracturas: gobernabilidad, reforma económica y transición en centroamérica.* San José, Costa Rica: FLACSO.

Stallings, Barbara. 1978. *Class Conflict and Economic Development in Chile, 1958–1973.* Stanford, CA: Stanford University Press.

Stallings, Barbara, and Robert Kaufman, eds. 1989. *Debt and Democracy in Latin America.* Boulder, CO: Westview Press.

Stallings, Barbara, and Wilson Peres. 2000. *Growth, Employment and Equity: The Impact of the Economic Reforms in Latin America and the Caribbean.* Washington, DC: The Brookings Institution.

Steinmetz, George. 1996. "The Myth of the Autonomous State: Industrialists, Junkers, and Social Policy in Imperial Germany," in Eley Geoff, ed., *Society, Culture and the State in Germany, 1870–1930*. Ann Arbor: University of Michigan Press.

Stepan, Alfred. 1978. *The State and Society: Peru in Comparative Perspective*. Princeton, NJ: Princeton University Press.

Stepan, Alfred. 1985. "State Power and the Strength of Civil Society in the Southern Cone of Latin America," in Peter Evans, Dietriech Rueschmeyer, and Theda Skocpol, eds., *Bringing the State Back In*. Cambridge, UK: Cambridge University Press.

Stepan, Alfred, ed. 1989. *Democratizing Brazil: Problems of Transition and Consolidation*. New York: Oxford University Press.

Stepan, Alfred. 2000. "Brazil's Decentralized Federalism: Bringing Government Closer to the People?" *Daedalus* 129(2): 145–169.

Stepan, Alfred. 2001. *Arguing Comparative Politics*. New York: Oxford University Press.

Stephens, John. 1979. *The Transition from Capitalism to Socialism*. London: Macmillan.

Stephens, John D., Evelyne Huber, and Leonard Ray. 1999. "The Welfare State in Hard Times," in Herbert Kitschelt, Peter Lange, Gary Marks, and John D. Stephens, eds. *Continuity and Change in Contemporary Capitalism*. New York: Cambridge University Press.

Stimson, James A. 1985. "Regression in Space and Time: A Statistical Essay." *American Journal of Political Science* 29(4): 914–947.

Strange, Susan. 1996. *The Retreat of the State*. Cambridge, UK: Cambridge University Press.

Swank, Duane. 2000. "Globalization, Democratic Institutions, and Policy Change in European Welfare States: The Corporatist Conservative Cases." Paper presented at the 2000 Annual Meeting of the American Political Science Association, Miami, August 31–September 3.

Swank, Duane. 2002. *Global Capital, Political Institutions, and Policy Change in Developed Welfare States*. Cambridge, UK: Cambridge University Press.

Swank, Duane. 2003. "Withering Welfare? Globalization, Political Economic Institutions, and the Foundations of Contemporary Welfare States," in Linda Weiss, ed., *States and Global Markets: Bringing Domestic Institutions Back In*. Cambridge, UK: Cambridge University Press.

Swank, Duane, and Cathie Jo Martin. 2001. "Employers and the Welfare State: The Political Economic Organization of Firms and Social Policy in Contemporary Capitalist Democracies." *Comparative Political Studies* 34(8): 889–923.

Tanaka, Martin. 1992. *Los espejismos de la democracia. El colapso del sistema de partidos en el Perú*. Lima: Instituto de Estudios Peruanos.

Tavares, Jose. 2004. "Does Right or Left Matter? Cabinets, Credibility and Fiscal Adjustments." *Journal of Public Economics* 88: 2447–2468.

Taylor, Alan, and Mark Taylor, 2004. "The Purchasing Power Parity Debate." NBER Working Paper no. 10607.

Thakur, Subhash, Michael Keen, and Balazs Horvath. 2003. *Sweden's Welfare State: Can the Bumblebee Keep Flying*. Washington, DC: International Monetary Fund.

Thorp, Rosemary. 1998. *Progress, Poverty and Exclusion: An Economic History of Latin America in the 20th Century*. Washington, DC: Inter-American Development Bank and Johns Hopkins University Press.

Tokman, Víctor, and Daniel Martínez. 2000. "The Impact of Labor Costs on the Competitiveness and Worker Protection in the Manufacturing Sector of Latin America," in Albert Berry, ed., *Labor Market Policies in Canada and Latin America: Challenges of the New Millennium.* Boston: Kluwer Academic Publishers.

Tsebelis, George 1995. "Decision-Making in Political Systems: Veto Players in Presidentialism, Parliamentarism, Multicameralism and Multipartyism." *British Journal of Political Science* 25: 89–325.

Tuesta, Soldevila, ed. 1996. *Los enigmas del poder: Fujimori 1990–1996.* Lima: Fundación Friedrich Ebert.

Ugarteche, Oscar. 1998. *La arqueología de la modernidad. El Perú entre la globalización y la exclusión.* Lima: Centro de estudios y promoción del desarrollo (DESCO).

Ulate Quirós, Anabelle, ed. 2000. *Empleo, Crecimiento y Equidad. Los retos de las reformas económicas en finales del siglo XX en Costa Rica.* San José, Costa Rica: Editorial de la Universidad de Costa Rica.

United Nations. 2003. *Trade and Development Report.* New York: United Nations.

United Nations. 2004. *Trade and Development Report.* New York: United Nations.

U.S. Social Security Administration. *Social Security Programs Around the World.* Washington, DC: Government Printing Office, various issues.

Valdés, Juan Gabriel. 1995. *Pinochet's Economists: The Chicago School in Chile.* New York: Cambridge University Press.

Van der Ploeg, Frederick. 2006. "Rolling Back the Public Sector: Differential Effects on Employment, Investment and Growth." *Oxford Economic Papers* 58: 103–122.

Vanden, Harry E. 2002. "The Effects of Globalization and Neoliberalism in Central America: Nicaragua and Costa Rica," in Gary Prevost and Carlos Oliva Campos, eds., *Neoliberalism and Neopanamericanism.* New York: Palgrave Macmillan.

Vega Ruiz, Maria Luz, ed. 2001. *La Reforma Laboral en América Latina: Un Análisis Comparado.* Lima: Organización Internacional del Trabajo.

Verdera, Francisco. 1994. "El mercado de trabajo de Lima metropolitana: Estructura y evolución, 1970–1990." Documento de trabajo #59. Lima: Instituto de Estudios Peruanos.

Verdera, Francisco. 1997a. "Mercados de trabajo, reforma laboral y creación de empleo: Perú, 1990–95." Documento de trabajo #87. Lima: Instituto de Estudios Peruanos.

Verdera, Francisco. 1997b. "*Seguridad Social y Pobreza en el Perú. Una aproximación.*" Documento de trabajo #84. Lima: Instituto de Estudios Peruanos.

Wagner, A. 1883. *Finanzwissenschaft.* Translated and reprinted as "Three Extracts on Public Finance," in R. A. Musgrave and A. T. Peacock, eds., *Classics on the Theory of Public Finance.* London: Macmillan.

Western, Bruce. 1997. *Between Class and Market: Postwar Unionization in the Capitalist Democracies.* Princeton, NJ: Princeton University Press.

Weyland, Kurt. 1995. "Latin America's Four Political Models." *Journal of Democracy* 6(4): 125–139.

Weyland, Kurt. 1996. *Democracy without Equity: Failures of Reform in Brazil.* Pittsburgh, PA: University of Pittsburgh Press.

Weyland, Kurt, ed. 2004. *Learning from Foreign Models in Latin American Policy Reform.* Baltimore: Johns Hopkins University Press.

Wilensky, Harold. 1975. *The Welfare State and Equality.* Berkeley and Los Angeles: University of California Press.

Wilson, Bruce. 1998. *Costa Rica: Politics, Economics, and Democracy.* Boulder, CO, and London: Lynne Rienner Publishers.

Wise, Carol. 1993. "In Search of Markets: Latin America's State-Led Dilemma." Working Paper no. 33, Institute of Latin American Studies, Columbia University.

Wisecarver, Daniel. 1992. *El Modelo Económico Chileno.* Santiago: Centro Internacional para el Desarrollo Económico (CINDE).

Wodon, Quentin, Norma Hicks, Bernadetter Ryan, and Gabriel González. 2000. "Are Governments Pro-Poor but Short-Sighted? Targeted and Social Spending for the Poor during Booms and Busts." World Bank, Manuscript.

World Bank. (Various Years.) *World Development Report.* New York: Oxford University Press.

Yashar, Deborah. 1997. *Demanding Democracy: Reform and Reaction in Costa Rica and Guatemala, 1870s–1950s.* Stanford, CA: Stanford University Press.

Index

and ISI model, 36
non-welfare state countries of, 31
party system study, 42
populism of, 240–241
pre-globalization period, 25
social insurance origins, 12
welfare state countries, 15, 29
welfare system, origins, 20–21, 26–31,
260–266
left-labor power, 41–48
additive index, 44
of Argentina, 44
of Bolivia, 46
of Brazil, 47
of Chile, 44
of Costa Rica, 46
of Mexico, 47
and QCA, 17
of Uruguay, 44
of Venezuela, 44
left-labor power weakness
of Dominican Republic, 47, 67
of Ecuador, 67
of El Salvador, 67
of Guatemala, 67
of Paraguay, 67
Llosa, Mario, 243, 248
logic of industrialism theory, 7–8, 32
low income group
democracy and interests of, 106, 111
social security expenditures exclusions of,
112

Mainwaring, Scott, 42, 113
Malloy, James, 3
manufacturing sector
of Brazil, 62
of Costa Rica, 221
and economic modernization, 80
employment reduction, 96–97
and expansion of informal sector, 98–99
growth of, 43
urban population size influence on, 43
marginalization, of public sector, 80
Mateos, López (PRI party), 47
Maximum Likelihood (ML) estimation
method, 131

McKinlay, R. D., 123
median voters
and democratization, 109
models, 107
theorem of, and selectorate expansion,
109–110
voter turnout importance, 121–123
Meller, Patricio, 181
Mesa-Lago, Carmelo, 11
Chilean welfare state expansion analysis,
176
class division analysis, 26
social security analysis by, 2
methodologies, for case study, 16–20
Mexican Revolution, 68
Mexico
collective bargaining of, 98
Confederación de Trabajadores de
México of, 68
decline of worker's social security, 98
default by, 87
GDP, per capita, 1930–1999, 32
labor movements, 68
left-labor power, 47
pluralism of, 68
PRI political party of, 47, 68
social expenditures, 15
welfare state non-development, 67
welfare system, 27
middle classes, top-down control attempts,
27
military coup
of Chile, by Pinochet, 177, 195
or Peru, by Bermúdez, 233–235
of Peru, by Alvarado, 232–235
of Peru, by Odría, 232
Ministry of Exports and Investment
(Ministerio de Inversiones y
Exportaciones)(MINEX), 219
Mixed Institute of Social Aid *(Instituto
Mixto de Ayuda Social)*, 210–211, 216
ML estimation method. *See* Maximum
Likelihood (ML) estimation method
MNR political party, of Bolivia, 46
Moene, Karl Ove, 108
monetary policy, and capital mobility, 101,
102

labor market deregulation, 250
macroeconomic chaos, 231
military coup, by Alvarado, 232–235
military coup, by Bermúdez, 233–235
military coup, by Odría, 232
Prado's return to power, 232
public expenditures, 245, 252–253
social expenditures, 15, 81–82
Social Fund law, 232
social policies of Fujimori, 244–256
as study choice, 18–20
SUNAT of, 245
temporary contracts in, 97
Terry's democratic leadership, 236–239
trade liberalization, 229
trade openness, 18–19
welfare system, 27
Peru National Fund for Social
    Compensation and Development
    (FONCODES), 246
Peruvian Social Security Institute (Instituto
    Peruano de la Seguridad Social)(IPSS),
    238
Pierson, Paul, 123
Pinochet, Augusto, 20
    authoritarianism of, 179, 184
    and Chilean economic reform, 188
    military junta of, 177, 180, 195
    plebiscite of, 187
    public/social expenditures under, 183,
        184–187
    reliance on "Chicago Boys," 195–196
    restructuring of welfare system, 181–183,
        188–191
    as "Supreme Chief of the Nation," 177
    welfare reforms, 190
PLN party, of Costa Rica, 46, 208, 213–214,
    216
pluralism, of Mexico, 68
political parties. *See also* Communist Party;
    Socialist Party
    APRA (Peru), 46
    center-left/left-oriented, variables, 44
    Christian Democratic Party (Costa Rica),
        209
    of Costa Rica, 209
    determining orientation of, 44

influences on, 118
leftist, weakness of, 117
MNR (Bolivia), 46
Peronist party, 44
PRI (Mexico), 47
Radical Party, of, 57
Social Democratic Party (Costa Rica), 209
in support of incumbent presidents, 119
politics, and power distribution, 2
poolability issue, in (TSCS analysis), 132
pooled time-series analysis, 131
populism, of Latin America, 240–241
poverty rates, and welfare states, 1
poverty relief expenditures, of Peru,
    252–256
power-resource theory, 9, 11–12, 117
Prado, Manuel, 232
pre-globalization period
    of Ecuador, 47
    of Latin America, 25
presidents
    coding of, 119–121
    popularly based, as variable (TSCS
        analysis), 138, 162
PRI political party, of Mexico, 47, 68
principal components factor analysis, 28
private sector
    savings balance deterioration, 87
    wages, public v., 80
Przeworski, Adam, 114
PSD. *See* Partido Social Demócrata
public expenditures
    of Chile, under Pinochet, 183
    disaggregated data (1973–2003), IMF, 128
    of Peru, 245, 252–253
public sector
    and Chilean welfare system, 183
    and economic development, 79
    expansion of, 92
    of Sweden/Austria/Netherlands, 92
PUSC Party. *See* Christian Unity Party
    (PUSC), of Costa Rica

Qualitative Comparative Analysis (QCA)
    basic features, 72–76
    Boolean approach, 16, 48–54, 76
    dichotomization of variables, 73